BOOK REVIEWER COMMENTS

"Change or die" appears to be the cry of contemporary organizations and indeed, any other kind of human institution because change is inevitable! Dr. Mujtaba's book "*Cross Cultural Change Management*" could not have been published at a better time as it provides a vast array of information, especially at this time of rapid change and recent 'world shaking' events!! Dr. Mujtaba creates a substantial contribution to the literature by providing broad perspectives on how effective change management is a mandatory necessity. The various chapters draw from existing theories those factors that provide insight, for example, into cultural differences in time orientation, global leadership practices, assessing organizational climate for change and guidelines for initiating and implementing change. I'm gratified that Dr. Mujtaba has included values and integrity issues as important variables for success, and posits, that individuals managing change, who respect humankind are more successful in their change management approaches. This book is a "must read" for academics as well as managers, supervisors and the general public. He has accomplished a remarkable task and has provided useful input into our vast armentarium of knowledge.

Timothy McCartney, PH.D; FCHS
Clinical Psychologist / Professor of Management
H. Wayne Huizenga School of Business and Entrepreneurship
Nova Southeastern University

Dr. Mujtaba's book, *Cross Cultural Change Management*, provides very keen insights into how cultures affect the work environment from a number of perspectives. He offers many well-known and tested methods of assisting everyone involved in this multi-cultural and multi-country, global business environment in which we work today. I think it is an exceptional work that every serious business leader will be better for having read.

Dr. Randolph A. Pohlman, Dean
H. Wayne Huizenga School of Business and Entrepreneurship,
Nova Southeastern University

Regardless of their size or location, today *all* businesses and organizations must learn to effectively deal with cross cultural change. *Cross Cultural Change Management* provides an excellent starting point for understanding and managing all the critical elements: leadership, individual change, team development, organizational learning, ethics, and social responsibility among others. This book provides examples of successful and unsuccessful cross cultural changes drawing on the experiences of Nike, Wal-Mart, and others. There are many tips and techniques for practicing managers including appreciative learning, conflict management, and stress management. This is a very comprehensive and practical book.

Dr. F. Barry Barnes, Chair and Professor of Management,
Nova Southeastern University

Dr. Mujtaba's *Cross Cultural Change Management* is a must read for all organizational leaders and managers. The book inspires and motivates, as well as provides valuable knowledge and guidelines on managing change effectively in contemporary and future contexts. It provides a broad overview of the process of change in all its facets, with unique examples and references, while bridging the gap between effective and ineffective change management approaches. Further information and guidelines on stress and conflict management are presented alongside the change process, thereby teaching leaders and managers of 21st century business organizations how to achieve success in this highly social-cultural, globally competitive environment. This well-written book is a timely and strategically significant addition to management knowledge, practices and literature!

Dr. Donovan A. McFarlane, City College of Fort Lauderdale;
Research Associate of the University of Metaphysics, Sedona, AZ

Dr. Mujtaba, in his masterful work, *Cross Cultural Change Management*, affords the reader a comprehensive and insightful examination of the concept, fact, and challenge of change, and from a variety of perspectives - personal, professional, global business, legal, ethical and moral, social, psychological, and spiritual. He discusses fully and explains clearly the role of the leader, executive, and manager - in both private and public sector organizations - in not only dealing with change but helping others to handle change, but also in initiating, leading, executing, communicating, and managing change. Accordingly, Dr. Mujtaba provides the reader with a variety of theoretical models and academic research, as well as practical strategies and tactics, to successfully handle change and to overcome resistance to change. His book emphasizes the reality and necessity of change, the positive benefits to be accrued from change - even conflict - and the critical need to take a broad "stakeholder" view when dealing with change. Dr. Mujtaba also discusses the role of personal growth, particularly by education, in promoting and producing beneficial change. Most importantly, Dr. Mujtaba throughout his thorough change analysis, underscores the dignity and worth of human beings, and thus very correctly asserts that no beneficial change will ever occur unless the change agent is a person of good character and integrity and the change contemplated treats all people as worthwhile human beings deserving of respect and dignity. His book is truly educational, efficacious, and uplifting, and a most enjoyable reading experience.

Dr. Frank Cavico, J.D., Professor
of Ethics and Law
H. Wayne Huizenga School of Business
& Entrepreneurship, NSU

Cross Cultural Change Management masterfully addresses the universal constant - change. Dr. Mujtaba's book empowers businesses and individuals alike to prepare for and ultimately embrace change, along with its vast consequences. Highlights include applicable literature on how to identify and properly cope with stress, as well as steps toward maintaining the work-life balance. Readers will gain the ability to confront and handle the psychosomatic effects of change, as they discover a plethora of information ranging from healthy diet tips to time management strategies.

Nicole A. Pirone, Psychologist
Health and Fitness Consultant-Curves
International

Cross Cultural Change Management is a very readable text that is well-founded in the literature while being quite useful for both students and practitioners. Mujtaba builds a compelling case that knowledge of cross cultural values is not central to building successful strategies for organizational change. This reader particularly enjoyed the chapter on "Making it Stick," which provides sound evidence for managers in making positive change a reality in their organizations.

> *Dr. Terrell G. Manyak, Professor of Management*
> *H. Wayne Huizenga School of Business & Entrepreneurship, NSU*

Cross Cultural Change Management lays a solid foundation for those interested in the management and human resource issues involved in doing business globally. This is an engaging and easy to read text which will open the reader's eyes to a wider world viewpoint and a greater understanding of how change affects each of us, individually, corporately, and internationally.

> *Mary Toledo, MBA Program Manager,*
> *Nova Southeastern University*

In our ever-changing world, Bahaudin Mujtaba's book is an invaluable resource. Presented in a practical manner, the reader is given a better understanding of the complexities of change, while providing genuine insight and advice. It's logical and common-sense approach to *Cross Cultural Change Management* makes this book a must read.

> *Jade Y. Chen, Assistant Director of Development-*
> *Office of Development*
> *H. Wayne Huizenga School of Business and Entrepreneurship, NSU*

CROSS CULTURAL
CHANGE MANAGEMENT

Bahaudin G. Mujtaba

Llumina Press

Bahaudin G. Mujtaba, 2006. Cross Cultural Change Management.

Produced by:
Dr. Bahaudin G. Mujtaba, Associate Professor of International Management
Nova Southeastern University
H. Wayne Huizenga School of Business and Entrepreneurship
3301 College Avenue
Fort Lauderdale FL 33314-7796
Phone: (954) 262-5000 Or (800) 672-7223 / (800) 338-4723
Email: Mujtaba@nova.edu
NSU's Website: www.nova.edu

ISBN: 1-59526-568-6

Printed in the United States of America by Llumina Press

Library of Congress Control Number: 2005938093

Dedication

This book on change is dedicated to those who bring about
positive changes in themselves and for others in
society. It is dedicated to my Mom (Uzra)
and my Dad (Ghulam) as they have
taught me that change
must always start
from one's
heart.

*
*
*
*
*
*

TABLE OF CONTENTS

Acknowledgements

There are many individuals that have formally or informally contributed to this book. *First,* I would like to thank the following colleagues for their contributions and guidance in preparing the content of this book:

- Timothy McCartney, Nova Southeastern University
- Kendrick D. Traylor, University of Phoenix-Online
- Elizabeth Danon-Leva, Nova Southeastern University
- Susan K. Key, University of Alabama at Birmingham
- Cyndy Jones, Nova Southeastern University
- Donovan A. McFarlane, City College of Fort Lauderdale
- Erica Franklin, Nova Southeastern University
- Philip F. Musa, University of Alabama at Birmingham
- Nicholas DiDomenico, University of Phoenix-Online
- Ruth Ferking, University of South Florida
- Harriett Carlton, Nova Southeastern University
- Mele K. Akuna, University of Phoenix- Hawaii
- Rose Marie Edwards, University of West Indies
- Tricia Osborne, Nova Southeastern University
- LeJon Poole, University of Alabama at Birmingham
- Margarida Karahalios, John Hopkins University.

Other researchers, graduate students, as well as direct or indirect contributors to this book are: Pauline Grace Richards, Furqan Nasri, Erin Raizen, Charlette Williams, Lamoy Coburn, Rasha A. Abbott, Dionne Mbanya, Anayansi Avila, Anita Edwards, Theresa Fitzpatrick, Charlette Williams, Jennifer Wohl, Gimol Thomas, Fred Barron, Lesmalene Morris, Paula Atkinson, Suzette Henry-Campbell, and Nicola Richards of NSU; and George Lucas, Cory Anderson, Aaron Butikofer, Blain Conway, Arley Enesa, Diana Michael, and Imran Manzoor from the University of Phoenix. Special thanks also go to the assistance of Randolph Pohlman, Jade Chen, Mary Toledo, Frank Cavico, Terrell Manyak, Nicole Pirone, Estuardo Jo, Shruti Salghur, Courtney Smith, and Sylvia Lanski of Nova Southeastern University as well as Shari Reimann of Llumina Press for their indexing, formatting, and review of the material.

Second, I would like to thank all those who have helped me both personally and professionally get to this point. I sincerely want to thank Lisa Mujtaba for her review, suggestions, and edits with the various chapters of this book.

Third, I thank you for reading this material on change management in a cross-cultural environment. For suggestions and questions, you can contact me (mujtaba@nova.edu) at any time. May you always have the hindsight to know where you have been, the foresight to know where you are going in every change, and the insight to know when you are about to go too far. Remember, if you can perceive and believe a better state of being through change, then you are very likely to achieve it as well.

Bahaudin.

PREFACE

Change is dynamic and a constant reality in today's business environment. In the new economy, change seems to keep picking up speed in all industries and professions. Today's employees and customers are living in a constant period of transition, and the shelf life of solutions keeps getting shorter since what works today can become obsolete a few months later. Where is all the change coming from in today's economy? Change is often coming from or caused by people, technology, new information, and globalization. The growing population is dealing with new technology everyday which feeds and sustains on itself. Experts suggest that it is best to think of technological change as something that keeps multiplying on a continuous basis. Still another source of this rapid change is knowledge or information which seems to be doubling about every four to five years. Some of the commonly addressed sources of change for businesses can include changes in nature of the workforce, economy, social trends, politics, leadership, management, organizational structures, products, services, customers, customer demands, and location of where the firm produces or offers its products.

Because of rapid changes, new knowledge and doubling of information every few years, the future promises more change than experienced thus far. Such rapid change can quickly or slowly destroy organizations that do not adapt to the new circumstances. Such rapid changes call for major personal and cultural shifts in behavior. Today's workers and organizational leaders cannot afford to ignore change and just do what comes naturally or as they have done in the past as that approach may not work. Workers must face the change proactively, surrender to the change, adjust to it, go with the change, adapt to it, and/or do what works in order to take advantage of the change.

Change can impact individuals, cultures, economies, countries, regions, and societies. Change can impact people positively or negatively, and to some extent, the impact of change is determined by one's response to it. As such, it is best to be proactive rather than reactive about responding to change. George W. Bush, President of the United States, mentioned that the American economy is moving, which is a sign of progress and development in the country. Jay Leno, late night television comedian, on August 2005 commented that yes the American economy is moving alright…it is moving to China, India, Indonesia, Mexico, and other such economies.

Change is a reality of life and all human beings go through it personally, professionally, physically, mentally, socially, and spiritually in the progression of their life. Realistically speaking, change happens regardless of whether it is desired, needed, wanted, or invited. Another reality is that responses to change are often predictable; thus resistance toward a new initiative can be reduced or managed through proactive planning efforts. *Cross Cultural Change Management* (CCCM) is about making sure that one is able to see the positive side of the issue and, as a change agent, make sure that every person impacted by the transition goes through the change process effectively and as smoothly as possible. The book on *Cross Cultural Change Management* provides a practical definition for change and change management and it discusses why change needs to be managed proactively. The book discusses how change can impact people, and how individuals often react to change. *Cross Cultural Change Management* offers change management models and strategies for overcoming resistance to change, while describing the roles and responsibilities of leaders, managers, and change agents in such initiatives. *Cross Cultural Change Management* advocates the use and skills of situational leadership concepts for effectively transitioning and influencing others as per their level of readiness to accept the change by telling them about it, selling the change to them, jointly working with them to implement the new process or change, and delegating the responsibility and accountability for the new processes' continuous success to them. Overall, the book offers various approaches and strategies for organizations and individuals to successfully initiate, execute, and manage change. Faculty members, corporate trainers and change agents that want to use this book for their classes and workshops can contact the publisher or author for available instructor's resources such as Power Point presentations for each chapter, exam material, lecture note suggestions, etc.

    Cross Cultural Change Management, in one respect, is about transitioning those who are impacted by the change and making sure everyone becomes a winner as a result. It is about understanding that everyone wants to be a winner and helping one get there through a smooth transition without a cost to others. Some individuals, regardless of how different they are, seem to understand life better than those who fall in the "norm," and people call some of these adults, children, men or women "disabled," and at times "differently abled." At a Seattle Special Olympics event, nine contestants, all with physical or mental disabilities, assembled at the starting line for the 100-yard dash. At the sound of the gun, they all started out, not exactly in a dash, but with a yearning to run the race to the finish and win. One little boy, who stumbled on the asphalt tumbled over a couple of times, and began to cry. The other eight heard the boy cry. They slowed down and looked back. Then they all turned around and went back…every one of them. One beautiful little girl with Downs Syndrome disability bent down and gently kissed him on the forehead while saying: "This will make it better." Then all nine linked arms and walked together to the finish line. Everyone in the stadium stood, some with tears in their eyes and on their cheeks, and the cheering went on for several minutes.

    Change management, at times, is about helping professionals heal physically, professionally, and mentally in their transition to the new destination. It is about understanding that all employees want to get there successfully along with everyone else. Change and winning are not mutually exclusive; therefore, both can happen simultaneously and everyone can and should become winners. As such, all leaders and change agents must be cognizant of this fact and perhaps slow down when needed so everyone on the team can become winners in this temporary race of life. *Cross Cultural Change Management* offers many of the skills needed to deal with major changes taking place in the work environment. The topics covered in *Cross Cultural Change Management* include culture, change management, conflict management, negotiations, time management, stress management, gender issues and discrimination, ethics, internationalization, repatriation, and examples of corporations that have become successful amid major societal, cultural, and economic changes.

Why should managers, leaders and change agents slow down to help others catch up when needed? Because deep down we know this one thing: What matters in this life is more than winning for ourselves. What matters in this life is helping others win, even if it means slowing down and changing course. As change agents and effective leaders, if you help others change successfully, rather than simply choosing to win at all costs, then we all may be able to change our hearts toward better societal goals, teamwork, and fairness for all. The fact is that a candle loses nothing by lighting another candle; however, everyone gains more light as a result. So, be the candle in this society and provide energy to others toward positive change by selflessly sharing your wisdom and knowledge with everyone who can benefit from it. Furthermore, while respecting the beliefs and ideologies of workers, global change agents must be persistent in selling the change by letting everyone know how it can benefit them both in the short term as well as in the long term. Calvin Coolidge has been quoted as saying, "Nothing can take the place of persistence. Talent will not; the world is full of unsuccessful people with talent. Genius will not; unrewarded genius is almost a proverb. Education alone will not; the world is full of educated derelicts. Persistence and determination alone are omnipotent." Change management is about being persistent and determined to manage change and stress effectively. Effective management of change means proactively planning, developing diverse scenarios and possibilities, and exercising one's body and mind to stay in good health. As the proverb states, "Those who don't find time for exercise will have to find time for illness." Those who don't find time to gain the right skills and get the education needed will have to spend time dealing with much resistance when managing change. For example, education in general "pays" personally and financially, because, according to the Bureau of Labor Statistics, those with a bachelor's degree will earn about $2.1 million over their work life while those with a master's degree will earn 20% more (a total of $2.5 million). One of the majors changes since 1992 has been the 33% increase in the number of college graduates and the fact that more fields now require a master's degree for career advancement. Acquiring more education can afford one more respect from one's colleagues and employees, while equipping one to make better decisions in both the planning and execution stages of change.

Thomas Crum (1987) states that in order for human beings to move beyond success, they need to make their life of work into a work of art. People need to naturally move into a "you and me" philosophy where they see the world as abundant and supportive in all aspects of their lives, from their health to their financial well-being. Crum defines *"alchemy"* as one's ability to change the ordinary into the extraordinary. The ability to change the ordinary to the extraordinary in the middle-ages involved changing common metals into gold; but the alchemy of today involves changing ourselves. Crum states that "It is the pressure of conflict, the interference patterns of energies caused by differences, that provides the motivation and opportunity to change" (1987, p. 25). Nature sees conflict in a positive light and uses it as a primary motivator for bringing about change. Similarly, human beings can and should do the same in order to effectively deal with the inevitable changes they face each and every day.

Change, the art of making things different, is a reality of life in every culture and organization. It is a natural part of evolution and human development. By nature, change is desired, wanted and expected.

Life and longevity are not about the number of breaths one takes between similar moments. Life is about the changing moments, actions taken, and the words spoken in these moments that take one's breath away!

CROSS CULTURAL
CHANGE MANAGEMENT

CULTURE AND CHANGE

C hange has always been a normal part of life, and perhaps more so today than ever before. While there may never be many consistent days of what is perceived to be a "normal" day in a person's professional life, it is very likely that a worker's day is filled with certain real or perceived changes; thereby making change a "normal" part of his or her day. With regard to a normal day, a writer by the name of Mary Jean Iron wrote the following:

> Normal day, let me be aware of the treasure you are... Let me not pass you by in quest of some rare and perfect tomorrow. One day I shall dig my nails into the earth, or bury my face in my pillow, or stretch myself taut, or raise my hands to the sky and want, more than all the world, your return.

One can always hope and expect the return of a "normal day," it is best not to wait too long as most days can be seen as "normal." Change is normal, and twenty-first century professionals might as well begin seeing it as such by consciously making every day a normal day for themselves and their colleagues. Change, or the art of making things different, is a reality of life in every dynamic culture and organization. Thus change management is needed in today's organizations to make things different effectively and efficiently. Similarly, every culture and organization tends to condition people toward consistent and predictable habits. Change is a natural part of evolution and human development. The average workweek for most full-time employees seems to be about 50 hours and "gone" are the days of 40 hour jobs. Some of the reasons for these changes are associated with more work and more business, while others relate to technology, new information, globalization, mergers, financial needs, job security, international travel, and dealing with people of diverse cultures.

By nature, change is desired, wanted and expected. Some personal, societal, professional, and cultural changes are positive and others can be negative as they tend to collide with one's values or they can "catch" and surprise individuals unexpectedly. For example, from a societal perspective, many couples today tend to experience a higher rate of divorce than their parents in the previous generations. As matter of fact, in some countries or cultures, nearly fifty percent of the marriages end in a divorce within the first few years, perhaps due to various personal and financial reasons or pressures of modern times. According to the U. S. Census Bureau-Statistical Abstract of the United States for 1980-2000, there are 6.2 divorces in the United States for every 1,000 individuals between the ages of 15-64 compared to only one in Italy (USA Today, 2005). The divorce rate for United Kingdom is 4, Sweden is 3.8, Germany is 3.5, Canada is 3.4, and France and Japan are 3.1 as reported by the USA Today. Of course, these high rates of separation tend to impact not only the couples but also their families and children, thereby creating unwanted stress, worries, and other unintended consequences affecting working adults both personally and professionally. These changes are difficult to prepare for, but one must deal with them appropriately when they do take place. It is important to mention that major changes in society or in one's personal life tend to have an impact on one's professional life as well.

Changes and Pressures of Modern Times

Change can impact people personally, professionally, financially, physically, spiritually, and emotionally. On August 31, 2005, there were over 1,000 innocent men, women and children who died in a Baghdad (Iraq) stampede while being on a spiritual event. The large crowds, about one million, of Shia pilgrims were heading towards the Kadhimiya mosque to mark the martyrdom of the 8th century religious figure Imam Musa al-Kadhim. During the panic, iron railings on the Aima Bridge leading to the shrine gave way and hundreds of people fell into the Tigris River. According to witnesses, panic spread because of rumors that suicide bombers were in the crowd. Thus, people began panicking and running away, while several people fell to the ground and the pattern continued. Thousands of victims were injured, crushed to death or fell in the river and drowned. Hundreds of men and security officials rushed to the Tigris River to search for survivors in the muddy water and to retrieve bodies floating downstream. The incident has caused the single biggest loss of Iraqi life since the US-led invasion in 2003. Such unfortunate incidents can negatively impact the lives of millions of people directly and indirectly, thus causing major change.

Another unfortunate incident that took place at about the same time period in late August was Hurricane Katrina which passed over the Grand Bahamas before coming to Florida; and the eye of this "category one" hurricane passed right over Fort Lauderdale and South Miami. After causing much destruction in South Florida and leaving over one million people without electricity for many days, it got stronger in the warm waters of the Gulf Coast going toward New Orleans. As a result of "category four and five" winds and about twenty feet water surges, Hurricane Katrina devastated thousands of families throughout the states of Louisiana, Mississippi, and Alabama. The results were nearly 1,100 people dead, and the city of New Orleans temporarily drowned since the levies built to protect the city got destroyed. Most homes had over ten feet of water, making these locations unfit to live in for months and years to come. Hurricane Katrina also showed that the American society and government was not ready to effectively handle such a crisis since many individuals died after the hurricane had passed as they did not have water, food, medication, and other essentials for survival. The local leaders and government officials for the cities impacted by Hurricane Katrina lost all contact with each other since their communication devices and other cyberspace technologies were under water. There seemed to be a chaotic situation with no one organization or official in charge, while thousands of victims were becoming more frustrated. Consequently, there were lawlessness throughout the cities and people were doing what they could to survive. The lesson learned as a result of Hurricane Katrina is that what can go wrong will go wrong (since the levies broke, leading to the drowning of a whole city), and the fact that the United States government was not ready to effectively handle such a crisis. FEMA was much more prepared for Hurricane Wilma's consequences which impacted West Coast and South Florida on October 24, 2005. After leaving much destruction in Cancun of Mexico and parts of Cuba as a category four hurricane, Hurricane Wilma came directly for Florida. Wilma left about 98% of the South Florida's population (2.8 million individuals) without electricity and telephone for days and weeks. While FEMA was much more prepared, the local authorities were not happy because the agency's trucks of ice and water did not make it to its points of distribution (PODs) as originally announced. People waited hours in long lines for FEMA trucks, only to hear that the ice and water were not coming. Furthermore, the local authorities were disappointed because FEMA officials did not consistently communicate with them about when the ice and water trucks would be coming to each location. The heroes during this hurricane seem to be the Florida Power and Light (FPL) employees and contractors who had gathered from around the nation and Canada to fix what had been damaged by Hurricane Wilma. Just because all things did not go well or as planned on the first few days after the hurricane does not mean that FEMA employees did not work hard because they adjusted quickly to the situational changes, and their assistance and response was much appreciated.

Overall, it is apparent that the government agencies need to put in place a better system for managing such a crisis in a timely and proactive manner. While unfortunate incidents, such as hurricane destructions, the stampede in Iraq, the earthquake which killed about 50,000 people in Pakistan during October 2005, and other made-made disasters can bring about major changes and high levels of stress, this book is not designed to deal with transitions and changes of such magnitude, as often times they require major interventions from government agencies and professionals. This book is designed for changes that impact business professionals and employees in the workplace who deal with national and international changes such as mergers, cultures, going to different countries, promotions, downsizing, layoffs, technology, globalization, etc.

For very valid reasons, many people are now worried or concerned about their safety in homes, workplaces, cars, trains, planes, malls, gas stations, and other places due to political unrests throughout the world. Of course, while people are worried about their security, many individuals in developing and developed nations do not want such worries or concerns to infringe upon every aspect of their day-to-day routines. According to Susan Page (2005), "The debate over where to draw the line between public safety and civil liberties is being waged, among other places, in the labyrinth of train and subway entrances." Page continues to say that many years after the attacks on New York City, Americans are still struggling on how to keep a balance between security and freedom. Of course, such incidents as London's transit bombings make this task even more challenging. According to a Gallup Poll (Page, 2005), while 81% of American respondents favored "Requiring every person entering into an office building or public place to go through a metal detector," only 6% favored "Allowing police to enter a person's home at any time without a search warrant." Furthermore, about 75% of the respondents opposed "Allowing the government to imprison U.S. citizens who are suspected of terrorism without putting them on trial for years." These issues were not of much concern to most people in various nations twenty to thirty years ago, since it was the job of the police officers, army officials, and other military personnel to protect the nation from being harmed. However, today, it is everyone's responsibility to be aware of their surroundings and take safety seriously. This is another major change that today's population has to deal with appropriately while balancing work, family life, and hobbies.

Another concern for working professionals and adults is dealing with the widespread presence of high officials cheating investors and employees by lying, being dishonest or deceitful, and by manipulating their company's data. As a matter-of-fact, former Cendant vice chairman, E. Kirk Shelton, received a ten year prison sentence and was ordered to pay about $3.3 billion to Cendant for his role in an accounting scandal that cost investors so much of their income. In another case, Time Warner settled a law suit by agreeing to pay $2.4 billion to shareholders over its 2001 merger with America Online. The lawsuit claimed that Time Warner had overstated its revenue around the time of the merger with AOL. Of course, there are similar charges which have been seen with WorldCom, Enron, Tyco, and many other low-profiled firms where executives lied to and cheated, both employees and investors out of their hard-earned income. Thirty to forty years ago, most people did not worry about being robbed by some of the highly respected categories of professional individuals, such as business people, entrepreneurs, police officers, clergymen, and politicians. However, this change in lack of trust with these professionals is an unfortunate sign of the modern times, and everyone must be prepared to deal with it appropriately instead of being caught unexpectedly.

The fast pace of today's work environment has created many workaholics who might be successful professionally, but personally they have a "bankrupt" life since they have forgotten about effectively balancing their time with family members. Perhaps, such work life is another variable playing into the high divorce rates in most countries and cultures. The fast pace of today's work world has caused changes in people's eating patterns as well. Instead of eating with family members, friends and colleagues many individuals have been conditioned to eat in between work or other activities. As a matter of fact, according to a USA Today survey in August 2005, the most popular places to eat on the go were in front of the television set (60% of the respondents), in the car (42%) and at work (40%). Fifty years ago, most traditional cultures did not encourage people to eat by themselves since eating was a social time for family members to talk and converse with one another. Because of such interpersonal conversation opportunities, there was little need for psychiatrists and psychologists which are highly in demand today by many individuals because they are the only professionals who would listen to one's modern day problems...provided that they are paid. In previous centuries, when children and teenagers faced a difficult task they usually approached a family member for advice. Today, most teenagers listen to strangers on the internet and their behaviors are often driven by the actions and trends of television stars, such as Ashton Kutcher, Lindsay Lohan, Orlando Bloom, Hilary Duff, Reese Witherspoon, Natalie Portman, Jessica Alba, Nick Cannon, and many other such icons. While these television icons and chat-room respondents on the internet may not always be good role models, many youngsters feel comfortable listening to them and doing what they do. These are major changes for parents and children who are brought up with traditional values and family members. Yes, they will have to effectively deal with these changes as well as the impact of such changes on their children and grandchildren. Today, the pressures of work life as well as other activities have brought many changes that impact one's personal and professional habits. Again, while many of such changes can be out of one's immediate control, one can be properly prepared to deal with them according to one's personal priorities and values. Even then, the most prepared individuals would have to show flexibility in choosing the best course of action for moving forward and achieving one's predetermined worthwhile goals in a changing world. While the changes in modern times might be a bit more challenging for those who are not brought up with them, the new generation must also develop skills to effectively deal with new changes as they too might have been conditioned by societal or organizational cultures that do not always welcome change.

Culture is a way of life, and it conditions people's behavior toward specific norms, customs, and societal expectations. One function of culture, therefore, is to regularize behavior within the society toward change and other life events. As such, by understanding the culture one can predict individuals' (living within that culture) general behavioral patterns toward prospective dilemmas, employment practices, change, and other day-to-day activities. Every individual comes from a society that conditions him or her to respond to challenges based on the specific values and customs of his or her upbringing. People of some cultures value change and new experiences, while others value consistency and predictability. Such differences accompany individuals in the workplace, thus leading to diverse responses and, at times, resistance to change. It should be noted that while years of conditioning can be a very strong influence on a person's behavior, each person can think for him/herself, and make decisions according to the situational factors surrounding the change. This is especially true in the workplace, as managers and professionals are expected to treat each other with respect and dignity, while proactively responding to changes according to industry practices. Therefore, it is extremely important for professionals, managers and leaders to have a good understanding of culture, change, and industry practices in order to make effective decisions. With a strong cross-cultural management foundation, every worker and manager can become a transformational leader by thinking critically and helping others reflect upon the facts before making changes that impact the lives of individuals both inside and outside the organization.

Cultural Differences

Twenty-first century managers work with different employees, suppliers and customers. As such, modern managers must be aware of cross-cultural and international management practices. *International management* is about the application of traditional management concepts and techniques in a global setting or environment. Hodgetts and Luthans (2003) defined culture as the "acquired knowledge that people use to interpret experience and generate social behavior." Of course, this acquired knowledge forms people's values, creates their attitudes, and influences their behavior in a predictable pattern (p. 108). Gert Hofstede (1980) defined culture as "the collective programming of the mind," which distinguishes one group of people from another. Today's managers, with diverse value systems, are global managers as they mostly manage people of diverse beliefs in an international environment. Consequently, understanding culture plays a critical role in international management. For an organization to operate in several countries with different cultures, it is important for the management team to understand the culture of the countries in order to efficiently and effectively operate interdependently among them. The norms and practices of one culture may not be the norms and practices of another. This book examines certain cultural challenges in national as well as international management, including, but not limited to, change, stress, conflict, and negotiations. It offers recommendations to assist managers toward a more efficient and effective operation with regard to change management both in small and large organizations. A starting place is to understand cultures as a way of improving management practices in the international work environment.

Table 1 – Values of People (Elashmawi & Harris, 1996)

United States	Japan	Arab Countries
1. Freedom	1. Belonging	1. Family security
2. Independence	2. Group harmony	2. Family harmony
3. Self-reliance	3. Collectiveness	3. Parental guidance
4. Equality	4. Age / Seniority	4. Age
5. Individualism	5. Group consensus	5. Authority
6. Competition	6. Cooperation	6. Compromise
7. Efficiency	7. Quality	7. Devotion
8. Time	8. Patience	8. Patience
9. Directness	9. Indirectness	9. Indirectness
10. Openness	10. Go-between	10. Hospitality

Note: "1" being the most important cultural value and "10" being the least important value.

Hall and Hall (1987) stated that each culture operates according to its own internal dynamic, its own principles, and its own written and unwritten laws. However, there are some common threads that run through all cultures. *Culture* can be likened to a giant, extraordinary complex computer. Its programs guide the actions and responses of human beings in every walk of life. This process requires attention to everything people do to survive, advance in the world, and gain satisfaction from life. Furthermore, cultural programs will not work if crucial steps are omitted, which happens when people unconsciously apply their own rules to another system (Hall & Hall, 1987). Culture and cultural conditioning of people can affect technology transfer, managerial attitudes, managerial ideology, and even business-government relations. Furthermore, and perhaps most important, "culture affects how people think and behave" (Hodgetts & Luthans, 2003, p. 109). An example of observing the differences in cultures is when researchers and managers compare the "Priorities of Cultural Values." As can be seen in Table 1, there are difference in priorities of cultural values between the United States, Japan, and Arab countries (Elashmawi & Harris, 1996, p. 63). Of course, similar differences exist between the cultures of other countries as well.

From the comparison of cultural values by Elashmawi and Harris (1996), one can observe that freedom and independence are the two main priorities in the American culture; while in Japan it is belonging and group harmony; and in Arab countries it is family security and harmony. In the United States, the constitution stands for freedom and independence while in Arab countries, it is taught that family is the most important aspect of life. Becker (2000) states that, "The technological innovations, demographic movements, political events, and economic forces have changed over time and are continuing to change human behavior in the future." As a matter-of-fact, one can say that "In today's increasingly competitive and demanding international free market economy, managers can't succeed solely on their domestic cultural understanding skills alone" (Becker, 2000, p. 1). It is important for global or international managers to understand the protocols of business operation in each particular culture / country, before making major changes.

Harris, Moran, and Moran (2004) provided ten basic categories that are important for understanding culture and these categories can be useful when studying another culture. The ten categories offered by Harris, Moran, and Moran include (2004, p. 5):

1. Sense of Self and Space
2. Communication and Language
3. Dress and Appearance
4. Food and Feeding Habits
5. Time and Time Consciousness
6. Relationships
7. Values and Norms
8. Beliefs and Attitudes
9. Mental Process and Learning
10. Work Habits and Practices

While the focus is on managing change in a culturally diverse environment and effectively managing the process of bringing about changes, one cannot escape a discussion of the other categories as they impact how people make decisions and why they behave the way they do. Accordingly, it is appropriate to begin with a discussion of culture and what change means to workers of an organization. Culture, as stated before and in its simplest form, is a way of life. While cultures cannot be changed easily, people's thoughts, words, actions, and behaviors can be changed and this change takes place best when it is intrinsically initiated through knowledge, education, awareness, critical thinking, and self reflection. Overall, each person is likely to achieve success in bringing about changes as per his or her own efforts, education, self reflections, behaviors, and ability to effectively work with others. George Adams, philosopher, said:

> There is no such thing as a 'self-made' man. We are made up of thousands of others. Everyone who has ever done a kind deed for us, or spoken one word of encouragement to us, has entered into the make-up of our character and of our thoughts, as well as our success.

Self-reflection about national and international change management issues is critical for personal growth and development as a global leader. Hopefully all scholars of management, human resources management, and global leadership do this often, and thus evaluate their actions and progress on a daily, weekly, monthly, and yearly basis. Of-course, one way to answer the question of why study change management issues or human resources development is to say that continuously getting more education in today's complex world allows for better leadership and upward mobility which can provide for a greater financial reward in today's dynamic work environment. While these are good goals, often times they are not the primary motivators for making the decision to such challenging endeavors. The opportunity to learn and grow personally tends to be the deciding factor for many individuals who choose to continue learning. As has been said many times, global knowledge can open many avenues and prevent embarrassments. Phillips (1999-2000) said, "...the opportunity to learn, enhance one's ability as a self-learner and explore the fascinating explosion of information is one that highly qualified students should not miss." It is the vast amount of knowledge out there that continues to provide motivation and excitement for today's learners.

The world is an ever-changing place, providing avenues of learning at a pace that most people cannot follow or keep up with in a timely manner. These changes can only occur as a result of continued learning. It is the need to question that drives change. It is always easy to do it the way that it has always been done, but if we never look past the obvious then how do we know what lies beyond. To truly learn one must open his/her mind and try to put away preconceived notions. Twenty first century workers must become critical thinkers in order to continuously learn and grow in understanding national and international change management practices. The goal of a formal education program is to increase one's knowledge and insight. It allows people to increase their understanding of change and business management. A formal education program allows one to take real life experiences and learn from them. The people participating in a formal program each bring a different background to the group, which allows for new perceptions to be shared and new interactions to occur. It provides a support group to "bounce ideas off" each other and gather encouragement from diverse perspectives.

With the current economic conditions, international firms are looking to fill vacant positions with people that have global experience and cultural sensitivity with regard to bringing about changes in organizational cultures. They are looking for the candidate that has the edge, the ability to understand and manage the business in a fair manner. Formal and informal education, especially in the area of international business and change, provides the framework for these qualities. For those already with a company, senior management often sends the message that a degree is needed to move up the corporate ladder. While promotion is a good reason to obtain global awareness, sensitivity, and education, the desire to accomplish one's tasks as a manager in a fair, just, ethical, and moral manner must come from a personal place – the inner-self. The opportunity for personal and professional growth should be a secondary accomplishment, not the primary. So, it is the ethical application of higher levels of awareness and education that can lead to the achievement of one's personal and professional dreams.

Understanding cultural differences and work practices are a necessity for the growth and success of doing business with others throughout the world and serving each market in an effective and efficient manner. International expansions have been on the rise in the past few decades, and they present managers with new challenges on how to deal with the differences in culture. One of the benefits that such expansions offer is the access to new markets for economies of scale. With globalization of markets, competition and organizations, individuals increasingly interact, manage, negotiate, and compromise with people from a variety of cultures. Over a quarter of century ago, Hofstede (1980, 2001) identified five dimensions of cultural values: Power Distance (PD), Uncertainty Avoidance (UA), Masculinity/ Femininity (Mas), Collectivism/Individuality (COLL), and Long Term-Short Term Orientation (LTO / STO) that characterize cultural differences among diverse countries or cultures. According to Hofstede (1993), a country's position, on these five dimensions, allows predictions on the way societies operate, including the management principles that are applied.

Other researchers developed theories to explain the extent to which one culture can affect others as people migrate and interact in the global marketplace (Dastoor, Roofe, and Mujtaba, 2005), and some of them include: convergence, divergence and crossvergence. *Convergence* describes the merging of different cultures due to the influence of globalization and other factors that bring them into close contact with one another. *Divergence* is the extent to which distinctiveness is exhibited by a specific culture despite interaction with other cultures. Finally, *crossvergence* is the development of a new culture with its own characteristics that result from cultures interacting with each other over time (Dastoor *et al*, 2005).

Many economies are shaping their management practices to model those of the United States (U.S.) and may, ultimately, transform their national cultures as well. According to some experts and writers, the export of U.S. management theories and practices through universities and management development workshops in other countries assumes that other countries are eager to become Americanized, that is, to converge with the culture of the U.S. Other researchers, however, think that there is a general lack of success in countries adopting the so-called "western management" practices to develop their economy (Hofstede, 1993; Dastoor *et al*, 2005).

Some of the Third World countries have adopted many of the Western and European management practices to achieve economic stability. For example, many foreign nationals work in the U.S. and many students study there as well. The diversity of the cultures within the U.S. presents opportunities and challenges as foreign students and workers are exposed to the Western culture for a prolonged period of time. Kim (2005) states that "according to the spillover theory, adjustment problems in non-work domains create stress for an expatriate and in turn negatively affect his or her adjustment in the work environment." Ramsey (2005) explained that the institutional distance between home country and host country groups exerts influence over how well expatiates adjust to their job, the new environment, the new culture. Institutional distance describes the extent to which there is dissimilarity between host and home institutions. In cultural distance countries, firms tend to face higher management and operational costs. Furthermore, cultural distance has been linked to increased difficulties and costs as well as increased challenges in managing a foreign workforce. Ramsey discusses Black and Stephen's 1989 expatriate adjustment facets which are work, general, and interaction: Work adjustment is the expatriate's psychological comfort with the job tasks for the foreign assignment; General adjustment focuses on the general living conditions and culture of the new country; and Interaction adjustment explores the interaction with the host-country nationals (Ramsey, 2005). Ramsey and other researchers have concluded that an increase in cultural novelty results in a decrease in general adjustment to the new environment and ethnocentricity of the host country national affects work adjustment. It is also argued that "The more similar (less distant) the rules and regulations of the host country group are to the foreign country group, the easier it will be for the expatriate to adjust to the new group" (Ramsey, 2005). Ramsey further explains that "the greater the discrepancy between the explicit or implicit rules of the home and host country groups, the greater the chance for error in adjusting to specific job responsibilities, performance standards and expectations, and supervisory responsibilities." International researchers state that people who are "other oriented," (concerned with the wellbeing of others and who are helpful to others), tend to understand foreign cultures better than people who are less "other oriented" (or selfish). A person who is high on "other oriented" is less self-interested and therefore is more likely to proactively adapt to the behavioral expectations of the local community members (Ramsey, 2005). Furthermore, it is believed that a person who is high on "other oriented" will be better able to close the distance between the home and host groups than a person who is low on "other orientation." Consequently, "other oriented" individuals are better able to deal with cross-cultural and industry-wide changes than those who are self-centered. "Other oriented" individuals generally tend to do well nationally and internationally, but they face similar challenges as anyone else in adjusting to major changes. Many "other oriented" individuals also high self monitors. Self-monitoring, according to Kim (2005), is "a personality characteristic define as the degree to which people are sensitive to the demands of social institutions and shape their behaviors accordingly." Kim explains that self-monitoring comprises a thorough knowledge of one's own actions and how one is perceived by others in terms of acceptable behaviors by the local community. According to Kim, "high self-monitors are those who are sensitive and responsive to social and interpersonal cues to situational appropriateness, they are more likely to be flexible in adjusting their behavior in an attempt to fit the demands of the new situation and culture in the host country." On the other side, "low self-monitors behave in ways that express their internal attitudes and dispositions; they therefore behave more consistently regardless of situational demands and audience" (Kim, 2005). People who are high "other oriented" and high "self-monitors" tend to gain the benefits of a social support system. Research shows that expatriates gain "feelings of reinforcement, recognition and affirmation from social support, and these feelings help facilitate expatriates' cross-cultural adjustment" during times of major change (Kim, 2005).

According to Dastoor, Roofe, and Mujtaba (2005), when expatriates return to their home country they sometimes discover that they no longer totally fit into the local culture's work practices, and many end up returning to developed countries on a permanent basis. Immigration has become one avenue for many individuals from some Third World countries as the thought of coming to the United States and other Western countries becomes more attractive. People are drawn to the free way of living and independence of the courts, the social security system, developed schools and education systems, as well as the thriving "gray market" or "shadow economy" (Dougherty, 2004; Dastoor *et al*, 2005). Irrespective of their education, immigrants and illegal residents often initially find employment in low-paying jobs that are unattractive for the local population. Such jobs might be in agriculture, catering, and housework, as well as in the building sector, mostly so-called 3-D jobs; "3-D" referring to the fact that these jobs can be *dirty, dangerous,* and *difficult* (Dastoor *et al*, 2005). These jobs are often better for some of the immigrants than the conditions in their places of birth or developing countries. Oftentimes, immigrants from developing countries are able to take whatever jobs are available to them and eventually, through hard work and continuous improvement, turn this job into an opportunity of a life time. For example, a person who is not able to fluently speak the local language might begin working as a dishwasher at a local restaurant or bakery, and within a few years acquire the ability, or begin, to manage the entire department. Such progress is partially so because these individuals often have a higher level of tolerance for hard work and long hours since they are likely to be goal-oriented. Another industrial change or trend in many industries has been the outsourcing of jobs which has created growth, entrepreneurship and promotion opportunities for experts of all professions. Outsourcing trends across industries and cultures impact people of all cultures and countries since it can mean major changes, i.e. loss of jobs for some and opportunities for others.

The late Peter Drucker, in his article entitled "Sell the Mailroom" that appeared in the November 15, 2005 issue of *Wall Street Journal*, states that "More and more people working in and for organizations will actually be on the payroll of an independent outside contractor." Drucker continued to explain that "Businesses, hospitals, schools, governments, labor unions -- all kinds of organizations, large and small -- are increasingly "unbundling" clerical, maintenance and support work." This "unbundling" process provides many promotion opportunities for blue-collar workers of all fields. Peter Drucker writes that:

> The most important reason for unbundling the organization, however, is one that economists and engineers are likely to dismiss as "intangible": The productivity of support work is not likely to go up until it is possible to be promoted into senior management for doing a good job at it. And that will happen in support work only when such work is done by separate, free-standing enterprises. Until then, ambitious and able people will not go into support work; and if they find themselves in it, will soon get out of it. Forty years ago, service and support costs accounted for no more than 10% or 15% of total costs. So long as they were so marginal, their low productivity did not matter. Now that they are more likely to take 40 cents out of every dollar they can no longer be brushed aside (Drucker, 2005).

According to experts, in-house service and support activities are de facto monopolies where the motivation to improve are often low. Oftentimes, workers of monopolized industries, in-house service departments, and state-owned enterprises have little incentive to improve their performance or invent new processes for getting the job done efficiently. Drucker explains that in the "typical organization, business or government, the standard and prestige of an activity is judged by its size and budget -- particularly in the case of activities that, like clerical, maintenance and support work, do not make a direct and measurable contribution to the bottom line." Therefore, for most workers and managers, "to improve the productivity of such an activity is thus hardly the way to advancement and success" (Drucker, 2005).

Similar to the conditions of state-owned enterprises, it is assumed that the workers and managers who are running in-house support services and departments are unlikely to do the "hard, innovative and often costly work" that is required to make service work productive. Thus, globally, there is a trend toward privatization of even state-owned enterprises that often do not much competition. Peter Drucker, who died in early November 2005, suggests that if clerical, maintenance, and support work is done by an outside independent contractor and entrepreneurs it can offer opportunities, respect and visibility for all white- and blue collar workers. Drucker used the example of how blue collar employees of a college, for example workers and managers of student dining, may never be anything more than "subordinates." However, these individuals working in an independent catering company can rise to be senior managers and vice presidents in charge of feeding the students in a dozen schools. According to Drucker, these blue collar employees might even become CEOs of their firms as they find specific niche markets to serve as per their interests and skills. Another example that Drucker mentioned in his article is how in "one large hospital-maintenance company, some of the women who started 12 or 15 years ago pushing vacuum cleaners are now division heads or vice presidents and own substantial blocks of company stock." However, as hospital employees, these blue collar workers would have still been pushing vacuum cleaners (Drucker, 2005). Such industry trends and cultural changes toward outsourcing and privatization mean threats to some workers and opportunities for others. Accordingly, responses to these major changes would vary from person to person and from culture to culture.

While there are many cultural and behavioral differences among various groups of people living in different parts of the world, most individuals tend to respond or react to change in similar patterns. Of course, based on the environmental and situational variables, some individuals are naturally conditioned to have a higher level of tolerance for change, ambiguity, uncertainly, and pain than others. For example, a person who has lived mostly in a warm climate is likely to quickly feel a slightly cooler weather than a person who has lived in a snow-climate majority of his or her life. During the winter season, while Floridians are likely to have their heaters on when the weather is about 65 degrees outside, some Northerners are seen swimming on the beach. However, when it comes to a major change (such as extreme temperature changes, getting terminated from the job, getting a reprimand, having a death in the family, etc.) that is personally impacting a person, individuals of all cultures are likely to respond to it in similar patterns by denying that it happened, being angry about it, justifying the situation with various reasons, exploring their options for dealing with it, accepting it, and eventually moving on to resume normalcy. It is apparent that major environmental, organizational, and interpersonal changes are likely to individually impact people in its path or vicinity. While cultural conditioning can certainly impact one's level of tolerance for change, uncertainty, and ambiguity, everyone, regardless of his or her culture, is likely to go through a similar continuum in his or her response to major changes. Thus, regardless of the culture, individuals who are impacted by a major change should deal with the transition appropriately, proactively, and productively. *Cross-Cultural Change Management* book and strategies can be of some assistance in moving individuals, regardless of their culture, from the continuum of denial and reasoning to the acceptance and motivation stages of dealing with the cycle of change. *Cross-Cultural Change Management* strategies can also help national and international managers and employees effectively deal with stress and conflict while working in diverse cultures around the globe.

Behavioral Differences

Cultures can condition people to behave toward others based on stereotypes and misinformation. A culture can also condition people to become extremists in their views, causes, and behaviors. Example of such conditioning can be seen in cultures and countries where there have been cases of suicide bombers, terrorists, massacre-style killings, beheadings, and racist activities. Since the hijacked airplane attacks on September 11, 2001 on New York City's Twin Towers and the Pentagon Buildings, there has been much focus on the activities of terrorists in foreign countries, especially poorer nations. However, terrorism views, thoughts and behaviors need not come just from poor nations since extreme beliefs can come from any culture and these beliefs can impact people's actions and activities. For example, according to the Southern Poverty Law Center and its founder Morris Dees, the United States is spending billions of dollars fighting terrorists in Iraq yet its Homeland Security Department is ignoring the threat posed by the right-wing domestic terrorist groups. The Southern Poverty Law Center, in its July/August 2005 *Intelligence Report* stated that "Since the devastating Okalahoma City bombing, there have been at least 60 right-wing domestic terrorist plots on our home soil." The Poverty Center continues to say that such plots can include, but are not limited to, bombings of public buildings, assassination of judges who oppose their beliefs, and amassing chemical weapons. Stereotypes and biases are not limited to extremism of political ideologies as they also show up in subtle forms in the workplace, thereby impacting behavioral patterns and decision-making.

Daryl Conner (1992), in his book entitled *"Managing at the Speed of Change,"* mentioned "People with each country demonstrate certain cultural idiosyncrasies in the way they respond to change, of course, but the basic human reactions to change are the same in everyone…executives who successfully implement change, regardless of their location, display many of the same basic emotions, behaviors, and approaches." While some managers demonstrate resiliency in their leadership style and change management, others are influenced by societal biases and stereotypes.

A manager once made a comment that based on his personal experience, Japanese employees work at a very slow pace. Based on limited observations with a few Japanese managers, he concluded that experienced Japanese workers are not concerned about efficiency (getting things done fast) and they work at a slow pace, focusing on one task at a time. First of all, while his observations may very well have been true, he didn't realize that one cannot generalize limited observations to a large group of people. Second, this manager did not realize that while the American culture conditions people to focus on *efficiency*, perhaps doing many things at one time and or doing them fast, other cultures tend to condition people to focus on *effectiveness*, doing the right things right. While many American firms spend very little time in the planning stage of projects, compared to some Japanese firms, American workers tend to end up spending much more time in the rework and fixing of problem process. Perhaps the Japanese culture conditions employees to start with a slow pace at first in order to produce quality products, so there is less rework and fixing of quality-related problems. It might be the result of such conditioning that has made the Japanese automotive industry stay focused on producing fuel-economy quality cars that have captured a huge market share in the United States at a cost to its American competitors. General Motors Corporation, an American firm, announced that they will be laying-off about 25,000 workers between 2005 and 2008 while their Japanese competitors announced that they will raise the prices of their cars in the United States to help American firms stay in business and compete more effectively with global competitors. Another example is the fact that the George Bush Administration in the United States is accused of invading Iraq without good intelligence about Saddam Hussein having Weapons of Mass Destruction (WMD), which were never found and probably did not ever exist. Some individuals from around the globe, including in the United States, are accusing the American government for acting too quickly on starting a war unilaterally without proper planning in advance or involving the United Nations. Some Republicans and Democrats in the United States have said that the war was a mistake. If this war was in fact a mistake, then it was a costly one since about 2,500 American soldiers have lost their lives in the past three years and thousands have been injured; not to mention that many soldiers and civilian contractors from other nations have died in Iraq as well as the fact that according to some reports, over 50,000 Iraqis may have lost their lives thus far because of the U.S. invasion. As a result, the lives of millions of individuals and their families in the United States, Iraq, and other countries have changed for the worse. Of course, the Bush Administration claims that the intention of the invasion was to remove Saddam Hussein from power and to bring democracy and peace in Iraq. Hopefully, the Iraqis will have peace and democracy since their wellbeing is important in the development of a peaceful world. Perhaps such examples show that the Japanese, despite their "perceived" slow pace, are very concerned about efficiency and long-term success. Perhaps, the lesson here is that change requires patience, assessment, analysis, planning, and teamwork.

Understanding personal, professional, and cultural differences requires effective analysis, planning, and training by culturally competent experts or facilitators who understand adults and their learning styles. While adult learning principles and fundamentals can be applied to all types of training, trainers and change agents must still remain sensitive to the audience's culture as well. There are other factors which trainers and change agents should always take into account, such as cultural differences, age, and generational differences among adults. Just as every individual has a learning style preference, some cultures have unique communication styles. These differences can also affect training methods and the participant's learning. Patricia Digh (2002) discusses how environmental cues play an important role in communication:

> Some employees respond better to messages in which everything is spelled out; they don't like nonverbal cues. At the opposite end of the spectrum…they attach much importance to nonverbal cues, and sometimes they derive a lot from what is not said. Some don't hesitate to challenge a message or say they don't understand it. Others prefer "saving face", which means they don't like to admit they disagree with the content of a message or are confused by it (pp. 2-3).

If trainers and change agents are not aware of cultural communication differences, the message can come across from an unintended perspective. Cultural diversity is found among every aspect of an organization, including in the area of training and change management. Experts agree that cultural differences do not disappear simply because people work together or toward a common purpose. When possible, trainers and change agents should attempt to pick up these differences in order to avoid miscommunication. For example, one can consider two specific cultural differences: power distance and uncertainty avoidance (Magnotta and

Mujtaba, 2004). *Power distance*, according to Gert Hofstede, refers to how cultures approach the role of power. For example, cultures that follow low power distance value trainee initiative. They focus on the amount of communication between the entire group including the trainer and anyone who can offer new knowledge. From this perspective, everyone is welcomed to contribute. On the contrary, high power distance follows strict, social roles. Because trainers are viewed as the professionals and are paid to deliver knowledge, trainees can only gain knowledge from them (Training Across Cultures, 1995, p. 3). Another way in which communication can differ is through a concept known as *uncertainty avoidance*. This style of communication deals with how members of a particular culture feel about unstructured or unplanned situations. For cultures that are not afflicted by unstructured circumstances, it is acceptable for trainers not to have a response for every question or concern. In fact, the group takes advantage of such a situation by utilizing diversity and critical thinking skills to come up with a resolution. In contrast, there are some cultures that do not welcome this approach. Instead, training professionals are considered intellectuals who should know the answer to every learner's inquiries (*Training Across Cultures*, 1995, p. 3). As one can see, multiculturalism is a huge factor that should always be closely observed as this may affect learning outcomes.

The art of training can be a challenge in a cross-cultural setting, especially when the trainer cannot easily capture the attention of the audience. Successful training involves understanding the cultural and personal diversity present in the audience and integrating diverse perspectives, interests, and cultural differences into the learning process in order to deliver knowledge effectively. A simple facilitation model can include five basic steps that facilitators can follow to assure effective training when working with a diverse audience (Magnotta and Mujtaba, 2004): 1) Assess the audience; 2) Assess the main purpose of the program; 3) Tailor the broadly structured training program to the audience's preferences and/or needs; 4) After completing the training, ask the audience to evaluate the program and their own learning through a reflective or action learning process; and 5) Evaluate training and audience learning. Trainers and facilitators of change have an important job to do and need to be aware of individual and cultural differences as they have the power to mold each individual's perception of the organization through knowledge.

Gert Hofstede defined culture as "The collective programming of the mind which distinguishes the members of one human group from another...Culture, in this sense, includes systems of values; and values are among the building blocks of culture" (Gert Hofstede, 1984a, p. 21). Along the same lines, Fonts Trompannaar (1993) differentiated between *Universalism* and *Particularism* and used dilemmas to see if respondents lean more toward universalism or particularism based on their cultures. *Universalists* believe what is good and right applies everywhere regardless of the situation or extenuating circumstances. *Particularists* emphasize obligations and relationships. The following are two typical scenarios asked of respondents, by Trompannaar, to see if they say "yes or no" or "agreed or disagreed":

Scenario One: "You are working for a large organization with over 10,000 associates. Your boss asks you to help paint his or her house this weekend." *Would you your help your boss?* The following results of over 15,000 respondents from different countries represent "*the percentage of people who would NOT paint the house.*"

–	Australia	96%
–	USA	89%
–	Japan	83%
–	China	28%
–	Hispanics	17%

Scenario Two: "You are riding with your friend who is driving 75 MPH in a 45 MPH zone. He accidentally hits a pedestrian and you end up going to court with him. His lawyer tells you "don't worry, you are the only witness." Would you agree or disagree with the following statement: "*My friend has NO right or some right and I will NOT help?*" The following are results of 15,000 respondents from different countries who said: "*My friend has NO right or some right and I will NOT help.*"

–	USA	95%
–	Germany	91%
–	France	68%
–	South Korea	26%

The answers from respondents from different countries and continents are often driven by cultural influences; as such, facilitators of change and trainers should take such diverse views into consideration when initiating change. Yes it is difficult, even impossible, for firms, trainers, managers, and facilitators of change to fully understand every aspect of other cultures in a short period of time, but the differences can be managed if they are proactively acknowledged, respected, and integrated into the change management process.

Managers and professional workers need to understand that each culture has its own pace and paradigm with regard to how fast or how slow things should get done. While some cultures are urgency-driven, others have a more balanced approach to tasks since they put relationships first. In the context of the manufacturing work environment, the balanced approach means spending more time on the planning stage so there is less rework, and spending time to get things done right the first time instead of experimenting until one gets it right. Understanding such differences about cultures and time orientations can help managers avoid stereotyping while leading people toward change according to their local norms and customs. Some of the well known researchers on culture and time are Hall and Hall. Consequently, the following paragraphs, summaries and concepts in the next section come directly from the articles, writings, and thoughts of Edward T. Hall and Mildred Reed Hall, which are comprehensively covered in their 1987 textbook titled *"Understanding Cultural Differences."*

Cultural Differences in Time Orientation (Hall & Hall)

Hall and Hall (1987) stated that each culture operates according to its own internal dynamic, its own principles, and its own explicit or implied laws. Even time and space are unique to each culture. There are, however, some common threads that run through all cultures that managers and change agents should consider when working with people from that environment. According to Hall and Hall, *culture* can be likened to a giant, extraordinary complex, subtle computer. It guides the actions and responses of human beings in every walk of life. This process requires attention to everything people do to survive, advance in the world, and gain satisfaction from life. Furthermore, cultural programs do not work if crucial steps are omitted, which happens when people unconsciously apply their own rules to another system. According to Hall and Hall, *cultural communications* are deeper and more complex than spoken or written messages. The essence of effective cross-cultural communication has more to do with sending the right responses than with the "right" messages. *Context* is the information that surrounds an event and it is readily available within the person. The elements, such as the events and context that combine to produce a given meaning, are in different proportions depending on the culture. A *high context* (HC) communication or message is one in which most of the information is already in the person, while very little is in the coded, explicit, transmitted part of the message. A *low context* (LC) communication is just the opposite; i.e., the mass of the information is in the explicit code. Twins who have grown up together can and do communicate more economically (HC) than two lawyers in a courtroom during a trial (LC). Most Japanese, Arabs, and Mediterranean people, who have extensive information networks among family, friends, colleagues, and clients and who are involved in close personal relationships, tend to be high-context. As a result, for most normal transactions in daily life they do not require, nor do they expect, much in-depth, background information (such information already exists or is common knowledge among them).

There are many kinds of time systems in the world, but the two discussed here, according to Hall and Hall, are most important to international business employees and managers. *Monochronic time* means paying attention to, doing and / or focusing on, one thing at a time. *Polychronic time orientation* implies and means being involved with many things at once. In monochronic cultures, time is experienced and used in a linear way. Monochronic time is perceived as being almost *tangible:* people talk about it as though it were money, as something that can be "spent," "saved," "wasted," and "lost." Monochronic time seals people off from one another and as a result intensifies some relationships while shortchanging others. Monochronic time dominates most businesses in the United States, Switzerland, Germany, and Scandinavia. For example, according to Hall and Hall, German and Swiss cultures represent classic examples of monochronic time.

Polychronic time is characterized by the simultaneous occurrence of many things and by a great involvement with people. There is more emphasis on completing human transactions than on holding to pre-determined schedules. Proper understanding of the difference between the monochronic and polychronic time systems can be helpful in dealing with the time-flexible Mediterranean workers. While the generalizations, listed in Table 2, do not necessarily apply equally to all cultures, they do convey a pattern. In monochronic time cultures, the emphasis is on the compartmentalization of functions and people.

Table 2 – Monochronic and Polychronic Time Orientations (Hall & Hall, 1987)

MONOCHRONIC PEOPLE	POLYCHRONIC PEOPLE
Do one thing at a time	Do many things at once
Concentrate on the job	Are highly distractible and subject to interruptions
Take time commitments (deadlines, schedules) seriously	Consider time commitments an objective to be achieved, if possible
Are low-context and need information	Are high-context and already have information
Are committed to the job	Are committed to people and human relationships
Adhere religiously to plans	Change plans often and easily
Are concerned about not disturbing others; follow rules of privacy consideration	Are more concerned with those who are closely related (family, friends, close business associates) than with privacy
Show great respect for private property; seldom borrow or lend	Borrow and lend things often and easily
Emphasize promptness	Base promptness on the relationship
Are accustomed to short-term relationships	Have strong tendency to build lifetime relationships

In polychronic Mediterranean cultures, business offices often have large reception areas where people can wait. Polychronic people feel that private space disrupts the flow of information by shutting people off from one another. In polychronic systems, appointments mean very little and may be shifted around even at the last minute to accommodate someone more important in an individual's hierarchy of family, friends, or associates. Some polychronic people (such as Latin Americans and Arabs) give precedence to their large circle of family members over any business obligation. Polychronic people live in a sea of information.

While working with international firms and diverse cultures, it is important to know which segments of the time frame are emphasized. Cultures in countries such as Afghanistan, Pakistan, Iran, India, and some of the Far East for many individuals are past-oriented; still others, such as those of Latin America, are both past-and present-oriented. In Germany, where historical background is very important, every talk, book, or article seems to begin with background information giving a historical perspective. The Japanese and the French are also steeped in history, and because they are high-context cultures, historical facts are often alluded to in a roundabout way.

Each culture has its language when it comes to *time*. For example, to function effectively in France, Germany, and the United States, it is essential to understand the local language of time. When people take their own time system for granted and project it onto other cultures, they fail to read the hidden messages in the foreign time system and therefore deny themselves vital feedback. For Americans, the use of appointment-schedule time reveals how people feel about each other, how significant their business is, and where they rank in the status system. In France, almost everything is polychromic, whereas in Germany monochronic promptness is even more important than it is in the United States. Often times, due to these differences, some Americans complain that the Germans take forever to reach decisions.

To conduct business in an orderly manner in other countries, it is essential to know how much or how little lead time is required for each activity: how far ahead to request an appointment or schedule meetings and vacations, and how much time to allow for the preparation of a major report. *Lead time* varies from culture to culture and is itself a communication as well as an element in an organization.

The way in which time is treated by some American and German Managers signals attitude, evaluation of priorities, mood, and status. Since time is highly valued in both Germany and the United States, according to Hall and Hall, the messages of time carry more weight than they do in polychronic countries. In the U.S. only those people with very high status can keep others waiting and get away with it. In monochronic cultures such as those in the U.S. and Germany, keeping others waiting can be a deliberate putdown or a signal that the individual is somewhat disorganized and cannot keep to a schedule. In polychronic cultures such as those of France or Hispanic countries, often times no such message is intended.

Overall, interactions between monochronic and polychronic people can be stressful unless both parties know and can decode the meanings behind each other's message and view of time. According to Hall and Hall, the language of time is much more stable and resistant to change than other cultural systems. In organizations, everything management does communicates; thus when viewed in the cultural context, all acts, all events, all material things have meaning (Hall and Hall, 1987).

There are many subtle and unique (not so subtle) differences in the time orientation of workers in Germany, France and the United States that must be considered by global managers and employees. According to Hall and Hall, as in most other countries and traditions, time lies at the core of German culture. For Germans, it is one of the ultimate means of organizing life. In general, German time and

American time are both monochronic and follow the same basic patterns. Germans are very high on the monochronic scale, and their consensus decision-making processes are often more involved and deliberate than the American. Because the Germans tend to approach decision making slowly and laboriously, once a decision is made they stand firmly and unalterably behind it. When Germans explain something to an audience, they often find it necessary to lay a proper foundation. Such lengthy explanations make the average American impatient and can be challenging to some of the French people. The German preoccupation with historical context brings up the matter of pace and how fast things are supposed to get done. Because decision making in Germany requires seemingly interminable discussion, a slow response to a business proposal does not necessarily mean lack of interest. The slower German pace can affect day-to-day life. The slow pace is hard on Americans, who must constantly remind themselves that Germans resent being tailgated. Polychronic people tend to adhere to a time system that emphasizes involvement with people and minimizes scheduling and compartmentalization. When a polychronic French manager is late to a meeting, the monochronic German is likely to misinterpret the tardiness as irresponsibility, egocentricity, or rudeness. Such judgments and interpretations can make change implementation very difficult when diverse individuals are involved.

French people tend to be high on the polychronic scale. This means they do many things at once; they can tolerate constant interruptions and are totally involved with people; they maintain direct eye contact and use all their senses: visual, auditory, and olfactory. Because they are highly polychronic, the French don't always adhere to schedules or appointments, delivery dates, or deadlines. The polychronic French also think nothing of changing plans at the last minute. This is very unsettling to most Americans and Germans, who consider such behavior irresponsible. Long-term planning is not the norm for the French. They are all too aware of the many things that may prevent their keeping a commitment as conditions and people may change. How can one predict the future? Many French people tend to see planning as a challenging task and tend to ignore it. This is because they expect interruptions and changes due to new knowledge, new technology, different demands, changing directions from managers, and other such variables. The French insist on enjoying life now, making the most of each day which is probably why they tend to ignore making rigid long-term schedules. In decision making, the French are able to move more rapidly than the Germans because they have a highly centralized authority structure. French executives can and do make independent decisions and don't have to go through several levels in the hierarchy for decisions, as is common in Germany.

The majority of American businesspeople are monochronic in how they approach time. For most Americans, time is scheduled and compartmentalized so that people can concentrate on one thing at a time. Schedules are sacred and time commitments are taken seriously. There are polychronic Americans, usually from families with origins in Latin America, the Mediterranean countries, or the Middle East. They handle time differently and are neither prompt nor necessarily scrupulous in observing deadlines. In their business and professional lives, however, most Americans adhere to the monochronic norms of Anglo-Saxon culture. American time and consciousness are fixed in the present. Many business-minded Americans tend to be impatient and generally do not like to wait; they want results now. They move at a rapid pace; everything about their business lives is hurried. Wanting quick answers and quick solutions, they are not used to waiting long periods of time for decisions and become anxious when decisions are not made promptly. This attitude puts them at a disadvantage in dealing with people such as the Germans, Jamaicans, Japanese, and Latin Americans, all of whom tend to take more time to reach decisions. American businesspeople tend to think in short-term intervals. When American businesspeople talk about the "long term," they usually mean no more than two or three years and this is not necessarily the mindset in other cultures. Such differences in time-orientation and pace can impact how managers initiate, plan for, and implement major organizational changes.

Cultural Values and Decision Making

Personal, organizational, and cultural values can be subconscious and impact a person's decisions. Values have an impact on one's everyday life and they shape as well as define one's character. Living by a personal code of ethics helps managers and leaders remain consistent when defining themselves and shaping the perception of others. The result of a decision oftentimes characterizes the process in which people follow when making decisions. Understanding the reasons behind decisions requires thoughtful consideration of the action one takes. Personal, organizational, or cultural values are the foundation on which decisions are made in the day-to-day operations. If personal values are a definition of who you are and what you do, then ensuring your actions are ethical is crucial to change and social development. Personal values are not always perceptible, so you can judge the effect you have on a situation by examining your actions.

American business culture typically views the global business arena as the marketplace where competition is encouraged. Although the American culture has always had an international flavor, many individuals living in the United States understand very little about the cultural values outside of their comfort zone (Cant, 2004). More than ever, boundaries in which global businesses were once limited, are now open, making it more important than ever for people to embrace their cultural values. Seeking to understand our values provide opportunities to reflect on who we are and gives us reason to explore the values of other cultures. However, there is a sense of individualism that exists in the American business culture and, at times it acts as a barrier to higher learning (Barnett, Weathersby & Aram, 1995). This individualistic approach can adversely affect the decisions we make when representing ourselves in the global environment. Therefore, understanding our values, specifically our cultural values, will provide us with the tools to make good choices when presenting ourselves outside of our own culture.

The values by which we live influence our everyday decisions, thus having a solid understanding of our values is essential in not only making good choices but also influencing the decisions others make. For example, according to one colleague's business trip to Bangalore, India (late 2004 and early 2005) to conduct training for new staff, a personnel conflict materialized where intervention was required. The conflict developed between an American business manager who worked for their most important business partner, and their Indian technical support outsource vendor. Upon arriving, members of the Indian outsource vendor greeted them with "open arms" and treated them extremely well. The vendor was a very large company, much larger than their company, and the level of respect in which they showed was supposedly impressive.

A couple of days into the month-long trip, the manager who worked for their business partner was becoming noticeably agitated by inconveniences outside of the work environment. Things such as the food choices, transportation challenges, solicitors, and communication barriers seemed to set him off on rants. This seemed quite odd because everyone else was having a wonderful time, despite facing major cultural differences, and these inconveniences were a minor price to pay for such a great experience. Unfortunately after a few days of this type of behavior, his attitude began to spill over into the workplace. This behavior caused tension between everyone involved in the project, including their hosts who seemed to sense the negative posture and withdrew some of their generosity. With the tension rising and the project at risk of falling behind schedule, the decision was made to counsel the business manager on the effects of his behavior. The complicated aspect of this dilemma was trying to rectify the situation without offending their most important client. Although the company's organizational values were not formalized, there was a clear understanding that maintaining the well being of business partner is a top priority. However, this colleague's personal and cultural values of treating all people with respect and total equality are values that follow him into any situation. Therefore, weighing the company objective against doing the right thing was obviously going to be a challenge. The first step in educating the business manager was to point out all of the wonderful things that India had to offer. Continuing to iterate that one of the core values of the Indian culture is being a great host, pointing out that their friends had gone to great lengths to ensure that all of their needs are taken care of, and by complaining they will most likely offend their Indian host. They also found out that one of the Indian executives had an MBA from the top business school in the U.S. and was once a professional golfer on the Nike tour. Moreover, the technical support agents that they were there to train all had advanced engineering degrees. The goal was to educate him on the culture and to make him realize his misunderstandings of a developing country, all the while assuring him that the people they are working with have similar goals and aspirations as this colleague's organization. Later that evening there was a noticeable change in his tone of voice, evolving from a condescending tone to one that showed more respect. Not surprisingly soon after, some of the issues that were bogging them down went away, putting the project back on track.

These types of decisions made along the way in international settings will most likely determine the level of success a business or an individual achieves. An executive or a senior organizational leader is a person who always decides; sometimes he or she decides correctly, but s/he always decides (Moncur, 2004). Making decisions is a way of life; but in order to make good decisions, one must have a firm understanding of the effects that morals, ethics, and values have on the outcomes.

Today, the United States is made up of a diverse population of people with different ethnic backgrounds, from different parts of the world, and with different cultural values. So, how does one define cultural values in such a society? "Cultural values can be viewed as a desirable or preferred way of acting or knowing something that has been reinforced by the social structure and, ultimately, governs one's actions or decisions (Leininger, 1985, pp. 209-212). These values can be reflected in a person's cultural perception of time, personal space, communication style, role of gender and family, as well as in their practices regarding such aspects of daily living as diet, modesty, self-care, and "hot" versus "cold" remedies. However, "a person's country and culture of origin and his or her current country of residence can complicate differences that seemingly reflect prevailing cultural norms" (Laukaran & Winikoff, 1986, pp.121-128). The diversity of the people in the world today has changed the way people view and understand what cultural values are and how they should be celebrated.

According to a colleague, named Mele K. Akuna (Personal Communication, March 2005) from Hawaii, the Hawaiian cultural values embrace the importance of family and the land. Respect for family and land are the most important values that continue to be practiced today. She further went on to say that many businesses in Hawaii are beginning to understand the importance of Hawaiian cultural values, and are incorporating these values into the way they conduct business as well as the way they treat their employees. Hawaii has its own culture that makes operating different for mainland and foreign companies. Businesses have survived on their long standing relationships with their customers, and continue to survive on loyalty. Unfortunately, new businesses have attempted to open up shop in Hawaii, but failed. Their failure was not because their product was not attractive to the people who live there, but the fact that they did not recognize the need to respect the cultural values of the people. Hawaii may seem like islands made up of a small population of people; however, the communities are very close-knit. Many people base their decisions on what the family has been doing for the past many years, or by word of mouth. People in Hawaii respect each other to the point that they do not always look into matters themselves, but they trust the word of their family and neighbors. Even with the opening of superstores like Safeway, Wal-Mart, and Costco so many "Mom and Pop" stores remain in business because of their loyal customers and personal relationships. Overall, to be a successful manager working for a business in Hawaii, cultural values of the local people need to be understood and practiced. Hawaii is such a diverse state that successful managers need to have a good understanding of who their employees are, where their values are formed, and how their ethnic backgrounds differ. Management must also take into consideration the family lifestyle in Hawaii; and thus how they decide to do business there will determine how successful the business will be in the long-term.

In addition to cultural values, personal ethics also play an important role in being a successful manager. How does one define personal ethics? *Personal ethics* have been defined as principles of good behavior. Simply stated, "*personal ethics* are nothing more than the rules we impose on ourselves that govern our daily actions" (David, 2003, p. 230). So, how do personal ethics and cultural values impact management's decision-making process in Hawaii? Well, just like the importance of cultural values and the impact it has on business, personal ethics are just as important. Like most small cities, according to Mele Akuna, the lifestyle of people living in Hawaii is so close-knit that news of someone or a company that does not conduct business in an ethical manner will travel quickly. It would not take the nightly television newscast to spread the news to the people of Hawaii. Therefore, as a manager, proper training in ethical conduct is a must. Friedman (1970) states that the sole moral responsibility of a business is to maximize profits while respecting the laws and ethical rules of the society in which it is located. Of course, this view is not accepted universally since much more is expected of organizations.

The success of a business is a reflection of management of the business and their cultural, personal, and organizational values. Cultures evolve and reflect the goals and values of an organization. In turn, "the organization's ethical decisions can have a strong impact on the organization's culture and this gives top management a degree of control on the composition of the corporate culture" (Reidenbach and Robin, 1989). As a manager in today's world, profits play a very important role in the success of a business; however, it can all be for nothing if people within the business are not practicing good ethical conduct, have no respect for the place where their business is conducted, and do not show respect for the people who help make the business a success. Continuous training in ethical practices, as well as cultural and organizational values will keep employees honest, and they will cherish the company's goals as if it were their own.

Cultural values which include freedom, prosperity, and security are the basis for the specific norms that tell people what is appropriate in various situations (Schwartz, 1999). Cultural values are shared in societal institutions such as family, political systems, religious references, and education or economic institutions. Therefore, the goals or ways of operation represent the values people believe in. The leaders of institutions, for example, parents, teachers, a CEO of a corporation, or a president of a country can draw on these values to select socially appropriate behaviors. These behaviors are communicated to the societal members through everyday exposure to family rules, regulations from the workplace, or laws (Schwartz, 1999). Societal members adapt to the functions of the institutions with whom they spend their time (Schwartz, 1999). In sum, a culture exists where a group of people share a set of beliefs, norms, and customs (Singhapakdi, Marta, Rawwas, & Ahmed, 1999). There are no national boundaries for a culture to exist; however, for nations that have been established for some time, the sharing of culture is substantial (Hofstede, Neuijen, Ohayv, & Sander, 1990).

In a capitalist society, individual ambitions and success are highly valued; the structures of the economic and legal systems are competitive. In contrast, the social culture tends to be in more cooperative economic and legal systems (Schwartz, 1999). A study was completed to compare consumers from Malaysia and the U.S.A. in terms of their corporate marketing ethics, and the result reveals significant differences between the two countries. Malaysians specifically and people in the developing nations in general tend to have lower ethical perceptions than the people from the United States or the industrialized countries (Hofstede, Neuijen, Ohayv & Sander, 1990). A research study was conducted on how business ethics is perceived across cultures among college students in different countries. The study confirms that cultural differences do exist and they affect how people perceive ethical business differently (Ahmed, Chung & Eichenseher, 2003). At the time of the study, Malaysia's economy had boomed along with its competition; therefore, the pressure was on for many Malaysian managers. Some believed it is acceptable to conduct business unethically. Similarly, the U.S. corporate executives continue to struggle with the unrealistic earning expectations (Tinkler, 2004). Could this type of pressure on management be the cause of the latest round of scandals with Enron, MCI, Tyco, Arthur Anderson, Worldcom, and others? Perhaps, and of course, there might be many other reasons and pressures as well. Unfortunately, there are some individuals who consciously subscribe to the paradigm of "buy, lie and deny" so long as it is advantageous to oneself without considering the harm to society or others.

Individual values are the products of shared cultures and unique personal experiences. For most individuals, family is the first institution in which values are instilled in children through their parents. Family is where the first and foremost fundamental training on ethics is acquired. Religious institutions are another avenue where values and beliefs are taught. Children are raised not to lie, not to cheat, to be responsible for their actions, to treat people as they want to be treated, etc. As such, most individuals seem to know the difference between right and wrong. Studies have shown that people who commit unethical acts know they are doing something wrong (Tinkler, 2004).

The most basic moral values are learned as children; and as children enter adulthood, more values are acquired at different institutions. When adults enter the workforce, there are rules of conduct imposed by companies and organizations that employees must follow. These professional values can be defined as "values relating to one's professional conduct that are commonly shared by the member of a particular profession" (Singhapadki & Vitell 1993b, p. 528). These organizational values are communicated through written codes of ethics, as well as formal and informal training. While there are no "right" or "wrong" values, there are values that are better aligned with the organization's culture and codes of ethics. Corporate values must be explicit, and they are applied to everyone in the organization including top management (Patten, 2004). Everyone must see that top managers are responsible for their ethical behavior, and employees need to be rewarded for ethical behavior and face consequences for unethical behavior (Patten, 2004).

In recent years, many corporate scandals have come to light. Ethics has become so important and often emphasized in society that it has become a major academic topic. The cultural values, the workforce and personal standards are interrelated; individuals exposed to these values will need to form their own rules of conduct. Life presents people with many choices; and decisions will be made based on personal rules of conduct. Of course, it is best not to choose the most convenient way to conduct business or personal affairs, but to instead choose the way that is aligned with one's overall life goals.

Asian culture is one of the many cultures in the United States, and it is different from the "American culture" in many ways. For example, Asian children are taught that it is impolite to talk back to the elderly, but in American culture it is a way for children to express themselves. People, who are exposed to both cultures, sometimes find it difficult to balance and/or determine which culture to adopt; especially for the younger generation. Religion also plays a strong role in shaping a person to act ethically toward another individual and have respect for a spiritual power. Again, while people know the difference between right and wrong, factors such as emotion, time constraints, and social pressures can become the major factors in their personal as well as professional lives. In challenging times of monumental changes, one needs to step back when faced with difficult decisions and find a balance where one would feel comfortable and happy while respecting everyone else's cultural norms.

Global Mindset and Learning

Managers, particularly top leaders and human resources managers, need to concern themselves with more than just profits or "making the bottom-line numbers" at the end of each week, month or year. They need to concern themselves with the well-being of their people. Carol Hymowitz, in her Wall Street Journal article on March 8 (2005, p. B1) titled *"When Meeting Targets Becomes the Strategy, CEO is on Wrong Path,"* stated that when companies become fixated on hitting quarterly or daily targets, oftentimes they don't produce sustainable profit growth. She quoted organizational psychologist Richard Hagberg, who said "It's hard to capture employees' hearts, and best efforts, with numbers alone." In a study of 31 corporations, Hagberg's staff found that the highest returns were achieved at companies whose CEOs set challenging financial goals, but also articulated a purpose beyond profit making, such as creating a great product, and convincing employees their work mattered. Similarly, Susan Annunzio, CEO of the Hudson Highland Center for High Performance in Chicago, found that the biggest impediment to high performance–defined by her as making money for the company and developing new products, services and markets – is short-term focus. In 2003, she and her staff researched 3,000 managers and knowledge workers at global companies such as Microsoft, Intel and J.P. Morgan Chase. About 10% of the respondents said they worked in high-performing groups, and 38% said they worked in "nonperforming groups." Yet almost one-third of the non-performers said their businesses used to be high performing (meaning that something changed this trend). Annunzio and her staff asked what had happened and the respondents had said "top management raised our targets, cut our budgets and staff, and we couldn't sustain results."

As global managers and agents of change, professionals need to concern themselves with the people side of the business. Global managers and change agents need to be concerned with culture shock syndrome - both upon arrival and departure, issues to be considered when relocating to another country, family issues, health care issues, education of children and family members, taxes, living quarters, salary, cost of living equity, transportation, local laws, etc. Overall, culture makes a big difference in how managers manage within each country. Besides culture, a country's political and economical consideration further complicates the equation for international human resources managers. An example of such complexity in the global management arena is the situation with the culture of Russians. Russia has been, and is, a market with huge opportunities for businesses, but most of its institutions are still in the infant stage, giving rise to economic instability and limited market conditions. Its high unemployment and lower GDP per capita also seem a constraint for a constant consumer purchase power. The Russian culture is evolving, helped by a rank of young Russian professionals that are becoming more individualistic. Cross-cultural training is a mandatory activity for all employees involved in international business. For expatriates, it is critical to also train the immediate family members and relatives as what to expect from the new culture. Otherwise, failure could come not only from the economic activities but also from political, marketing, interpersonal, and cultural differences.

Summary

In today's world, change is a constant for almost all individuals. For global managers and professional employees, business-related crisis seems to be a continuous dynamic causing unexpected change and stress. Culture seems to be one factor that conditions people, at least to some extent, toward the acceptance or resistance of change. Cultures can also drive people toward certain behaviors, at times subconsciously.

With the convergence of a global workplace, there is a need to ensure that people are not discriminated against nationally or internationally. So, to ensure continuity amid major changes in a culturally diverse environment, and to create an inclusive work environment throughout the company, everyone should be required to attend sensitivity training. Sensitivity training involves understanding different cultures and how people of different cultures act in various situations. Cultural diversity in the workplace is becoming common in today's society, especially in the United States, where more businesses are becoming global and the diverse workplace is becoming more apparent. Not to mention the fact that most firms are becoming a melting pot of different cultures and ethnic backgrounds. This global diversity and the increase in import penetration in the United States are forcing more and more companies to create a diverse workplace and to have diversity training to promote a wide range of different cultures without being afraid of expressing one's view or losing business unnecessarily. So, companies shall continue to conduct cultural awareness training that will create awareness of the different cultures and how these cultures are an asset to the overall success of the company in the long-term. Such awareness and improved interpersonal relationships can enhance the change management process.

Chapter Two

SOCIALLY RESPONSIBLE CHANGE

G lobal leadership and effective change management are essential elements of business success in the twenty-first century. Effective international change management strategies in business tend to vary from country to country; therefore, global leaders should be aware of the culture and social standards of foreign nations before embarking on major changes. Global leaders in the twenty-first century environment should make decisions that are effective and aligned with both local and international norms and policies. These leaders need to ensure that work practices throughout the global organization are accurate, that all the subsidiaries are treated fairly, or equal to the parent company, and their organizations are socially responsible in implementing change.

Cross-Cultural Communication

The book entitled *Cross-Cultural Communication- the Essential Guide to International Business* was published in 2003 and edited by John Mattock. The book is dedicated to companies that are marketing towards the global economy. International business is now the ongoing trend for most large organizations. When dealing with companies outside the United States, managers must consider the cultural values; and then find a way to broaden communication and its effectiveness. By communicating effectively, employees and managers learn how to empathize with the traditional roles and leadership styles of other organizations. *Cross-Cultural Communication* offers suggestions on ways to foster communication and understand cultural influences when doing business internationally. It also discusses various negotiation strategies, better ways to interpret indifferences of behavior and managerial styles, avoiding stereotypes, and overcoming culture shock. *Cross-Cultural Communication* is informative in that the concepts can be practiced in organizations today.

Over the past century, the traditional barriers of distance and culture have decreased with the diversity of each nation's workforce and convergence of technological advances. The dot-com era brought about a revolutionary change, by just the click of a mouse. Managers can now interact with organizations worldwide and increase their economic success. The dot-com era then influenced the desire of companies to go global. Going global was then seen as tangible, and companies wanted to increase profit, consequently competing better in the marketplace. However, marketing and communicating cross-culturally in the global environment were not easy tasks. There were many risks/threats that could be faced by targeting foreign markets around the globe.

Communication, the art of exchanging information, is one of the most fragile tools in global marketing. Companies and their managers communicate daily, discussing different business processes in their everyday decisions; therefore, it is essential to communicate both efficiently and effectively. When it comes to cross-cultural communication, cultures are different and managers must be sensitive to the public's perception of their business practices in order to create trust. There are many participants in the communication process, such as suppliers, competitors, distributors, and customers. Political and legal forces influence businesses to comply with rules and laws regarding fair business practices. The business society, in many countries, has shifted from a totalitarian management approach towards a free market society. Some argue that the totalitarian regime is no way for a government to run an economy because free markets allow people to act at their own pace. Therefore, a shift has been triggered by the realization that government involvement in the economic activity often impedes a country's economic growth. Consequently, more organizations are breaking away from the old approach to management. Joint ventures are commonly used to balance command economy instabilities. Exxon Mobile is a company that has excelled as a global organization, ranked number one with regard to revenues. Exxon, the leading oil company, merged with Mobile to become a global power, taking advantage of corporate synergy. Its successful communication strategies led to the company's success.

In *Cross-Cultural Communication*, the main success elements mentioned for an organization are: culture, company, character, tactics, timing, and talk. These processes are broken down into a pyramid of six upward steps. The concepts can assist business and entrepreneurs in formalizing a better communication chain amongst business partners. The six processes list the word *culture* at the bottom of the pyramid and *talk* at the top of the pyramid.

Culture. At the bottom of the pyramid there is the word *culture.* When people think of cultures, they look at the norms of attitudes and behavior amongst people within the community or nation. One may notice and make a distinction between the food, conversation, dress, and even ethics of the culture. It is stated that "the business stands or falls on the understanding of the other side, what motivates them, what their priorities are, and how they will change as the relationship matures" (Mattock, 2003). These assumptions are very normal. However people must be careful about the assumptions they make, not to be stereotypical. Stereotypes create barriers in the communication process; stereotyping is a form of prejudice and generalization. It shelters the mind to a perceived reality that disallows one to see the actual facts. Stereotypes are not necessarily always based on "the mistakes of facts, but they do tend to mistake the part for the whole. They are often out of date, twisted by the media, and popular mythologies" (Mattock, 2003, p.14). People must do away with stereotyping in order to better communicate across borders. John Mattock demonstrates how to create a model to better understand the cultural patterns, which enable managers and global employees to seek out the facts in predicting behavior, which goes beyond distorted observations. Culture shock is a feeling that a manager or individual may face when working, or visiting a foreign company. At first, the new things and ways may fascinate one, and after time one can become afraid because when reality sinks in, adjusting gets more difficult. Communicating can become harder, and difficulties with functioning in everyday life may arise. People must research the culture, not just the place and get prepared accordingly, when deciding to go abroad since going into a new culture is a major change.

Company. The *Company* culture is the second stage of the pyramid. The *company* operates in the contexts of the culture. Employees must learn the culture of the organization. Japan's form of government is parliamentarian democracy under the rule of a constitutional monarch. The dominant religion is Shinto, which is exclusive to Japan. By knowing such factors one can tell that many Japanese tend to be somewhat introverted in their ways of doing business. They generally are not receptive to outsiders. Loyalty and relationships are crucial when doing business. Japanese have traditionally valued lifetime employment, company unions, and the seniority system of pay and promotions. When deciding on conducting business in Japan, American companies must realize that relationships and loyalty to the group is critical for success. They should analyze how the

Japanese company officials might think, and what are their motivations and expectations, raising questions such as:

- Are workers people oriented?
- Do they focus on product or service quality?
- Are decisions centralized or decentralized?
- Who are their competitors, and what do they value?
- Do they empower?
- Who are the workers (gender, age, class)?
- Who are the suppliers, customers, and how are they treated?

When managers and employees figure out the answer to these questions then they can better communicate and find ways to motivate all employees. When people have an understanding of the culture, the language, and the hierarchy approach, everyone can better understand the differences.

Character. The third variable of the pyramid is *character.* A person's *character* reflects on the drives, moods, and personality of the individual. It is important not to let one's expectations of say, Chinese behavior, blind one to the behavior patterns of a particular Chinese person one is dealing with (Mattock, 2003, p.71). How can someone's character be defined? Does he/she have a high or low tolerance for change or ambiguity, is s/he well respected, dedicated, intrinsically motivated, reactive, and so on will help describe a person's character. One should also look at the values of the global organization, and the behavioral patterns. Study the culture's way of life, instead of just formulating judgments of character. For example, instead of saying he/she is quiet and non-social look into the customs, and analyze the background of the individual to see why he/she is an introvert; is it because of the cultural influences? In high-text cultures verbalizing is low; people rely on facial expressions, body language, inflections of the voice, and eye contact as a way to communicate. Therefore, "those raised in such an atmosphere can get impatient with low context communicators" (Mattock, 2003, p. 70). In low context cultures, verbalizing is essential to communicating; communication is fostered through phones and face-to-face conversations back and forth; "these people sometimes think that high context communicators are chaotic, secretive, unreliable, and emotional." Gert Hofstede's model of national culture discusses power distance as "the degree to which societies accept the economic and social distances in wealth, status, and well being that result from distances in individual capabilities" (Jones & George, 2003, p. 201). One must determine whether or not there is a high or low power distance. Some cultures are also low on uncertainty avoidance and are afraid to take risks; therefore, they do everything to avoid conflict. By knowing the character of individuals and how they communicate, global employees and managers will have a clear understanding of communicating across borders.

Tactic. Tactic is the fourth variable of the pyramid. *Tactic* is defined as a planned action for accomplishing an end. People want end results and get it by enforcing planned strategies and policies. They ask the questions, what disciplines can be used, are they effective, what are some ways of negotiating, how will the organization, or individual benefit from the tactics? Japanese people tend to do this by establishing their work and authority effectively. They negotiate by discussion, meeting protocols, socializing, and gift giving. *Cross- Cultural Communication* tells managers to know the attitude of the company or the individual. It will gives clues on what is the right tactic to use; are they persuasive, loyal, honest, or manipulative? Furthermore, a global manager should:

- Know his or her own attitude,
- Know the company's or individual's attitude,
- Know their bargaining range, and
- Deliver a message to suit the partner.

Timing. Timing is the fifth variable of the pyramid. *Timing* in every organization is essential. Many organizations revolve around different time frames and measures. Beware of time differences and know when is a good time to market to an organization or its management. Depending on the culture, it may take a longer or shorter time to do things. Consider technology when thinking of time, other organizations may not be as flexible or as advanced. The Internet and conference calling has made it faster and easier to communicate. Video conferencing is another attribute that is used to communicate effectively and fast.

Talk. The pinnacle of the pyramid is *Talk.* One can communicate effectively by learning the language, learning about the language, or teaching the language. Listening and understanding verbal and non-verbal signs are essential. The moment of contact is crucial in the business process because money, respect and trust can be abandoned if things are misunderstood. It is best to encourage individuals to learn more than one language. In American schools, many foreign languages are taught and managers can certainly take advantage of these programs before moving into a new country. Managers must eliminate any barrier to communication, and open their minds towards cross-cultural communication. With the diversity of today's nations it is essential to learn ways to build strong relationships with foreign organizations. It is very important to maintain a relationship that provides trust, dependence, cooperation, information exchange, and commitment. Cross cultural managers also must rid the transactional model of communication and enforce relationship modeling in order to create long-term value for all parties involved. Managers can do this by first educating themselves; then, they must strategically plan for long-term improvement which may be time-consuming and a bit challenging. Companies must then conduct seminars to talk, teach, promote, and discuss cross-cultural communication.

Cross-Cultural Communication and its concepts are helpful for the twenty-first century managers because it focuses on ways to communicate and add value not only to the organization, but to people in all cultures. It also helps foster teams and intercultural long-term relationships. Value over time can be developed through these practices and understanding of one's culture and the norms of behavior. *Cross-Cultural Communication* teaches the importance of people, and that there isn't only one style of managing. Managing styles may have to shift or be adjusted to fit the organizational culture. *Cross-Cultural Communication* teaches global managers and employees about workforce diversity, and how to be effective in cross-cultural communication strategies.

The Principles of Entrepreneurship

The textbook, published in 2003 by Yerkes and Decker, entitled *Beans* is the story of The El Espresso, a coffee shop in Seattle, Washington. The book describes how The El Espresso conducts business in a world facing constant change in the business arena. According to the authors, *Beans* is the story of a return to the "old ways" of doing business. This book identifies the factors which go into the making of a successful business at times when change is inevitable. Once a hugely successful small business firm, The El Espresso began to see a decline in sales. The decline was caused by not focusing on quality and the fact that nearby offices that provided much business moved out of the area. As a result, they had to examine the quality of customer service that was being provided. It was decided that they needed to seek the advice of a consultant who would observe the business and make suggestions to get back to how things used to be, growing. The story demonstrates that "often the secret to success in bad times is to do what you did when you created the good times to begin with" (Yerkes & Decker, 2003, p. 90).

Yerkes and Decker identify and examine five concepts that are important to successfully operating and running a business in the twenty-first century environment. They are the four Ps: passion, people, personal, and product; and the Eye of Intention. According to the authors, the four Ps "cover all the essential ingredients for success." These principles can be applied to any business, regardless of its size or particular industry, to help it run more successfully and improve business processes and service quality.

Passion. Passion for life and work forms the basis of an individual's attitude that he or she brings to work everyday. Passion for work or a particular industry is the reason that people select the career that they do. Many people settle for jobs that they are not passionate about, and as a result, their job performance suffers. Jack Hartman, the owner of The El Espresso, had tremendous passion for the coffee shop. He and his wife devoted themselves to learning all that they could about coffee. Every cup of coffee that they produced was the best that it could be. One thing that they realized, however, was that no matter how much passion they had for their jobs, their customers needed to have a similar level of passion if they were to stay in business. In other words, customers needed to become raving fans and cheerleaders. Therefore, Jack and Dianne, his wife, sought out to generate passion in their customers every day. One way in which they accomplished this was by making every cup of coffee a double shot while still selling it for the regular price of a single. In a sense, Jack and Dianne created a competitive advantage over the other coffee shops, because their coffee would always be twice as good as the competitors. Both employees and managers must possess a passion both for the business and for making people happy. It is has been said that "When you allow your passion to be the center of your work, your work becomes play. And that makes work fun, and ultimately successful" (Yerkes & Decker, p. 93).

People. The second P stands for people, including both employees and customers. Jack was somewhat disturbed with the "work-think of the last hundred years," which stated that "employees were a necessary evil – that every business would run much more smoothly" without their moods and problems. Jack sought out employees who shared his values. One of those values is the idea that "work is more than the money" (Yerkes & Decker, 2003, p. 23). Jack looked for potential employees "who first had passion and second had the right attitude" (Yerkes & Decker, p. 23). It is important to look for people who share your values, who can then be trained on the skills required by the job. Another method that Jack uses to bring people together is encouraging his employees to engage the customers. There are several reasons for doing this. One reason is so that customers develop a strong relationship with employees, the company, and the product or service. A second reason is that when customers develop a connection with the company, they will be less likely to spend their money with a competitor. Passion and people greatly impact one another. When employees enjoy their work and are passionate about what they do, their loyalty to the company and to customers increases. Several positive effects result. Of course, loyal employees produce and offer better products and services. Better products and services attract better and more customers, and better customers are loyal, which ultimately means greater value to a business (Yerkes & Decker, p. 94). It is also important to create shared expectations with employees in order to ensure that both parties are clear at all times about the intentions of the company. This way, employees will always know what is expected of them at all times. Rather than using "fear or force" to achieve results, managers should "honor all employees and value their contributions" (Yerkes & Decker, p. 95).

Personal. Keeping things personal is the third P and Jack treats his "customers as friends first instead of customers" (Yerkes & Decker, p. 43). For example, learning customer names is one method Jack uses to differentiate his company from the rest. Jack even takes this concept one step further and tries to learn what his customers like to do when they are not working or how many people they have in their family. This creates a stronger connection between Jack and customers. Jack makes sure to incorporate this strategy throughout the company by hiring employees who have passion, who "just sort of pick up on making things personal" (Yerkes & Decker, p. 47). Of course, the more connections that exist between customers and employees, the greater will be the bond, the greater the loyalty, and the greater the financial success of the organization (Yerkes & Decker, p. 47). Customer loyalty has a direct relationship with employee loyalty: when employee loyalty wanes, so does customer loyalty. Employees who are loyal act selflessly and put both the company and the customer first. However, when employees lose loyalty to the company, they often distance themselves and "become antagonistic" in their behavior toward the customers and the company. Making it personal creates "a connection between the customer and the business that extends beyond the product, a connection that builds loyalty" (Yerkes & Decker, p. 95). Making it personal creates the kind of experience that customers seek – the kind that they will share with their friends and family.

Product. The fourth P stands for product. An important issue when considering a company product is consistency both in the product and its complementary services. Maintaining consistency can ensure that customer expectations will never be let down. According to Yerkes & Decker, "Having the right product is a combination of the right beans, knowing how to prepare them the right way, and training employees to pull each drink the same way each and every time they make it." In other words, quality, knowledge, and technical skill all contribute to the development of a great product. Product consistency creates a confidence in customers that will often increase loyalty to the business. Service plays a large role in addition to product quality. As Yerkes & Decker state, bad or poor service can drive customers away from a good product; "yet not even superlative service can overcome bad product" (p. 66). Jack sets standards for his business and makes sure that everyone keeps them. For example, if the wholesale price of beans went up, Jack would not switch to a cheaper bean; rather, he would maintain the quality of the product and take the hit himself or pass along the price increase to customers. In this case, customers usually do not mind paying a little extra if they know why there was a price increase. To be successful in business, "the first thing is …to get the fundamentals right…fundamentals start with the product" (Yerkes & Decker, p. 68). Product quality should be job one. In fact, quality is no longer the responsibility of just one department. Research has demonstrated that "the most successful businesses are those in which the employees take ownership, accountability, and responsibility not only for their actions, but for the quality and consistency of the product itself" (Yerkes & Decker, p. 70). Research also has demonstrated that "as the quality of the product rises, so does employee loyalty" (Yerkes & Decker, p. 70). In essence, business owners should be passionate about the quality of their product and service and encourage employees to do the same (Yerkes & Decker, 2003).

The eye of intention. The Eye of Intention, in essence, is the idea of being clear about organizational goals and milestones. Yerkes and Decker state that "If you don't know where you're going in business or life, or what you intend to have happen along the way, you can't effectively decide what to do next or if you're even on the road to success…without a plan, it's not possible to accurately determine what success is" (p. 80). In other words, results must be examined in terms of a company's intentions. They continue to say that "Every result you achieve can only be evaluated with regard to your intention." Before a company, or an individual, can become successful, success must be defined for the person, company and the specific project or task. When the results match the intentions, then you have arrived at the train-stop known as success (Yerkes & Decker, 2003, p. 98).

Beans and the theories and principles discussed by Yerkes and Decker are helpful for the twenty-first century's global management practitioners. Some companies and organizations today have forgotten what is important when running a business. Many entrepreneurs tend to focus on profit and short-term value for the company and forget what it is that really makes a company successful. Yerkes and Decker (2003) identify five principles for running a business, which are the four Ps and the Eye of Intention. In many organizations, employees are not passionate about their work. Remembering to select individuals who have similar values as the organization and who share a passion about the business should reduce the numbers of individuals who lack passion in the workplace. More than ever, organizations are creating an environment where employees cannot openly express ideas or make suggestions without a fear of recrimination. Yerkes and Decker suggest creating an atmosphere that is supportive and does not involve the use of fear or force in managing employees. In such an environment, change can happen without much resistance since employees tend to trust managers. Some companies today forget that the customer comes first. It is crucial for managers to ensure that the organizational culture is customer-oriented and that employees remember to value the customer. Some organizations tend to compromise quality in order to increase their bottom-line profits. Yerkes and Decker (2003) suggest that a focus on quality can provide greater value over time than a focus on short-term profits.

Global Leadership Practices

Leadership; the art of influencing others, is one of the main elements of successfully managing change in international business. Global leaders contribute inspiring ideas and implement flourishing strategies for the success of a company. According to Thomas and Mujtaba (2004), "Leaders play a significant role in the company; therefore employing leaders or executives with appropriate leadership skills generally determines the victory of the company." Being a leader in a company is fundamentally a complicated task, and when one is a global leader the chore becomes more complex. Global leaders work with a vast diversity, which includes many different nations so they should have the knowledge of various cultures. Since the opportunities in international business are growing rapidly, the necessity for proficient global leaders are promptly increasing. In previous centuries, businesses were practiced differently due to values, beliefs or major cultural differences. However, because of globalization and technological convergence there are many commonalities of how things get done in different nations. Thus, in order to be successful in the twenty-first century, it might be necessary to change one's business and management style from prior years. In global organizations, global leaders are usually responsible for instituting new transformations for the company's future prosperity.

Global leadership, influencing people throughout the world, is described as a blend of global business, managing diversity, encouraging employees, responsibility, and broad thinking, etc. (Mendenhall, Kuhlmann and Stahl, 2001). Global leaders and managers interact with people worldwide; therefore they should have the ability to encourage and influence people from all over the world. These managers and leaders think globally instead of locally, which is the primary method to conduct business and effectively bring about changes. For companies to have knowledgeable leaders in the twenty-first century, they should provide plenty of opportunities for the employees to attain extensive knowledge regarding their worldwide operations and the different processes around the world. The companies also can provide opportunities to increase the knowledge of their global leaders by letting them have practical experience in overseas operations. There are various ethical decisions that leaders will have to make in their daily activities. Sometimes they depend on their personal experiences and beliefs to make these decisions, which might not be a suitable method since people have different ethical perspectives and these decisions affect many people (Cavico & Mujtaba, 2005). In international business, managers and leaders can face some difficulties in making ethical decisions since those decisions have to be appropriate and acceptable for the local culture.

Global companies in the twenty-first century demand global leaders who have the capabilities to work adequately throughout the world. Today's leaders should be able to change themselves according to the environment without varying their values and morality. Marquardt and Berger (2000) said that "To be an effective leader in the twenty-first century one will need to possess eight key attributes: an ability to develop and convey a shared vision, a service/servant orientation, commitment to risk-taking and continuous innovation, a global mindset, comfort and confidence with technology, competence in system thinking, recognition of the importance of ethics and spirituality in the work place, and a model for lifelong learning." The global leaders with these attributes can direct the company in a new path to achieve success.

The twenty-first century often is titled as "the global age." Businesses are practicing, and people are thinking and acting globally; and these performances directly affect businesses and people sharing more common values and systems. There are at least four common elements or forces that have led businesses to be in the global age and they are technology, travel, trade, and television (Thomas & Mujtaba, 2004). According to experts, "an organization is globalized when the organization has developed a global corporate culture, strategy, and structure, as well as global operation and global people" (Marquardt & Berger, 2000). More companies are globalizing, therefore the need of global leaders is rapidly increasing. Dealing with the international market means interacting with people of different ethnicities, ages, and value systems throughout the world; therefore global leaders need to be aware of the cultural and market differences between countries in order to be successful in the twenty-first century.

The new business environment is different from prior years, and there are still differences among cultures despite much technological convergence around the world. While some management and leadership practices are global, there must be room for local adjustments and practices. Local people are not as willing to accept leadership practices by foreign managers that disrespect their ways of doing things. Consequently, global leaders have to recognize this transformation from twentieth to twenty-first century and perform accordingly. A twenty-first century leader should have the capability to view the world and businesses with a global mindset and local adjustments, and it would guide them to understand the international business practices effectively. The global leaders with a global mindset have a broader way of thinking, they are aware of the cultural diversity, and they make appropriate decisions from a global perspective while acting locally. Global minded leaders think globally but usually act locally, since they understand that adjusting to the local culture is sometimes a necessity out of respect for the norms and traditions. They are usually open to adapt and exchange new ideas and techniques. They generally try to equalize local and global needs in order to be successful locally, nationally, and internationally (Marquardt & Berger, 2000).

In most cases, while the ultimate goal in business is to make profit, the business systems vary from country to country and culture to culture. According to Cavico and Mujtaba (2005), "when companies do business with developing countries they should not always expect the developing nation to have the same economic systems as their native country."

Furthermore, the authors state that "Every country has its own economic system, political system, and other local customs that influence its infrastructure. It is the foreign company's obligation to follow the country's rules while enforcing high ethical standards and safety measures." The global leaders should try to follow the social standards of the country where they are doing business. Following moral values of the native country in a different nation might not be appropriate for the local standards. However since the ethical standards in all countries are similar, following those standards will be appropriate for business success and stability in the foreign country (Cavico & Mujtaba, 2005). According to Marquardt and Berger, leaders are teachers, coaches, and mentors who lead people in the successful business direction. It is their responsibility to teach, mentor, and coach others in the company in order for others to have effectual knowledge regarding the business. Today's leaders must also be great teachers as they need to effectively impart knowledge and develop their people appropriately. This may allow people to learn the processes instantaneously and efficiently (Marquardt & Berger, 2000) while working collaboratively with their superiors.

Leadership, the process of influencing others, is fundamentally a continuous teaching and learning process. A leader should have the capability to influence people and change their views and actions to improve their performance in an organization. The most effective method to have more leaders for the twenty-first century is by having the current leaders develop new leaders. The current leaders need to teach the new leaders every aspect of the business and help them to form a new and effective leadership style and this will guide the company's future success. The twenty-first century business environment is very fast paced; therefore if the companies transform slowly, they might not persevere in the industry. Action learning appears to be one of the most effective methods to learn business, since it involves real practice and it would allow people to handle complex tasks (Marquardt & Berger, 2000). In today's global environment of business, emerging leaders need to be sent overseas and have the hands-on practice to learn the culture and local business style. Globalization opens new doors that demands new aptitudes; however these capabilities are not attained in a short period of time. The need for the global leaders is increasing because of the method of the globalization (Black, Morrison, & Gregerson, 1999). Since majority of the large companies are globalized in this century, it is very important for the companies to have skilled global leaders and that they receive adequate overseas training. Such global leaders must then become effective teachers and developers to their people so they can all function effectively in the context of cultural differences (Thomas & Mujtaba, 2004). Effective leaders and teachers understand that learning is about exploring the unknown, and that such exploration begins with open ended questions and personal reflection. One also needs to remember that teachers are not there to just be passing out information. Educators are also teaching people how to think and deduce conclusions. The last thing teachers want to do is stand up and tell people what to do, or give them the answers that they want to hear. The best educators are less interested in the answers than in the thinking behind them. One final thing that all leaders and educators should keep in mind is to never stop teaching as it is the best source of learning. Effective teaching is about the quality of the relationship between the teacher and the student (or leader and employee). It doesn't end when the workday is over. One should remember that effective leaders are also effective coaches that coach their players before the game, during the game, and after the game for future successes. It is a continuous learning process for both the coach and the players. Effective global leaders must become effective teachers and coaches as they lead their organizations to avoid disasters in developing countries while securing their trust and business.

Guidelines for Initiating and Implementing Change

As presented in Figure 1, human resource professionals can apply the following steps to better manage the introduction of new policies and expectations and, thus, effectively manage change.

1. Understand the culture and cultural attitudes towards the new change.
2. Clarify cultural, national, and international laws applicable to employment practices in the organization. Measure current organizational practices.
3. Develop policies and implement procedures appropriate to the organizational values.
4. Elicit support from senior management.
5. Disseminate organizational policies and communicate expectations to all managers and employers.
6. Educate and train all managers and employees about the need and necessity of the new changes. Prepare and develop their new skills.

7. Consistently monitor and evaluate program and consistently enforce policies.

8. Improve the program, policies, and procedures with regard the new practices.

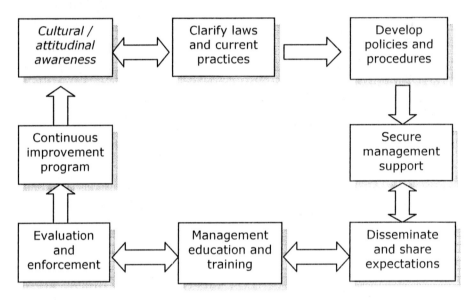

Figure 1 – Cultural Change Management Procedures

Introducing new practices, policies and procedures into an established organization can be cumbersome. However, models that have a structured outline and provide step-by-step guidelines can be a great way to initiate change management. As such, managers and change agents can adopt an existing model or procedure that can be followed by everyone initiating the change, or they can create a model or procedures that are specifically designed to meet the needs of the department or organization.

Nike Corporation[1] Responding to Cultural Expectations

Bringing change is a difficult process in itself. It is even more difficult when it involves a society's values and beliefs. Today's organizations are being forced to be environmentally and socially responsible since how they work and how they treat their employees and society at large impacts

---

[1] - Initially published by Mujtaba, Cavico, and Jones (2005) in the *International Business and Economics Research Journal*.

all human beings. So, one of the changes that corporations must deal with is that they need to manage changing toward socially responsible strategies, which is one way to achieve economic prosperity. According to Cavico and Mujtaba (2005), social responsibility is about taking an active role in the social, cultural, and charitable causes and the civic life of one's organization and community. Nike has received much attention and criticism for its global suppliers using low wage workers to produce sneakers. Of course, Nike's success came from its strategy to purchase sneakers from the lowest cost sources, without any Foreign Direct Investment (FDI) in its own manufacturing plants. Furthermore, the company's other success strategy was its use of high-profile celebrities, such as Michael Jordan, to popularize the desire and demand for its products. While the company has done well, Nike has been battling negative perceptions to bring about positive changes in the communities and plants producing their products, and to inform those who actually buy their sneakers. Nike's troubles initially began when various media outlets ran stories about conditions in factories under contract with Nike in China, Vietnam, and elsewhere. The stories contended that the workers were paid below minimum wage, abused verbally and sexually, and exposed to dangerous working conditions, including working with hazardous chemicals.

Nike grew from a $60,000 athletic shoe company to a $49 billion multinational athletic shoe and apparel enterprise in less than ten years. Then, in the 1990s, Nike found itself in a high profile scandal regarding the use of the low cost labor pool in developing countries. Nike's growth and reputation was jeopardized as it became the target of labor activists and then the global press as safety concerns, human rights violations and oppressive labor practices were uncovered in the factories of Nike's manufacturing partners. In the early 1990's, daily wages in the Indonesian firms were reported to be approximately $1 as compared to daily rates in South Korea at $24.40 and $64 in the United States. There were almost six times as many strikes in the Indonesian factories in 1991 as compared to 19 strikes in 1989. As the strikes continued, Nike was accused of encouraging its business partners to mistreat workers through the use of low wages, long hours, unhealthy working conditions, and underage workers. Nike insisted that it had no legal or moral responsibility for the actions of its independent contract partners. Nike maintained a very ethnocentric attitude in its approach to its contractors and did not set specific expectations or standards of conduct for its contractors (for example, as has been done by some of Nike's competitors or even Wal-

Mart). Unlike its competitors, however Nike did not embrace its corporate responsibility and respond to the charges. Nike did engage a newly hired public relations staff, Dusty Kidd, to develop a series of regulations for its contractors, called a Code of Conduct and Memorandum of Understanding and attached these as part of its new contracts. Yet, these measures were not enforced and Nike continued to be criticized for worker exploitation in the U.S. media. Nike engaged Ernst and Young to conduct formal audits of the factories. Since Ernst and Young was paid by Nike, the reports were not considered to be objective, and consequently criticism against Nike continued. In 1996, not only the US press, but the government began to investigate the area of child labor. Nike was the first company to join a Presidential task force to study the issue. It also established a Labor Practices Department to "help make things better for workers who make Nike products" (Bartlett et al., 2004, p.141). Originally, Nike tried to ignore the rising criticism stating that issue of wages was beyond its control. When poor working conditions were revealed in a factory in Vietnam, Nike reported that these conditions had been addressed, resulting in even more criticism, as well as the California consumer lawsuit.

Nike did not see any impact on its sales until late 1998 from this negative publicity. As can be seen in Figure 2 (Barlett, Ghoshal, and Birkenshaw, 2004), annual revenue declined in 1999. Nike denied that this downturn was related to its negative image; however Nike began to lose market share to its competitors and lost some of its major contracts with universities.

Finally, in 1998, Philip Knight introduced a series of reforms that included raising the minimal age of workers, adopting OSHA clean air standards, expanding its monitoring program, expanding worker educational programs, and making micro loans to workers. In addition, Nike became more involved in government-based reform efforts, including participation in the Apparel Industry Partnership. When this organization dissolved, Nike became active in the Fair Labor Association and worked to get other corporations involved with the organization.

Figure 2: Nike Ten-Year Revenues Trend

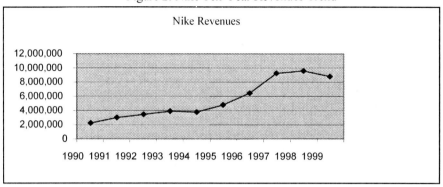

In 1999, Nike ran extensive training programs for its contractor managers. All managers needed to learn the native language of the host country as well as to understand the cultural differences; and the company worked with international organizations to improve the lives of workers in the developing countries. These measures helped to improve Nike's image and reputation. However, even with these changes, Nike was criticized for not dealing with the real issue of minimum wage for workers.

Multinational companies, like Nike, can no longer afford to ignore the global ramifications and responsibilities associated with its business activities. It is imperative for companies to understand the cultural profiles of the areas in which they operate. For example, "Power distance indicates the extent to which a society accepts the unequal distribution of power in institutions and organizations. Uncertainty avoidance refers to society's discomfort with uncertainty, preferring predictability and stability" (Bartlett et al., 2004, p.156). Nike falls in the category of low uncertainty avoidance and low power distance, indicating the need for less formalized rules and procedures, less hierarchical and more decentralized and people are free agents. Nike's contractors while they also fall in the low uncertainty avoidance category, the power distance is high. This fact indicates the need for a centralized, paternalistic structure where loyalty and personal relationships are important. The implications for Nike is the need to have more formalized procedures and structures with its partners, and to develop more personal relationships with workers in the host countries.

While Nike did address many labor issues, it did not effectively deal with the issue of wages. In this area, Nike continued with its avoidance strategy. Throughout the early and middle 1990s, Nike denied any responsibility for the poor labor conditions in the manufacturing facilities. In 1992, the company's general manager in Jakarta said: "I don't know that I need to know" (Bartlett, et al., 2004, p.139). Nike did not consider that the labor and safety issues in the contractor factories were its responsibility. While this approach may be legally accurate, it was not well received by the "activist" community.

Figure 3: Indonesian Monthly Wage Rates in Rupiah

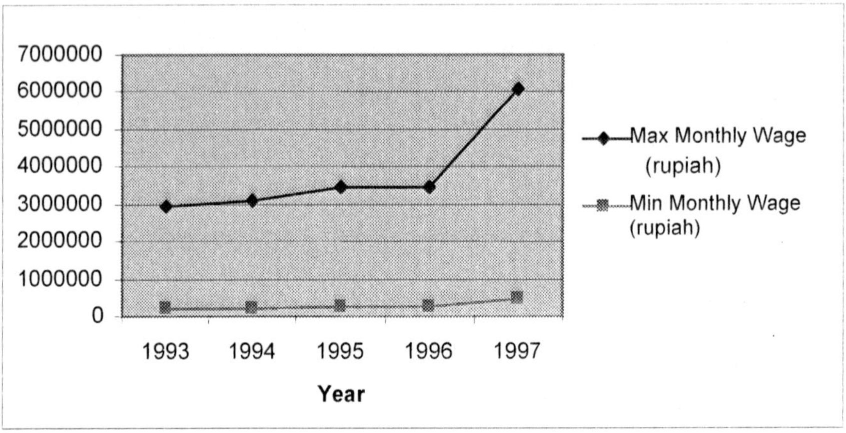

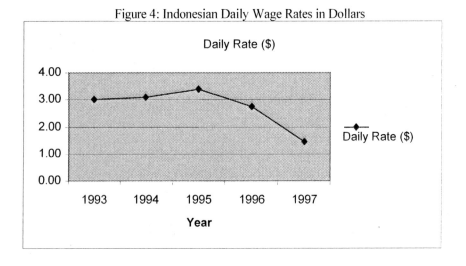

As shown in Figure 3 (Barlett, Ghoshal, and Birkenshaw, 2004), both the maximum and minimum monthly wage rate in rupiah increased from 1993 through 1997. When converted to dollars, as shown in Figure 4, using the exchange rate for each year, the daily rate in dollars decreased in 1996 and plummeted to less than $2.00 in 1997. A study of wages in Vietnam indicated that the daily wage for an average worker was $1.67. This compares to a daily rate of approximately $64 for US workers.

Figure 4: Indonesian Daily Wage Rates in Dollars

Due to the measures that Nike did take to improve working conditions in the factories in the developing countries, its revenues as shown in Figure 5 did rebound in 2000, and continued to grow over the last several years. Nike's continued reluctance to deal with the labor wage, however, may continue to erode the image and reputation of the company. Nike accordingly needs to consider analyzing the compensation structures in the countries where its contractors operate. It needs to develop policies and procedures that provide compensation guidelines that are consistent with the industry and the host country standards.

Figure 5: Nike Fifteen-Year Revenues Trend

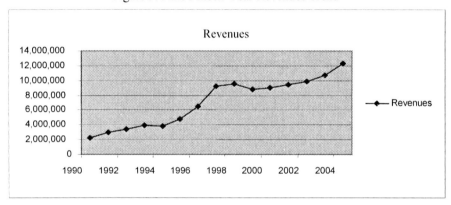

Based on Nike's experience and what others have done in this age of globalization to retain a good brand name as well as to be successful in the twenty first century's competitive environment of business, Nike needs to:

- Recognize its status as a multinational company and change towards a more "transnational" mentality and to be flexible and responsive to country-level operations.
- Change toward a more geocentric orientation and set global standards for its operations and develop greater identification with national interests of the host countries.
- Move from its internal-oriented and protectionist posture to an integrated business approach.
- Develop more formalized procedures and structures that are adopted by its partners and to develop more personal relationships with workers in the host countries.
- Continue to train its employees in these formal processes and procedures. Nike also needs to analyze compensation practices in the developing countries that it operates.

- Work with vendors to adjust workers' wages in the international markets. Wage guidelines should be incorporated in the contracts with its manufacturing partners.

The major risk to these strategies is that there may be a decrease in profits in the short-term. This result could be outweighed by the positive impact on Nike's reputation and image, which in turn may translate to greater sales and market share in the long term. Another risk that Nike may face is the instability of the governments in the region. This could be mitigated by a better understanding of the culture in the region and by developing personal relationships with government officials.

Since Nike outsourced all its manufacturing, strikes in any of its plants could adversely affect the supply chain in that goods may not be produced and delivered to fill customer orders on time. Nike's continuing efforts to improve labor conditions could mitigate this risk. Another mitigation strategy is for Nike to deal effectively with the wage issues of workers in the factories, and accordingly to be viewed as a "socially responsible" organization.

Understanding Social Responsibility

Social responsibility is different from legal responsibility. Social responsibility is not simply about morality. Social responsibility is not altruism – which is about taking the interests of others into account in such a manner that one's intentions and actions afford some real degree of preference to others. Furthermore, social responsibility is not heroism, or sainthood (Cavico and Mujtaba, 2005). So, what is "Social Responsibility"? According to Mujtaba, Cavico, and Jones (2005), social responsibility can be defined as "taking an active part in the social, cultural, and charitable causes and civic life of one's organization, community, and society a whole."

Why should a company be socially responsible? The social responsibility "obligation" of business suggests that global or national society may demand that business consider the social implications of its actions, and concomitantly to act in certain socially responsible ways (Mujtaba, Cavico, & Jones, 2005). Otherwise, perhaps, society will compel business by international or legal mandate or increased taxation to fulfill its perceived social obligations. Business, as illustrated by the Nike case, also gains an improved public image by being socially responsible. An enhanced public image will attract more customers and investors, and thus provide positive benefits to the firm and its shareholders. Academic studies generally are supportive of the proposition that there exists a positive relationship between socially responsible behavior and favorable financial performance. Employees also may possess a heightened social consciousness, and consequently will want to be associated with a firm that not only is concerned with making profits but also with the welfare of society. A corporation that acts more socially responsible not only secures public favor, but also avoids public disfavor. Sir John Brown, the CEO of British Petroleum, astutely comprehends that society wants and expects business to be socially responsible. Social responsibility, at least in some reasonable degree, is thus in the long-term self-interest of business. Furthermore, a corporation cannot long remain a viable economic entity in a society that is uneven, unstable, and deteriorating. It thus makes good business sense for a company to devote some of its resources to social betterment projects. To operate efficiently, business needs educated and skilled employees. Education and training, therefore, should be of paramount interest to business leaders, and a company can center its social responsibility efforts in these critical areas. Finally, in recent years, there has been a steady growth of organizations that rate corporate social responsibility and that supply these ratings to investors and consumers. It obviously is beneficial to a company to earn a favorable corporate social responsibility rating. The conception of social responsibility as envisioned merely asks business to take a longer-term, more expansive, stakeholder view of its traditional profit-maximization role (Cavico and Mujtaba, 2005). Enlightened self-interest and rational egoism, therefore, provide the justification for the firm's social responsibility efforts and contributions.

How should a company be socially responsible? There are many ways that business can fulfill its social responsibility obligation. A corporation, for example, can be socially responsible by providing computers to community schools and by releasing employees on company time to provide the training. British Petroleum (BP), for example, markets itself as "Beyond Petroleum," and has been regarded as a very socially responsible firm for its global environmental and alternative fuel efforts. BP also is engaged in job training and building schools in the communities where it does business. Nike now offers small business loans to the family members of its employees. The pharmaceutical companies have been providing AIDS drugs at greatly reduced costs to African nations. Coca Cola has been using its extensive delivery system to transport the drugs to even the most remote African village. Pfizer loans a cadre of trained business and scientific professionals to aid groups in developing countries. Intel has computer clubhouses that provide Internet access and technology training to children in over 30 countries. General Electric is constructing hospitals in Ghana. Avon provides breast cancer programs and subsidizes mammograms in over 50 countries. Starbucks has built a health clinic in Guatemala. Home Depot is extensively involved with community efforts to develop and rehabilitate affordable housing. Office Depot has sponsored an international "best practices" conference on corporate giving. These are just a few of many examples of praiseworthy social responsibility contributions by business. Moreover, there is absolutely nothing wrong in a company's publicizing such social responsibility actions, and thereby receiving well-deserved acclaim.

To what degree should a company be socially responsible? Regardless of how meritorious a firm's social responsibility actions may be, a company nonetheless must be careful in the degree of its commitment to the societal welfare. As to the proper extent of a company's social responsibility efforts and contribution, Aristotle has provided the answer. According to his seminal principle, the Doctrine of the Mean, Aristotle counseled that the correct and virtuous choice is a rationally determined mean between two extremes of deficiency and excess, which if present in a moderate degree will be a virtue. The intelligent and virtuous person will choose the mean between the two extremes, which constitute the corresponding vices. Accordingly, regarding the degree to which a company should be socially responsible, Aristotle would advise the firm not to concentrate on profits only, and abjure good deeds, because such deficiency is a vice. Similarly, Aristotle would advise the firm not to subordinate profits to good deeds, since too much attention to good deeds at the expense of profits is also a vice. Rather, Aristotle would counsel a company to aim for the mean of social responsibility, that is, profits first and then prudent good deeds (Cavico and Mujtaba, 2005). So, for example, "Chainsaw" Al Dunlap would represent the one extreme, and thus vice of deficiency in social responsibility. Ben & Jerry's would represent the extreme and vice of excessive social responsibility. Such companies as Target, Hewlett-Packard, Proctor & Gamble, Johnson & Johnson, Coca-Cola, Bank of America, and Microsoft would represent the virtuous means of moderate and prudent social responsibility. A corporation, of course, exists in a competitive global environment and thus is limited in its ability to solve the multitude of social problems. Business cannot and should not be expected to substitute for government or a "world government." If a corporation unilaterally or too generously engages in social betterment, it may place itself at a disadvantage when compared to other less socially responsible business entities. In a highly competitive market system, corporations that are too socially responsible may lessen their attractiveness to investors or simply may price themselves out of the market. The Ben and Jerry of Ben & Jerry's, as a matter of fact, were forced by shareholders to accept a buy-out offer from Unilever, the multinational conglomerate. Yet a corporation that disdains any social responsibility, especially in a supercilious manner, may find itself less attractive to consumers and employees who likely will prefer to do business with and work for a socially responsible firm that provides good value. The Nike case clearly underscores the practical importance of prudent social responsibility.

Overall, it is concluded that a global organization in the twenty first century environment cannot afford to be socially irresponsible, at least, not for long. As can be seen from Nike's case, profiting from the international community often carries with it some obligations as well. Above and beyond the responsibility of business to act legally and morally is this very prevalent, undeniable, and practical issue of the social responsibility of business. The law determines legal accountability; philosophical ethics determines moral accountability; but ascertaining the definition, nature, and extent of social responsibility emerges as a serious challenge for today's business leaders, executives, and managers, especially in a global context.

Summary

The purpose of a business is normally perceived as making money for its shareholders or owners. As such, many believe that business is not supposed to be concerned with moral and social values. However, the values of ethics and morality has become part of the changes in today's work environment and, as such, it is integrated into business policy and planning. Very recently, yet a new value, social responsibility has emerged to challenge business leaders and business educators. Social responsibility had not been viewed as a concern, let alone an obligation, of business. Yet, today, business leaders and organizations are being forced to change in this direction and concern themselves in a practical way with the social dimensions of their activities and the welfare of society. Therefore, global social responsibility becomes an important aspect of managing change in today's workforce. These changes need effective global leadership.

Global leadership plays a significant role in a cross-cultural business environment. It is important to have highly skilled leaders in an organization to encourage and train employees. Since global leaders work with people throughout the world, they need to be aware of the cultural differences, especially when implementing new changes. Using the same business and change management style as the parent company in another nation may not always be a successful method to bring about changes. Global leaders ensure that the global organization is operating smoothly and all the changes are being executed effectively. Companies need to send their leaders to foreign nations for them to understand the culture and social standards. Business in the twenty-first century is different from previous generations and leaders need to make sure their people are adapting quickly to current and prospective changes through effective communication, knowledge dispersion, change management skills, time management guidelines, and conflict management techniques. Due to the rapid growth of international business, companies require more global leaders and global-minded employees. To develop more global leaders, current leaders need to provide adequate training for the new leaders. The best methodology in developing global leaders is by providing employees more exposure to the international arena of the organization, and by offering them training from other experienced global leaders in the company.

Harris and Moran (1996) emphasize that skillful and socially responsible global managers understand the significance of cultural differences and local ethical mores. These global managers understand that they need to manage cultural differences by developing the requisite skills that are needed for participation in the global business environment. Harris and Moran offer the following nuances and cultural differences (1996, p. 3):

1. Japanese culture tends to promote a sense of group identity through its collective patterns. Creating ambiguity is an unconscious cultural process that often leads to foreigners to draw false conclusions based on Japanese appearances.

2. During the first business meeting in Saudi Arabia, one should not conduct business, but rather use this time to get to know the parties involved (develop the personal relationship).

3. In matters of recruitment and selection, Asian managers interview and often select family and trusted friends to fill positions, while Western managers use more impersonal measures of recruitment.

4. When doing business in Indonesia, shaking hands with either gender is acceptable, but using the left hand for taking food or giving a gift is not recommended. In some other cultures, shaking hands is not recommended with the opposite gender as a form of bow might be preferred.

5. The cities of Los Angeles, Miami and New York are diverse, multicultural and have a multilingual population. In Los Angeles, Spanish and Korean are the second and third largest foreign-language groups. Cultural sensitivity greatly influences the success or failure of a product or service.

6. The Business Council for International Understanding estimates that international personnel who go abroad without cross-cultural preparation have a failure rate much higher than those who had the benefit of such training.

Harris and Moran (1996) theorize "that all management and professional development requires some global intercultural education and skills" (p. 4). They suggest that change agents, workers, and global leaders must move beyond the mere coping with cultural differences to create more synergistic processes and embrace the wellspring of diversity.

Chapter Three

UNDERSTANDING CHANGE

Human behavior is a complex phenomenon. Human behavior in the twenty-first century's cross-cultural work environment can have as many dimensions as the number of workers in the organization. According to Geller (1994), a person's behavior and response to change can range from simple to complex, from functional to dysfunctional, from group orientation to selfishness, and from highly productive to highly ineffective. A simple behavioral response to change can include a two-way discussion for understanding it, while a complex response can be difficult to understand, leading to stress and physiological illnesses. For example, Dean's four-year old nephew (Zaki) was staying with them and got to see his uncle first thing in the morning and said: "Uncle, you don't look normal until you put your glasses on." Not seeing his uncle without the eye glasses was a major change for Zaki. Mateen once asked h is uncle, "Hi Uncle Bahaudin, how is life treating you?" Bahaudin (Dean) said "It isn't, I am paying for everything." Based on Dean's facial perspective, one could see how "paying for everything" could mean dealing with so much change, stress, chaos, natural disasters, man-made disasters, human right violations, etc. These are life-changing events that impact people's lives every day causing both simple and complex reactions.

There is no panacea or structured magical solutions to managing human behavior during change implementation which can cause complex human responses. The solution depends on the situation and the progressive and dynamic readiness levels of each individual going through the change. As such, understanding and effectively managing human behavior requires assessment, management, and leadership skills. Human behaviors toward change can be best influenced by gathering the right information, understanding the situation through a careful assessment, having a holistic perspective, and truthfully communicating with everyone who is impacted by the change. After a careful analysis and assessment of the culture, managers and change agents can proactively develop an action plan to modify behaviors, or at least reduce the ones, that can hinder the progress of change initiatives and the empowerment of employees (Geller, 1994).

Human beings now live in a world where natural disasters and "manmade" crisis seem to be a relatively common occurrence. According to Ian Mitroff (2005), for global managers and employees who are responsible for seeing their businesses through crises, the question is not whether they will experience unexpected events, but rather when and how much of a change will it be from the norm. Managing this change and effectively navigating through such unexpected events on a continuous basis will depend on the responses of today's leaders. Mitroff (2005) draws on years of experience in the field of crisis management to challenge change agents so they can meet unexpected crisis and challenging events head on. Mitroff (2005) suggests seven distinct competencies that global change agents and twenty-first century's learning organizations must demonstrate to be successful in this changing environment. The seven competencies or intelligences are:

1. Accepting that crisis can occur,
2. Using creative thinking to consider types of crisis,
3. Understanding that businesses are affected by challenges that are universal in nature,
4. Seeing crisis and solutions as complex, but understanding that preparation can simplify the path to survival,
5. Using controlled paranoia to discover where a business is vulnerable,
6. Making crisis management central to all business activity, and
7. Understanding the connection between our work and our spirit.

Mitroff (2005) states that the prevention of crisis requires examining the business with a "controlled paranoid" mind, which implies that change agents and managers must determine their weaknesses and vulnerabilities by thinking like a terrorist, computer hacker, and thief. Mitroff uses examples of modern companies that hire investigators to gather intelligence by snooping around to find loopholes in the firm's security. These investigators also launch mock attacks on the firm's products, in an attempt to identify possible challenges and prepare for handling prospective challenges that can happen. If it can happen, then it may very will happen; so, one might as well prepare accordingly for the worst case scenario. Of course, change does not always result from unexpected events or unforeseen crises, since change also can come from the regular day-to-day nuances that make human beings different from one another.

Compared to people working within a country or culture, those who work on international levels have had to deal with greater levels of change because of cultural, social, economical, and environmental differences that exist within and among people of various countries. These international business and non-business people must become aware of subtle differences and nuances in other people's conversation, body gestures, sensitivities, motivations, table manners, business dealings, general contracts and agreements, gender differences and perceptions, time and stress management styles, attitudes, values, religious beliefs, and many other variables that might be more prominent in some cultures than others. This chapter concludes that all people deal with change to different degrees and everybody goes through similar processes in dealing with change. However, how they move through the process may vary based on their subtle differences which could be influenced by personal, organizational, and/or cultural elements. This section reveals how successful people namely global managers and change agents, regardless of their culture, use the general change management process to become exuberant catalysts for change in their societies, organizations, and families.

According to Albert Einstein, "Everything should be as simple as possible, but not simpler." This is a good philosophy to keep in mind when implementing, executing, and communicating change initiatives. Of course, change does not always appear simple, as it involves gaining new and different habits or ways of doing things. Just as almost all people have a natural tendency to initially resist change, people also have abilities to adapt to change as well.

According to Daryl Conner (1992), the basic human reactions to change seem to be similar in everyone…managers and change agents "who successfully implement change, regardless of their location, display many of the same basic emotions, behaviors, and approaches." These change agents and managers demonstrate resiliency in their leadership style and change management; resiliency refers to their capacity to absorb high levels of change while displaying minimal dysfunctional behavior (Conner, 1992, p. 6). Conner states that light travels through space at a constant speed of 186,281 miles each second as the laws of universe dictate this pace with no deviation. However, workers travel in their life and at work often without a fixed speed or velocity. People move at variable pace which fluctuates according to their capacity for assimilating new information and influences. How well human beings absorb new information and make good use of it determines how well they manage and re-direct change to their benefits or pre-determined goals. Life is more comfortable, effective, and efficient when it is moving at a speed that allows one to appropriately assimilate the change one faces. The appropriate speed is one at which one is able to effectively absorb change with a minimum of dysfunctional behavior (Conner, 1992). When one is no longer able to effectively deal with the actual and perceived change, one is likely to display dysfunctional behavior. Since the future is guaranteed to bring about more ambiguity, change and chaos than what is present today, learning to raise one's individual and team resiliency is an imperative for effective change management. As Conner states, people respond to change at different intellectual and emotional rates. As people adjust to organizational change, they often enter a pattern of observing that a change has occurred or is possible; developing their opinion toward the change; making a decision to support or resist the change; and taking action on that decision (Conner, 1002, p. 155).

Introduction

One meaning of change in the work environment is basically as any modification in the way things are currently being done. Therefore, minor and major modifications in the way things are done can be seen as a "fact of life" if people are to live happily and successfully in the progression of life. As such, change is constant, global, ubiquitous, and unequivocally a fact of life. Change can be, but it does not have to be, arduous, cumbersome, unpleasant, and/or a total surprise. Change, happiness and success are not mutually exclusive; therefore all three can happen simultaneously. Many people suffer from bad circumstances while others benefit from these types of situations. Many individuals claim that if we don't take advantage of opportunities they are lost. Of course, opportunities are not lost they simply go to someone else. In every crisis there can be a bright spot and one should look for it rather than feeling bad and complaining about its bad consequences. This can be seen from the Chinese characters which represent crisis. From the two Chinese characters, one of which is a symbol for danger and the other is a symbol for opportunity, the word crisis emerges. Today's global environment is changing and evolving toward greater diversity which opens up a whole new world of challenges and opportunities which can be advantageous, changing how managers and employees do things. The changing and diverse global population will continue to influence new and innovative methods of completing tasks, offering services, and achieving results. This influence may prove to be positive or negative depending on whether we take advantage of it or not. The competitive advantage of firms lies in valuing and celebrating these differences which exist among today's diverse workforce. It is through valuing and using everyone's input that disasters can be prevented and opportunities can be taken advantage of during changing times. For example, when astronaut Jim Lovell uttered "Houston, we have a problem," most people including the astronauts thought that their chances of a safe return were very slim or impossible. However, with concurrent engineering among all parties and changing their usual operations both on earth and in the space, the crew of Apollo 13 returned safely back to earth within four days. By changing the usual way of doing things as well as teamwork between the Apollo 13 astronauts and the people of mission control in Houston, a prospective disaster was turned into a successful mission, which taught many lessons about the aggregate capability of the human mind. The global manager knows that effective management of change in a borderless environment requires persistence, perseverance, and an understanding of people in a general level. Furthermore, as Kenichi Ohmae (1989) in his article, published in the May-June issue of Harvard Business Review and titled "*Managing in a Borderless World*" wrote, "approaches to global management and products vary…However, persistence and perseverance are the keys to long-term survival and success."

On the other hand, we have witnessed many unfortunate situations which have proved to be disastrous for humanity in general and changed the lives of many people for the worse. These types of cases require patience, understanding, time, a shoulder to cry on, and hoping for the best in the worst of times. For example, the Chernobyl disaster which was caused by two electrical engineers on April 26th of 1986 killed hundreds of people immediately and affected thousands throughout the world. The explosion caused radioactive cesium 137 and iodine 131 to vertically rise up three miles into the sky. The damage (cost of cleanup) has been estimated to be over $14 billion which according to researchers might be more than the Russian's entire investment in the nuclear power industry from its beginning in the mid 1950s. For safety purposes, the Chernobyl ground and its surroundings must remain intact for many centuries. So, part of the Ukrainian land cannot really be considered to be a forest or human community anymore. The Chernobyl disaster has meant major changes for thousands of individuals.

Wars are another "man-made" disaster that causes much negative change for human beings. In World War II, the Russians lost over 20 million soldiers and were happy that they were winners because they were able to defeat Hitler's Army and bring the war to a halt. The hatred for people of other religions by Adolf Hitler and his supporters caused millions of people to die through torture and mass killings of children, men, women, and senior citizens who could not even defend themselves. It has been estimated that over six million Jewish people lost their lives because of Hitler and his men's hatred toward them. He was a charismatic leader, like Alexander the Great, and changed the lives of many individuals for the worse. Yet, there are many other unfortunate incidents that have caused much change for human beings. In March 24th of 1989, the Exxon Valdez oil spill caused much damage to people, environment, birds, fish, and other inhabitants in the ground, water and air. The Russian invasion of Afghanistan in 1979 caused four million people to change their lives forever and become refugees in Pakistan and Iran. For the following ten years over two million Afghan men, women, and children died through bombings, summary killings, and torture. It has been estimated that the economic condition of Afghanistan has reverted back to what it was in the early 1900s. The Bhopal accident at Union Carbide (India), Limited (UCIL) which is a subsidiary of Union Carbide, U.S.A., located in the central part of India caused much damage. On December 2nd of 1984, the pressure in a tank containing methyl isocyanate (MIC), which is a deadly potent and very volatile gas used to make pesticides, was rising and a leak occurred. The leak got out of hand and could not be controlled. So, the gas covered the air before the tank was sealed. The cloud of gas all over the city killed 2,500 people and injured about 200,000 others. This accident was named to be one of the worst industrial disasters in the world. Even though in 1975 the municipal corporation officials had asked for moving the plant into an unpopulated area because it was too dangerous, nothing was done. One thing that did happen was the official who initially requested the move was removed from office and terminated. Several prior audits had shown that there was inadequate training and employee morale was low at this plant in Bhopal; thus additional employees, as well as experienced managers, were needed. There were also some technological problems related to the design of the plant, equipment, materials, and operating procedures that needed to be improved or eliminated. However, change did not take place because the remaining workers were probably afraid and did not speak their minds with regards to these unsafe working conditions. Finally, on February 14th of 1989, the Indian Supreme Court awarded the Indian government $470 million on behalf of the victims who are still feeling the aftereffects of the disaster.

Hurricanes Andrew, Charlie, Ivan, Dennis, Katrina, Rita, Wilma, the earthquake in Pakistan, and the tsunami in Indonesia changed the lives of many people throughout the world. Hurricane Andrew, which is estimated to be one of the costliest natural disasters in the United States, attacked South Florida in the early dawn hours of August 24th of 1992. It left over half million people homeless and interrupted the daily working conditions of about 123,000 people and some 8,000 businesses. Publix Super Markets, one of the businesses in South Florida, sent trucks of water and food to be distributed to people in that area at no cost to them. The trouble was that people could not find their way because the street signs were all down, so it was difficult to find the exact locations of different areas. The main point here is that change can be caused by many situations that cannot be predicted or planned for, however as human beings we can transcend such situations by envisioning a better future. In the mean time, the individuals impacted by these changes need to have patience, understanding, and a winning spirit in order to overcome it. While these types of changes cannot be predicted, there are many changes in the corporate world of business that can be predicted and managed appropriately. This book focuses on such changes in the work world and how to plan for making these changes successful despite resistance. It further attempts to help global managers become change agents who can help themselves and others implement change successfully and efficiently in a culturally diverse environment. Robert B. Reich (1991) in his article titled "*Who is them?*" published at the March-April issue of Harvard Business Review, wrote, "Ultimately, our wealth and well-being depend on the value that the world places on the work we do, on our skills and insights." Therefore, global managers must be able to deal with change effectively because their firm's reputation and their shareholders' bottom-line are at stake.

The current work environment is full of changes at the organizational level as well as the interpersonal level which affects managers and employees. Change is cumbersome and uncomfortable; yet the human mind can be programmed or influenced to see change as opportunity and turn the hassles of a routine workout into the muscles of beauty and achievement. It is through change that ordinary people can create extraordinary results. It is only through change that people can expect different results. If we keep doing what we have always been doing, then we will always get exactly what we have gotten in the past. It is ludicrous to expect different results from the same actions or without doing things differently. We need to realize that "if it is to be, it's up to me," and nothing happens as a result of our thinking alone, but things do happen when we think, act, and adapt in accordance with predetermined goals.

What Is Change?

Change, in its simplest form, is the art of making things different. It is a modification to the way things are, or how things are done. In other words, change is a modification to the status quo (Geller, 1994). *Change* is the process of turning things from one state to another. *Change management,* then, is the art of effectively and efficiently making things different. Change is not something that only top executives or community leaders decide to bring about. Change is brought about often by outside forces that are beyond one's immediate control. It is driven by technological advancements, a better workforce, globalization, diversity, natural environmental forces, and other variables that one may not be able to fully control. Therefore, human beings are pressured into adapting with these changes and making the best of each change. There are at least three types of change which are "passive or natural," "mandated," and "self-generated" that affect individuals throughout their lives.

1. *Passive or natural changes* are those changes that are not noticeable at the personal level but nonetheless do take place, i.e. growing, crawling, walking, etc.
2. *Mandated changes* come from top down to the individual level in the form of laws, demands and/or policies.
3. *Self-generated or proactive change* is usually initiated by an individual, a team or an organization. Its successful implementation needs research, support, reliability, reasons, credibility, and/or strong leadership.

People learn or adapt to the passive or natural changes by osmosis and usually there are not many things one can do to prevent or stop these changes. For example, parents and care-takers usually attempt to help or encourage children to walk or crawl but these will take place regardless of outside forces or influences. This passive change can be very dangerous at the organizational level because often top executives are caught by surprise when they are not prepared for it. Mandated changes are usually decided upon by the top people of the society or an organization to prevent chaotic situations from taking place. For example, having traffic rules saves many lives while not having such general rules can be very costly. These are usually based on the Golden Rule principle which states that one should do unto others as he or she would have them do unto him or her. Finally, the self-generated changes are the best types and usually the most difficult to deal with in the initial states. It is the self-generated changes that create the planned results in the long-term. Self-generated changes are proactive and value-driven. Therefore, they can be goal oriented and focused toward self-chosen ends and targets. This deals with Newton's principle of physics which states that a body in motion moving to a certain path tends to stay in motion in that path until acted upon by outside forces. So, if you generate purposeful changes toward certain goals then you are likely to get those results unless you are confronted by resistance which cannot be overcome.

One of the most stressful situations throughout the world, especially in the Untied States, is balancing work and family lives because while people may value being connected to their families they often may be away from them in order to work and produce the basic necessities of life in order to have a family. This is why many professionals plan to work and go to school at the same time to get more advanced education. As the Proverb states, "Those who don't find time for exercise will have to find time for illness." Those who don't find time to gain the right skills and get the education needed will have to spend time dealing with much resistance when managing change. For example, education in general "pays" personally and financially, because, according to the Bureau of Labor Statistics, those with a Bachelor's Degree will earn about $2.1 million over their work life while those with a Master's Degree will earn 20% more to a total of $2.5 million. One of the majors changes since 1992 has been the 33% increase in the number of college graduates and the fact that more fields now require a Master's Degree for career advancement. Acquiring more education can afford one more respect from one's colleagues and employees, while equipping one to make better decisions in both the planning and execution stages of change. For example, those who are in human resources departments tend to get more formal certifications and advanced degrees in specialized fields for effective human development and change management. According to Pamela Babcock (September 2005), author of the article entitled "*A Calling for Change*," more and more company leaders are trying to make human resources a truly global function so the department's professionals can always be a strategic partner. She states that experts want the HR function to be more transformational as it involves transitioning people through major changes. Babcock (2005) writes that "CEOs often want HR to help shape organizational culture, or to place more emphasis on executive development and succession planning." Babcock advises HR professionals in charge of managing change to keep in mind that "Just because the CEO is ready for a change doesn't mean everyone else is ready to accept a transformation." Therefore, one must not assume that everyone wants change and welcomes it. As such, change agents must try to get others to "buy-in" to the new change before beginning the implementation process. It is also critical to remember, Babcock states, "Change can be stressful and disruptive for anyone." Effective change management through the human resources personnel and change agents requires the right skill sets and an approach that balances speed with inclusiveness and collaboration since engaging everyone impacted by the change in the system is critical if the change is to be sustained. The attributes require to bring about effective change include integrity, a proven track record, leadership skills, the ability to capture the respect of other business leaders, and a vision for what the future can be. Other important traits that change agents need to possess are financial acumen and great presentation skills in one-on-one format and to large audiences (Babcock, 2005). Overall, change agents need to initially learn the organization's culture and assess its problems by getting the company's pulse and developing a good relationship with leaders and their staff.

According to Geller (1994), change is present all around twenty-first century workers; its momentum, volume, and complexity are increasing at speeds to which many workers show difficulty adjusting. Geller states that the driving forces for change can include, but are not limited to, "an increasingly diverse workforce, technological advancements, faster communication, increased (global) competition, social and political pressures, and limited resources." So, what can be done to deal with so much change? Geller recommends that managers and leaders manage change and its corresponding resistance through proactive planning and anticipation of its consequences. Furthermore, twenty-first century employees need to learn to accept disruptions, while taking advantage of new opportunities that accompany it. Of course, the first step should be to understand the change, and assess both organizational and individual readiness for its acceptance.

Assessing Organizational Climate for Change

Some change programs succeed while others are not so successful due the high level of resistance and/or lack of proper assessment of the culture for change. As such, assessment of change readiness is important in order to prepare a change initiative. The change agents can design an appropriate instrument to assess the readiness of their organization before moving forward with designing a process of change management. The Survey of Organizational Climate for Change, located at the end of this chapter, is a simple assessment tool for assessing the organizational climate or an organization toward change. It is based on the research by Symmetrix, as Massachusetts consulting firm, as mentioned by Stephen Robbins in his 2001 textbook entitled *Organizational Behavior*. The higher the total score on the *Survey of Organizational Climate for Change*, the greater is the likelihood that the change initiatives and efforts will succeed in this organization. Questions that receive low ratings from a large number of employees in the organization are areas of opportunities for improvement in the reduction of resistance to change.

Work-Family Conflicts

The competitive environment of international business has driven many individuals to become "workaholics." In many cases, these workaholics get rewarded and are encouraged to expect others to do the same in order to remain competitive. In many countries, materialism is not a great value as compared to spending time with family and friends. There are many managers who are unorganized and not prepared to deal with unexpected circumstances; so they end up asking others to work late or overtime on short notices, work on their days off, or work fifteen or sixteen hours in a given day in order to complete tasks. Incidents like this can cause people to hate their jobs, get ulcers, develops unhealthy eating habits as well as unhealthy relationships. Incidents like this can cost organizations money, productivity, and experienced workers because most people will not take this for very long since they would want a change for the better and may end up quitting. The work-family conflict is a reality for many professionals, and it is having a deeper impact on organizations than most people think. Despite a good career and financial freedom, people do want a balance between their personal and professional lives. An 18-month study, completed at Baxter Healthcare, showed that work-life conflict is a major concern because it is afflicting males, females, single and married individuals, and both low and high income individuals. The study showed that 30% of employees at Baxter, which has many family-friendly programs, had some type of work-life conflict every week. The study further showed that about 42% of these individuals had looked for another job because of the work-life conflict. Another study at Mary Young of Boston University's Human Resource Policy Institute found that long hours and a lack of clearly standardized work-time fed dissatisfaction among all employees. In today's world, most young people are not willing to work long days or on weekends because they want to accomplish many of their interests and hobbies simultaneously.

There are many companies and organizational leaders that acknowledge and recognize the concerns of their associates in a nominal way and provide lip-service to give people the impression of caring and responsibility. However, lip-service, monetary rewards, and frothy perks are not great substitutes for a balanced life and does not make up for lost time and opportunities with one's family and friends. In order to eliminate or reduce work-life stress and increase morale, companies need to:

1- Respect and appreciate each individual,
2- Help people balance their work-lives with their private lives by being flexible in scheduling,
3- Empower employees through education and professional development programs so they have a "say" about the decisions that affect their company, and
4- Provide continuous training so employees are competent and updated in their professions.

As individuals, leaders, and responsible citizens, we must take responsibility and create self-generated changes that are aligned with our goals and values and eliminate conflicts between our work and personal lives. In order to do this effectively, one must be able to become a change agent and manage change appropriately in the context of a diverse culture. Before talking about change agents, one must understand what change management is all about. *Change Management* is the process of identifying, interpreting, aligning, facilitating, and implementing new procedures, policies, and innovations according to purposeful goals in such a way that efficiency and productivity is maximized. It has been said that "even if you are on the right track, you will get run over if you just sit there." Therefore, change management is about managing and directing the energy which exists in the environment toward predetermined goals and objectives. Martial artists do this all the time, as they focus on using their opponent's energy along with careful strategies to make the best out of a situation without using too much effort. So, change management is beneficial and a necessity if one is to remain healthy, competitive, and live a balanced life. In general, change management is about the most important asset of any organization, the human resource asset, its people.

The Importance of Managing Change

Managing change means managing human behavior because robots, machines, and computers are very easy to change and these machines do not resist change. It appears that the main reason change implementation is difficult is because people are resistant to it. Therefore, change management is about helping people understand the need for change, accept change, implement change, and to become advocates of change. Change management takes more than knowing how to create function trees, models, Pareto charts, dazzling presentations, activity lists, or making fishbone diagrams to determine how work should be performed. Change managers must be able to not only help and influence people at all levels to overcome their resistance to change but also to gain their consensus for implementing it quickly. Change is naturally difficult for everyone because it causes people to move away from their comfort zone into unfamiliar territory. For example, if people are asked to fold their arms the opposite of how they usually fold their arms then it might feel uncomfortable to them. This change can be awkward, and can cause people to think whether they are doing it right or wrong, whether they are doing it efficiently, whether this change has a purpose to it or not, and whether they are doing it for the right reasons. Change management means controlling the elements involved in the change process, knowing why change is needed, proactively planning for change, understanding the phases of change, understanding the roles of communication and involvement in the change process, learning how to appreciate and reduce resistance positively, and how to create a fire within each person through clear values and a meaningful mission statement in order to make change a successful reality.

As effective leaders and change managers, we need to listen intently to the concerns of all stakeholders, acknowledge them and then act accordingly to walk our talks. Those who are doing the job and those who are affected by the final products and/or services can provide helpful clues for identifying, interpreting, facilitating, and implementing change. Effective change management requires dealing with change in the long term by being patient, proactive and resilient. While some managers who focus on short-term results to provide quick pain relief medication to deal with the symptoms of change on temporary basis, it is not very effective in the long run.

Many organizations are suffering from the delay of adapting to change and from the delay of satisfying customers' expectations. Companies are losing market share and profit margins because they are unable to keep up with the increasing rate of customer expectations. The faster individuals and organizations change, the more they will minimize their losses in the industry. In order to stay competitive in any industry, employees need to create innovative ways of adapting faster than before. Corporate executives need to realize that a firm's success depends on its flexibility to quickly internalize, adapt and meet customer expectations better than its competitors. This realization has focused many corporate executives to become better change managers and to adapt as well as accept change as quickly as possible. All business people, according to Ed Crenshaw – President of Publix Super Markets Inc., need to do some work in four areas in order to manage change and remain successful. These four areas are: 1) know the business; 2) know the product; 3) know the customer; and, 4) develop and train people who can duplicate these efforts. These four elements, which can contribute to the success of individuals and firms, require continuous change and adaptation to the needs of customers, businesses, associates, and products.

Change can be positive or negative. It may affect one for the good or perhaps somewhat negatively, but that is not a good reason to view change as negative because one cannot be sure of the situation or its future results. Also, one should keep in mind what actually happens does not necessarily make or break a person but it is one's response to the situation that can make or break a person. So, there are changes that will affect one positively, and then there are changes that can affect one negatively. For example, getting married, promotions, moving to one's dream home, and going to high school are considered to be positive changes. While deaths, accidents, demotions, getting laid-off from a good position, and other unexpected or traumatic changes are considered to be negative changes that require patience and future oriented focus in order to overcome their negative side effects. Both positive as well as negative change can be very stressful and may cause an individual to respond negatively to it. Change, especially if it is unexpected, can be scary, difficult to deal with or accept, cumbersome, and at times very frustrating. Human beings are all expected to die sooner or later, but most people are not properly prepared to deal with such circumstances appropriately. Accidents, illness, violence, and mature age take the lives of many people every day. This can be difficult emotionally and financially, especially if people are not prepared at all. According to the National Funeral Directors Association and based on personal experiences, the average cost of a funeral in the United States is running at about $5,000 to $10,000 these days. There are many companies that are using "reduction in force" strategies to become more competitive or because of survival which causes much frustration to many people both emotionally and financially. However, human beings have dealt with change from the beginning of time, and the only difference is that now it comes much faster than it has ever come. Therefore, people need to learn to adapt to change as quickly as possible in order to minimize or eliminate the negative impact of change. Generally, there are two responses to change from a company or individual perspective: reactive and proactive.

Reactive. Reactive responses are unplanned and their purpose is to catch-up with the industry or competition before the firm, or industry along with the people, are out of the "picture." Reactive responses are negative because they are often based on emotions, feelings, and circumstances without much consideration for or reflection on one's mission or purpose in life. Reactive companies and people are usually on the defensive and this can lead people to live lives that are based on urgency. In this situation, people are driven into many directions which creates a very stressful life because they cannot find time to plan.

Proactive. Proactive people and firms are opportunity-minded and they plan for the future as much as possible, and they plan for and expect change. Proactive people are visionaries and see things from a larger perspective. They see things from a bird's eye view as well as a worm's eye view. Proactive responses are anticipated, planned and aligned with the company or one's personal purpose and mission in life. Proactive people do not resist or meet change through a head-on collision. When proactive people encounter change, they move from having a point of view to a viewing point in order to see all the possibilities and perspectives of change. They use change to their advantage and thrive on it similar to martial artists who go along with change in the same direction and simultaneously gain more power and fluidity as they strike the target. Proactivity allows a person to turn a life of work into a work of art. Proactive people do what they love and consequently love what they do. Therefore, they never have to "go to work" because they choose to do things they love and things they want to accomplish for personal joy.

Change is one thing that employees of national and international firms can be certain about in today's environment. Highly effective individuals are prepared to constantly accommodate change. Highly effective individuals know that it is not change that hurts or makes one feel bad in the long-term; but it is one's response to change that really hurts the future. Change happens and then its negative affect can be over faster if, and only if, we allow ourselves to focus on the future and plan to make the best of it rather than moaning about the past. The leaders of today need to remain open and flexible in order to deal with *planned and unplanned changes* that will be affecting them and their organizations. Sometimes people know about a policy or technology which will be implemented and its prospective benefits are clear and known to everyone. Therefore, employees can purposely plan to deal with such changes appropriately and people will not be shocked because they were expecting change. However, individual employees face many unplanned changes which require them to adapt without much prior planning. Obviously, it would be helpful to forecast change and plan accordingly, but unfortunately that is not always possible. Therefore, employees need to be prepared and adapt to the unplanned changes that affect them from all directions of life. For example, if one person on a manufacturing assembly line is not able to perform his or her job then many more individuals will be affected by this because they are waiting to receive the work-in-process or completed parts in order to continue. This can cost the company money, time, products, customers, morale, jobs, and of course productivity.

Of all the living mammals in the world, human beings are the only ones that can proactively change and adapt to their environment easier than any other. Human beings have been able to use their intelligence and make their lives better from generation to generation since the beginning of time. Every generation has had to endure some uncomfortable changes in order to make their lives and/or those of future generations better. Human beings have always been able to adapt to change in their environment by working with it, around it, but not against it. For example, human beings have adapted to sleeping mostly at nights, because it was effective, and working during the day, which does not necessarily have to be that way in today's environment. Changes in technology have helped people work at anytime they choose to do so. People can travel around the globe in matter of days by airplanes, shuttle, high speed boats, and other methods of transportation. People can make telephone calls, complete bank transactions, and approve credit card charges from anywhere in the world in about five seconds through modem and computers or the internet. All this has become possible through the advent of technology, and thus has made living better, easier, and more enjoyable, but not before the acceptance and adaptation to change. It is known that change is beneficial, yet many people resist it because the future may seem uncertain. However, it is clear that not everybody resists change because wet babies welcome and love change and so do their loved ones who take care of them. Nonetheless, individuals have different feelings and experiences when it comes to dealing with change. Geller (1994) states that workers may have the following experiences and feelings when dealing with change (circle the ones that applied to you in the last change you experienced):

- Rewarded
- Isolated
- Uncertain
- Quiet
- Frustrated
- Frightened
- Empowered
- Refreshed
- Invigorated
- Energized
- Enlightened
- Puzzled
- Happy

- Stressed
- High
- Angry
- Confused
- Depressed
- Weighted down
- Strengthened
- Open to opportunity
- Disrupted
- Good
- Bad
- Low
- Sad

Some people enjoy change while others loathe it. Generally, responses to a major change can include the stages or feelings of immobilization, denial, anger, bargaining, depression, and testing before eventually accepting the change (Conner, 1993; Geller, 1994). Geller states that, on a psychological or attitudinal level, one may have strong emotional reactions to changes; the reaction can be so strong that one may become numb and unable to respond appropriately. Change agents, managers, and leaders must be aware of such diverse reactions and respond according to the needs of each person and situation in order to help him or her transition effectively.

Regardless of the feelings experienced, employees must keep in mind that change does not always mean totally abandoning an existing way of doing things. Sometimes innovations can lead to major changes and at other times innovations can mean more options to choose from or options to fit a variety of circumstances. For example, Johnson and Johnson created the easy-to-open Fast Cap bottles of Tylenol for people who may be suffering from arthritis and others who have a hard time opening the "nail-breaking" bottles. So, innovations and changes do not always have to be replacements but sometimes they can serve as an enhancement for productivity or better service to more stakeholders.

In regard to resistance to and acceptance of change, Judson (1991) states that there is a spectrum of behaviors that can be categorized as responses to change; the spectrum of behaviors, as shown below, can range from deliberate sabotage to enthusiastic responses in the categories of active resistance, passive resistance, indifference, and acceptance of change.

Active resistance	⇒ Deliberate sabotage ⇒ Spoilage ⇒ Committing "errors" ⇒ Personal withdrawal (time away from work) ⇒ Slowing down
Passive resistance	⇒ Doing as little as possible ⇒ Working to rule ⇒ Protests ⇒ Non-learning ⇒ Regressive behavior
Indifference	⇒ Doing only what is ordered ⇒ Apathy; loss of interest in the job ⇒ Indifference ⇒ Passive resignation
Acceptance	⇒ Acceptance ⇒ Cooperation under pressure from management ⇒ Cooperation ⇒ Enthusiastic

Another example of change is the way people shop and where they shop. Many of today's large retailers have made it easy for their customers to shop in their locations. Wal-Marts, K-Marts, Publix, and other retailers have shopping carts available for carrying products, wheel-chair carts; rain coats, and umbrellas to help customers carry their products to their cars; photo labs; and pharmacies to accommodate the "one stop shopping" needs of their customers, and many other little things that enhance the shopping experiences of their shoppers. Not offering these luxuries might be the cause for reduced sales volume in some major outlet malls which do not offer many of the conveniences mentioned above. In order for them to attract more people, they will need to make some changes or additions to their existing services. These changes may not be easy but are necessary to compete profitably with others in the industry.

According to Lodge and Vogel (1987), professors at Harvard University, a country can be successful if its ideology is "coherent and adaptable," enabling it to clarify and achieve its goals, and when the gap between the prevailing ideology and practice within the nation is minimized. Ideology is seen as the aggregation of ideas which institutions use to clarify values in a relevant context. These professors define values as those timeless and agreeable notions which communities throughout the world have always cherished and pursued. Lodge and Vogel further define "relevant context" as the aggregation of events, insights, facts, forces and so on that affect communities. Lodge and Vogel state that common values of communities stay the same over time, however its ideology may change and if it is not aligned with their dominant communitarian or individualistic ideologies then it may cause some problems. Every culture or community wants the value "justice" which basically means fair treatment. Every community always has wanted and will want justice, so that fact has not changed over the course of history; however what constitutes "fair" has changed in regard to contextual changes. Therefore, one can conclude that the value "justice" has remained the same in all communities; however ideology varies between communities and over time. Lodge and Vogel mention that an institution or community can be successful when it is able to "manage ideological change while maintaining institutional efficiency and legitimacy in the face of contextual change." They further conclude that change is continuous, and successful Western institutions have responded and adapted quickly to these changes while unsuccessful institutions have found the transition cumbersome because of traditional ideological assumptions which have caused much waste, chaos and in some cases bankruptcies. So, being able to change quickly is not only beneficial to organizations and communities but it is a necessity for their survival. Of course, as individuals people are at the core of their communities and organizations. Managers and change agents can help them change from the inside as well as the outside.

People respond to change differently with regard to their speed of adjusting to change, and this is not usually at the speed of light. Most people respond to sudden changes suddenly, but tend to ignore the slow and gradual changes called passive or natural changes. This is true of frogs as well because they tend to ignore gradual changes even if it is life threatening. During experiments, frogs responded to sudden changes and not to gradual changes at all. This was proven by putting frogs in water and heating the water quickly where the sudden heat caused the frog to jump out of the water. On the other hand, when the water temperature was gradually increased the frog did not respond to this and eventually the frog's energy deteriorated and it could not do much to save itself. As proactive individuals employees need to not only be aware of the gradual changes, but they must attempt to predict and plan appropriately for them. As Stephen R. Covey (1989) states, in his book titled *The 7 Habits of Highly Effective People*, the best way to predict the future is to create it, plan for achieving it, and then work the plan on daily basis.

Dealing with change requires skills of resilience, patience, and experience. There are individuals who claim that "people are always trying to do me in" and surviving this gives them experience to deal with change accordingly. While this may or may not be true, one can learn from any experience which is different than what students learn in the conceptual framework of academics. In many cases, college students learn facts, figures, dates, and theories which help them pass their coursework, but lack real experience and learning ability. In today's changing world the facts and figures alter very rapidly due to the technological advancements and increased productivity. So, it is not very important to solely focus on them; however it is important to learn new theories and concepts by critically thinking about them on the individual level. Students should have the ability to learn new concepts, methods, and theories while remaining flexible to abandon old concepts and adapt to new ones in the new and competitive global environment. In other words, students need to learn how to manage, thrive, and welcome change. Of course, the same is true for all national and international employees if they are to effectively deal with change.

Roles Involved in the Change Process

There are three types of people in this world: 1) Dependent people - those who wonder what happened; 2) Independent people - those who watch things they want to happen; and 3) Interdependent people - those who make things happen along with others. *Dependent* people, those who feel helpless and vulnerable, do things that are expected of them from others in order to receive recognition and rewards. *Independent* people, those who always want to be in control or else, do what they want to do which are things that they can accomplish by themselves regardless of what others think or say. *Interdependent* people are those individuals who understand that they can only go so far in this world through their own individual efforts since everyone needs someone else if they are to live happily and realize their full potential. These are holistic or "systems thinkers" and see the impact of individual components on the whole. Interdependent people understand that they cannot be engineers, doctors, masons, carpenters, home builders, architects, and army generals to do everything for themselves. As such, they realize that they need to trust other professionals and rely on others if they are to make progress in the society. Interdependent people let independent people accomplish their tasks by their own methods and help dependent people build confidence and self-esteem to become independent and eventually interdependent. Furthermore, they are not scared to share, ask, listen, risk, or delegate authority to others. Interdependent people are not afraid to explore their fears and are able to empower others to their fullest capacity so they too can develop and mature toward interdependency. These individuals are able to meet people where they are and take them one step at a time to where their potential can take them. Interdependent people are also able to wear different hats and play different roles simultaneously. They have the capability to see things and let themselves wonder what happened, they can watch and enjoy seeing things happen, and most importantly they can make things happen individually and with or through people. In order for organizations to become successful, independent people need to let go of their controlling behavior and the dependent people need to let go of their dependency on others in order to function effectively as interdependent individuals. Interdependent people believe in moderation, balance, and flexibility toward gradually getting things done. Interdependent people are flexible enough to serve in various roles that are involved in the change process. Interdependent people can be successful sponsors, agents, and targets in the change process which are the common roles in any organization that is changing.

Managers in the twenty-first century environment need to be both successful and effective. Research shows that successful managers spend about 48% of their time in networking activities and 28% in communication activities, while effective managers spend about 44% of their time in communication and about 11% in networking activities (Robbins, 2001). In order for managers and professionals to be successful in their roles as change agents, they need to be involved in both networking and communication activities. The following are the common definitions of these roles in the change process: sponsors, agents, targets, and others.

Sponsors: These are individuals who want the change and legitimize it. Sponsors initiate the need for change, the change itself, and may or may not be involved in implementing the change. Sponsors can choose to be the change agents or they can delegate the implementation process to others. Sponsors can also be the targets as well.

Agents: These are individuals who are the driving force and are leading and guiding the process of change in the society or in the organization. Success as a change agent depends in large part on the capabilities and strengths of the human resources team and the department's leaders as well as their credibility with employees in the organization (Babcock, 2005). Effective change agents are interdependent and have the following qualities:

1. *Knowledgeable and self-developers* – they do their homework and become knowledgeable about the benefits and dangers of change, commitment of the sponsors, and understand their targets. They take care of themselves physically, mentally and spiritually. They routinely take time to improve themselves because that is the best way to help others. They understand that the best way to live a good life is to stay healthy, open-minded, humorous, and enjoy life at the present while keeping a focus on the future.

2. *Risk takers* – change agents understand that a risk-free life does not exist and every move one makes or even does not make has risk associated with it. Effective change agents are able to mentally calculate the potential reward of each decision, thereby taking calculated risk as often as possible. Successful people are successful from the outset because success is found within the journey and not necessarily always in reaching the destination. Effective change agents understand that they deal with emotions, fears, feelings, and anxieties that are caused by uncertainties of change. They respect and empower others to make their choices according to their own values and behaviors.

3. *Resilient* – change agents are able to learn from the past, mentally focus on the future, and function in the present. Resilient change agents are able to bounce back from extreme levels of discomfort caused by change and become as productive as possible in the most efficient possible manner. They welcome and expect change especially in times of crises.

4. *People oriented* – change agents are able to network with people throughout the organization and the community. They understand that in order to eat an apple from one's own tree, one must first plant the tree, nourish it and give it time to grow before one can expect the fruit. They understand that in order to have more friends they must become friendly. They also understand that one must earn support from other people before one can expect them to support his/her ideas. Effective change agents understand that you must do before you can be, and you must be before you can have. Effective change agents understand people and they further understand that before you can put yourself in someone else's shoes you must first take your own shoes off. Effective change agents are also good listeners. They understand that sometimes people feel frustrated and there is nothing that can be done but to listen and acknowledge their feelings and make sure they are heard. Effective change agents do not respond autobiographically, which is responding based on one's own past experience without fully understanding the present situation. They want to get to the core of the problem by being open-minded and listening empathically.

5. *Responsible and active role models* – change agents are action oriented and experience the change personally before expecting others to do so. They understand that a person with experience is never at the mercy of a person with an argument. They follow Gandhi's philosophy of leadership and become the change which they would like to see in their people. They also do what they say; therefore they are people of high integrity and strong character. Effective change agents are action oriented and actively seek to get their questions answered from the original source. Effective change agents become part of the solution, and not the problem, by supporting others who are having a difficult time dealing with change. They usually focus on the positive despite negative circumstances.

Targets. Targets include the group, population, department, or individual that should, need to, or must actually change. Change agents may include systems, processes, and/or people or individual(s) in departments and organizations. The best way for the target to adapt to change would be to become change agents themselves.

Others. Those who are indirectly affected by the change. These people may be advocates, adversaries, or neutral to the change. Sometimes, the people of the community could be the driving force or the restraining force for change. Their support or discontent could mean taking two distinct routes. For example, lobbyists are not change agents, but they could be supporters of the change and that would make a big difference in the decision of the company or government. There could be many internal and external advocates or adversaries of change such as employees, stockholders, and customers.

Initiating and leading major organizational changes is not an easy task. However, making or bringing about major changes requires experience, skill, and integrity. Human resources experts state the "quite frankly, as a profession we haven't done a good job of giving people enough opportunities to lead and sustain organizational change efforts." Change agents must remember not to underestimate the power of the culture they are about to change. Change agents and managers also must be clear, concise, and consistent in their roles as communicators of the new change and process. In their roles as change agents, human resource professionals and managers must "have a very strong ownership culture where all employees are involved and engaged" (Babcock, 2005).

Playing Multiple Roles

In some cases a person may be required to play many roles in the change process. A person can be the sponsor, agent, and target for the change. There are advantages and disadvantages to playing multiple roles in the change process. While the disadvantages of playing multiple roles might include lack of time, lack of resources, lack of support, lack of different points of view, and in some cases lack of initiative, the advantages might be more involvement, awareness, control, and understanding of the change from the outset. Procrastination can hurt the change process if one does not begin the process quickly. The best way to overcome procrastination is to clearly envision the end-results, the overall task, and then break large tasks into small chunks that one can manage on a short-term basis. Short-term may include hourly, daily, or weekly goals and activities. As you break large tasks into small ones, you can use "ACTION" to fulfill your responsibilities.

- **A**cknowledge and accept your role(s) in the change process,
- **C**ommunicate your goals, needs, and plans to other stakeholders,
- **T**hink tolerance, teamwork and target,

- **I**nitiate the change,
- **O**bjectively observe nuances and responses to change,
- **N**egotiate noteworthy observations and suggestions into the strategy.

Summary

Change is a natural part of life and inevitable in professional organizations. As a matter of fact, change is a natural part of human development as people progress through the continuum of conception, birth, adolescent, maturity, golden years, and the ultimate departure from this physical world. This chapter has introduced change as one may experience it through his or her personal or professional lives, the challenges associated with change, and the various roles that managers and employees can play in the change process. It has also discussed various reactive and proactive responses to change initiation and implementation. Finally, the chapter discussed the "ACTION" model when one plays single or multiple roles in the change management process. Since change is inevitable, global employees and organizations might as well prepare for it and proactively seek it in a purposeful manner.

Survey of Organizational Climate for Change

The Survey of Organizational Climate for Change is based on the research by Symmetrix, as Massachusetts consulting firm (Robbins, 2001). Answer each question in a Likert scale format on the continuum from strongly agreeing (5), agreeing (4), neutral (3), disagreeing (2), to strongly disagreeing (1) with each statement. Circle a number from 1-5 on the ratings column and then total the choices by adding them.

Survey of Organizational Climate for Change

Questions	Ratings (1-5)
1. The sponsor of change is senior, powerful or influential enough to effectively deal with foreseeable change.	1 2 3 4 5
2. The leadership of the operation is supportive of the change and committed to it.	1 2 3 4 5
3. There is a strong sense of urgency from senior management about the need for change and it is shared by the rest of the organization.	1 2 3 4 5
4. Management has a clear vision of how the future will look be different from the present.	1 2 3 4 5
5. There are objective measures in place to evaluate the change effort and reward systems are explicitly designed to reinforce them.	1 2 3 4 5
6. The specific change is consistent with other changes going on with the organization.	1 2 3 4 5
7. Functional managers are willing to sacrifice their personal interest for the good of the organization as a whole.	1 2 3 4 5
8. Management prides itself on closely monitoring changes and actions taken by competitors.	1 2 3 4 5
9. The importance of the customer and knowledge of customer needs are well accepted by everyone in the workforce.	1 2 3 4 5
10. Managers and employees are rewarded for taking risks, being innovative, and looking for new solutions.	1 2 3 4 5
11. The organizational structure is flexible.	1 2 3 4 5
12. Communication channels are open both downward and upward.	1 2 3 4 5
13. The organization's hierarchy is relatively flat.	1 2 3 4 5
14. The organization has successfully implemented major changes in recent past years.	1 2 3 4 5
15. Employee satisfaction and trust in management are high.	1 2 3 4 5
16. There is a high degree of cross-boundary interactions and cooperation between various units in the organizations.	1 2 3 4 5
17. Decisions are made quickly, taking into account a wide variety of suggestions.	1 2 3 4 5
Total Score =	

The higher the total score on the *Survey of Organizational Climate for Change*, the greater is the likelihood that the change initiatives and efforts will succeed in this organization. Questions that receive low ratings from a large number of employees in the organization are areas of opportunities for improvement in the reduction of resistance to change.

Chapter Four

LEADING AND MANAGING CHANGE

People resist change mostly due to the loss of control over what they do or the perception of such a loss; therefore, it is the change agent's role and responsibility to reduce and eliminate this fear by instilling a sense of confidence in workers who are impacted by change, in the context of the employee's level of readiness to accept the change or successfully complete the new task. It is recommended that managers and change agents use the situational leadership concept and appropriate leadership styles to effectively transition workers in the change management process. Overall, this chapter continues to offer various approaches and strategies for organizations and individuals to successfully initiate, execute, manage, and lead change in today's cross-cultural workplace. This chapter encourages the use and skills of situational leadership concepts for effectively transitioning and influencing others as per their level of readiness to accept the change by telling them about it, selling the change to them, jointly working with them to implement the new process, and delegating the responsibility and accountability for the new process to them.

Change and Leadership

Change management is about managing productivity and progressively increasing the effectiveness of each person (including oneself). Hersey and Campbell (2004) state that studies indicate that managers who employ general, as opposed to close, supervision of their employees, tend to have higher production in their work groups. This seems to be a general tendency. In reality, as demonstrated through the self-fulfilling prophecy principles or the Pygmalion effect, employees do respond positively to genuine high expectations from their superiors and managers with attempts to justify those expectations with high performance. As a result, managers and leaders naturally feel that their confidence was not misplaced, and continue to believe their subordinates are capable of, and willing to achieve, high performance (Hersey and Campbell, 2004). According to Paul Hersey and Ron Campbell, in such a way an *effective cycle* is created, with each repetition resulting in high confidence by the managers and high performance by subordinates. Of course, as stated by Hersey and Campbell, change agents and managers must be aware that the same tendency can create an *ineffective cycle*. When leaders, managers, and change agents focus on output variables (such as production), they often limit their concerns to short-term and task-oriented behaviors; thereby killing the "goose" in hopes of getting a few extra "golden eggs" in the present. In such a case, the leaders and managers tell their employees what to do, and when to do it, without developing a high sense of confidence in them. According to experts, often employees respond to these low expectations with low performance; as a result, leaders and managers feel justified in their low expectations, and lower them further, and so on (Hersey and Campbell, 2004). The ineffective cycle is difficult to break, often requiring major changes in management.

Hersey and Campbell recommend that change agents, leaders, and managers use situational leadership concepts to bring about effective changes in the readiness of each individual in their departments. Situational leadership concepts and leadership styles are excellent tools for the developmental cycle of each employee and his or her level of readiness to deal with new tasks. According to Hersey and Campbell (2004), "*The developmental cycle* is a tool that managers can use to increase the task–relevant readiness level of their personnel. It is a growth cycle through which managers can work toward making their people winners." With such a plan and before moving into the developmental cycle, the manager must determine the current readiness of the employee in dealing with the new change, task or job. A manager or change agent can ask: how able is the employee, and how willing is that person to meet the expected level of good performance in the new task or job? The manager and change agents can also determine readiness by asking the employee, do you know how to do this task according to the new process? Do you like doing it according to the prescribed manner? Or, managers and change agents can determine readiness of their employees by observing them at work performing the new task, job, or new process. Once the employee's readiness is determined, Hersey and Campbell (2004) recommend the following leadership styles (telling, selling, participating, and delegating) for twenty first century leaders, managers, and change agents:

1.   If the manager determines that the employee is both unable and unwilling to undertake an aspect of the new job, change or task, the person has a low readiness level for that task or new method of performing it. The appropriate leadership style, with this level of readiness, is *telling* (close supervision or high–task, low–relationship style).

2.   If the person is willing to accept the change or new process but is unable to do the task, the person has a low to moderate level of readiness. Thus, the manager should engage in *selling*, being both directive and supportive toward the person using a high–task, high–relationship style.

3.   If the employee or worker is able to do the new task, but is unwilling to accept the change or new process, then the manager or change agent's role is to be supportive, to help the person develop the confidence to do the task. This is *participating*, a low–task high–relationship leadership style.

4.   Finally, if the person is both able and willing to accept the new process, then the manager or change agents need not initiate the developmental cycle for that aspect of the job as the individual is already at high readiness. The manager should simply engage in *delegating*, a low–task low–relationship leadership behavior. Furthermore, besides making the manager's job easier, employees at this level can become change agents and champions of the new process or change in the organization.

The leadership styles of telling, selling, participating, and delegating are used by the Center for Leadership Studies, founded by Dr. Paul Hersey. The same styles are also known as directing, coaching, supporting, and delegating by the Blanchard Management Corporation, founded by Dr. Kenneth Blanchard (Blanchard, Zigarmi & Zigarmi, 1985). Dr. Blanchard states that every person has peak performance potential, it is the job of managers and leaders to know where they are coming from and meet them there. After assessing the current readiness level of a subordinate in a particular job aspect and determining the appropriate leadership style to employ, the leader's or change agent's job is to help that subordinate increase readiness in that task by helping them go where they need to be. This requires that the manager delegate some responsibility, in a progressive manner, to the individual that is slightly above the person's current readiness level. Hersey and Campbell (2004) state that it is important to remember that employees are not all motivated by the same things when it comes to change management incentives. For something to act as a positive reinforcement of an individual, it must be something that person identifies as desirable. For desirable behavior to be obtained in a change initiative, a reward must be made for appropriate behavior, and it must be delivered immediately after the desired behavior. Naturally, as demonstrated by the above discussion prior to beginning the change management cycle, a situational leadership model is recommended for all change agents, managers and leaders as they initiate and executive change.

The Situational Leadership Concept

The concept of situational leadership claims that there is no one "best" way of leadership when it comes to increasing one's productivity and success on the job, since effectiveness depends on the situation. Therefore, effective leaders adapt their styles to fit a broad range of individuals and variables impacting their situations. Dr. Paul Hersey states that "leadership is any attempt to influence the behavior of another person or persons," and effective leadership is adapting one's behavior to the performance needs of the person or persons. Effective leaders diagnose, adapt, and communicate based on the readiness of their followers in the workforce and other situational variables. Dr. Hersey defined a person's *readiness* level as their ability and willingness to perform the task at hand and this definition considers two types of readiness: job and psychological. Knowing a person's (follower's) readiness level and effectively adapting one's leadership style to match the readiness level is an important element of making sure the job gets done successfully. Consequently, situational leadership applies to professionals in business, government, the community, volunteers, religious leaders, as well as to parents, and others who have a need to influence the effort of others while initiating a change. The Situational leadership model proposes that managers and change agents can and should change their leadership style (behavior) depending on the situation and the readiness of the follower.

The situational leadership model keeps a balance between high tech (task behaviors) and high touch (relationship behavior). Once the followers' readiness is determined, a change agent or a leader can choose from the four leadership styles that focus either on task behavior or relationship behavior. *Task behavior* is the extent to which leaders engage in top-down communication by explaining what the follower is to do, as well as when, where, and how each function is to be accomplished. *Relationship behavior* is the extent to which leaders engage in joint communication with followers while providing socio-emotional support. The four corresponding leadership styles that match the four different readiness levels (R1-R4) are as follows:

1. *R1- matches best with "Telling," high task-low relationship.* The manager or the leader defines the roles needed to the do the job and tells followers what, where, how, and when to do the tasks.

2. *R2- matches best with "Selling," high task-high relationship.* The manager or leader provides step-by-step and disciplined guidelines to get the job done while being supportive.

3. *R3- matches best with "Participating," low task-high relationship.* The managers, or the leader, along with followers (employees and/or colleagues) jointly decide how to get the job done with the required quality standards.

4. *R4- matches best with "Delegating," low task-low relationship.* The manager or leader provides little directions and little support to the followers since they know how to get the job done and they are very willing to do it independently.

Of course, there are perhaps thousands of situations that could use many different leadership styles; yet, they have been categorized into four for better management and easier application by managers, change agents, and leaders. Thus, the situational leadership model has four leadership styles to keep it simple and easy to understand, so it can be applied by individuals of different skill levels and competencies. In each situation, the model encourages managers to match the style with the followers' level of readiness thus providing the most appropriate amount of task behavior and relationship behavior for the specific task on hand. Hersey and Campbell (2004) provide the following recommendations for each of the four leadership styles:

- Style one or *telling* is best when attempting to influence low levels of readiness. Alternative words that describe the telling style are guiding, directing, and establishing.
- Style two or *selling* is best when attempting to influence low to moderate levels of readiness. The leader attempts to get the follower to buy into doing the task psychologically. Alternative words that describe the selling style are explaining, clarifying and persuading.

- Style three or *participating* is best when attempting to influence moderate to high levels of readiness. The key is to encourage the follower to participate and get involved. Alternative words that describe the participating style are encouraging, collaborating and committing.
- Style four or *delegating* is best when attempting to influence high levels of readiness. This is where the follower has almost all of the decisions for both decision-making and implementation of the activities to get the job done. Alternative words that describe the delegating style are observing, monitoring and fulfilling.

As the readiness of the follower (person performing the specific task) increases in terms of performance or adaptation with the new process or change, the leader (managers and change agents) should adapt by reducing task behavior and increasing relationship behaviors. As the follower becomes totally ready by showing successful performance in the new process or task, the leader should reduce both task and relationship behaviors to the lowest level possible. Overall, a manager or a change agent must first diagnose the follower's level of readiness with the new task or change, and then act with an appropriate leadership style. Diagnosis, or assessing ability and willingness of the follower to see what leadership style is needed, should be followed by matching an appropriate leadership behavior and then implementation of the leadership style to make sure the job gets done with the required quality in the allotted timeframe. Situational leadership is a very effective tool for managing the change cycle and it is recommended for all leaders, managers, and change agents. Dr. Ken Blanchard once stated that every employee is a potential high performer and some of them need a little extra help in realizing their potential in getting there. It is the responsibility of managers and leaders to assess the readiness of each person for the task or change and help them develop to their full potential. Blanchard, Zigarmi and Zigarmi (1985) state that, "The three secrets of one minute management make situational leadership a dynamic model" (p. 81). The one minute management model states that managers and leaders should consciously take time every day, every week, or every month as appropriate to set performance goals with their employees, to praise employees for doing their jobs right as a means of reinforcing or improving performance, and to stop employees from continuing with poor performance. It is important to note that the one minute management practices are situational and the feedback should be honest, based on facts as observed, and it should be timely to effectively change, improve or reinforce performance. It is also very important for change agents and leaders to remember, as stated by Blanchard, Zigarmi and Zigarmi (1985, p.84), that "situational leadership is not something you do to people but something you do with people." So, effective management of the change cycle requires everyone's involvement and input as to better understand individual, interpersonal, organizational, and environmental consequences of change.

Managing the Change Cycle

Just as each individual can have an impact on the society, a society can have an impact on the individual as well. Change can originate from an individual and move toward the society or it can begin in the society and impact the individual. However, it is the individual that makes a difference in regards to the success of the change and the well-being of humanity. Change can take place at the societal or environmental level, organizational level, interpersonal level, and individual or personal level. No matter where change begins, it will always affect people at the individual level and sometimes their interpersonal relationships with other individuals as well. It takes people at the individual level to make change a successful reality by adapting to it and taking advantage of it. Creating personal and interpersonal change must precede organizational and environmental change. Therefore, making changes at the personal and interpersonal levels would be the first steps toward creating cultural or organizational change. The Change Management Levels' model, shown in Figure 6, shows that change can affect an individual from various levels including the society in general.

Figure 6 – Change Management Levels

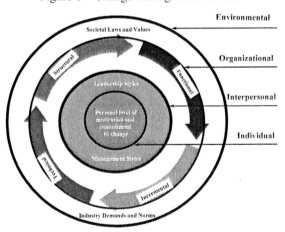

Individual Level

Change will have positive or negative effect on the individual depending on how the individual responds or adapts to change. Change can affect a person's motivation, morale, desire, skills, attitude, level of control, commitment, as well as his or her level of performance. Changes in some of these areas will take more time than others and, similarly, some will be a little more difficult to change than others. Every individual goes through an intrinsic emotional change cycle when he or she is changing his or her usual method of doing things. This cycle can be described in terms of five gradual stages (DREAM).

1. **D**enial and anger.
2. **R**easons and justification.
3. **E**xploration of alternatives and benefits.
4. **A**cceptance of the change.
5. **M**otivation to be a catalyst in the change process.

People can choose to respond positively, negatively or be totally indifferent to change. However, most individuals will go through an emotional cycle which has positive and negative consequences. Flexible and successful people will attempt to shorten or minimize the gap between the first and the last stages in the process. Normally, an individual can go through five stages of emotional change and experience denial and anger, reasoning, exploration, acceptance, and finally motivation to make the change happen. Each individual may go through these stages at his or her own pace. Some people go through them faster than others and some people never seem to make it to higher stages. Stephen R. Covey mentions a blind person by the name of S.B. who gained his sight through an operation. After he saw the sunset for the first time, he said, "we came down the hill and it disappeared" and apparently chose not to be happy with his new paradigm of the world. This was a huge change for him and he could not handle it positively, so a year later after much denial and reasons he went into a deep depression and died. He never made it into the full cycle of emotional change. It is also possible for individuals to skip or revert back a stage or two in the change cycle depending on their level of resilience and flexibility to change. Let us discuss some of the characteristics of people in each stage.

Figure 7 – The Emotional Cycle of Change (DREAM)

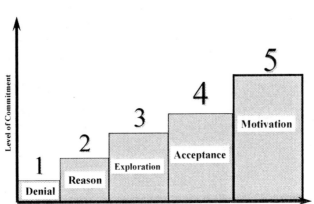

1. *Denial and Anger-* People are usually shocked that the change is actually taking place. They cannot believe it is happening to them. They may be angry at the world or themselves for being put in such a position. Individuals at this stage may have a tendency to talk with others, complain, and seek affirmation of their thoughts and feelings about the new process or change. They may be resentful of the company and those who are implementing the change. They may even plan to work against the new change and sabotage the new plan or process that is affecting them.

2. *Reason-* At this stage, people usually attempt to justify their own reasons in order to reject the change in a logical fashion. They try to come up with all types of reasons which to them would logically support why the change will not work. This can have an aggregate effect on the individual because the more one sees the negative aspect of a situation, the more reasons he or she will be able to gather in order not to go along with the change. People may choose to blame the change on others and reason that the initiators of the change, sponsors and change agents do not really know everything about the change or the job. They only attempt to see why the change is wrong for them and for their jobs, tasks or departments. This would be a cause for staying longer in the first two stages of DREAM.

3. *Exploration-* At this stage, people realize that the options of denial, reasons, and negativity have not produced positive results; therefore they are not happy with them. By this time, people are usually more

knowledgeable about the change and can see their role in the new process as important. They also may realize that change is inevitable if they want to feel better, work more productively, get along with the team, and support the upper echelon. Now, people are able to see different options and opportunities in the new process or change. At this stage the possibilities and benefits of change become much more clear to the individual and he or she may attempt to discover many ways of dealing with the change positively.

4. *Acceptance*- At this stage, the individual has already dealt with his or her emotions, anger, reasons, and frustration. The individual has concluded that he or she can accept and effectively deal with the new change and perhaps support it. At this point the individual is at peace with him or herself and will want to be part of the team and support the team to simply implement the change.

5. *Motivation*- This is where the person totally understands the change, is aware of the consequences of the change, agrees with the change, wants the change, and is totally committed to make the change happen because his or her involvement is an integral part of the process. The individual sees himself or herself as having the sole responsibility for making things happen and he or she is proud to be a part of it.

Highly proactive and effective individuals are able to reach stage five of the change cycle in the shortest period of time and with minimum loss of productivity. Change always causes some uncertainty to individuals and firms; however successful firms are able to bounce back to the top quicker than others because they are flexible, ready, and expect opportunities from change. Those individuals who are flexible, resilient, open-minded, and those who welcome change will be better able to complete the first stages of the "DREAM" cycle than those who fear or resist change. Individuals can experience "DREAM" because of a change in any part of the system. One level of change can affect other levels because in many cases they are interdependent. Change can take place at environmental, organizational, or interpersonal levels, and still affect the individual(s).

Interpersonal Level

Change can take place because of new management, new models, theories, concepts, mission, objectives, goals, and other formal structures, rules, or policies that are being applied or transformed. Also, the relationship of people among departments, teams, and team members may change as well. The reporting systems may alter which can bring about major changes in the interpersonal relationship of individuals. People may have to report to different individuals or departments and some may experience dual matrix systems where they would have to report to more than one person or department.

Organizational Level

There are at least four different ways which a change can take place in the organization and change managers must aware of the harmony among them. The various changes can be:

1. *Structural.* Structural changes can include the reorganization of the systems or the hierarchy throughout the company.
2. *Technical.* These changes are brought by the new technology and innovations which may require new skills and training.
3. *Incremental.* Incremental changes involve addressing a few or the most urgent needs at one time and taking care of them accordingly. This is easier to control and manage because it is specific and one can plan and adjust appropriately.
4. *Functional.* Tasks can be designed in such a way that a totally new and different set of skills may be required in order to complete the job.

Environmental or Societal Level

Societal innovations, ideological changes, customer demands, values among people, global competition, international treaties or disasters, wars, technological advancements, and other such variables can create environmental changes. Environmental changes can bring about changes in the organizational, interpersonal or individual levels. The Chernobyl chemical disaster, for example, changed the lives of thousands of individuals, and nothing productive can take place in the surrounding areas of the land for another century, because it is dangerous for people to work or live there. Similarly, the September 11, 2001 attacks on the Twin Towers of New York, the invasion of Iraq by the American military forces, the invasion of Afghanistan by the former Russian army, and other such formal and informal wars have negatively impacted the environment as well as the lives of thousands of people throughout the world. On the other hand, the internet, teleconferencing, and email communication technologies have positively changed the society and the quality of life for many individuals throughout the world.

Managing Change and Stress Effectively

Change is equivocally ubiquitous and constant throughout our lives. At times, these changes will create stress which needs to be managed quickly, continuously, and at a personal level. That means that workers have to take personal responsibility for their own well-being and routinely attempt to manage and overcome stress in a positive manner. There are three steps that individuals should take to reduce stress in their lives. First, set specific times during the day and/or week to relax and enjoy doing things that bring joy into your life. This requires knowing or learning about your favorite readings topics, games, exercises, and perhaps meditation techniques. You need to continuously practice relaxation techniques both on and off work environment. Second, find out what causes stress in one's life, why they cause stress, and work on reducing and/or eliminating the root causes of these stress-creators immediately. Be aware of situations that cause stress and proactively work to eliminate its root causes. Third, be a source of positive light and energy while maintaining an open mind and a positive attitude toward change, life, and new opportunities. When life gives you lemons, make lemonade and enjoy drinking it along with other friends and family members as if it is a sunny summer day. There are certain "Tension Releasers," also called "Immediate Pressure Release Techniques," which can be helpful in stressful situations when one is with others or by oneself.

Change with Others. When you are with others, try the following tension releasers: Active listening (good eye contact, listen to the words, clarify discussion), empathic listening (reflect the other persons feelings seeking first to understand), self-talk "remain calm," be open-minded and objective, remember that other factors could be contributing to the stressful situation, don't take it personally, keep emotions in control, find a conducive environment for discussion, eliminate any barriers to discussion (interruptions), respect the other person's feelings (even if you disagree), use appropriate body language and be relaxed, keep personal space between yourself and the other person, approach solutions to the conflict when possible, stop, think and select an appropriate response, count silently to yourself, take a deep breath, have a physical signal that reminds you to stay calm (such as index finger touching thumb or hands placed flatly together), know when to politely excuse yourself (situation getting out of hand—explosive), and refer the person to others when necessary or appropriate.

Change with Oneself. Take a break, remind yourself, "if it doesn't kill you, you'll be OK," take a stress walk, get some fresh air outside, give yourself time to calm down, step back to review situation, consider your personal stress level conditions, go outside and scream, delegate duties when possible, do work that is physical—stocking, loading, stacking, gardening, cleaning and so on, eat foods that you like moderately, use positive self-talk, focus on what you can control, plan to do something fun (later that day or on weekend), talk with a friend, become quiet and meditate, pray, review your schedule, plan ways to gain control of your time, listen to calming music, and release energy by hitting a punching bag or by challenging yourself to doing one hundred pushups in one minute. The Change Management Process Flowchart (Figure 8) represents the process and steps for implementing change successfully.

It is extremely important to manage change appropriately and consciously. Change management requires proactive planning and working the plan efficiently. People do not plan to fail, however, people do fail to plan. Planning can prepare individuals to deal with unexpected circumstances in a positive fashion. Human beings are very complex; however there are certain patterns that are pretty much characteristics of all individuals. If one can predict these patterns of behavior then one can be prepared to eliminate its negative impacts through planning.

Figure 8 – Change Management Process Flowchart

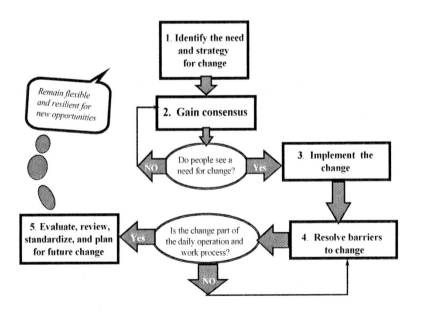

One must keep in mind that people often go through several stages before they can be productive with the new change. People often *hold on* to their old habits as long as they can before they *let go;* and ofcourse they have to let go before they can *move on* to the new methods. According to the bulk of research, in a major change people may experience shock, denial, anger, bargaining, and/or depression- which are the first three stages of "DREAM"- before they can move to acceptance.

As an effective change agent, one can properly prepare and manage change proactively. As shown in Change Management Process Flowchart, there are five stages to the change management process and they are:

1. Identifying the need and strategy for the change,
2. Gaining consensus of the target,
3. Implementing the change,
4. Resolving and removing barriers to change, and
5. Following up and evaluating the implemented change.

1- Identifying the Need and Strategy for Change

The suggested change management model has five stages which will take managers and change agents from the beginning stage of a change to its conclusion and follow up process. During each stage, the sponsors and change agents may have different responsibilities unless the sponsors are also change agents. Originally, the sponsors should identify the need and strategy for the prospective change. This need should be determined according to the vision, mission, and purpose of the company or team. The sponsors should also distinguish and state whether the change is mandated or self-generated because this may play a role in the strategy-making process. The sponsors should also clearly state why the change is needed as well as the results if the change is implemented successfully. They should further determine the timeline for accomplishing the change along with identifying the levels which will be affected by the prospective change. The individuals affected by the change should also be determined by the sponsors of the change. Overall, the sponsors should determine the following strategy for implementing the change:

1. Clearly state the need for change,
2. Determine the best strategy to implement the planned change,
3. Determine change agents,

4. Determine driving forces for change:
   - Determine the available forces that would support the change,
   - Every driving force can create an equally strong opposing force; therefore decreasing these opposing forces can be effective tools to drive the change forward,
5. Determine restraining forces for change. Determine possible forces that may prevent this change from being implemented successfully, and
6. Clarify and provide resources to support change.

2- Gaining Consensus for Change

The best way to make change happen successfully is to make sure everyone agrees with and supports the change before it is implemented. Change requires planning, preparation, education, skill, teamwork, and involvement from all stakeholders. Change agents can use the seven "RESPECT" steps to better prepare targets for agreeing and accepting the new change. Skills for gaining agreement to change are:

1. **R**ecognize resistance and create a common vision,
2. **E**ducate and train people beforehand,
3. **S**upport people and provide them with resources to successfully deal with change,
4. **P**ersonalize rewards, training, and support for change,
5. **E**mpower and involve people in the process,
6. **C**ommunicate the change along with its consequences clearly and listen empathically, and
7. **T**reasure and value people as well as teamwork.

The following thoughts are included in the "RESPECT" model, and need to be done in order to expect the target group to agree and support the change:

Recognize Resistance and Create a Common Vision – Resistance can provide new information that was not seen in the beginning. Resistance can also make the organization a little safer because people are not accepting the status quo, but are taking a leadership role by asking why something needs to be done. Resistance can mobilize people to take action and responsibility for their jobs. It is important that everyone on the team is pushing or pulling in the same direction and not in opposite directions. The best way to create a buy-in for the mission is to involve them in the process of building it up from the ground floor. This mission should be clear, concise, and understood by everyone on the team. Make sure the mission statement is capable of energizing people to work in its direction because when you are going in the right direction, you will eventually get there through hard work and dedication regardless of failures. A journey of a thousand miles begins with the first step and eventually it can be completed as long as one is going in that direction. The principles of physics support this notion because a body in motion tends to stay in motion in the same direction unless acted upon by outside forces.

Educate and Train People Beforehand – Education is important because it provides knowledge about the change and of course a little knowledge is appreciated by everyone. Training is the key to transforming knowledge into production. People say that "knowledge is power" which may not be totally true because knowledge that is not put into use is no better than not having it. A person who is able to read, but does not read is no better than one who cannot read. So, it is the application of knowledge that creates results which may or may not create power depending on other variables such as the need for the result, the availability of the results from other sources, and so on. So, when people are trained and educated about the change then they may be fully prepared to deal with change, and change will not be a threat to them as much as before. Education helps people grow and growing is a biological imperative unless one wants to die. Most fruits are either green and growing or ripe and dying. People are the same as well: they are either green and growing or ripe and rotting. The only way to prolong the growing part is through continuous learning. Education is the only way to keep growing continuously. Educating the team also helps everyone see their part in the overall scheme of things. For example, when a worker at the Houston space center during the mid-1960s was asked what do you do here? He responded by saying "I am helping put a man on the moon." This worker was a janitor and did his work with pride and commitment because he was part of a team that wanted to accomplish something worthwhile to everyone in the society. This person was aware of the long-term mission and had "bought" into it.

Support People and Provide Resources for all Associates – Any change involves some cost and it should be taken into consideration before implementing the change. If the cost is spent appropriately, it can eliminate crisis, chaos, and inefficiency throughout the implementation process. It is suggested that companies provide awareness programs about the new change, stress management workshops, time for people to work through their grief and frustration, as well as an ongoing resource to support them climb the ladder of change.

Personalize Rewards, Training, and Support – People are motivated internally by different needs, and those needs may become fulfilled by different rewards, incentives, or recognition programs. It is important that people are rewarded at the right time, for the right reasons, and for the right values. One cannot water flower A, which is on the next block to flower B, and expect flower B to grow. Watering the right flower at the right times and using the right amount is very important and extremely crucial to its survival. It is important that appropriate monetary and non-monetary rewards are associated with implementing the change successfully. In order for people to change their way of doing things the change should be supported or aligned with recognition and reward programs that are of some value to the people.

Empower and Involve People in the Process – When you empower people to the fullest extent, they will give you maximum performance. One of the greatest human needs is involvement and recognition of one's contribution to worthwhile causes and services. Everybody wants to be involved and contribute to a greater cause or service, therefore involving people in the change process and asking for their cooperation from the outset would be the best way to expect successful implementation of change. Involvement and contribution creates "buy-in," which helps people become much more accepting of the change. Involving people from the outset helps them understand the need for change and consequently agree with the change. Once people see the obvious benefits of change, agree with the change and accept it, then they will not be tempted to go back to their old methods. For example, how many teenagers or adults do we see that would crawl instead of walk in order to get from one place to the next. Involvement also increases trust and commitment on everyone's part thereby making them formal or informal change catalysts or agents. Some people fear that involving people in the process will create chaos and they might lose control; however, they do not realize that not involving them will create more hassles and chaos because people may remain resistant for a long time and may resort to shirking.

Communicate the Change Along with its Consequences Clearly and Listen – Tell everyone about the prospective change as much in advance as possible. Have an open door policy so concerned associates can voice their opinion to appropriate authorities without fear of losing their jobs. Make sure everybody's input is sincerely appreciated and their feelings are acknowledged. Become an empathic listener by seeing people's emotions, hearing them from the heart, and acknowledging their resistance. Try to sincerely understand their point of view and once you fully understand them, they feel understood, and they have overcome their anger, then try to explain the reasons for change and their role in making this change successful. It is important that change agents listen to employees at their pace and not rush them because most people become strongly attached to how they have been doing things and change is usually seen as the enemy. So, be patient, listen with empathy and then help them understand the need for change and provide emotional support. Another key element of listening is finding out the right time to communicate back to associates what they need to know. Feedback should be specific, meaningful, accurate, relevant, and timely (SMART) in order for it to be effective. Feedback to associates has been proven to be one of the most important factors in job satisfaction among employees. It has been said that feedback is the breakfast of champions and an effective strategy for change agents.

Treasure and Value People as well as Teamwork - Human beings are the most important asset for any organization or society. Henry Ford once said, "You can destroy my cars, you can destroy my buildings and my factories, but give me people and I will build them right back." Walt Disney and Oliver Wendell Holmes have been cited as saying that the greatest waste in the organization is not the waste of natural resources, although that could be a great waste, but the greatest waste is the waste of human resources. Change agents need to respect the opinions of others and value their contributions to the organization. This is the power of diversity and should be taken advantage of to create competitive advantage. The true power of teams lies within each individual and not in the team leader, although he or she may have a very important role in the process. When geese fly together they fly about 70 percent faster as opposed to flying individually. They support and encourage each other during their flight and they further switch leadership roles on a continuous basis. They also help and accompany the sick geese until they feel better or die. So, when a goose is sick and can't keep up with the team, two or more geese stay with the sick goose till the sick goose is better and able to fly. Similarly, human beings should respect and value each other just like the geese until their last moment in life because each person is unique and he or she should be treated that way.

The success of any change is dependent on the targets' acceptance and implementation of the proposed change. So, in order to gain their acceptance and agreement then they must be involved in the process as much as possible. They must also be educated and trained on the new process as well as the skills needed to be productive. Uncertainty about the future should be minimized as much as possible so people can feel safer and more in control as they are looking ahead. One should also keep in mind that the consequences of not changing successfully could mean loss of learning and/or advancement opportunities, loss of reputation and social image, bankruptcy or loss of competitive advantage, and the risk of survival or progress in the long-term. Change at each level may affect other levels because they are highly interdependent.

3- Implementing the Change

For the success of implementing change, it is absolutely necessary that people are well educated about the change before the implementation stage begins. This is especially important in cases where people's routine habits are affected. The implementation can change and vary according to the situation and feedback from the recipients or as more information becomes available from various sources. There are three tasks involved in the implementation process, and they are initiating the change, supporting the change, and coaching the target to deal positively with the change.

Initiating the change. Before the change is implemented, make sure that everyone is well aware of the change, their respective roles, their responsibilities, their rewards in making the change successful, and the importance of this change for them. Then roll out the change to targets and make a public statement about the change. Make sure people understand that this change is not a fad, but a real solution or opportunity to the situation. It is important to be aware that some individuals will be playing multiple roles in this change process. Many well respected and influential individuals may be change agents and targets simultaneously and may need time and project management skills to juggle all their responsibilities. So, some just-in-time training may be necessary to help people manage different roles and projects successfully. People may need to use project management skills and planners to organize their activities in order of importance to use their time efficiently. This will help them to keep track of important dates, activities, responsibilities, things to delegate, and all other activities involved in the change process.

Supporting the change. Supporting the change means total commitment without any hesitation whatsoever. It means being an adamant advocate of the change consciously and subconsciously. It requires continuously talking about the change, celebrating the change, and reaffirming the change in a public way. In order to encourage the new behavior (change), change agents and managers may reward those who are successful at implementing the change or even those who are attempting to implement the change. So, the change needs to be supported economically, publicly, privately, and in terms of human talent and muscle.

Coaching the target(s). The change sponsors and change agents can serve as mentors, coaches, guides, and resources for the target group. Sometimes long-term change requires time, patience, and experimentation (heuristics) for trial and error purpose at the individual level. Therefore, having a resource and guide would be helpful. Coaching would require welcoming, appreciating, and integrating targets' feedback to the new process. Coaching also requires giving people emotional support and guidance so they can positively deal with change and overcome the change cycle quickly. Coaching the target means meeting people where they are and gradually taking them to the desired place at their pace, and not yours, otherwise the situation may become too stressful.

4- Recognizing and Resolving Barriers to Change

Implementing change can be very difficult because most often it involves people and new ways of doing things which can be somewhat cumbersome. However, it can be helpful to anticipate some of these obstacles beforehand and prepare everyone accordingly. According to James A. Belasco (1990), the author of *Teaching the Elephant to Dance*, change often takes longer than anticipated because it is virtually impossible to predict all the elements which may get in the way. Adults, in general, learn very slowly and have a tendency to forget easily, therefore more time and repetition may be required to reinforce desired habits and procedures. The key is to be consistent and stay with the plan. Vince Lombardi, a longtime coach of the Green Bay Packers, once said, "Mental toughness wins more games than great skill and fancy game plans." It is also important not to exaggerate too much result too quickly because if the success or results are not delivered on time, then people get disappointed. It may be best to under-promise or promise the least and deliver the most as quickly as possible. Some people also procrastinate starting new and cumbersome tasks, behaviors, or acts. Therefore, it might be wise to follow up with people regularly or break large tasks into small chunks that can be managed on hourly or daily basis. James A. Belasco wrote, "If you want to get things moving in your organization, your first task is to create a fire that people can see and smell, a fire that empowers people to change." It is important to keep this fire under control and not let it get out of hand. To achieve success in change implementation, Belasco suggested three things;

1- *Build a sense of urgency.* Make sure you are prepared to deal with change because change is constant, and so should be your response to it.

2- *Create a clear tomorrow.* The best way to get people's agreement and support is to show them a better tomorrow. Make sure they are clear about the "promised land" because it can be a pulling or driving force for the change.

3- *Show the way.* Create a clear mission or purpose for the people and the company with everyone's involvement. A sense of a worthwhile and worthy purpose can be a great motivator for change. Be the model which you would like to see your people become.

Recognizing barriers to change. The change sponsors along with the change agents must have predetermined key performance indicators (KPIs) that would determine whether the change is accomplishing the expected results or not. KPIs are predetermined results or key points which must be accomplished in order for the change to be successful. These KPIs are means of measuring progress and then aligning accomplishments with expected goals. Anything that prevents the progressive realization of the expected change can be seen as a barrier or resistance. Barriers can come from people, systems, structures, environment, rules, policies, machines, and other indirect or direct variables. Most barriers would fall in the category of resistance or systems that do not support or are not aligned with the expected change. One way to make sure that change happens successfully is to make sure the rules, structures, compensation programs, and policies are totally aligned with the change. The other method would be to reduce or eliminate resistance. Resistance to change can be a source of opportunity because it can let the change agents know some of the things that may not work very well. People are different and each person has his or her own personality or individuality; therefore individuals may respond differently to change based on their paradigms. While some individuals are able to adapt to change easily, others may resist the change. *Resistance* serves as a guard and is the mobilization of energy during a perceived or real threat. Common reasons for resistance include the feeling of being controlled, loss of skill or span of control, lack of adequate information, not being able to meet the new requirement, stress of uncertainty, having difficulty learning, personal goals do not match organizational goals, informal processes may be rewarding production and not the new change or process, misalignment of goals between departments, too many things to do in a given period of time, etc. This resistance may come in many different forms, and some of the common forms of resisting change are passive, overt and covert.

1. *Passive resistance*: This is where people choose to remain quiet, not share their ideas with the group, and not follow the predetermined plan. People may also voluntarily choose not to use their new skills or tools on the job.

2. *Overt resistance*: This is where people refuse to change their way of doing things because they do not see the need for change. They may avoid a very important workshop because they are very busy with current customers or workload. They verbally oppose the change and express their anger and disagreement openly. They may also sabotage the company, department, new process, and/or even the change agents in variety of ways.

3. *Covert resistance*: In this situation, people may not go along with the agreed changes even though they agreed with it. People may withhold information and reduce productivity as well as participation. They may attempt to keep busy to avoid important activities and delay the process. They may also either directly or indirectly advise others not to follow the new procedures. They are sabotaging the new change without appearing as though they are against it.

According to John P. Kotter and Leonard A. Schlesinger's 1979 March/April article in Harvard Business Review, which was titled *"Choosing strategies for change,"* there are four common psychological reasons among people for resisting change and they are:

1- Potential loss of something valuable such as authority, control, loss of job or status, freedom in procedures, etc.

2- Misunderstanding of prospective change and lack of trust in those initiating or implementing change. The common phrase is that top echelons are trying to get more (usually in terms of profits) out of people without giving anything in return to their associates.

3- A belief that new change is not necessary and not needed which may very well be based on incomplete information or totally wrong paradigms.

4- A belief that one may not be able to adapt to new change and may lose face among peers. Believing that one cannot tolerate change at current stage or period of his or her life or skills.

Resolving barriers to change. There are many approaches to handling problems, some of which may be inappropriate to use in all situations. There are positive ways of dealing with resistance, and then there are negative ways which may include force, manipulation, and an autocratic style of leadership. Kotter and Schlesinger's (1979) further suggested the following strategies, along with their appropriate uses, advantages and disadvantages, for handling resistance.

1 *Education and Communication*- Explaining the rationale and the necessity of change to all stakeholders. Use when there is a lack of information or inaccurate information and analysis. After people are persuaded, they will help implement the change. Can be time-consuming when there are many individuals or groups involved.

2 *Participation and Involvement*- Asking stakeholders to help design the change process(s). Use when the change sponsors or agents do not have enough information to design the change or when high resistance can be predicted. Involvement will create buy-in and more or better ideas could be integrated into the change plan. This can be very time-consuming if the participants design the change inappropriately.

3 *Facilitation and Support*- Offer retraining, emotional support, understanding, etc. to people affected by change. Use when people are resisting because they cannot adjust to change. No other alternative approach works better with adjustment problems. Can be costly, time-consuming and still not be successful.

4 *Negotiation and Agreement*- Negotiating with those who may resist, may solicit letters of understanding. Use when a powerful individual or team loses out in a change. It can be a relatively easy way to avoid major resistance to change. Can be costly if it alerts others to negotiate for compliance.

5 *Manipulation and Co-optation*- Putting key people in desirable roles during the design or implementation processes of change. Only use when other techniques will not work or when they are too expensive. It can be a quick and inexpensive way of solving resistance problems. If people feel manipulated, this approach can lead into problems.

6 *Explicit and Implicit Coercion*- Threatening to eliminate people's jobs, power, status, promotions, etc. Use this approach when speed is a necessity and when change agents possess

considerable power. It is speedy and can overcome any type of resistance; yet can be very risky if it leaves stakeholders upset with the change agents or sponsors.

In his 1989 book titled *Juran on Leadership for Quality,* Joseph M. Juran suggested eight specific ways of dealing with resistance in the workplace. Juran's "Rules of the Road" for handling resistance in the work place can be useful in resolving barriers to change.

1. Involve people that are affected by the change in planning and executing the change.
2. Provide enough time for those affected to evaluate the merits of the change and reach an accommodation.
3. Start small with a test site. Do a pilot and then expand slowly through the levels before implementing the change to everyone.
4. Change the reward systems and involve upper management on quality improvement teams and processes.
5. Respond positively to unexpected problems and obstacles.
6. Work with recognized leaders among affected groups.
7. Treat people with dignity.
8. Keep it constructive. Emphasize benefits and solutions, not prior deficiencies or blame.

The most effective way of successfully implementing change would be to reduce restraining forces while increasing driving forces, which can further help reduce resistance to change. In physics, it is learned that for every action there is an equal and opposite reaction. Therefore, for every driving force, there will be an equal and opposite restraining force that will be attempting to stop the change. So, reducing restraining forces can be very helpful in implementing change successfully. The following are some of the methods to reduce restraining forces:

1) Create dissatisfaction with maintaining the status quo.
2) Eliminate the fear of losing control, status, or power.
3) Eliminate the fear of losing existing benefits and rewards.
4) Eliminate incentives for maintaining group norms if the current norms do not support change.
5) Eliminate target complacency with current methods.
6) Make use of current skill and experience in the future so people can feel fulfilled.
7) Diminish uncertainty about the future as much as possible.
8) Acknowledge, understand, and handle resistance positively.

It should be mentioned that if the "RESPECT" process has been implemented properly, then most of the target group should go through the "DREAM" stages somewhat quickly. One should find out what is prohibiting the change from proceeding before doing anything, because rewarding the wrong thing may prove to be chaotic and increase confusion. It also can be helpful to increase driving forces in order to successfully implement change. The following are some of the things that can be done to increase driving forces:

1) Increase "RESPECT."
2) Training for the use of new process, method, and/or technology.
3) Innovation and technology can be great change drivers.
4) Increase the commitment level of management and key leaders.
5) Encourage advocates to share their thoughts, reasons, and benefits about the change.

5- Following Up and Evaluating the Implemented Change

It is very important to follow-up on implemented changes to make sure they were carried out as planned and have produced the expected results. The follow-up process is also important for documentation of the final processes, activities, and future planning. An Afghan proverb states that "those who forget the past are likely to repeat it, those who only live in the present are likely to be hedonistic, those who do not plan for future are not likely to have a good one. However, those who remember the past, plan for future and live in the present are likely to be happy and enjoy a prosperous life." So, planning with proper follow up is very important in change management. There are four stages in the implementation process and they are evaluation of the results, reviewing and documenting the change, standardizing the implemented change, and planning for future.

1. *Evaluate the results of the implemented change.* Find out if the initial change has been implemented and become part of the daily routine as originally planned. Find out any alterations, causes for those alterations, and the results. Finally, find out if the results of the change are positive and satisfactory to all stakeholders.

2. *Review and document the implemented change process.* If the process has changed from the original outline, then document the new process and its results. Document the time, cost, resources, skills, people, and other important elements that contributed to the success of the process. Can the process be duplicated in the future or other areas in the organization? In

some cases, unique situations may require a unique solution which cannot be implemented in other places because of the contextual elements and variables involved.

3. *Standardize the implemented change.* Make sure the new process is documented and communicated as the new method of doing things. This needs to be clear so everyone including new associates can understand and follow them without any difficulties. The new process should also be integrated into training programs.

4. *Plan and prepare for future change.* Change is the only constant and experience can certainly be helpful to plan for future changes. Experience means nothing unless it is documented for future references and usage. People change in organizations, so it is important to document things for future changes and decisions. Make sure people understand that change is constant, that they should be flexible and appreciative of change. Document and plan toward prospective changes that may affect the environment, organization, interpersonal relationships, and/or the individuals in the near future.

Summary

Global thinking and local acting have become the norm in today's small business world. International joint ventures, mergers, partnerships, and cooperatively working in complementary businesses have become a prevalent mode of business and are not considered anomalies anymore. All of the above has been caused by the advent of new technology, global competition, and the availability of resources around the world in short periods of time. Of course, an abundant amount of information is available and can be accessed in a matter of five to ten seconds through a telephone or a computer and the Internet. So, change has become a way of life and it comes in a variety of shapes, sizes, and forms. Change can be passive or inactive, mandated, and self-generated or proactive. Each type of change may have different effects on people because the variable and elements may be different. However, we know that successful implementation of international change entails both learning how people go through the "DREAM" stages of the change cycle and learning how to use "RESPECT" in order to get people excited about change and move them into a brighter future, perhaps a little quicker and with less stress in the process. The resilient individuals or change agents will have a better chance of moving from the denial and reasoning stages to the acceptance and motivation stages much more quickly and more successfully. Today's environment demands that each individual becomes a change agent and takes responsibility for his or her own future by mentally creating it, and then working toward accomplishing it on a daily basis. Once the vision of the future is clear, then people can align the changing world to fit their goals and objectives. There is something valuable in each learning experience even if it is just experience. At the local, global, or national levels of leadership, having a world of wealth means nothing, having good health and a vision of the future means something, however, having integrity and a great character, amid major changes, means everything.

Change is a constant reality in the business environment. In the new economy, change seems to keep picking up speed in all industries and professions. Today's employees and customers are living in a constant period of transition, and the shelf life of solutions keeps getting shorter since what works today can become obsolete a few months later. Where is all the change coming from in today's economy? Change is often coming from or caused by people, technology, new information, and globalization. The growing population is dealing with new technology everyday which feeds and sustains on itself. Experts suggest that it is best to think of technological change as something that keeps multiplying on a continuous basis. Still another source of this rapid change is knowledge or information which seems to be doubling about every four to five years. Some of the commonly addressed sources of change for businesses can include changes in nature of the workforce, economy, social trends, politics, leadership, management, organizational structures, products, services, customers, customer demands, and location of where the firm produces or offers its products.

Because of rapid changes, new knowledge and doubling of information every few years, the future promises more change than experienced thus far. Such rapid change can quickly or slowly destroy organizations that do not adapt to the new circumstances. Such rapid changes call for major personal and cultural shifts in behavior. Today's workers and organizational leaders cannot afford to ignore change and just do what comes naturally or as they have done in the past as that may not work. Workers must face the change proactively, surrender to the change, adjust to it, go with the change, adapt to it, and/or do what works in order to take advantage of the change. Change can impact individuals, cultures, economies, countries, regions, and societies. Change can impact people positively or negatively, and to some extent, the impact of change is determined by one's response to it. As such, it is best to be proactive rather than reactive about responding to change.

Change is a reality of life and all human beings go through it personally, professionally, physically, mentally, socially, and spiritually. Change management is about making sure that one is able to see the positive side of the issue and, as a change agent, make sure that every person impacted by the transition goes through the change process effectively. Change management is about transitioning those who are impacted by the change and making sure everyone becomes a winner as a result. It is about understanding that everyone wants to be a winner and helping them get there through a smooth transition without a cost to others. Change management, at times, is about helping professionals heal physically, professionally, and mentally in their transition to the new destination. It is about understanding that all employees want to get there successfully along with everyone else. Change and winning are not mutually exclusive; therefore, both can happen simultaneously and everyone can and should become winners. As such, all leaders and change agents must be cognizant of this fact and perhaps slow down when needed so everyone on the team can become winners in this temporary race of life.

Why should managers, leaders, and change agents help others to catch up when needed? Because what matters in this life is helping others win, even if it means slowing down and changing course. As change agents and effective leaders, if you help others change successfully, rather than simply choosing to win at all costs, then we all may be able to change our hearts toward better societal goals, teamwork, and fairness for all. The fact is that a candle loses nothing by lighting another candle; however, everyone gains more light as a result. So, be the candle in this society and provide energy to others toward positive change by selflessly sharing your wisdom and knowledge with everyone who can benefit from it. Furthermore, while respecting the beliefs and ideologies of workers, global change agents must be persistent in selling the change by letting everyone know how it can benefit them both in the short term as well as in the long term. Calvin Coolidge has been quoted as saying, "Nothing can take the place of persistence. Talent will not; the world is full of unsuccessful people with talent. Genius will not; unrewarded genius is almost a proverb. Education alone will not; the world is full of educated derelicts. Persistence and determination alone are omnipotent." Change management is about being persistent and determined to manage change and stress effectively. Effective management of change means proactively planning, developing diverse scenarios and possibilities, and exercising one's body and mind to stay in good health. As the proverb states, "Those who don't find time for exercise will have to find time for illness."

Thomas Crum (1987) states that in order for human beings to move beyond success, they need to make their life of work into a work of art. People need to naturally move into this "you and me" philosophy where they see the world as abundant and supportive in all aspects of their lives, from their health to their financial well-being. Crum defines "*alchemy*" as one's ability to change the ordinary into the extraordinary. The ability to change the ordinary to the extraordinary in the middle-ages involved changing common metals into gold, but the alchemy of today involves changing ourselves. Crum states that "It is the pressure of conflict, the interference patterns of energies caused by differences, that provides the motivation and opportunity to change" (1987, p. 25). Nature sees conflict in a positive light, and uses it as a primary motivator for bringing about change. Human beings can do the same with change, conflict and stress. The future chapters continue to discuss change and relevant skills needed to manage time, conflict, and stress that often accompanies change.

CHANGE AND TEMPERED RADICALS[2]

L earning organizations educate and empower their employees to make the needed changes in a timely manner. The holistic-thinking leaders of learning organizations encourage employees to bring about appropriate changes in their own behaviors first and then expect others to change. Tempered radicals use various strategies to initiate, champion, and bring about the needed changes quietly at the right times. Organizations and their members around the globe inherently resist change, yet there are individuals in the workplace today, who have felt the need for change and initiate it very effectively. However, individuals who wish to drive change sometimes face a dilemma: if they speak up, resentment from those accepting the status quo can build toward them; if they remain silent, resentment and stress may build inside them. In essence, these individuals must eventually find a way to rock the boat silently without hurting their reputation or future opportunities. These individuals are referred to as "tempered radicals" because they choose to bring about incremental changes in moderate ways. Accordingly, this chapter presents an opportunity for studying and appreciating the various techniques and styles "tempered radicals" utilize that enable them to make changes in their departments or industries. This section further discusses how appreciative inquiry can be used by tempered radicals as an effective tool to bring about successful change and cultural transformation.

System Thinking and the Learning Organizations

The "systems thinking," or a holistic paradigm, allows all senses to work synergistically in the creation of a learning environment through their interactions with the external environment. Perhaps the effectiveness of the five senses working together can result in the awakening of the sixth

---

[2] This chapter is co-authored with Nicholas DiDomenico, University of Phoenix-Online.

sense, the ability to see beyond time and space. The twenty-first century organization is much more complex, and the best way to effectively address this complexity is to see the interconnectedness of the parts through the five senses from the detail to general as well as from internal to external variables while predicting the future. Instead of managing through a "critical eye" or micro-managing, managers need to unleash their potential to see other systems beyond their limits to lead disparate generations in the twenty-first century workforce. Also, as the organizations become more complex, managers will need to teach employees to think from a holistic and systemic perspective in order to discover new methods of leading diverse generations. They need to help employees see how their jobs affect the next step in the chain or process, and how their functions positively impact the environment. The skills and systems thinking process can be learned to support diverse generations. Human beings, as change agents and managers, have the ability to effectively adapt according to the needs of their employees in the workforce. Capra (1997) stated that the human mind is powerful enough to facilitate the conceptualization of system thinking including chaotic (complexity) theory and non-lineal mathematical models. The twenty-first century manager cannot rely just on the past to effectively move forward and lead diverse generations into the future. As effective supervisors and intellectuals, managers should realize that their self-imposed ideologies of reality must evolve with nature, science, and time in order to foster new strategies for leading today's diverse workforce. These managers must learn to embrace the diversity of various generations and ethnicities in the workforce through the creation of an inclusive learning environment throughout the organization.

In the twenty-first century's fast paced global environment, as well as in today's changing economy, organizations need to embrace change as a constant motivating force that provides both opportunities as well as challenges. The concepts presented in Senge's (1990) book, titled *"The Fifth Discipline: the Art and Practice of the Learning Organization,"* assist individuals in overcoming the illusion that the world is created of separate or unrelated forces (p. 3). It is the letting go of such an illusion that makes a learning organization a possibility. Learning organizations, according to Senge, are "organizations where people continually expand their capacity to create the results they truly desire, where new and expansive patterns of thinking are nurtured, where collective aspiration is set free, and where people are continually learning how to learn together."

Decision-making is one of the most interesting and pervasive concepts in all organizations because people make decisions concerning various concepts such as leadership style, motivation, productivity, conflict management, human resources management, and so on based on their experiences and perceptions. As a matter-of-fact, Peter Senge (1990) states that the ability to learn faster than one's competitors for making effective decisions might be the only true competitive advantage for twenty first century managers and organizations. One always can think and reflect upon the importance of decision-making and the consequences of making both good and bad decisions. One can also evaluate some of the major decisions and think of how leaders could have approached them differently from a holistic perspective. There have been many examples of major decisions made by corporate managers and world leaders in hopes of either making the society a better place to live or their organizations more competitive in their industries. Some of these decisions have been good while others have been disastrous to the well-being of people either financially or physically causing deaths to many innocent individuals on all sides. As can be seen through the media, there also has been a crisis in corporate governance in the United States due to unethical decisions, short-term focus on quick profits, excessive senior management pay, weak vision for direction, corrupt analysts, complacent boards, and questionable accounting practices in some of the largest organizations. With the controversies surrounding Enron, Arthur Andersen, Tyco and a host of other large organizations that have admitted to, at the very least, having used "poor" judgment in managing stocks and acquisitions, the public trust will have to be restored in the credibility of business. In order to remedy such problems in the business environment and improve the level of trust among the stakeholders, perhaps the senior managers can set the company's moral tone, ban stock sales by directors for the duration of their terms, send some senior leaders to jail, and a host of other suggestions might be appropriate as well. However, none of these suggestions will be complete when the focus is on short-term profitability, with no consideration on how one aspect impacts all the other elements both inside and outside of the organization. The leaders must see the impact of their decision from a systems perspective as they attempt to create an inclusive learning organization.

In a learning organization, managers can increase everyone's ability to make non-programmed decisions, those that allow them to adapt, modify, and alter their tasks by creating an effective and inclusive learning environment. A *learning organization* is one in which managers do everything possible to maximize the potential for organizational learning to take place. *Organizational learning* is the process through which managers seek to improve understanding and meet employees' desire and their ability to understand and manage the organization (Jones & George, 2003). This type of environment allows a free flow of ideas from decisions, to dealing with their consequences and further creativity. In order to create a learning organization, senior leaders and managers must integrate such creativity and brainstorming in the organization and allow every person in the organization to develop a sense of personal mastery (Senge, 1990). Peter Senge goes on to say that such organizations also need to encourage employees of all generations to develop and use complex mental models. Managers must do everything they can to promote group creativity and team learning. Leaders and managers must emphasize the importance of building a shared vision. Managers must model and encourage systems thinking because building a learning organization requires them to radically change their assumptions. Incorporating systems thinking into the organizational structure provides a vehicle to effectively deal with change at the planning phase as well as the problem analysis phase. The "systems thinking" paradigm provides an avenue for organizations to continuously improve their processes and embrace change using new perspectives and new methods of thinking. Today's organizations can no longer operate in "silos" or closed systems, and expect to be competitive with other national or international firms that effectively operate using all of the resources available to them in the open environment. As such, these organizations must embrace change as well as new ways of seeing and doing things as per a systems thinking mentality.

"Systems thinking" is a multidisciplinary approach that involves the "wholeness" of an organization. While basic analysis by any means can result in knowledge, systems thinking results in understanding as well as lasting changes. In the application of systems thinking, the entire organization and its subsystems can be investigated to understand each segment of the operation. Understanding the interdependence and interconnections of systems in operation and employees can provide a more holistic environment that embraces change. "Systems thinking" is basically a method of analyzing organizational problems of modern technology, society, and organizations from a new "*weltanschauung*," or a new perspective.

Most organizational leaders understand that their firms need to stay efficient, effective, and sensitive to their environments in order to remain successful and socially responsible. This applies equally to both for-profit and not-for-profit organizations. Because of cultural and technological changes, organizations are required to make internal changes periodically in order to continue to be sustainable. These internal changes are a result of the organization's ability to effectively use their human resource assets, which can be inclusive of different generations of workforce with varied levels of education and skill. The degree to which organizations are successful in these change efforts is in part a function of the degree to which they keep members of different generations in mind and aware of specific required changes and the general need for continual change. Systemic change without considering the culture or the needs of each generation of the workforce in which they are contained is doomed to failure. For this reason, organizational managers need to understand the needs, desires, and work habits of diverse employees in the workforce before planning or implementing major changes. Organizational leaders, managers, and change agents should educate and empower employees to bring about changes both privately and publicly as often initiated by tempered radicals.

The Quiet Leader's Leadership Style

There are many individuals, who desire change in their learning organization, yet believe that direct, angry confrontation will get them nowhere. Rather, they choose to work quietly to challenge the status quo and gently provoke their organizations to change at the right times, in the right ways, to get the right results. Meyerson (2001) refers to these individuals as "tempered radicals" because they choose to effect significant changes in moderate ways. Meyerson suggests studying and appreciating the various techniques and styles which these individuals utilize, as these techniques allow them to not only make significant changes to their organizations, but to emerge as leaders at the same time.

In today's business environment, rapid changes in technology and the globalization of markets require that organizations keep a watchful eye on developing trends in their respective markets. As easy as this may sound, it can be quite difficult for organizations to accurately predict such trends in which technology, customer preferences and global markets can change dramatically in the span of several weeks.

A clear parallel can be made between organizational and ecological evolution, in which the inability to respond to a changing environment ultimately threatens survival, whether it be a plant, animal, or an organization. Conversely, rapid or disruptive ecological or organizational changes can occur abruptly and quickly, yet the mortality rates of such changes are typically high. Therefore, organizations must be flexible, adaptable, and have the ability to judge and gauge their responses to changes in their environment in order to remain a viable entity.

Yet, organizations inherently resist change, as do many of the individuals who make up these organizations. Nearly two-thirds of all major changes in organizations fail, and Fortune 500 executives state that resistance is often the primary reason (Schiemann, 1992). Organizational resistance can be multi-dimensional and can include many factors such as the failure of commitment and ownership, fear of chaos and being controlled by expert syndrome and parental management (Holder, 2002). Resistance on a more personal level tends to stem from insecurity regarding one's job, fear of the unknown, and loss of status. However, many individuals in the workplace today have, at some point in their careers, felt the need for change in their organization. This need for change can be prompted by many reasons including, but not limited to, dissatisfaction with their organization's values, interests, practices, or actions. Yet, individuals who wish to drive changes that are not being initiated by formal leaders often face a dilemma: if they speak out loudly, resentment will build towards them; if they play by the rules and remain silent, resentment builds inside them. In essence, these individuals must find a way to rock the boat at the right times and in the right way without falling out of the boat (Meyerson, 2001).

In her article, *Radical Change, the Quiet Way (2001)*, Debra Meyerson describes individuals who desire change in their organization, yet believes that direct, angry confrontation will get them nowhere. Rather, they choose to work quietly to challenge the prevailing wisdom while progressively provoking their organizations to change. In their approach, "tempered radicals" exercise a form of leadership that is different from traditional leadership in that it is more localized and modest. Typically these individuals are dedicated to their organizations and excel at making organizational changes at the grass roots level. As such, they are invaluable to top management in helping to identify fundamental causes of discord. Tempered radicals recognize alternative perspectives and can adapt these to changing needs and circumstances. With support from above and some freedom to act, tempered radicals prove to be excellent leaders. In order to gently provoke their organizations to adapt and change, tempered radicals utilize various incremental approaches which Meyerson (2001) describes as disruptive self-expression, verbal jujitsu, variable-term opportunism, and strategic alliance. Each of these approaches is used in many ways and in many different circumstances by tempered radicals.

Disruptive self-expression is a behavior that quietly disrupts other's expectations (Meyerson, 2001). This disruption may be as innocuous as an article of clothing, yet have profound effects. Meyerson (2001) offers the example of Dr. Frances Conley who is a leading researcher and neurosurgeon at Stanford Medical School and Palo Alto Veteran's Administration hospital. Dr. Conley, as the sole female in a male dominated environment, struggled to maintain her femininity and integrity amid gender discrimination. Dr. Conley did not want to make a huge issue of her gender and yet felt she had to make a stand. To do so, Dr. Conley began wearing lace ankle socks with her green surgical scrubs. In of itself, this is not a Gandhian act of civil disobedience, but in the stolid masculinity of the surgical environment, this act stated clearly, "I can be a neurosurgeon and be feminine." Dr. Conley made her point, quietly, intelligently and forcefully with a very small act.

Verbal jujitsu and *variable-term opportunism* are techniques that tempered radicals use to take advantage of situations that arise to further their message of change. Meyerson (2001) defines verbal jujitsu "as reacting to undesirable, demeaning statements or actions by turning them into opportunities for change that others will notice." While these small acts cannot and may not force immediate change in organizational culture, they tend to accomplish several important things. First, these acts reaffirm the tempered radical's convictions. Second, it pushes the status quo door slightly open by introducing alternative modus operandi. As with the drops of water, these actions gain strength and power slowly over time.

Strategic alliance building is when tempered radicals work with allies, those who are of like mind, to gain a sense of legitimacy, access to resources, contacts, technical and task assistance and advice (Meyerson, 2001). Tempered radicals understand and acknowledge the fact that people who represent the majority perspective can be important allies in subtle ways. In their efforts to change the status quo, tempered radicals must navigate between their desire to change the status quo and the organizational requirements that uphold it. Therefore, they seek the advice and counsel of those allies or "insiders" in their networks who know just how hard to push for change and recognize the opportune time to do so.

Tempered Radicals in Action

Since many organizations may be resistant to outward change, tempered radicals achieve reforms without widespread notice. They continually and gently push against the prevailing culture, making small yet steady changes and setting examples from which others can learn. The changes can be so incremental that they are barely noticed, which is perhaps why they work so well. Like drops of water, these approaches are innocuous and non-threatening. But over time and in accumulation, these drops of water can erode granite (Badaracco, 2001). The form of change utilized by tempered radicals has many similarities to evolutionary change models such as *"incremental experimenting," "appreciative inquiry"* and *"attunement bonding."* These types of changes often evolve slowly and deliberately with interpersonal skills driving the changes that manifest themselves as adjustments to the corporations' status quo. The dynamics of organizational change utilized by tempered radicals to alter their corporations' status quo is indeed evolutionary, yet it requires specific behaviors to accomplish.

One of the laws of physics, and Peter Senge's "Fifth Discipline" with respect to resistance, is that the harder one pushes, the harder the system pushes back (Senge, 1990). This is apparent in an organization's inherent resistance to change, and the high rate of failure of change implementation "attempts" due to widespread resistance. However, tempered radicals seek organizational change in evolutionary means; they are firm in their commitments, yet flexible in the ways to fulfill them; their actions are small, but have the potential to spread like a virus. Tempered radicals yearn for change, but trust in patience and realize that change often requires time, commitment and the patience to endure (Meyerson, 2001). Change initiated by tempered radicals, like a spreading virus, can be such that the organization's defense mechanisms are not aware of its presence or if aware, the threat is deemed too insignificant to merit a response. The slow, measured and non-threatening changes inspired and championed by tempered radicals can avoid evoking organizational defenses, the "system pushing back," and allow for assimilation of changes without prompting significant resistance.

The types of actions by tempered radicals, seemingly small and unimportant, like a virus, have the potential to create tremendous changes in what can be likened to a "ripple effect." One small action, a ripple, by itself, is perceived as insignificant, yet this action can prompt another and another and soon a ripple has turned into a wave. This was never more apparent than in the case of a tempered radical by the name of Rosa Parks. Rosa Parks could be the epitome of a tempered radical in that her actions parallel those characteristics of disruptive self-expression, verbal jujitsu, and strategic alliances. With the seemingly insignificant action of refusing to give up her seat to a white man in December of 1955, Rosa Parks, who has been called the "mother of the civil rights movement," created a ripple that sparked a boycott, and this boycott raised a then unknown clergyman, Dr. Martin Luther King, to prominence. Rosa Parks, in one quiet and non-threatening action, one small and insignificant ripple, initiated a series of events, which turned a ripple into a wave of civil rights.

Tempered radicals that prove to be excellent leaders may not be as apparent when one considers that tempered radical behaviors do not follow those behaviors frequently expected and observed in leaders. A general comparison of leadership characteristics of the tempered radicals' quiet leadership style to that of the typical leadership style (as seen in Table 3) illustrates this difference in personality and approach to leadership.

Table 3: Leadership Style Characteristics

Typical Leadership Style	Tempered Radical's Quiet Leadership Style
Competitive	Unassuming
Confident	Modest
Assertive	Firm
Outgoing	Reserved
Motivating	Inspirational
Dynamic	Persistent and focused
Widespread influence	Localized influence
Risk taker	Measured approach
Lead from the front	Lead from within
Focused and determined	Flexible and patient
Individualism – one leader, one vision	Collectivism – multiple leaders, multiple visions
Broad change leader	Focused change leader
Change from the top down	Change from the bottom up

Stereotypical leaders are confident, outgoing, competitive, take-charge individuals, who normally lead from the top or visible positions within an organization; "they realize that being timid will not get them where they want to go" (Sugarman, 2000). Yet, tempered radicals operate beneath their organization's radar, achieving reforms without widespread notice and attempt to stay "behind the scenes." Tempered radicals emulate a leadership style, which can be characterized by Lao Tzu, who wrote in *Tao Te Ching*; "A leader is best when people barely know that he exists. Of a good leader, who talks little, when his work is done, his aim fulfilled, they will say, 'We did it ourselves.'"

One of the primary advantages of the tempered radical's quiet leadership style over that of the typical leadership style is due to the personality of tempered radicals. The position and authority normally required and attributed for typical leadership, is not as essential for tempered radicals since they typically use non-formal means such as strategic alliance to further their message.

This combination of personality and use of strategic alliances by tempered radicals also results in a synergistic and non-competitive approach to leadership, as opposed to the often competitive, individualistic approach common to typical leadership styles. In essence, the more tempered radicals involved in a "change," the better the chance of their success. Whereas, the more typical leaders involved in a "change" the better the chance of failure as a result of conflict due to competition for "leadership" and perhaps, a clashing of egos. The clashing of egos reaffirms the old adage that "too many cooks spoil the stew!"

Table 4: Emotional Intelligence Behavior Categories

Behaviors Category	Actions
Self-awareness:	Observing oneself.
Managing emotions:	Handling feelings so that they are appropriate.
Motivating oneself:	Channeling emotions in the service of a goal; emotional self control.
Empathy:	Sensitivity to other's feelings and concerns and their perspective; appreciating the differences in how people feel about things.
Handling relationships:	Managing emotions in others; social competence and social skills.

A second advantage to the tempered radicals' quiet leadership style is their apparent capacity for, and the use of, emotional intelligence. Emotional intelligence "is a type of social intelligence that involves the ability to monitor one's own and other's emotions, to discriminate among them, and to use the information to guide one's thinking and actions" (Mayer & Salovey, 1993). These characteristics associated with emotional intelligence are the essence of using a tempered radical style of leadership. According to Salovey and Mayer (1990), emotional intelligence can be categorized into several "behaviors" as can be seen in Table 4.

Researchers have long investigated related concepts such as social skills, psychological maturity, interpersonal competence and emotional awareness, which they now attribute to the dimension of emotional intelligence. Additionally, social scientists are just beginning to uncover the links of emotional intelligence to leadership (Ashford & Humphrey, 1995), and group performance (Williams & Sternberg, 1988). This ability of tempered radical leaders' to recognize and manage both their own personal emotions, and more importantly, those emotions of other's around them, provides them with a tremendous advantage over typical leadership styles, especially when challenging prevailing organizational culture and attempting to gently provoke change in the face of resistance. Socrates was a master of making people think and this is one strategy he used to reduce rumors. He knew that sharing information with others is a fact of life but sharing misinformation with others is also a reality. When someone is about to pass on rumors to a tempered radical, he or she can ask him/her to consider the *"Triple Filter Test"* before continuing, as used by Socrates:

- The first filter is *Truth*. Have you made absolutely sure that what you are about to tell me is true?
- The second filter is *Goodness*. Is what you are about to tell me something good?
- The third filter is *Usefulness*. Is what you want to tell me going to be useful to me?

One way to bring about transformational change to the culture of a department is to change one person's mindset or paradigm at a time, and using the "Triple Filter Test" is a good strategy that can be used by tempered radicals at any time. On the other hand, if the manager or change agent is the target of rumors and/or "insulting" statements, it is best to not let it bother one and go about one's objectives as planned. In such instances, it is best to remember that when one gives another person a gift and the other person does not accept the gift, then the gift stays with the original owner. The same concepts can be true of "insulting" statements; let them stay with the originator since some things cannot always be changed or they are not deserving of, or "worth," one's time. However, with respect to organizational change, there are many critical success factors that determine the selection of any form of change process, whether evolutionary, revolutionary or systematic, and they are as follows:

1. Identification and understanding of the change needs
2. Organizational type and culture
3. Constraints, boundaries and barriers
4. Identification of resistance, who, where, and why
5. Cost in terms of time, money and resources

Understanding, planning, and effectively managing these success factors are essential for managing change in today's turbulent times.

Effective planning also requires understanding that conflict will be inevitable when initiating changes and as such tempered radicals must use an appropriate conflict resolution model to overcome it.

Ethical and Cultural Conflicts in the Workplace

The United States, along with many other countries, continues to become more culturally diverse each year and this trend is expected to continue as the minorities eventually will become the majority within this century. This diversity is setting the stage for an increasingly multicultural workforce which can be very beneficial to an organization when used appropriately. The differences between the cultural backgrounds and ethical beliefs contribute to the conflicts people deal with in their workplaces (Mohebbi *et al*, 2004). A study conducted by Professor Catherine Tinsley, from Georgetown University, identified that members from different cultures hold distinct preferences for how conflicts should be resolved (Adams, 1999). Managers tend to underestimate the importance of an ethical criterion and focus more on their own personal gain (Virovere, Kooskora, & Valler, 2002). With the continuous growth that is taking place in the corporate world today, the importance of taking into consideration the cultural backgrounds and ethical beliefs of each individual within any given company when attempting to resolve conflict has also grown. The ability to recognize these differences, being proactive to rectify them, and putting in place a code of conduct can change a negative atmosphere in the workplace into a positive work environment. This change allows a company to use its diversity as an advantage and as an agent to strengthen their business.

Recent figures from the Bureau of Labor Statistics (U.S. Department of Labor, 2001) showed that, "In 2000 white males comprised only 44% of the U.S. workforce, compared to 51% in 1980." The number of workers from Hispanic background alone has more than doubled, and the numbers of non-white workers in nearly all job sectors continues to increase. According to the Workforce 2020 report (Judy & D'Amico, 1997), whereas in the 1980s new immigrants accounted for approximately one-fourth of the increase in the U.S. workforce, in the 1990s they accounted for over one-half of the increase. Today, an estimated 500,000 legal immigrants are added to the United States workforce each year (Broom, Turk, Kristiansdottir, Kanata & Ganesan, 2002). This increase in non-white employees is allowing the workforce to become increasingly multicultural. Because of this multicultural existence, the probability of having conflicting cultural and ethical backgrounds increases. This is mainly because individuals from different cultural backgrounds have different ethical perceptions (Burns, 1993).

The situation of having a diverse workforce has been a major challenge for corporations around the world. Erica G. Foldy (2004) mentioned, in her article *"Learning from Diversity: A Theoretical Exploration,"* that cultural diversity refers to identities such as race, ethnicity, nationality, religion, gender, and other dimensions of difference derived from membership in groups. These groups are socio-culturally distinct, that is, they "collectively share certain norms, values or traditions that are different from those of other groups" (Cox Jr., 1994). This diversity has led many organizations to become familiar with the cultures and ethics that represent their workforce, in addition to, learning how to deal with conflicts that arise because of this diversity. Research, as previously mentioned, suggests that people of different cultures hold distinct preferences for how conflicts should be resolved. Therefore, to avoid secondary problems that arise from mishandling disagreements, it is important for managers to understand the cultural preferences for conflict resolution of the parties involved (Adams, 1999). In a multicultural environment, having clear rules and guidelines about how conflicts should be resolved to avoid further disagreements about the resolution strategies would be appropriate. According to Shelton and Darling (2004), "Conflict is unavoidable, but is necessary for individual and organizational evolution…Each conflict situation offers organizations, and individuals opportunities for transformation…Conflict challenges the status quo, providing a breeding ground for innovation…Managers who try to eliminate conflict are operating under an outdated paradigm. (p. 23)."

Thomas Capozzoli (1999) added that resolving conflicts effectively can result in a more productive environment. Furthermore, he stated that conflicts can be considered constructive if it creates personal change and growth in people, increases the involvement of everyone affected, builds cohesiveness among the members and results in a solution to a problem. Capozzoli (1999) proposed the following process for a productive conflict resolution (1999):

1. Explore the reason for the disagreement
2. Alternative solutions must be presented by the parties involved
3. The parties should agree on the most appropriate solution
4. The solution should be implemented and evaluated
5. Alternative solution should be sought if necessary
6. The process should be practiced, successes and failures should be analyzed and applied to the next situation

An important element in a successful diversity related conflict resolution is establishing a dialog across cultures (Mohebbi *et al*, 2004). Participants in a successful dialog should abide by the following presuppositions: "respect one another as competent subjects; treat one another as equal parties; assume one another's truthfulness; cooperate with one another" (Singh, 2002). It is also important for everyone to follow rules, such as they should only assert what they believe to be true and may not contradict themselves; they should be consistent with their values, and everyone should be allowed to express their attitudes, desires and needs (Singh, 2002).

Diversity can be an asset to an organization if respected and addressed correctly. Management should establish a training procedure that allows each group to learn and become familiar with the different backgrounds and ethics of each culture. Diversity brings different ideas and perceptions to each situation which could be valuable to an organization when confronted with difficult managerial decisions (Mohebbi *et al*, 2004). Research suggests that a group's diversity perspective is central to learning in culturally diverse groups. Ely and Thomas (2001) proposed the idea of "diversity perspectives" as the key moderator of the relationship between diversity and performance. Diversity perspectives are a work group-level phenomenon; different work groups within the same organization can hold different perspectives. A diversity perspective is the way that group members think about the cultural differences among them, whether they are important, and how to harness them to improve the group's work (Foldy, 2004).

One way for an organization to be successful in dealing with cultural differences and conflicts that arise from diversity might be to embrace the different cultures and recognize them in their organization's calendar of events and holidays. William A. Guillory (2004), in his article "*The Roadmap to Diversity, Inclusion, and High Performance*," offered ten steps for achieving an inclusive culture:

1. Develop a customized business case for your organization.
2. Educate and train your staff to develop an understanding of diversity, its importance to your organization's success, and diversity skills to apply on a daily basis.
3. Establish a baseline by conducting, a comprehensive cultural survey that integrates performance, inclusion, climate, and work/life balance.
4. Select and prioritize the issues that lead to the greatest breakthrough in transforming the culture.

5. Create a three to five year diversity strategic plan that is tied to the organizational strategic business objectives.
6. Secure leadership's endorsement and financial commitment for the plan.
7. Establish measurable leadership and management objectives accountable to top leadership.
8. Implement the plan, recognizing that surprises and setbacks will occur along the way.
9. Continue training in concert with the skills and competencies necessary to successfully achieve the diversity action plan.
10. Conduct a follow-up survey one to one and a half years after initiation of the plan to determine how inclusion has changed.

When managed effectively, conflict can be very informative, allowing one to see the status of organizations in general, as well as the problems, which occur as a result of rapid growth and differences between people (Virovere, Kooskora, & Valler, 2002). Ethical conflict occurs when managers attempt to solve problems with their authority and do not consider the ethical standpoint of their employees and/or customers. They only have concern for their own success, personal gain, prestige, and power (Kooskora, 2001). Tim Thatcher (2003), in his article *"Ethical Compass,"* explains that being ethical is based on a combination of personal, religious, and family-based values, as well as skills, knowledge, and attitudes that can be developed through training and education. In order to build their integrity within a community, company leaders must build an ethical infrastructure (Mohebbi *et al*, 2004). Thatcher provides seven strategies for building this infrastructure:

1. View strategic learning initiatives through ethically and socially responsive outcomes.
2. Consider ethical issues and social performance in needs assessments.
3. Use core process analyses to spot ethical bottlenecks and leverage points.
4. Emphasize ethical behavior and social responsibility in training and management development.
5. Evaluate the effects of technology on ethical issues.
6. Develop globally conscious people through training.
7. Consider the importance of work-life issues.

Overall, one strategy in resolving conflict in the workplace between individuals with diverse cultural backgrounds and ethical beliefs is the willingness to communicate between individuals, perhaps using the Four-F model (addressed in the next session) whenever needed. With proper training, management will have the ability to recognize when conflicts exist, take the proper measures to resolve them, and at the same time insure the well being of those associates under their supervision. Emphasizing cultural and ethical diversity in the workplace will enhance conflict management and integrity within the community.

Regardless of the make up of the organization in relation to diversity, conflict is a reality of life, which everyone must face at one time, or another. Leaders, managers and team members of all tempered radicals need to understand the cause and effects related to conflict. Furthermore, they need to know how to respond in the best interest of all members concerned, and the desired vision. Conflict is often a characteristic of change and comes as one form of resistance. Any attempt, whether by tempered radicals or others, to adjust the status quo in an organization can result in conflict. If effectively handled conflict can be a healthy way of airing differences and discovering other alternatives. However, constant conflict can be anxiety inducing, debilitating, and destructive. Conflict resolution includes recognition, awareness, and choice. It occurs within and between individuals, groups, teams, organizations and societies.

Generally speaking, individuals react differently to conflict as per their conditioning and personality. Some people seem to thrive on conflict while others abhor it and others remain unruffled by the most conflicting situations. Individuals also deal with conflict in different ways, some people attack, while others tend to defend. However, most people are consistent in their individual responses to conflict, tending to react the same way over time, developing a behavior pattern.

Conflict is the struggle that results when two or more individuals perceive a difference or incompatibility in their interests, values, or goals. Every interaction has a potential for conflict and some conflict is good for productivity and team performance. Too much conflict causes team leaders to spend much time and energy responding to such behaviors. Conflict Management is the process of dealing with conflict in an effective manner. Positive conflict (conflict that is managed effectively) is great for team performance, and negative conflict can be very hurtful. One can manage individual conflict by:

•Increasing awareness of the source of conflict,

• Increasing diversity awareness and management skills,
• Effectively communicating and listening to the different sides,
• Practicing job rotation and temporary assignments,
• Using permanent transfers and dismissals if needed, and
• Changing team's structure.

Furthermore, during an interpersonal conflict with a team member or colleague, tempered radicals can remain focused on stating the facts, their feelings and future expectations rather than attacking the other person. For example, when hearing an offensive comment or joke about women in the workplace, tempered radicals can immediately use the Four-F Model (facts, feelings, future expectations, and following up) by calmly saying: "*When you make comments like that about women... I feel angry and disappointed because...they are false and inappropriate in the workplace. Please don't make comments like that again.*" Managers and change agents should also follow up on this request to make sure the inappropriate statement or behavior is not repeated. In most cases, repeating the facts of what was said by the person, one's feelings as a result of hearing what was said and future expectations would take care of the situation as it brings this concern to the attention of the person making the comment. The person is likely to either clarify the misunderstanding, if that was the case, or change his or her behavior as a result of this awareness. As such, there may not be a need to place an official complaint with the Human Resources Department or the company's lawyers since the goal is to have a healthy work environment. This is a very effective method used by many skilled tempered radicals to bring about positive changes in their departments one person at a time thereby eliminating the existence of a hostile work environment. Of course, if the candid discussion, based on the Four-F Model, does not work and there is a repetition of inappropriate comments then one must take appropriate actions to inform the organization. After all, the best way to resolve conflict is to seek cooperation from all parties involved, and to create a win-win solution for everyone. This way tempered radicals can meet their own needs as well as their colleagues' needs in bringing about moderate, incremental or significant changes.

Table 5 – Strengths and Weakness of Tempered Radical's Change Model

Elements	Strengths	Weaknesses
Slow and deliberate changes	Individuals and organizations have time to adjust to the change, the process is flexible and adaptable. There are no time lines or time constraints so the process can move as slowly or as quickly as it needs.	This model may not be suitable for addressing those change needs that require immediate corporate-wide changes.
Grass roots approach	Many organizational changes fail due to lack of support at the individual employee level. This change approach builds from the bottom up and gains momentum as it progresses.	Management support is required in any change. A bottom up change will eventually need management support and may stall or be delayed if not obtained.
Change Leaders or Champions	Individuals with vested emotional interest drive the change. As the changes progress, the number of change leaders increase as individuals adopt the changes.	Individuals with vested emotional interest are needed to drive this change. This model is dependent on a "leader or champion" to step forward.
Powerful	The changes are driven slowly and deliberately, but gain momentum as individuals adopt the changes. Momentum becomes a driving force.	The changes are driven slowly and deliberately, but gain momentum as individuals adopt the changes. However, power lies with the individuals behind the change. If individuals lose interest or become discouraged, the change will quickly lose its "power."
Change resistance	Change efforts are slow, persistent, determined and patient. They do not "provoke" organizational "defense" mechanisms.	Change leaders need patience and perseverance. Discouragement must be avoided or change will lose momentum.

The change model and approach for tempered radicals and their style of quiet leadership has many strengths and weaknesses. The primary strengths and weaknesses of the change model and approach are stated in Table 5.

In addition to their value in championing organizational change, tempered radicals' quiet leadership style and their use of emotional intelligence, are also very beneficial for managing multicultural organizations and workforce. The effect of cultural diversity on an organization creates many new challenges for effective management of such a multicultural environment. Ethics, values, beliefs, and diverse perspectives have the potential to alter the efficiency and, therefore, profitability of organizations with a diverse workforce when managed ineffectively.

Advantages of diversity and a multicultural environment within an organization are numerous and the following are several examples (Cox, 1991, Fernandez, 1991, et al.): Multicultural organizations:

- Have an advantage in attracting and retaining the best available talent.
- Can compete in wider and diverse markets.

- Display higher creativity and innovation.
- Demonstrate better problem solving skills
- Are better able to adapt to change and exhibit more organizational flexibility.

The key to taking advantage of the power and potential of a culturally diverse workforce is to create an organization and environment in which all members of various socio-cultural backgrounds can contribute and achieve their full potential. This is where the benefits of the tempered radicals' quiet leadership style and use of emotional intelligence will prove to be invaluable.

The behaviors of tempered radicals quiet leadership and use of emotional intelligence; self-awareness, managing emotions, motivating oneself, empathy and handling relationships, are the very behaviors needed by managers and leaders of multicultural organizations in order to foster and promote openness and tolerance of such a diverse workforce. Jonathan Tisch (2004), in his new book, titled *The Power of WE: Succeeding through Partnerships,* which appeared on Wall Street Journal's October 26th issue, discussed the value of teamwork as follows:

> Managing through partnerships may sound idealistic. Actually, it's profoundly practical. In an increasingly complex world, no single organization is capable of mobilizing all the resources required to accomplish everything it needs to do. We literally have no choice but to work together. And whenever managers, employees, communities, shareholders, owners and even competitors join forces in pursuit of shared goals, everybody wins (Tisch, 2004).

While tempered radicals can influence change to some extent by themselves, it is much more practical to involve others when the change impacts many individuals in the department or the organization. With all that has been discussed regarding the aforementioned change model or approach, and the given examples, the following recommendations and conclusions are offered:

- The tempered radical change model may not be an appropriate choice for organizations which are already open to change. Rather a systematic change model with a relevant design and development steps would be more suitable in this situation.

- The tempered radical model is an excellent choice for situations in which organizational change is resisted. This resistance could take any form, but the tempered radical approach, when conducted as described, can slowly overcome almost any form of resistance. The success of the change effort will be dependent upon the commitment, perseverance and determination of the change "leaders" and those who are impacted by them. Like the seemingly innocuous drops of water falling on granite, tempered radicals and their followers quietly and slowly erode organizations resistance to change and most importantly, they accomplish this without conflict.
- The emergence of a new type of leader, the quiet leader, has many advantages over the typical leadership style and as such, can and should be encouraged and used in situations other than organizational change.

The tempered radical style of leadership is not a stand-alone model for bringing about change; but rather it is a model that can be used in conjunction with other models, such as appreciative inquiry, to systematically involve everyone in the process and eventually transform the culture of a department or an organization.

Appreciate Inquiry and Transformation: Applied to Educational Institutions

"Appreciative Inquiry," as a tool, can serve as the basis for formal transformation and change by tempered radicals within any organization (Cooperrider and Whitney, 2005). Once it is apparent to all individuals that change is needed then a formal tool such as Appreciative Inquiry can be very effective to bring about the needed changes. *Appreciative Inquiry* (AI) is an organizational transformation tool that focuses on learning from past and current successes as opposed to focusing on deficits and problems. According to Cooperrider and Whitney (2005), "Appreciative Inquiry is the cooperative, coevolutionary search for the best in people, their organizations, and the world around them" (p. 8). Cooperrider and Whitney further write that AI "involves systematic discovery of what gives life to an organization or a community when it is most effective and most capable in economic, ecological, and human terms." Using AI, managers can begin the change process with a rigorous, "organization-wide" search, discovery and analysis of the "positive core" or the root cause of success analysis (Cooperrider and Whitney, 2005). Cooperrider and Whitney define positive change as "Any form of organization change, redesign, or planning that begins with a comprehensive inquiry, analysis, dialogue of an organization's positive core, that involves multiple stakeholders, and then links this knowledge to the organization's strategic change agenda and priorities" (2005, p. 12). Through the making of simple managerial changes, sharing of information with more employees, and inviting employees to participate in the affairs of the organization, companies can be transformed (Cooperrider and Whitney, 2005). The Appreciative Inquiry (AI) strategy focuses on discovering what works well, why it works well, and how success can be extended throughout the organization to further encourage change initiatives toward the vision. It is both the vision, and the process for developing this vision, that creates the needed energy to drive change throughout the organization (Johnson & Leavitt, 2001). Appreciative Inquiry (AI) can be seen as a systematic discovery of what gives "life" to a living system when it is most alive, most effective and most constructively capable, in economic, ecological, and human terms. Appreciative Inquiry involves, in a central way, the Socratic strategy and practice of asking the right questions that strengthen a system's capacity to comprehend, anticipate and heighten positive potential (Carr-Stewart & Walker, 2003).

Appreciative inquiry (AI) from the perspective of an educational institution is best understood as a strategy for initiating micro-level reform within a single institution; reform that is both affective and analytical. The process would reconnect teachers and administrators to their passion for teaching and to their sense of mission; for students the process can enhance school pride and foster recognition of the bonds that students have with peers and teachers alike. Moreover, AI's approach counteracts exclusive preoccupation with problems that all too often de-energize teachers, staff, and sometimes administrators themselves at educational institutions (Ryan *et al.*, 1999). According to researchers, AI is about appreciating and valuing the best of what is, envisioning what might be, dialoguing what should be, and assuming that an organization is a mystery to be embraced (Cooperrider and Whitney, 2005, p. 13). Cooperrider and Whitney (2005) state that the AI process has four phases which include: discovery, dream, design, and destiny. Cooperrider and Whitney explain that:

> ⇒ *Discovery* emphasizes the mobilization of the entire system by engaging all relevant stakeholders in the articulation of the department or firms' strengths, core competencies, and best practices.

⇒ *Dream* requires the creation of a clear result-oriented vision and purpose. This image of the future can and should guide everyone's behavior in the organization.

⇒ *Design* stage mandates that managers and the organization create "possibility propositions of the ideal organization." It should provide a roadmap that people can follow for realizing the dream.

⇒ *Destiny* involves the strengthening of the affirmative capability of the entire system, in hopes of enabling it to sustain momentum for ongoing productive change and higher performance (Cooperrider and Whitney, 2005, p. 16).

In order to effectively implement an intervention strategy in an institution that requires some form of transformation, those involved in the process and those that are impacted by the process will need to be categorized as stakeholders. The stakeholders involved in an institution's change strategy are often the support staff, teachers, parents, administrators, accrediting bodies, government authorities, and students. Each of these stakeholders represents a specific group and various levels of the internal and external organization. The stakeholders can also be viewed as agents of change who will be involved in the development, implementation, and process of sustaining recommended changes. Involving the stakeholders in the change process serves as a basis for a "site-based compass" for reforming specific, micro-level components of the educational program, while preserving the "sense of community membership" that is frequently threatened by the reform process itself (Ryan *et al.*, 1999).

With the Appreciative Inquiry (AI) model, one must begin with the discovery process. During this process, tempered radicals will look for at least one aspect of the school system that is doing particularly well. They can also begin by interviewing members of other successful schools in the area to learn about the underlying processes that make them successful. This will give the staff opportunities to look for the positive elements within the successful organization. Such a process "taps the collective wisdom, vision, and excellence already inherent in the group, and has the potential to resolve significant organizational problems as a by-product" (Newman & Fitzgerald, 2001). Rather than dwelling on which problems must be 'fixed,' this process allows tempered radicals the opportunity to use these successful elements as models. It also opens up avenues for conversation among the staff as to what will work better and what will not. It leads the staff into the step of dreaming where they can begin to build a vision of what they would like their institution to become. They, as a group, can also begin to devise ideas to help change the system to their dream system. They all have input into this vision, so they are likely to "buy-in" to the vision. Since this perspective does not include tearing down what is wrong with the current system, the staff may feel that they are on safer grounds.

If an institution is to implement drastic changes, there will need to be support at all leadership and management levels (Cooperrider and Whitney, 2005). The most effective form of leadership, under these circumstances, may be transformational leadership for tempered radicals. Newman and Fitzgerald (2001) stated that team members working synergistically can often generate a powerful vision of open, just, and inclusive leadership. Whichever form is used, all leaders must be trained to be supportive, encouraging and above all, willing to implement the needed changes into the organization. According to Kreitner and Kinicki (2003), the first step in leading change is to "establish a sense of urgency." This is best initiated through unfreezing the organization's culture by creating compelling reasons for why change is needed (Kreitner & Kinicki, 2003, p. 683). The leaders must be the champions and agents of the desired changes. The leaders also must be able to effectively communicate and transmit the vision and the needed reasons for achieving it to the general staff. The tempered radicals and formal authority figures must be capable of involving their staff and colleagues in bringing about needed changes. The leaders must be involved in the changes, willing to educate others, and capable of motivating those who may not be willing to implement the changes called for in achieving the desired vision. In order to implement the Appreciative Inquiry (AI) model, the core steps need to be put into practice since "the five core principles when translated to action become Appreciative Inquiry's five generic processes" (Watkins & Mohr, 2001, p. 6).

1. The first generic process to implement is choosing the positives as the focus of the inquiry. This is done to avoid the traditional problem solving techniques usually implemented and instead framing the intervention objective in a positive light.

2. Then, the interviewing process takes place to get everyone to interact and discover their desires. An Appreciative Inquiry interview is unlike any other interview as two organizational employees are paired together with the goal of telling each other stories about their best experiences, personal values, organizational values, and finally, to express three wishes.

3. In the third step of the process "the interview data from the previous step are parsed for common themes" according to Watkins and Mohr (2001). Several of the most inspirational and interesting stories are selected that reflect several common themes and these stories are used to build practical models to spur the development of organizational goals.

4. The fourth step in the generic process gathers together common themes from these stories in order to spur the organization to articulate a vision of the future. Of course, the "objective of this step is to invite the participants to imagine an organization in which those special moments of exceptional vitality found in the stories become the norm rather than the exception" (Watkins & Mohr, 2001). The purpose of the first four steps is to lead relevant stakeholders to the articulation of a preferred future state.

5. Finally, step five is where this materializes into the final generic process which is to find innovative ways to create the preferred future.

According to Johnson and Leavitt (2001), the Appreciative Inquiry is "a process which takes shape differently in different organizations, and in different contexts." This being said, the process in a small department or institution, may take as little as a week or two to complete, or even as long as several months to complete. Depending on how well the process is planned and implemented along with the determination of employees to put forth a consistent and committed effort into the successful completion of the tasks will go a long way in determining how long the intervention will take to implement.

The implementation of appreciate inquiry intervention strategy is often expected to take months to implement when done effectively. The baseline implementation strategy can be broken down into several phases with each phase lasting some weeks or months in duration. During each of the phases, objectives and measurements should be defined and implemented. Additionally for process control purposes weekly, monthly and end of quarter review sessions can take place with all stakeholders. Such review sessions are intended to provide status updates and an opportunity to fine tune existing and future action plans for moving forward. Another benefit of these sessions can be reinforcement of the vision for all stakeholders involved in this journey towards change. Additionally, the institution can consider developing a long-term (three to five years) roadmap to examine current and prospective objectives with strategies and action plans for sustaining permanent changes. Of course, permanent and sustained changes take years; therefore, monitoring the results of initiated changes along with executing a "roadmap" for change are of significant value to the institution. Finally, in any change initiated by tempered radicals there should be appropriate metrics and measurements associated with each change objective for monitoring and reporting purposes. At the end of each evaluation period, the strategies toward the vision should be adjusted appropriately to make sure the transformation is taking place as planned.

The philosophy of Appreciative Inquiry allows managers and organizations to engage the hearts, minds and souls of their people. AI is a process that can move people and their organizations upward on the ladder of success in today's competitive global environment business. Overall, AI is perhaps one of the most feasible and "implement-able" strategies for initiating transformational changes in an organization (Cooperrider and Whitney, 2005). Perhaps, and most importantly, the appreciative inquiry approach provides all direct stakeholders an opportunity to celebrate what is being done successfully within the institution, rather than what is not done or being done incorrectly. In an organization where the stakeholders are "bombarded" with negativities, the focus needs to be shifted to the organization's positives and their future dreams as envisioned by everyone. If people continue to focus on negatives, things will inevitably remain the same and much energy will be wasted on things that cannot produce their desired futures. Thomas White, President of GTE, asks, "In the long run, what is more likely to be useful: Demoralizing a successful workforce by concentrating on their failures or helping them over their last few hurdles by building a bridge with their successes?" (Lord, 1998). Tempered radicals, through effective communication skills, should help everyone build a bridge to success in their institutions. They can do this with the help of all relevant stakeholders and leadership support, as they jointly build a culture that is focused on achievement, learning, and an institution-wide system that will be envied by others. Just as tempered radicals do not allow barriers to get in the way of achieving their objectives, every worker and manager should understand, analyze, and eliminate the common barriers that hinder understanding in his or her communication and interactions with others.

Understanding Barriers to Communication

A classic article entitled *"Barriers and Gateways to Communication"* was written at the Harvard Business Review in 1952 by Carl Rogers and

Fritz Roethlisberger which still applies to today's work environment. Carl Ramson Rogers (1902-1987), a psychologist and psychotherapist was a professor of Psychology at the University of Chicago for twelve years. Fritz J. Roethlisberger (1898-1974) a Harvard graduate, has been called "one of the founders of the modern Human Relations movement."

In their article Carl R. Rogers and F. J. Roethlisberger collaborated to look at some of the *Barriers* and *Gateways* to communication. Rogers postulates the view that *"failure in communication"* is one of the main factors necessitating psychotherapy. He believes that failure in intrapersonal communication results in failure in interpersonal communication. This effectively causes a breakdown in relationships, at which point professional third party intervention is sought to facilitate resolution. Both authors cite the tendency to evaluate and make assumptions as one of the main reasons for the failure to communicate effectively. Rogers describes the urge to evaluate as *"natural"* and indicates that acquiring and practicing good listening skills, that is, active and effective listening may control this tendency.

In Part I of the article Dr. Rogers suggests that, *"we all have a natural urge to judge, evaluate and approve or (disapprove) another person's statement."* Rogers also indicates that where *"feelings and emotions are deeply involved"*, mutual understanding is less likely, although this is when it is most important. According to Rogers *"real communication"* can be achieved and evaluative tendencies avoided when *"we listen with understanding"* Rogers assures us that this apparently simplistic approach to a global, societal, organizational, and individual dilemma is not to be taken at face value. Listening with understanding requires full attention.

Rogers has some suggestions about practicing effective listening. These include *restating* the other person's argument to establish mutual understanding of what is being said. This approach should effectively make the participants in the communication exchange less defensive, reduce feelings of threat and create empathy. Rogers also suggest that some amount of *courage* is necessary to practice effective listening. This is because listening may influence changes or even threaten one's position if greater understanding of the other's views is achieved. Hence, fear of change can encourage an unwillingness to listen. A third barrier to effective listening and effective communication is heightened emotions. Rogers states that though *'good listening'* is essential during moments of heightened emotions, it is at those times that persons are less inclined to engage in this practice. At such times, people are less likely to achieve mutual understanding, this usually result in the need for third party intervention to achieve resolution. Finally, Rogers examined the impact of group structures on effective listening and ultimately on communication.

Although he only had experiences with small group face-to-face interactions, Rogers believes that listening with understanding to each other even on a global scale could resolve many important issues (such as religious and racial differences). As with small group and individual interactions Rogers suggest that an unbiased third party may be used to aid the process of mutual understanding. This is because as the participants accept that they are not being evaluated and judged they tend to become less defensive and trust is established.

Essentially, Rogers takes a more technical approach to the problem of poor listening and its impact on communication and the psychological effects on relationships. He outlines the possible benefits of employing the appropriate listening skills to the communication process and lists the various causes and effects of the barriers to this process.

In Part II Roethlisberger uses two practical scenarios to outline how listening with understanding can effect an opposite positive outcome compared with preconditioned listening where the listener enters the interaction with his or her own assumptions and makes an evaluation based on those assumptions. The kind of listening suggested by Roethlisberger shows consideration and compassion. This builds trust because there is mutual respect in the interaction. Roethlisberger indicates that pure logic and intellectual capability may not be enough to effect good communication. However, compassionate, empathic listening can result in both *"an emotional and intellectual achievement."*

In the two scenarios created by Roethlisberger, he first outlined a situation where the manager (Smith) enters an interaction with a subordinate (Bill) by making an evaluative assumption about how best Bill should do his work. Bill's response of "Oh yeah?" to Smith's stated assumptions is rather ambiguous. However, Smith takes no time to clarify this response, Smith does not listen to find out if that is an opening to proceed or a sarcastic disagreement, and why. He simply proceeded to apply logic and intellect to qualify his evaluation without ever taking into consideration Bill's position. Naturally, Bill becomes more defensive and Smith more frustrated as this diametrically opposed discourse continues. Eventually, Smith assumes that Bill is rather "thick headed" and Bill decides that Smith neither understands nor respect him; therefore, he cannot trust him. Bearing in mind Rogers views on the need for good listening during moments of heightened emotions it is no surprise that no mutual understanding is reached in this scenario.

On the other hand, another manager (Jones) in the same scenario responds to Bill's "Oh yeah?" as an invitation to hear Bill out. She, therefore, decides to *"pay strict attention"* only seeking to clarify Bill's feelings so she may be able to reach an amicable solution. This becomes a learning process for Jones; she begins to see Bill through different eyes. Eventually, Bill becomes less defensive and more trusting of Jones's motives. He eventually decided to try things a new way (Jones's way) and report his results to this newfound management ally at a mutually agreed time.

According to Roethlisberger, the differences in both approaches reflect some general factors namely: (1) Misevaluations results in misunderstanding. (2) Misunderstandings result from ignoring such factors as assumptions, intentions, audience, interpretation, status, process, genre, and product. (3) When these factors are ignored emphasis is placed on logic and denotation, which can lead to communication barriers because words in themselves mean very little. (4) Recognizing the other person's feelings and value in the interaction can result in *"a psychological chain reaction of reinforcing feelings and perceptions that eases communication."* Roethlisberger concludes by reinforcing the view that empathic listening is the more effective approach not just to managerial communication but also to any human interaction and interpersonal relationship.

Although this article was first published in 1952, it has significant relevance to communication in contemporary management and effective leadership. In fact, its relevance extends to interpersonal interaction in general. The authors both emphasized the common error in most interaction, that is, the natural tendency or urge to evaluate. This is a condition which still prevails (probably more so) some fifty years after the article. Current statistics reveal that most individuals practice good listening at a rate of less that 30% of their capacity. Many problems, including work related and personal, stem from this difficulty most persons have to resist the urge to evaluate and make assumptions. When we evaluate we use our own beliefs, values and experience to form judgments. As a result, we only hear some of what is being said, that is, the part that fits our paradigm and we base our assumptions on that. This eliminates the other person's individuality, ignores context, non-verbals, and purpose and influences defensiveness.

In 1991, John J. Gabarro presented a retrospective commentary on this *Barriers and Gateways to Communication* article. He aligned the articles relevance then with the dynamics and diversity within organizations, which he indicated, made communication even more difficult than in

1952. Ten years later, the situation is compounded by work and information overload leaving little time to practice *"good listening."* Greater diversity in the workplace introduces cultural and language barriers which creates noise in the communication process.

Also, the new generation of knowledge workers are not inclined to indulge in psychological self-assessments to discover what they believe they already know about themselves; that is that they are *right!* Additionally, the constant restructuring of organizations and increased competition engenders a certain degree of insensitivity and disloyalty. There appears to be little place for empathy and a desire for mutual understanding. Management has to be careful not to take advantage of the power of their office by subordinating the feelings, beliefs and values of employees.

More and more organizations are recognizing employees as their most important asset. It is, therefore, incumbent on management to factor mutual understanding among employees as a source of motivation. Empowerment, which is a popular contemporary management concept, recognizes the significance of employee input both to the employee and the organization. It is interesting to note that the principle of mutual understanding impacts society at all levels, especially when major changes are taking place.

Summary

There are many individuals who desire change in their organization, yet believe that direct, angry confrontation will usually not be very effective. Rather, they choose to work quietly to challenge the prevailing wisdom and gently provoke their organizations to change at the right times, in the right ways, to get the right results. These individuals are *"tempered radicals"* because they choose to effect significant changes in moderate ways. Once there is sufficient support for the change, tempered radicals can use such tools as appreciate inquiry to formalize the transformation process. This chapter presented a brief review of the various techniques and styles which tempered radicals utilize to bring about changes while emerging as leaders in the eyes of many colleagues.

Some organizational leaders inherently resist change, as do many of their employees who represent their organizations. Yet, there are individuals in the workplace today who have at some point in their careers felt the need for change in their organization. This need for change can be prompted by dissatisfaction with organizational values, interests, practices, or actions. These individuals can use a "tempered radical" style of leadership to effectively bring about transformation and the needed changes in due time using Appreciative Inquiry. They can use Appreciative Inquiry in a formal manner to initiate transformational change in an institutional system.

CONFLICT MANAGEMENT
AND NEGOTIATIONS[3]

C ulture can be seen as customs and achievements of a particular
civilization or group because culture is comprised of the values,
beliefs, customs, and norms shared by people in a society. In today's
global economy, cooperation among diverse cultures is imperative for a
company's success because cultures are now tied together by information.
Technology has made communication and travel easier and has increased
the amount and speed of global interaction. Therefore, technology has
made the world a smaller place (Tucker *et al.*, 2002). Similar to the
convergence of technology, there are useful global strategies for effective
communication, negotiation, and conflict resolution that are common to
global managers. The purposes of this chapter are to explain the
significance of effective cross-culture communication in the negotiation
and conflict resolution process and to provide recommendations for global
managers.

Conflict is often assumed to be a contest and it is not. Conflict is part
of nature; neither positive nor negative, it just is, said Thomas Crum
(1987). People can choose whether to make conflict a contest, a game
which requires that some players become winners and some losers.
Winning and losing are generally the goals of games but not the goal of
conflict management. Effective conflict management requires "thinking
win-win" with the goals of jointly learning, growing, and cooperating.
Thomas Crum states that conflict can be seen as the interference pattern of
energies as seen in nature: "Nature uses conflict as its primary motivator
for change, creating beautiful beaches, canyons, mountains, and pearls"

---

[3] - Parts of the material in this chapter come from the research and writings of Tricia Osborn, Rosemarie
Hinds, Lesmalene Morris, Paula Atkinson, Suzette Henry-Campbell, and Nicola Richards of NSU in
Kingston, Jamaica.

(1987, p. 49). It is not whether one has a conflict in his or her life because everyone experiences it; but rather it is what one does with the conflict that makes a positive or negative difference. Crum states that in order for human beings to move beyond success, they need to strive for turning or making their life of work into a work of art. People need to naturally move into a "you and me" mentality where they see the world as abundant and supportive in all aspects of their lives, from their health to their financial well-being (Crum, 1987, p. 25). Crum defines "*alchemy*" as one's ability to change the ordinary into the extraordinary. The ability to change the ordinary to the extraordinary in the middle-ages involved changing common metals into gold; but the alchemy of today involves changing ourselves. Crum states that "It is the pressure of conflict, the interference patterns of energies caused by differences, that provides the motivation and opportunity to change" (p. 25). Nature sees conflict in a positive light and uses it as a primary motivator for bringing about lasting changes. For human beings, the strength, the will and the needed skills are available so long as they are willing to let go of tension, fear, stereotypes, biases, and boundaries.

Effective Communication by Management

Just as effective communication is both an art and a science, so are negotiation and conflict resolution strategies. Now, more than ever in the global economy, it is critical to understand the skills of effective communication, negotiation and conflict resolution. In the last decade, managers have witnessed the changing needs of professional working adults and have concluded that the traditional methods of communication may not be enough in today's global world. The workforce has changed a great deal and so should the way managers communicate with their employees, colleagues, and suppliers throughout the value chain. With outsourcing, mergers, and reorganizations being constant in today's global business environment, middle managers, directors, and senior executives alike are being forced to learn effective communication skills and acquire new knowledge as to ensure effective negotiation and conflict resolution with diverse professionals around the world.

Effective communication is the single most important element of any manager's success with regard to the negotiation and conflict resolution process in today's diverse workforce. Therefore, effective communication is an essential component for success in dissemination of information as well as negotiation and conflict resolution. Hence, communication plays a key role in the success or failure of national and international managers.

As such, managers should understand the basics of communication in order for them to be effective negotiators and solve conflicts in a timely manner.

Management communication involves the realistic expectation of communicating effectively in organizations from the individual to the corporate level. From traditional written and oral forms to electronic presentations and proficient use of the Internet, the effective manager must communicate with brevity and clarity (Darden, 2004). It should be noted that since the number of channels for communication in business is rapidly increasing, a manager's ability to persuade and motivate has never been more important. Management communication involves all aspects of communication between various constituencies in management settings. Managers must be able to think about communication strategies and select the proper strategy for each situation and audience, especially when it comes to resolving conflicts and negotiations.

Today's global environment requires managers to be highly skilled and knowledgeable in several areas regarding management communication. Such skills include strategic communication, negotiations, conflict resolution, interviewing, giving and receiving feedback, and facilitation skills (Darden, 2004). The primary principle is that communication forms the lifeline of a system in an organization, thereby conveying directions, expectations, processes, products, and attitudes (Beck, 1999). Therefore, managers must promote a positive climate of communication within the organization, and this will create an atmosphere of camaraderie, which will add to their organizational value. Communication involves the transmission of information; and managers must be aware that communication refers to the message perceived rather than to the message sent (Beck, 1999). Hence, managers need to be sure that the information that they intended to send is what is received; thus leaving no room for misunderstandings. Misunderstandings can seriously hamper an organization's growth and development. Furthermore, misunderstandings can greatly hurt negotiations and, in some cases, lead to conflicts.

In today's global workforce, communication is critical as competition is regional, national and international. Therefore, companies need to have a strategic advantage over their competitors, and one way of acquiring this advantage is by mastering management communication, conflict resolution and negotiation skills. Therefore, it is essential that managers develop communication strategies that take into account the audience, genre, space, culture, purpose, and channels. In addition, workers must acquire the required expertise of how to listen, write, speak, and how to judge non-verbal actions. These skills will enable workers to be able to argue compellingly and coherently in a contested arena in which others vie for airtime and resources. In addition, managers need to employ active listening skills to elicit information and opinions of others to build trust with others in today's global workforce. Culture affects communication and a person's cultural values and beliefs can become a crucial barrier in the communication process. Managers must recognize the challenges in cross-cultural communications. Communicating with colleagues, at meetings, during disagreements or conflicts, and at negotiations requires skill, thoughtfulness and the ability to take responsibility for others' understanding. Communication and negotiation are not something that should be left to chance.

Introduction to Conflict

Conflict can be defined as a process that "begins when one party perceives that another party has negatively affected, or is about to negatively affect, something that the first party cares about" (Robbins, 2001). Regardless of the exact definition, conflict always includes some type of perceived threat.

The traditional view of conflict was that it is dysfunctional and should be avoided at all costs. Managers, if effective, would spot conflict brewing and do whatever was necessary to stamp it out. More currently, however, conflict is seen as a healthy measure of organizational creativity. Without any conflict, organizations would stagnate. Conflict is seen as a normal part of organizational life; and the absence of any conflict would be seen as symptomatic of employee apathy and a withering organizational culture.

There is, of course, both functional and dysfunctional conflict in all organizations for a variety of reasons.

Causes of conflict. Alan Filley in his 1975 book, "*Interpersonal Conflict Resolution,*" identified nine conditions related to conflict:

1. Unclear jurisdictions between individual responsibilities.
2. Conflict of interest because of scarce resources and the resulting competition.
3. Barriers to communication such as perception, language, and status.
4. Dependency for accomplishment of organizational and personal goals.
5. Increasing differentiation and the resulting levels of authority and specialization.

6. Increased interaction because of participative management and shared authority.
7. Need for agreement because of the desire for group consensus.
8. Regulations for behavior in terms of workplace standards.
9. Presence of previous, unresolved conflict.

Levels of conflict. Organizational conflict can occur at the intrapersonal, interpersonal, group, and interorganizational level. *Intrapersonal conflict* usually involves goal conflict. The three main types of intrapersonal conflict are: (1) approach-approach conflict which occurs when an individual desires two mutually exclusive goals; (2) avoidance-avoidance conflict which occurs when a person must choose between two unattractive and mutually exclusive goals; and (3) approach-avoidance conflict which occurs when a person experiences conflict over the same goal. In the beginning, the goal is viewed as very desirable, then, as the person nears the goal, he or she starts having second thoughts.

Interpersonal conflict can be exemplified by two people competing for scarce resources or disagreeing over an issue. In this type of conflict, personality conflicts, value differences, and generation gaps often present themselves. *Group conflict* refers to conflict between groups, to the "we-they" mentality that breeds dysfunctional competition. *Inter-organizational conflict* refers to organizations having conflict with other organizations. An example would be friction between Company A with its supplier, Company B, because Company B is delaying shipment until its previous bill has been paid. Management authors often talk about a five stage conflict process. The five stages are: (1) Potential opposition or incompatibility; (2) Cognition and personalization; (3) Intentions; (4) Behavior; and (5) Outcomes.

Conflict Management Strategies. Good managers must have effective conflict management strategies. The following are short descriptions of some of the most common strategies for conflict management (Robbins, 2001).

- *Avoidance*: Some managers do not feel comfortable dealing with conflict situations so they simply ignore them.
- *Smoothing*: Other managers offer platitudes to cover up conflict similar to what a mother might do with her two small children, saying in effect, "Don't fight with your brother; let's all watch TV together."
- *Expansion of resources*: In the event conflict is over scarce resources, like a new position in the budget, it is sometimes

possible and wise to expand resources, e.g., add an additional position to the budget so that both managers can have a new employee.

- *Compromise*: In compromise, everyone wins something. There is no winner and no loser; of course, nobody is completely happy either.
- *Authoritarianism*: With this style, the manager simply dictates the answer to the conflict.
- *Mutual problem solving*: This is probably the best way for long-term conflict resolution, this method requires all conflicting parties to hear each other out and work on a solution together.

One cannot have discussion of conflict without considering the topic and skills of negotiation. *Negotiation,* according to some experts, is a decision-making process between several individuals where they agree upon how to allocate available resources. It has been stated that there are three main elements in this definition of negotiation: judgment, interdependence, and cooperation. Negotiation involves logical and rational thinking, thus judgment. Interdependence of the negotiating parties is obvious or there would be no reason to negotiate. Cooperation is necessary for the parties to reach a mutual agreement.

Dr. Jane Gibson, in her book, titled "*Organizational Communication: A Managerial Perspective,*" defines negotiation as "the process of arranging or settling something through such means as discussion or conference." Here are some suggestions from Jane Gibson about dealing with negotiation in organizations:

1. Remember that if you are negotiating with people in your organization, tomorrow is another day and you will have to work with them again. Use a win-win approach. Very few people make it to the top by continually besting their peers. As you approach the upper managerial level there is great emphasis on teamwork.
2. In dealing with subordinates, always try to use a win-win strategy. This approach is very helpful in creating and increasing your referent power. It points you out as a person who can be trusted and relied upon.
3. When negotiating with subordinates, remember that it is important to balance a concern for the needs of the organization with a similar concern for the needs of the people. Both need to be given attention.

Understanding Conflict Resolution

Conflict is a reality of life, which everyone faces at one time or another. Managers, therefore, need to understand the cause and effects of conflicts and how to respond in the best interest of all concerned. Conflict is often a characteristic of change, fear and unmet expectations. Any attempt to adjust the status quo in an organization can result in conflict. If effectively handled, conflict can be a healthy way of airing differences and generating alternatives. However, constant conflict can be anxiety inducing, debilitating and destructive. Conflict resolution includes recognition, awareness and choice. It occurs within and between individuals, groups, organizations and societies.

Each individual may react differently to conflict. Some people seem to thrive on conflict, while others abhor it, and others remain unruffled by the most conflicting situations. Individuals also deal with conflict in different ways, some people attack, while others tend to defend. However, most people are consistent in their individual responses to conflict, tending to react the same way over time, developing a behavior pattern.

Conflict within organizations is a major concern of management, and is usually a result of various grievances ranging from human to industrial relations. Issues such as remuneration, work allocation, methods of communication, working conditions, performance appraisals, gender, racial, and religious differences are just the major commonly disputed sources of conflict. Due to an obvious awareness of the need to resolve conflicts effectively, experts in the fields of psychology and human resources have identified formal methods and processes to do so.

What is Conflict?

Conflict can be good or bad, positive or negative, and constructive or destructive to the functioning of a group or unit depending on how it is handled. Conflict has been defined from a communication perspective as "an expressed struggle between at least two interdependent parties who perceive incompatible goals, scarce rewards, and interference from the other party in achieving their goals"– Joyce Hocker and William Wilmot as quoted by Devito (Beck, 1999). Interpersonal conflict has been defined as "a process of antagonism that occurs when one person or organizational subunit frustrates the goal attainment of another" Gary Johns (Beck, 1999). Devito differentiates two major types of conflict: *Content conflict* and *relationship conflict.* *Content conflict* "centers on objects, events and persons that are usually, but not always or entirely, external to the parties involved in the conflict." *Relationship conflicts* "do not concern some external object as much as relationships between the individuals– issues such as who is in charge, the equality of a primary relationship, and who has the right to set down rules of behavior."

According to experts in the field, the following are some general signs for the existence of conflict, which may alert management of existing or potential conflict:

◊ People begin to avoid one another or become less cooperative.
◊ Rumors and gossip become more frequent or exclusive.
◊ Humor disappears between groups or individuals.
◊ Sick leave, absenteeism increases.
◊ Apathy increases, productivity slows.
◊ Boycotts, strikes, or demonstrations are planned, and escalate to gain negative media coverage.
◊ Individuals or group begins undermining or sabotaging decision-maker or that which is associated with decision-maker.
◊ Phone calls, memos and e-mails don't get returned.
◊ Tension or outright hostility increases.
◊ Outside channels, such as the media, are used to air grievances.

There are also some specific benefits to conflict. Conflict is normally viewed from a negative perspective; however, Beck (1999) listed five positive benefits of conflict as follows:

◊ Prevents stagnation,
◊ Stimulates interest,
◊ Stimulates curiosity,
◊ Serves as a medium to air problems, and
◊ Serves as a medium for solving problems.

Conflict can take an "ugly" turn when personal glory is staked on the outcome. This simply means that one party may not wish to concede, even if he/she sees it as a possible solution, for fear that this will be seized by the other party as a victory and will probably be used for future advances. This is what is referred to as a "win-lose" scenario. If the parties refuse to let go of their particular problems, then ultimately the result is a "lose-lose" situation. All parties lose sight of the real goals during the conflict. One thing that a manager must pay keen attention to is the fact that conflict may be overt, leading to a rehearsal at every meeting. If it is covert, then the parties may continue to mask what the true issues are and this, over time, can develop into serious problems within the organization.

Managing Conflict

People get into conflict whenever their interests and or values are threatened or it may also occur when their needs are not being met. Usually, each individual is directed consciously and unconsciously, toward various goals. Some of these goals are obvious and some are not, however, they are all important to the individual. In an attempt to fulfill these goals, individuals can face challenges, and dealing with these challenges sometimes result in conflicts. The way conflicts are handled is an important factor in managerial effectiveness. To successfully negotiate a solution when a conflict arises, it is necessary to:

◊ Listen to and try to understand the point of view being expressed by the other party- try to avoid reiterating your own viewpoints.

◊ Be alert for trade-offs- is there something that you are able to concede to the other party that is actually more meaningful to them and costs little to you?

◊ Avoid capitulating the conflict into a personal battle- focus on the real issues and facts.

These aforementioned suggestions are the foundations on which one can most often build a "win-win" situation. All too often though, personality is the root of many conflicts and this is a factor managers must take into consideration when analyzing the nature of conflicts at the work place. There are many obstacles for managing conflict, and some of the typical obstacles to the effective management of conflict are:

◊ Fear of change,

◊ Language Barriers,

◊ Fear of losing the advantage /power,

◊ Attempts at disempowerment,

◊ Lack of trust,

◊ Ignorance,

◊ Inability to articulate the issues,

◊ Impatience,

◊ Power Imbalance, Ego,

◊ Emotions, and

◊ Threats.

Suggestions for conflict resolution

According to Beck (1999) and other experts, there are some common "dos and don'ts" in conflict resolution; and some useful hints for conflict resolution are:

◊ Dos:
  o Do *fight fair.* Avoid hitting where the other person is defenseless, such as criticizing something over which there is no control.
  o Do *fight actively.* Confront conflicts purposefully. Do not tune out or walk out on the other person.
  o Do *take responsibility.* Take ownership for your thoughts and feelings and for expressing those thoughts and feelings.
  o Do *be specific.* Limit your focus to the issue at hand. Do not bring up past grievances or involve other persons unnecessarily.
  o Do *use humor wisely.* Use humor only to ease the tension, but never sarcastically. Do not ridicule or embarrass the other person.

◊ Don'ts:
  o Do not *avoid. Avoidance* is ignoring (tuning out) or redefining the issue. It sometimes takes the form of actual physical fighting.
  o Do not *force. Forcing* may involve either physical or emotional coercion and may actually result in physical attacks.
  o Do not *blame. Blaming* involves a refusal to accept responsibility and actually holding another person responsible.
  o Do not *silence. Silencing* includes the use of an array of fight techniques that literally silence the other person; such techniques include crying and yelling.
  o Do not *manipulate.* In *Manipulation,* there is avoidance of open conflict. One person may use charm to disarm the other in order to win.

Personality Types and Conflict Resolution

Everyone has a basic personality type, which causes him or her to exhibit certain consistent behaviors and temperaments. The renaissance era refers to temperament as persons prevailing mood patterns that were based on the dominance of four body fluids (Keirsey 2002). According to Dr. David Keirsey and other experts, the blood, phlegm, black bile, or the yellow bile, ruled a person and this determined his response to his environment. Whichever fluid/humor emerged dominant was considered the persons' truest self. Hence a person was choleric, phlegmatic, melancholic, or sanguine.

Modern psychological terminologies that relate to these temperaments are Choleric/Idealist, Phlegmatic/Rationalist, Melancholic/Traditionalist and Sanguine/Hedonist. Such varying temperaments can undoubtedly result in negative conflict from time to time and it is important that the manager understands them, what drives them and their most negative conflict handling styles. According to David Keirsey, clinical psychologist, the following are some common motivators and conflict resolution suggestions for such personality types.

Choleric/Idealist.

◊ *Motivators:* Perfection and Superiority. The Idealist is goal and detail oriented and can be an advocate. He or she strives to do the right things first, tends to be organized, efficient and accurate. He or she is a high achiever. He or she however needs time to process information. The Idealist tends to be diplomatic and ethical. He or she desires intimacy, but won't die without it.

◊ *Conflict handling styles*: Collaborative at best compromising at worst.

◊ *Most frequent source of conflict:* not having enough information to work with,

◊ *What to do:* Use scenarios in resolving issues. Appeal to his or her greater sense of logic present the facts, show how they can help others and acknowledge contributions to the organization. Go through processes and procedures step by step without condescending.

Phlegmatic/Rationalist.

◊ *Motivators*: Power and Control. The Phlegmatic seeks greater understanding, educational, social, economical progress and also seeks to learn new skills. Although a high achiever he tends to be dictatorial in his approach and thus intimidate others. The Phlegmatic can be bossy, often rage or shout at persons. He or she (he from here on to simplify) is often verbally caustic and is very arrogant. As a supervisor he wants things done his way and now. He can be systematic and attentive to details.

◊ *Conflict handling style:* Competitive. This person takes the offensive readily. They tend to use "you messages" to freely discount stereotype, label, hold accountable, accuse, and blame others.

◊ *Most frequent source of conflict:* personality clashes and demanding dictatorial approach.

◊ *What to do:* Research and present the facts of the situation straight away. Argue logically without emotive terms and most of all remain calm and in control. Promote win-win.

Melancholic/Traditionalist.

◊ *Motivators:* Desire for peace and belonging. The Traditionalist believes in the norms, rules and regulation of the organizational structure. He is loyal to the core, is supportive, and cultivates unity. He is very sincere and desires reciprocity in relationships. He desires status and responsibility but is not committed enough to be a strong leader. However he is prepared for the worst, is good at motivating and inspiring others and thus makes a good coach.

◊ *Conflict handling style:* Accommodating, avoiding, and agreeing to disagree. He will be accommodating to keep the relationship going at any cost to his own detriment. He is submissive under pressure and puts aside his own feelings and values in order to feel a sense of belonging. He will avoid that is, he will spend time minimizing discomfort and restoring harmony. On his good day when he decides to stick to his guns he will agree to disagree but will seek out an opportunity later on with due consideration to re-enter the conversation. He is unpredictable and so can also be quite competitive.

◊ *Source of conflict:* The Melancholic procrastinates, spends too much time empathizing with issues and persons and doing extraneous work. As a result of being busy doing nothing, he often does not meet deadlines.

◊ *What to do:* Listen to him sincerely. Show him you like him, highlight his positives first and focus specifically on the issue at hand. Suggest alternatives. Use him where his strengths lie, in public relations, gathering support, and team building / coaching.

Sanguine/Hedonist.

◊ *Motivators*: Need for popularity and freedom. The Sanguine desires freedom to choose to act and not be acted upon. He is optimistic cheerful and exciting. He focuses on action activities that are related to the achievement of a goal. He is people orientated. He is innovative and is led by inner vibes. A charismatic leader, he has bursts of energy, but this is not sustainable in and of itself but it is contagious. He does not desire public acclaim or glory because he is already popular. He is therefore content in putting forward ideas and having others run with it and support it from the sidelines, he knows his shortcomings. He is also quite talkative.

◊ *Conflict handling style:* Compromise at worst and collaborative at best. As a compromise he seeks a quick fix if he sees them to be a non-priority. He reveals only the surface needs of the other party and glosses over underlying needs. He can therefore put results before principles. However as a collaborator he promotes win-win situations as an expert negotiator.

◊ *Source of conflict*: Perceived waywardness, level of prioritization when overly supervised. Tight inflexible work environment and wrong job fit. He is generally forgetful and forgiving.

◊ *What to do:* Be enthusiastic about ideas. Listen to the Sanguine without interrupting and without being judgmental. Use body language to show your support for his ideas. Address problems immediately and do not take him for granted.

Twelve Steps to Conflict Resolution

In order to communicate effectively, managers must be cognizant of the different ways in which they can resolve conflicts. Conflict resolution builds stronger and more cohesive organizations and more rewarding relationships. The following are twelve steps for effective conflict resolution:

1. *The win/win approach.* The win/win approach is about changing the conflict from an adversarial attack and defense, to cooperation. It is a powerful shift of attitude that alters the course of communication. One person continually applying a joint problem solving approach can make the difference. Until we give it some thought, we usually are unaware of the way we argue. We often

find ourselves with a knee-jerk reaction in difficult situations based on long established habits combined with the passing mood of the moment. When challenged we experience loneliness, we feel disconnected from those around us. While people argue over opposing solutions-"Do it my way! No, that is not good! Do it my way!" the conflict is a power struggle. What is needed is to change the agenda in the conversation. The objective should be "I want to win and I want you to win too." It is about "thinking win-win" as explained by Stephen R. Covey in his popular *Seven Habits of Highly Effective People* book which was originally published in 1989.

2. *Creative response.* The creative response to conflict is about turning problems into possibilities. It is about consciously choosing to see what can be done, rather than existing with how terrible it all is. It is in affirming that you will choose to extract the best from the situation.

3. *Empathy.* It is deemed necessary to develop communication tools to build rapport. Use emphatic listening to clarify understanding. Charles Beck (1999) defines emphatic listening as when one "fully understands the speaker's views, values, attitudes, emotions, and feelings" (p.63).

4. *Appropriate assertiveness.* It is imperative that managers apply strategies that attack the problem, and not the person. The emphasis of appropriate assertiveness is being able to state your case without arousing the defenses of the other person. The most important factor is saying how it is for you rather than what they should or should not do. "The way I see it..." attached to your assertive statement, helps. A skilled "I" statement goes even further. When you want to state your point of view helpfully, the "I" statement formula can be useful. An "I" statement says how it is on my side, and how I see it.

5. *Co-operative power.* It is very important to eliminate the "power over" to build "power with" others. When faced with a situation that has the potential to create conflict, ask open questions to reframe resistance. Explore the difficulties and then re-direct discussion to focus on positive possibilities.

6. *Managing emotions.* Express fear, anger, hurt, and frustration wisely to effect change. Additionally, these messages should

demonstrate sincerity and trustworthiness matching the intent of the communicators.

7. *Willingness to resolve*. It is important for managers to maintain a willingness to resolve. The more someone inflames, angers or upsets you, the more one realizes the need to learn more about themselves. We must constantly look within ourselves to see whether or not, we are projecting or if there is anything that has interfered with our willingness to resolve. Projection is when we see our thoughts and feelings in the minds and behavior of others and not in ourselves.

8. *Mapping the conflict*. Sometimes issues are simplified when they are written down. A good idea is to define briefly the issue, the problem or conflict in neutral terms that everyone would agree on.

9. *Broadening perspectives*. Everyone should learn to respect and value differences. Just as we are unique and special, so are other people. We all have distinctive viewpoints that may be just as valid from where we stand. Each person's viewpoint makes a contribution to the whole and requires consideration and respect in order to form a complete solution. This wider view can open our eyes to many more possibilities.

10. *Mediation*. The third party mediator should endeavor to be *objective*. They should validate both sides, even if they silently prefer one point of view or even when only one party is present. Secondly, the mediator should be *supportive*. They should use caring language. Provide a non-threatening learning environment, where people will feel safe to disclose personal issues. Thirdly, the mediator should be *unbiased*. They should actively discourage judgments as to who was right and who was wrong. Ask questions such as: What happened? How did you feel? The mediator should endeavor to *encourage participation*. Encourage suggestions from participants. Do not give advice. If your suggestions are really needed, offer as options not directives. *Strive for a win/win situation* - Turn opponents into problem-solving partners. One can follow the following steps for effective mediation:

    ◊   *Open* - Introductions and agreements.
    ◊   *Establish* - Overview: What is the matter? Ask each person to express their view of the conflict, the issues, and their feelings. Details: What is involved? Lay out the needs and

concerns. Clarify misconceptions. Identify other relevant issues, mirroring if needed.

◊ *Move* - Where are they now? Identify areas of agreement. Encourage willingness to move forward. Negotiation: focus on future action. How would they like it to be? What would that take? Develop options. Trading build wins for everyone.

◊ *Close* - Completion: Contracting. Plans for the future, including appointed time to review agreement. Clarify and offer closing statements.

11. *Designing of options*. It is best to explore all possible options and perhaps break the problem into smaller parts. Furthermore, one should research the situation, gather more information, and establish the constraints involved. When exploring options, always consider the following questions:

◊ Is the option satisfying the win/win approach?

◊ Does the option meet many needs of all parties?

◊ Is it cost effective?

◊ Is it fair?

◊ Does it solve the problem?

◊ Can the problem be settled with only one option?

12. *Negotiation*. The emphasis is on the work relationships among team members. The strategy involves a series of controlled negotiations between participants. One should remember that negotiations involve several principles:

◊ The emphasis should be on the problem, and not on the person.

◊ Focus on the needs, not on positions.

◊ Emphasize common ground.

◊ Be inventive about options.

◊ Make clear agreements.

One must always focus on the issue while maintaining the relationship and trying to resolve the issue. After clarification, members must decide which items they want most and form into pairs to negotiate, usually with a third party to help in the process. Finally, there should be a written role negotiation agreement. The outcome of the negotiation is written down and spells out the agreements and concessions, which each party finds satisfactory.

Cross Cultural Negotiations

Globalization has made cross-cultural negotiations a way of life for both individuals and organizations as business is often the first link established between societies (Tucker et al., 2002). It should be noted that culture has an impact on how two persons converse; they rarely communicate the same subject, for each person's own cognitive world and cultural conditioning can affect the meaning. Therefore, when negotiating internationally, this concept needs to be acknowledged and translated into anticipating culturally related ideas that are most likely to be understood by a person of a given culture. Negotiations are frequently hampered because the two sides tend to pursue different paths of logic; in any cross-cultural context, the potential for misunderstanding is great (Herbig, 2005).

It is naïve for individuals and organizations to enter into international negotiations with the attitude that since we are similar in appearance and share the same interests, we have a similar value system. The people of each nation have different negotiating styles that are shaped by their cultural systems such as history, politics, and geography. The negotiation style used can have serious repercussions when dealing with persons from another cultural background. Hence, when participating in cross-cultural negotiations participants need to have heightened sensitivity, and pay close attention to details such as changes in behavioral patterns. However, no one can usually avoid bringing along their cultural assumptions, images and prejudices when negotiating (Herbig, 2005)

There are at least three ways in which culture impedes the negotiation process (Ting-Toomey, 2005). The first factor is cognitive constraints. These are frames of references with which new information is compared. Most individuals tend to view situations from a narrow-minded point of view, and will not be open to any ideas that do not fall within these references. The second factor is behavioral constraints as each culture has its own rules about what is proper etiquette; this includes verbal and non-verbal communication. For example, whether one looks the other person in the eye or not; whether one says what one means explicitly or talks around the issue; how one deals with personal space when communicating, all of these and many more are rules of politeness, which differ from culture to culture. The third factor is emotional constraints. People in different cultures may display emotions differently. Also, people of some cultures get very emotional when debating an issue. Some individuals have the tendency to yell, cry, and exhibit their anger, fear, and frustration openly. However, people in other cultures keep their emotions hidden, exhibiting or sharing only the rational aspects of the situation. These different tendencies can lead to communication problems, which manifest itself in the negotiation process. Therefore, when conducting cross-cultural negotiations, the individuals involved need to become aware of these differences or they are likely to fall victim to them.

Negotiations are usually entered into for the purpose of reaching an agreement. An agreement is an exchange of conditional promises in which each party states that it will behave in a particular way that both parties behave in accordance with their promises (Herbig, 2005). Depending on which culture is involved, sometimes breaking a promise is tolerated, expected, or desired. According to research, there are two types of agreements: explicit and implicit. *Explicit agreements* are detailed, written contracts that cover all aspects of the negotiation and bind the parties through an outside enforcement mechanism. This contract assumes that there is no personal relationship between the parties. The only relationship that exists is to allow for the exchange of information. Communication in this type of negotiation is limited only to substantive issues. Therefore, it is formal and relies heavily on technical language. Obligations are also limited to those specific, detailed actions provided in the contract. *Implicit agreements* are broad, oral agreements that accept unforeseen changes as normal and leave room for the parties to deal with problems. Formation of personal relationships is expected. Implicit agreements assume that the importance of the relationship overrides other concerns. These agreements are more concerned with personal non-economic satisfactions than substantive exchange. Communication is extensive, covering subjects apart from the substantive concerns of the negotiations, formal and informal, and verbal and non-verbal. Obligations are unlimited and un-measurable. The future cannot be foreseen or included. The negotiations process, especially in international settings, is long and drawn out (Herbig, 2005).

According to experts, culture affects the different phases of the negotiation process. These various phases of negotiation are the preparation phase, the beginning, middle, and the end. It also should be noted that the various ways the negotiations process is decided are culturally loaded. For high-context negotiators, the preparatory stage focuses on building personal relationships with the other side. Accustomed to acting within a rich framework of interdependent relations, high-context negotiators start by attempting to build such a network with the opponent. Negotiators in low-context cultures see issues separable from personal relations and prefer to act in relatively anonymous ways. Negotiators in high-context cultures also tend to take a long view, focusing on cultivating and improving the parties' relationship. Low-context cultures tend to have more short-term focus on the issue at hand. Maintaining face is generally more important in high-context cultures than in low-context. Because of the importance of maintaining face, high-context negotiators generally try to minimize uncertainty and prevent crises, confrontations and surprises. Being caught by surprise is likely to result in a loss of face for someone involved in the negotiation process. Low-context cultures are less concerned with the issue of face and are more open to uncertainty, competition and confrontation. Low-context negotiators tend to open negotiations by first setting forth their position, assuming that the other side will respond by stating their opposing position. Low-context cultures view declaring an open position to be risky and confrontational. The opening positions generally reveal each party's level of interest. When this statement of positions is not reciprocated, it gives the reticent party an advantage. Cultures also differ in their preference for agreement on specifics or on general principles. Low-context negotiators focus on examining the facts at hand and crafting a conclusion to fit those facts. High context negotiators tend to seek agreement on general principles to the case at hand.

Different cultures may have different expectations as to what should occur during the middle phase of negotiations and how much time this phase should take. Low context cultures such as the U.S. expect that the middle phase be a period of bargaining, a process of trade-offs and concessions in which the parties gradually converge on a shared position. People in high-context cultures use a process of haggling as appropriate to price negotiations, but do not negotiate in matters of principle. High status individuals do not lower themselves to haggle over small points. Negotiators in polychronic cultures are usually willing to draw out the middle phase. Monochronic cultures are usually in a hurry to reach an agreement. Monochronic cultures are often at some disadvantage when negotiating with polychronic cultures, since their sense of urgency can prompt them to make concessions in order to close the deal quickly.

Different cultural approaches to authority also can complicate the middle phase. Collectivist cultures tend to base authority relations on the father-child model. Authority is centralized, hierarchical and tends to be absolute. Individualist cultures tend to disperse power and authority and encourage questions and even challenges to authority. Different cultures favor different means of negotiation and persuasion. The emphasis on personal relationships, as well as group harmony in high-context cultures, mean that persuasion focuses on cultivating a close, trusting relationship with the other side. High-context cultures are generally uncomfortable with overt aggression, confrontation and adversarial style of interaction. Low-context cultures find facts and reasoned arguments to be persuasive and tend to favor a more direct explicit and even aggressive style of communication. According to Herbig, culture influences negotiation through its effects on communication and through their conceptualizations of the process, the ends they target, the means they use and the expectations they hold of counterparts' behavior. Culture affects the range of strategies that negotiators develop as well as the many ways they are tactically implemented. In international negotiations, people bring to the negotiating table the values, beliefs and background interference of their culture and normally will unconsciously use those elements in both the presentation and interpretation of the data (Herbig, 2005).

Cross cultural negotiation has become a topic of interest due to today's shrinking world and there have been several studies done on the importance of cross cultural issues. One researcher is Fons Trompenaar who is a "world authority" on managing cultural diversity. Trompenaar developed a model to analyze cultural differences, known as the *'Seven Dimensions of Cultural Model,'* to show how managing complexity in a heterogeneous environment is a challenge for international managers. Taken from Trompenaar (1993) and ChangingMinds.org, Trompenaar's *'Seven Dimensions of Cultural Model'* involves (ChangingMinds, 2005):

1. Universalism vs. Particularism. *Universalism* is about finding broad and general rules. When no rules fit, it finds the best rule. *Particularism* is about finding exceptions. When no rules fit, it judges the case on its own merits, rather than trying to force-fit an existing rule.

2. Analyzing vs. Integrating. *Analyzing* decomposes to find the detail. It assumes that the message is in the details and that decomposition is the way to success. It sees people who look at the big picture as being out of touch with reality. *Integrating* brings things together to build the big picture. It assumes that if you have your "head in the weeds," you will miss the true understanding.

3. Individualism vs. Communitarianism. *Individualism* is about the rights of the individual. It seeks to let people grow or fall on their own, and sees group-focus as stripping the individual of their inalienable rights. *Communitarianism* is about the rights of the

group or society. It seeks to put the family, group, company and country before the individual. It sees individualism as selfish and shortsighted.

4. Inner-directed vs. Outer-directed. *Inner-directed* is about thinking and personal judgment, in our heads. It assumes that this is the most powerful tool and it considers that ideas and intuitive approaches are the best way. *Outer-directed* is seeking data in the outer world. It assumes that we live in the real world, and that is where we should look for our information and decisions.

5. Time as sequence vs. Time as synchronization. *Time as sequence* sees events as separate items in time, sequence one after another. *Time as synchronization* sees events in parallel, synchronized together. It finds order in coordination of multiple efforts.

6. Achieved status vs. Ascribed status. *Achieved status* is about gaining status through performance. It assumes individuals and organizations earn and lose their status every day and other approaches are recipes for failure. *Ascribed status* is about gaining status through other means such as seniority. It assumes status is acquired by right rather than daily performance, which may be as much luck as judgment. It finds order and security in knowing where status is and stays.

7. Equality vs. Hierarchy. *Equality* is about all people having equal status. It assumes we all have equal rights, irrespective of birth or other gift. *Hierarchy* is about people being superior to others. It assumes that order happens when few are in charge, and others obey through the scalar chain of command.

Another significant contributor to this topic is Gert Hofstede, who is responsible for what is the most widely used topology and assessment vehicle for intercultural difference among cultures (Tucker et al, 2002). Hofstede believes that there are five different dimensions that affect cross-cultural communication, negotiation, and conflict resolution (Jones & George, 2003).

1. Individualism vs. Collectivism. *Individualism* is a worldwide view that values individual freedom and self-expression and adherence to the principle that people should be judged by their individual achievements rather than by their social background. Countries such as U.S.A, Great Britain and Australia are highly individualistic. *Collectivism* is a worldwide view that values subordination of the individual to the goals of the group and adherence to the principle

that people should be judged by their contribution to the group. Countries such as Indonesia, Jamaica, and Columbia are highly collectivistic.

2. Power Distance. This concept means the degree to which societies accept the idea that inequality in the power and well being of their citizens are due to differences in individuals' physical and intellectual capabilities. Societies in which inequalities are allowed to persist or grow over time have high power distance. On the contrary, in societies with low power distance, large inequalities between citizens are not allowed to develop. *High power distance* ranking indicates that inequalities of power and wealth have been allowed to grow within the society. *Low power distance* ranking indicates the society de-emphasizes the differences between citizen's power and wealth.

3. Achievement vs. Nurturing Orientation. *Achievement Orientation* is a view that values assertiveness, performance, success and competition. Countries such as Japan and United States are achievement oriented. *Nurturing Orientation* is a view that values the quality of life, warm personal relationship and services and care for the weak. Netherlands, Sweden and Denmark are nurturing countries.

4. Uncertainty Avoidance. Societies *low in uncertainty avoidance* tends to be easygoing, value diversity and tolerate differences in personal beliefs and actions such as the United States and Hong Kong. Societies *high in uncertainty avoidance* are more rigid and skeptical about people whose behavior or beliefs differ from the norm.

5. Long term vs. short term orientation. This dimension describes a culture's attitude towards work and life. Societies with long-term orientation rest on values such as thrift and persistence in achieving goals. Short-term orientation is concerned with maintaining personal stability or happiness and living for the present (Jones & George, 2003).

Trompenaar and Hofstede's cultural models are useful instruments for organizations and individuals to use in cross cultural negotiations as they help one understand how culture contributes to participants' behavior. According to Neil Payne (2005), cross-cultural negotiations are more about the process than how foreigners close deals. It involves looking at all factors that can influence the proceedings. Therefore, it should be noted that in the United States, United Kingdom, and much of Northern Europe, strong and direct eye contact are seen as a sign of confidence and sincerity, and in South America it is a sign of trustworthiness. Japanese and people in some other Asian countries consider prolonged eye contact to be rude. Europeans and North Americans normally leave a certain amount of distance between themselves when interacting. However, in South America or the Middle East, business people like to get up close. In Japan or China, it is not uncommon for people to leave a gap of four feet when conversing.

Western societies are extremely time-conscious, they view time as money and punctuality is crucial. In Asian countries, such as Japan or China being late would be considered an insult. However, in South America, southern Europe and the Middle East, being on time for a meeting does not carry the same level of urgency. Most international business people meet with a handshake. However, in some countries, such as Afghanistan and Pakistan, a handshake is not always appropriate between genders. Some cultures view a weak handshake as a sign of weakness, where as others would perceive a firm handshake as aggressive.

In Japan and China, gift-giving is an integral part of business protocol, however in the United States and United Kingdom, it can have negative connotations related to bribery. There are three interconnected aspects that need to be considered before entering into cross-cultural negotiations (Payne, 2005):

1. *The Basis of the relationship.* In much of Europe and North America, business is contractual in nature. Personal relationships are seen as unhealthy as they cloud objectivity and lead to complications. In South America and much of Asia business is personal. Partnership will only be made with those they know, trust and feel comfortable with. It is, therefore, necessary to invest in relationship building before conducting business.

2. *Information at negotiations.* Western business culture places emphasis on clearly presented and rationally argued business proposals using statistics and facts. Other business cultures rely on similar information but with differences. For example, visual and oral communicators such as South Americans may prefer information presented through speech or using maps, graphs and charts.

3. *Negotiation styles.* The way in which we approach negotiation differs across cultures. For example, in the Middle East rather than approaching topics sequentially negotiators may discuss issues simultaneously.

American negotiators from the United States tend to rely on individualist values, imagining self and other as autonomous and self-reliant. They tend to be competitive in negotiations, including coming to the table with a fallback position but beginning with an unrealistic offer. These negotiators have the tendencies to be energetic and persistent; they enjoy arguing their positions and see things universally. They concentrate on one problem at a time. They focus on areas of disagreements, not areas of commonality or agreement.

Many African nations have indigenous systems of conflict resolution that have endured into the present, sometimes quite intact and sometimes fragmented by rapid social change. These systems rely on particular approaches to negotiation that respect kinship ties, elder roles and structure of local society. In Nigeria and many parts of Afghanistan, for example, people are organized in extended families, village, lineage, and lineage group. A belief in the continuing ability of ancestors to affect people's lives maintains social control and makes the need to have formal laws or regulations minimal.

The following values tend to influence Japanese communication: focus on group goals, interdependence and a hierarchical orientation. In negotiation these values manifest themselves in awareness of group needs and goals and deference to those of higher status. Japanese negotiators are known for their politeness, their emphasis on establishing relationship and their indirect use of power. Japanese negotiators tend to put less emphasis on the literal meanings of words in negotiations and more emphasis on the relationships established before negotiation begins. European styles of negotiation vary according to region, nationality, language spoken and many other contextual factors. The French tend to be more aggressive negotiators using threats, warnings and interruptions to achieve their goals. German and British negotiators are often rated as moderately aggressive.

Latin American style and role expectations influence negotiation in Latin American contexts. Responsibility to others is generally considered more important than schedules and task accomplishment. Their negotiation approach relates to the polychronic orientation to time and patterns of high-context communication and communitarianism. Thus, negotiations are done within networks; relationships are emphasized; and open ruptures are avoided (LeBaron, 2005, pg. 7-9). Overall, global negotiators understand and effectively manage conflict.

Summary

Individuals and groups are driven by different cultural as well as personal values, beliefs and goals. As a result, conflict is inevitable in today's diverse work environment. The effective global manager must, therefore, be prepared to negotiate effectively and handle conflicts in such a way that it is in the best interest of the organization's stakeholders. The requisite knowledge to support effective conflict resolution includes an understanding of the nature of conflicts, the dangers and benefits of conflict and the various methods or approaches to handling conflicts. A better understanding of such factors as personality types, cultures and communication styles will assist the manager in the conflict resolution process. A combination of techniques and approaches may be used to resolve a conflict. What is important is to be adequately prepared *before* the conflict, so that a positive atmosphere may be quickly restored when there are opposing issues to be addressed.

The international negotiation process is filled with challenges and perils. To achieve success in these negotiation processes, companies and their managers must improve their knowledge of the other participants and their culture. Managers and negotiators must invest time in preparing for these meetings with the use of translators and cultural experts. The road to success in cross-cultural negotiations is recognizing that a foreign negotiator is different, in perceptions, motivation, belief, and outlook. It is important to identify, understand, accept, and respect the other side's culture. As such, one must communicate and operate on two separate and different cultural wavelengths. It is very important to be culturally neutral; hence, negotiators should not cast judgment on the other's cultural traditions and values as they feel the same way about their culture as you do yours, even if some of the customs appear fickle, cruel or even insane (Herbig, 2005). In addition, be sensitive to their cultural norms, "dos," and taboos; try to understand who they are and how your behavior may impact them even if it causes you discomfort or emotional stress. It is necessary to accept and proceed with business without showing distress if one wishes to come home with an agreement beneficial to both parties and the start of a long-term healthy relationship between two companies from two different cultures (Herbig, 2005).

"The Magic of Conflict: Turning a Life of Work into a Work of Art," a beautifully written book by Thomas F Crum in 1987, states that conflict is neither good nor bad, it just is as "Our lives are not dependent on whether or not we have conflict. It is what we do with conflict that makes the difference" (Crum, 1987, p. 21). Thomas Crum states that, during changing times and major conflicts, "instead of seeing the rug being pulled out from under us, we can learn to dance on the shifting carpet." Thomas Crum quotes Woody Allen who said that "More than at any other time in

history mankind faces a crossroad. One path leads to despair and utter hopelessness; the other to total extinction. Let us pray we have the wisdom to choose correctly." The key in managing conflict effectively is to learn how to convert frustration to fascination and disappointing and upsetting thoughts into growth. John Denver, who wrote the foreword for *The Magic of Conflict*, said the following:

> Tom takes us simply, clearly, and profoundly through the nature of conflict and the principles of the Aiki Approach for resolving conflict and moving beyond success, and provides us with real, practical applications of these principles to our daily life. These principles work on an individual level, in the simplest of relationships, and in the most complex, even those between societies and nations which espouse differences in language, heritage, politics, and faith. Transformation takes risk and courage. This is no longer a world of you or me. We must recognize that it is you and me and that together we can create the world, the life that we have dreamed of forever, a world of peace and goodwill among men. A world without hunger. A world without the threat of nuclear disaster and the possible extinction of humanity. Peace is a conscious choice (John Denver, 1987).

Thomas Crum states that discovery is one essential component of effective conflict management because *discovery* is a place that does not know, does not evaluate, and is willing to see what is; *discovery* sees beyond the fight to an open realm of possibilities; *discovery* enables people to let go of the filters of their past and the blinders of their expectations; *discovery* perceives not right and wrong, only inquiry and creativity; and *discovery* turns frustration into fascination and work into play (1987, p. 129). Discovering the right response in each changing moment requires having an open mind as well as an open heart to see new opportunities and the way things are, and then the way they can be. The origin and evolution of every living species has been a lesson of change as various living species adapt to and evolve with their changing environments in order to flourish. The same means of adaptation applies to human beings since change in nature is not an ideological choice but rather one of survival. Change is a choice for learning, creativity, flexibility, and growth; and effective conflict management is the key to bringing about change in an efficient manner. Amid all the change, it is best to remember that flexibility allows one to stretch rather than shrink, and proactively welcoming and embracing change is about choosing a better or predetermined future. Furthermore, choosing to be synergistic, while involving everyone in the change management process, can transform a "personal" vision into a "professional" vision for everyone in the department or the organization.

Chapter Seven

STRESS MANAGEMENT STRATEGIES

Change can bring about an invisible pandemic known as stress. Major and continuous change can create a strong culture, where core values are intensely held and widely shared, where a high level of stress is the norm. Today's rate of change has been much greater than the past; yet, this is perhaps an initial start compared to the changes for tomorrow. Just look at the population growth which, for the first time ever in recorded history, reached one billion in the 1860's. In the 1930's, the population doubled to two billion, and then it doubled again in 1975 to four billion people. As of 2006, there are over six billion individuals on earth that within a decade should pass seven billion, despite the fact that many couples in developing nations are having fewer children. In the early 1980s, people did not have personal computers; yet, many professionals today cannot effectively do their jobs without a computer and access to email or the Internet. Pritchett and Pound, in their booklet entitled *"A Survival Guide to the Stress of Organizational Change,"* suggest that people should accommodate change, align their behaviors with it, and use it to their advantage instead of seeing it as an enemy. Pritchett and Pound suggest that in today's rate of change, sometimes one just has to "give up" or surrender to the change; another option would be to simply "toughen up" by developing higher levels of tolerance for adapting to change; and yet at other times, one has to "wise up" by not allowing self induced stress to take over one's life.

Stress management is about being healthy and happy. With regards to happiness, Mahatma Gandhi states that "Happiness is when what you think, what you say, and what you do are in harmony." This relates to the consistency of what goes in one's heart, mind, and daily habits. Such a consistency can be best achieved when one's purpose and mission in life are clear. Dr. Viktor Frankl, a psychologist, states that "Everyone has his own specific vocation or mission in life; everyone must carry out a concrete assignment that demands fulfillment. Therein he cannot be replaced, nor can his life be repeated, thus, everyone's task is unique as his specific opportunity to implement it."

For effective management of stress, one should work on building good rapport with one's colleagues and surroundings by adapting to changes that cannot be altered. Kevin Hogan, speaker and author, is reported to have said that "Building rapport begins with you. The entire process of building rapport is built on the foundation of concern, caring, compassion, interest, and a desire for the well-being of your customer." Besides having a good rapport with others, one must learn to "play." Brian Sutton, professor of education, states that "The opposite of play isn't work. It's depression. To play is to act out and be willful and committed as if one is assured of one's prospects." Good rapport with others and having fun at work can go along way in creating happiness and success. It has been said by Orison Swett Marden, author, that, "The greatest thing a man can do in this world is to make the most possible out of the stuff that has been given him. This is success, and there is no other." It should be noted that success and happiness do not come from perfection, but rather action. Ralph Marston, author, said "Hold yourself to a high standard, to be sure. But don't let that stop you. Though perfection is a worthy aim, there's plenty of good you can accomplish before you get there."Anne Frank, diarist, said "How wonderful it is that nobody need wait a single moment before starting to improve the world." One must remember that "It's not the load that breaks you down, it's the way you carry it," as stated by Lena Horne, singer and actress.

Dr. Randi Sims, professor of stress management at Nova Southeastern University mentions that "Since it is neither possible nor advantageous to prevent or avoid all stress, control or management of stress becomes the key to success." Perhaps it is true that "the absence of stress is death." According to Sims (2005), the first step in effectively managing stress is recognizing that there is excessive stress in one's personal or professional life, or both. The first step requires one to recognize the typical symptoms associated with stress, while linking the causes with the consequences. In general, the typical symptoms of excessive stress can be physical, psychological, behavioral, or any combination of these or other such illnesses. The second step, after recognizing the symptoms, is to begin to look for the causes. Of course, the fact is that some stress cannot be avoided or controlled. As such, its awareness, proper planning, and balancing one's important goals can help in managing it. It is best to remember that stress can come from how one interprets an event or person, and not necessarily from that event or person directly. The effective management and control of stress is the final step or objective of an effective stress management program. Sims (2005) recommends that "The individual differences between people must be taken into account when planning a stress management program." Sims further states that the best way to know if a person will be comfortable with a stress management technique is to try it. While using a particular technique just one time will not always provide the maximum benefit possible, a person will be able to tell if he or she would be comfortable in giving the technique an opportunity for long-term stress management. According to Sims, once a specific technique has been used repeatedly for stress management, the individual begins to experience the benefits of it more quickly. Once a person becomes an expert at one to two techniques, he or she will begin to feel relaxed just by getting ready to initiate the technique (Sims, 2005).

Working Hard: Why?

Are you working too hard to get more money, to do a really good job, to gain more power, to get a promotion, to be one of the "in-group" members, to have insurance, to have prestige, or to simply feel good? You probably work for many reasons that are personal to you and because you enjoy it. Sometimes people work a bit too much and a bit too hard, and the best way to manage stress is to balance one's personal and professional activities. Davidson (1997) offers ten ways to know when you have been working too hard; see if any of them apply to you:

1. You have become good pals with the nightly cleaning crew and the security guards.
2. You think "Ross Perot," and "Bin Laden' are new types of beverages to be served with evening meals.
3. You and your PC have become "one."
4. You have filed for an extension to complete your taxes for the third year in a row.
5. You think *Dead Man Working* refers to poltergeists.
6. You have equipment in your office that you have never used, and you can't recall what it does.
7. You have installed a cot in your office and keep forgetting to bring in a pillow, so you roll up your jacket.
8. The word "vacation" has no meaning to you.
9. You missed a gala awards dinner at a splashy hotel, in your honor, paid for by your company.
10. You got lost on the way home last night.

If the above items closely apply to some aspects of your life, then you have been working too hard and need to take time for reflection and prioritization. You need to schedule this time for reflection as your time is probably already booked up and things are not going to get better unless there is a conscious intervention. If you want a change and different results, then you must begin doing things differently.

The future promises greater rates of changes with higher levels of complexity which can bring about more stress, when not managed properly. In many cases, the rate of change cannot be changed, but one's behavior can be managed appropriately to effectively deal with unforeseen events, thereby reducing stress. Stress, the invisible pandemic, is neither good nor bad by itself when balanced. There is good stress (*Eustress*), such as the tension caused by marriage or graduation; and there is bad stress (*Distress*), such as those that are brought upon one by organizational politics, inconsistent or unrealistic demands, and the abuse of one's power or status. Too much stress can make one unproductive or sick at best, and it can cause death at worst. There are many variables that cause stress. Stress causing factors can include, but are not limited to: being attacked or blamed for something one did not do; the control of information when one needs it; the formation of coalitions against one's change initiatives; having too many obligations; mismanaging impressions; and dealing with too many organizational politics. Organizational politics represent attempts to influence others using discretionary behaviors to promote personal objectives. Of course, organizational politics can be good or bad. Problems with organizational politics are that it is often the most common reason for decision-making delays, inefficiency, and "backbiting." It is estimated that business leaders spend nearly one-fifth of their time dealing with organizational politics (McShane, 2003). McShane states that employees who experience high levels of organizational politics tend to report higher stress, psychological withdrawal, and turnover.

Power, which is the capacity of a person, team, or organization to influence others, is often associated with organizational politics. Ineffective use of power creates stress in the workplace. There are many forms of power and people can use them to get what they want or to delay the progress of work done by others. There are legitimate, reward, coercive, expert, referent, information, and connection forms of power that can effectively or ineffectively be used. According to Hersey (2004),

McShane (2003), Robbins (2001), and other authors, the common forms and definitions of power are as follows:

- Legitimate power is an agreement among organizational members that people in certain roles can request certain behaviors of others.
- Reward power is derived from the person's ability to control the allocation of rewards valued by others and to remove negative sanctions.
- Coercive power is the ability to apply punishment.
- Expert power originates from within the person.
- Referent power is when people have others identify with them, like them, or otherwise respect them.
- Information and connection power relates to having access to specific "know-how" for tasks or networks. In such cases, power is about control over the flow and interpretation of information given to others. Through impression management, one can develop a "perceived" ability to effectively cope with organizational uncertainties as a result of his/her connections or access to information.

Power is not a bad thing. However, the purpose of its use and how power is used can determine if it is a good thing or a bad thing. Unfortunately, many people tend to use power to get their way with employees through a command and control system or culture. This type of an organizational culture can create much unneeded stress for employees, colleagues, and customers. Medical professionals estimate that over 70% of all medical complaints are likely to be stress-related (The Stress Management Handbook, 1995). The most common stressed-related illnesses seem to be insomnia or sleep disorders, sexual dysfunction, vomiting or indigestion, ulcers, diarrhea, headaches, muscle aches, high blood pressure, heart attacks, strokes, chronic illness (flu, colds, sweating), hives, and others. Of course, such illnesses and their symptoms can lead to lost workdays, lost productivity, accidents, injuries, and lost customers for modern organizations. Continuous and ongoing stress, or its symptoms, can include isolation from family and friends, abuse of illegal drugs or alcohol, smoking, depression, anxiety, irritability, rapid mood swings, compulsive eating or dieting, spouse or child abuse, and increased conflict in the workplace. Stress can impact one's personal or home life, work life, and financial life, thereby overwhelming a person. As such, it is important to understand stress and determine what one needs to do to manage it effectively or at least have control over it.

Stress: What Is It?

The stress people experience today is much more intense than what was experienced by previous generations of the workforce. According to the *Stress Management Handbook,* 1995, stress which is a reaction to change is the body's mental, emotional, and physiological response to anxiety-producing events and situations. According to "*Conquering Stress,*" a little book by KRS Edstrom (1993), less stress equals more success in whatever one does. Stress is basically what one thinks it is and what one perceives it to be. Stress is the epidemic of twenty-first century's hectic work life. While stress has been around since the days of Adam and Eve, the increased emphasis on stress is due to the fact that too much of it can cause major physical, psychological, and behavioral illnesses. One must learn to proactively fight stress, flee it, and "flow" with it, in order to effectively deal with the changes that cause stress. Nearly 75% of Americans describe their jobs as successful and 34% have considered quitting their jobs due to high levels of stress (Edstrom, 1993). Research shows that 90% of workers tend to experience high levels of stress at least once each week and over 75% of all visits to primary-care physicians are stress-related disorders (Edstrom, 1993). Over 112 million Americans take medications for stress-related illnesses and symptoms. Stress costs American employers over $200 billion each year in absenteeism, lost productivity, accidents, and medical insurance; and over 60% of industrial accidents are incurred by extreme levels of perceived stress (Edstrom, 1993). It is extremely important that change agents and global employees learn effective means of conquering stress and managing it before it leads to any type of illness, absenteeism, loss of productivity, accidents, or mental problems.

Stress, an unavoidable consequence of life, occurs at all levels in organizations as a result of many factors including time pressures, personnel conflicts, and the quantity of work expected to be completed at a given time. According to Stephen Robbins (2001), *stress* is a dynamic condition where one is confronted with either an opportunity, constraint, or a demand for which the outcome is perceived to be uncertain and important. These dynamic conditions, when not managed effectively, can lead to physiological, psychological, and behavioral symptoms. Hans Selye, known as the Father of Stress Management, said that stress is the wear and tear on the body that occurs in daily life; more specifically, stress is "the nonspecific response of the body to any demand made upon it" (*The Stress of Life*, 1976). The word "nonspecific" implies that everyone responds differently to stress at different stages of his or her life. The body goes through many changes when under stress, including physical changes. Originally, these physical changes served to protect early humans against environmental stressors: "the fight or flight syndrome."

The Fight or Flight Syndrome. The "fight or flight syndrome" is credited to Walter Cannon who taught that when faced with an enemy in the environment, animals and early humans had to muster their strength to do one of two things: run away or stand and fight. Therefore, the body's physical reactions during stress help prepare people for fight or flight. Some of the most common physical changes are as follows: increased heart rate, increased respiration rate, increased skin perspiration, increased dilation of the pupils, increased blood pressure, increased muscle strength, decreased gastric functioning, decreased abdominal and surface blood flow, and increased secretion of adrenaline. Unfortunately, today, people cannot always fight or run away, so the chemical reactions of the body to stress make people sick instead.

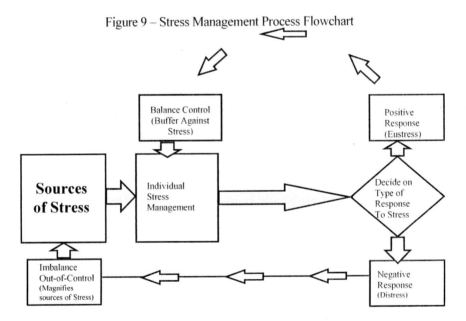

Figure 9 – Stress Management Process Flowchart

The General Adaptation Syndrome (GAS). Hans Selye proposed that stress goes through three stages that together make up the General Adaptation Syndrome. *Stage one* is the alarm stage. At this point, the stressor has just been recognized and the body has become mobilized for fight or flight. The body's homeostasis (normal balance) is disrupted and internal organs become ready for action. *Stage two*, the resistance stage, is the longest stage of the GAS. It begins when the body is persistently exposed to the stressor. The body struggles to resist the alarm reactions and to return to a homeostatic stage. *Stage three,* the exhaustion stage, occurs if stress continues longer than the body can resist. At this stage organ systems break down. The body can no longer adapt to the stress load placed on it; and the result of the exhaustion stage is a disease of adaptation such as ulcers or cardiovascular disease.

As demonstrated by the Stress Management Process Flowchart, in Figure 9, individuals can choose their responses to stress by balancing their life responsibilities, obligations, and pace. According to estimates, about 50-80 percent of all physical diseases tend to be stress-related. Stress is believed to be a principal cause of many cardiovascular diseases, perhaps the number one killer in "workaholic" cultures (for example, in the United States of America). It also may be a main contributing factor to the development of cancer, the number two killer in the United States. Also, stress can place one at higher risk for diabetes, ulcers, asthma, migraine headaches, skin disorders, epilepsy, and sexual dysfunction. Each of these diseases, and a host of others, can be psychosomatic in nature; that is, it is initially either caused or exacerbated by mental conditions such as stress.

Subjective effects of stress include feelings of anxiety, aggression, frustration, guilt, or shame. Individuals are also apt to feel irritable, moody, tired, tense, nervous, or lonely.

Behavioral effects of stress represent readily visible changes in a person's behavior. Among these effects are things such as increased accidents, use of illegal drugs or alcohol, outlandish or argumentative behavior, laughter out of context, very excitable moods, and/or eating to excess.

Cognitive effects refer to diminished mental ability, and may include such effects as impaired judgment, rash decisions, forgetfulness and/or hypersensitivity to criticism.

Organizational effects take the form of absenteeism, diminished productivity, high turnover, poor relations with workers, and/or general job dissatisfaction. Stress wreaks havoc on organizational productivity. Highly stressed employees, based on personal experience, seem to have more frequent accidents, are often irritable, and are unable to cope with daily situations.

Another organizational consequence that has received much interest is corporate liability for employees whose illness is linked to job stress. Some people are suing and winning legal cases where work-related stressors cause burnout. Burnout is the work-related equivalent of a nervous breakdown. The burned-out employee has succumbed to long, continuous stress and is no longer able to function at a reasonable level of effectiveness. Where does all this stress come from? One can divide general causes of stress into at least three categories: environmental, personal, and sudden stressors. *Environmental* stressors include conditions in the environment that cause mental or physical stress. These conditions include noise, pollution, temperature, diet, toxins, and drugs. *Personal* stressors include factors, such as family or financial problems, as well as amounts of change with which a person has to cope. *Sudden* stressors refer to intense stimuli, such as narrowly averting an automobile accident, or the surge of nervous energy felt when someone startles or scares one unexpectedly.

Pritchett and Pound, in the booklet entitled "*A Survival Guide to the Stress of Organizational Change*," highlight many of the destructive behaviors that people must abandon if they are to manage change without being too stressed. Pritchett and Pound mention 15 common mistakes and assumptions people make and they are as follows:

1. Expect someone else to reduce one's stress.
2. Decide not to change.
3. Act like a victim.
4. Try to play a new game by the old rules.
5. Shoot for a low-stress work setting.
6. Try to control the uncontrollable.
7. Choose your own pace of change.
8. Fail to abandon the expendable.
9. Slow down.
10. Be afraid of the future.
11. Pick the wrong battles.
12. Psychologically unplug from the job.
13. Avoid new assignments.
14. Try to eliminate uncertainty and instability.
15. Assume that "caring management" would or should keep employees comfortable.

Of course, the above assumptions are common mistakes that professionals in the twenty-first century environment should avoid if they are to reduce the level of stress and change with the times. As mentioned by Pritchett and Pound, as well as other experts, there are numerous forces driving major changes that impact people's day-to-day activities; and the major forces seem to be people, technology, information, innovation, and globalization. Instead of making the wrong assumptions in this new economy, it is perhaps more productive to surrender to upcoming changes by aligning one's behavior and expectations with it, while using the changes to one's advantage. Pritchett and Pound, in the survival guide, suggest to everyone that one not should expect others to come along and relieve one's stress. Instead, today's professionals should put themselves in charge of managing the dynamic pressure since they are probably the best persons in their lives who will be able to do much to lighten their psychological load. When you seem to be going against the tides or against the whole world, just think of what Robert Orben said: "Sometimes I get the feeling that the whole world is against me, but deep down I know that is not true as some of the smaller countries are neutral."

Stress Management Techniques

Choices of personal stress management techniques depend on the individual's personality. Four of the most popular techniques, are time management, physical exercise, biofeedback, and meditation. *Time management* helps one control stress by better organizing time and setting priorities. *Physical exercise* is an appropriate substitute for the fight or flight response of long ago. It provides a physical release for the chemical reactions caused by stress. Exercise not only "burns off" the physical effects of stress but also strengthens the body's organ systems to be better able to withstand stress. *Biofeedback* refers to a number of techniques that give concrete feedback to the individual regarding bodily functions such as pulse rate, blood pressure, body temperature, and muscle tension. By being cognizant of these physical phenomena, one can learn to control them, thus bringing the body to a more relaxed state. *Meditation* encompasses a variety of mental exercises that focus one's attention on something other than daily thoughts. Regardless of the type of meditation, it is remarkably useful in lessening one's sensory reactivity and in quieting the stress response. Best of all, when practiced with some regularity, meditation has a carryover effect; that is, it lowers one's normal reactivity even when not actively meditating.

There are at least three different organizational stress management strategies. Job redesign strategies start with an effort to determine what is causing job stress and then proceed to change the job so as to relieve this stress. Overload is often found to be a chief contributor. In this case supervisors may follow one of several strategies. Jobs can be redesigned in such a way that less coordination of effort is needed and thus less information processing is required. Alternately, supervisors could identify liaisons who are responsible for coordination efforts, and improve management information systems to provide what is needed at the appropriate time. In other cases jobs may be frustrating because of lack of decision-making authority. Traditional job enrichment approaches can work well because they give workers increased responsibility for decisions in their work area.

Environmental reengineering focuses on changing the physical environment by reducing stressors such as lighting, temperature, noise, vibration, and toxins. Supervisors might adopt one of two strategies for dealing with these stressors.

1. The first concentrates on protecting the workers from the negative consequences of the stressors: workers are required to wear goggles, earplugs, or masks. This strategy is often resisted by some workers due to habit patterns and must be firmly enforced by the supervisor.

2. The second strategy focuses on lessening the negative environmental stressors by reducing noise, improving lighting, and lessening the exposure to toxins. This latter choice is far more acceptable as a stress reducing alternative, but it rests largely on a company's economic analysis of costs and benefits. Managers follow this alternative whenever possible instead of waiting for court settlements that force companies into compliance.

Of all corporate stress management efforts, wellness programs have been receiving the most attention in recent years. Corporate wellness is part of the trend to be concerned about the total human being. Programs vary from companies that shuttle employees back and forth to a local health spa during lunch hour, to those that install their own health spa facilities complete with nutritional experts and meditation rooms.

Type A Behavior

Friedman and Rosenman, cardiologists, provided the famous profile of a high stress individual known as a Type A Personality. This behavior pattern is highly correlated to coronary heart disease and is typified by such characteristics as:

1. Always moving, walking, and/or eating rapidly.
2. Feeling impatient with anyone who is moving "slowly," or not talking about something of interest to him / her.
3. Indulging in polyphasic activity--that is, doing two or three things at the same time.
4. Feeling unable to relax or abstain from working.
5. Trying to accomplish more and more things in less and less time.

The Type A person is in a constant race against time, the stereotypical "workaholic." People of this personality type can cause stress not only for themselves, but also for those around them. Friedman and Rosenman described the Type B personality as a low stress individual with varied interests, and a relaxed but active approach to life. Spera and Lanto (1997) provided the following description of Type A and Type B personalities.

TYPE A's	TYPE B's
Always in a hurry	Seldom in a hurry
Does several things at once	Does one thing at a time
Speaks, walks, and gestures rapidly and forcefully	Speaks, walks, and gestures slowly and calmly
Works late, brings work home	Works regular hours
Likes things clear-cut	Can tolerate ambiguity
Listens impatiently	Listens patiently
Easily angered	Slow to anger
Hard-driving, aggressive	Easygoing, nonassertive
Competitive, striving	Noncompetitive, satisfied
Expresses feelings easily	Tends to bottle feelings up
Restless, unable to relax	Enjoys relaxing, doing nothing

Should everyone strive to be a Type B? Not necessarily. Some Type A personalities seem to thrive on a hectic pace and actually feel invigorated by the pressure of time urgency. New evidence seems to indicate a difference between coronary-prone Type A's and their healthier cohorts. Those who combine their Type A tendencies with hostility and anger seem to be the most likely to suffer serious health problems. Overall, an individual's response to stress is not predetermined by his or her gender, personality type or body size. The reality is that most people are a blend of both types of personalities and respond differently to similar circumstance at different stages of their lives. To determine your tendencies toward Type A or Type B personalities, take the Glazer-Stress Control Life Style Questionnaire at the end of this chapter.

Managing Stress[4]

This mind/body adaptive mechanism due to change which is a constant factor has been labeled stress. Our reactions to stress, however, are unique to each individual. Also when good interesting things happen to us - promotion on the job, increase in the quality of one's life, challenging work, new love, travel, good food and wine, spiritual peace; positive interpersonal relationships, good friends – cause adaptative reactions of this mind/body continuum as well. The remarkable factor is that whether good or bad, the body reacts the same physiologically. Change, therefore, can bring about an invisible pandemic known as stress. Continuous and major change can create a strong culture, where core values are intensely held and shared, and where high levels of continuous, mind/body adaptation is the norm.

In order to understand how to manage stress, one has to understand what stress is. We are fortunate that the development of theories, concepts and management techniques have evolved into a remarkable plethora of research results allowing anyone to not only understand the process, but to be stress management specific! It is also important to become acquainted with other concepts of human behavior because as Hans Seyle stated in 1956, *"Life without stress is death."* The methodology has to be holistic with approaches that understand mind-body connections.

The concept of stress has its history in the early experiments and writings of Cannon, Seyle, Freidman & Rosenman, Wolff & Wolff, Benson, Holmes & Ras, Oixfeill, Eysenck and Lazarus to name a few. The earliest pioneers, Seyle and Cannon, provided the basic framework for the evolving understanding of the stress response as later researchers pursued their specialties. Hans Seyle was an endocrinologist who was able to study the body's reaction to various stimuli. Although he experimented with rats in the laboratory, he saw many patients in hospital in which he could not find a specific cause for their illness, virus, germs, etc. to determine a diagnosis; he eventually labeled them as suffering from a "syndrome of being sick." It is alleged that Seyle was having an after dinner drink at the

---

[4] - This is material is co-authored with Timothy McCartney, Nova Southeastern University

home of a friend who was an engineer. His friend was working and calculating the stress and strain of certain metals as important information for the construction of bridges throughout Canada. Seyle likened this to the human body as it responds to the many stresses and strains of their internal and external environments. It is at this time that the term stress was used to describe Seyle's idea of the human body as reacting to stress in a three phase process which he called the General Adaptation Syndrome (G.A.S.).

1. Phase I is the *alarm* phase: The body's first reaction to a stressor. This phase is comparable to Cannons' "fight or flight syndrome."
2. Phase II is the *reaction* phase: When the stressor is continuous the body reaches a "plateau" and resistance rises above normal.
3. Phase III is the *exhaustion* phase: When the stressor persists for a long time and the adaptation energy is exhausted; manifestations of physical and/or emotional illnesses and sometimes death appears.

Seyle (1974) also describes positive, energizing stress, as *eustress* and negative non-motivating stress as *distresss*. The interesting phenomenon is that both are experienced the same physiologically. The first definitive research on stress was done by Walter B. Cannon, a well known physiologist from Harvard Medical School. He was the first to describe in detail the body's reaction to stress. Cannon experimented initially with cats and the kinds of manipulations he did to them would be condemned today by the society for the preventions of cruelty to animals. Cannon (1932) indicated that a reaction to stress could elicit either a confrontation (attack) on the stressor; running away from it or being in such a state of shock that one becomes immobilized. He proved that the body prepares itself by attempting to get as much energy as possible to the muscular-skeletal system in order to fight or run away. He called this reaction the "fight or flight syndrome." The body systems that are associated with strength and energy speed up their activity; those that are not involved slow down or shut down. There are also "surface reactions" like perspiration, pupil dilation and pilo-erection. These two pioneering researchers paved the way for experiments in the U.S.A., England, Germany, Japan, and other parts of the world. Some experts have focused on other causes and reactions to stress, stressors, physiological and emotional responses, mind-body connections, and stress and disease. There explorations have attempted to find effective methods to manage stress and to possibly resurrect some of ancient methods for stress management, i.e. prayer, yoga, meditation, and hypnosis as being effective.

Understanding and Managing both Good and Bad Stress

Stress has many meanings to different people. It also depends on what aspect of stress that a researcher is organizing their focus. Simply, anything to which the body has to react to or adapt to can be termed stress. Seyle's description of stress is still valid in that eustress describes the good or positive things that happen. *Eustress* is motivating and can initiate creativity and positive mental attitudes. *Distress* describes negative de-motivating stress that can oftentimes place an individual in a situation of inactivity or inertia.

There are, inevitably hundreds of definitions that can be found in the literature. The most common may be that it is defined as a response or as a stimulus. It would appear that the most popular accepted concept of stress is that there is a stressor(s) (which can be anything) that triggers off or has a response to (stress) either Eustress or Distress.

Research over the years has established this fact: The body and mind are consistently adjusting to balance and equilibration. *Homeostasis*, the term used for physiological "balance," and *equilibration*, the term used to indicate emotional balance, must be maintained. Any change or threat to equilibrium can be either eustress or distress. This is a psychosomatic response reaction. Some examples of this would be, learning of the accidental death of a spouse; being fired from a job; and being diagnosed with cancer. The term originates from the Greek word "psyche" meaning (mind/soul) and 'soma' meaning body. On the other hand:

1. The body/mind are in states of homeostasis and equilibration.
2. There is a stressor (s) trauma to the body which destabilizes mind and body.
3. The effect of the destabilization, if continued, causes mental/emotional states. That is, the body's adaptative processes, affect one's mental state.

This is a psycho-somatic reaction and must be understood in the context that the physiological state of the body triggers off, through the evaluative processes of the mind, emotional states that are either eustress or distress. One example is having a mastectomy for breast cancer. The depression caused by having cancer, the self-esteem concept after a mastectomy and the constant worry as to whether cancer would come back, can trigger off a distress response. It should be noted that these are real body/mind states. They are not imaginations or delusions. When an individual experiences for no known reason, illnesses, and is constantly imagining a disease, taking lots of medication, and complaining all of the time about one's health, may be described as a hypochondrical reaction. The person is usually labeled as a hypochondriac. This reaction is in the mind. Stress, therefore, develops when the pressures and demands in one's life exceed one's ability to cope (distress). When the individual is motivated, creative, and finds balance in the three major environments in which they function, the stress becomes eustress.

Stress has been around from the inception of the beginning of life and even though stressors change with every year and stage of human development, much more is known about this process. More than 200 million Americans take medication for stress-related illnesses and symptoms. American organizations are losing more than $ 200 billion each year in workplace accidents, absenteeism, drug abuse, violence, medical insurance, and productivity (Edstronm, 1993). To summarize what we now know about stress (eustress and distress), the following should be noted:

1. Stress is a neuro-endocrine process that affects the metabolism of the body and has an input on every system of the body. Nervous System, Immune System, Cardiovascular System, Digestive System, the Skin and the Muscular-Skeletal System.

2. A stressor is a stimulus that 'triggers off' the "fight or flight" response which is comparable to Seyle's Alarm state. Stressors can be physiological, biological, psycho-social, external and/or internal.

3. Psycho-somatic disease is real. It is not just "in the mind" (which is a hypochondrical reaction). It involves the mind and the body.

4. Stress related diseases include migraine headaches, backaches, asthma attacks, some cancers, allergies, stroke, coronary heart disease, hypertensions, tension headaches, and neck and shoulder pains.

5. Distress, especially chronic distress, tends to make your immune system more susceptible to colds, infections, inflammations, lupus, some cancers, and allergic reactions.

6. Stress begins with life situations that become very difficult to understand and which overwhelms individuals in any of the three environments in which humans primarily function (intimate, workplace and leisure).

7. After years of research and the understanding of mind/body processes, stress management techniques are "management-specific."

8. Work related stressors and those internal and external factors that impact employer and employees in organizations have been

identified. Stress management techniques can restore health and improve productivity.

9. Knowledge, techniques and practice allows for the proper control and well being of the individual as distress can be transformed into eustress.

Thus far, we have defined and described stress as being an adaptative reaction to a stimulus which holistically effects the individual at emotional, mental, neurological, biochemical, and physical levels at any given instant of time. Job and workplace stress have their own peculiarities. The individual reacts to workplace stressors in a manner by which his/her individual characteristics (e.g. personality traits, anxiety levels, and behavior patterns) deal with organizational and extra organized sources of stress (stressors). We have also examined the expensive "fall out" of job and workplace stress in absenteeism, drug and alcohol abuse, poor decision making, hospitalizations, rising health benefit costs, violence, burnout, negative interpersonal relationships, and decreased productivity. Stress management experts provide managers and supervisors with information that can be useful in prevention, intervention and employee assistance advice. Researchers state that "Stress prevention and management strategies include (1) making person-environment fit (2) organizational programs such as employee assistance and wellness (3) individual approaches such as cognitive techniques, relaxation training, meditation and feedback."

Job-related stress is of particular concern to the study of change and stress management. Some jobs are more stress-producing than others. For instance, air traffic controllers, who face the daily pressures of protecting the lives of thousands of people, have an occupation that is considered highly stressful. Although this is one example, every job has potential stressors. Some of the most common stressors for the 21st century's global employees and managers are as follows:

1. *Information load.* Whether individuals are overloaded or under-loaded, they are likely to experience stress. The under-loaded individual is apathetic and bored from being cut off from necessary communication, whereas the overloaded employee feels harried and frantic. In either case absenteeism and turnover increase, and productivity decreases.

2. *Role ambiguity.* Whenever employees are not sure what their job is or the way it relates to other jobs in the organization, role ambiguity occurs. This in turn leads to confusion, lack of focus, and stress.

3. *Role conflict.* Stress occurs when various people seem to be expecting different things from a person. Supervisors are particularly susceptible to role conflict because both management and their subordinates often look to them as their representative. As they try to satisfy everyone's expectations, they often experience considerable personal stress.

4. *Occupational change.* Whenever the work environment changes, stress is inevitable. All change brings some uncertainty with it, and uncertainty interferes with one's mental and physical homeostasis.

5. *Stress carriers.* Employees are often brought into contact with Type A persons, who force stress upon them. The grumpy boss, the forgetful secretary, and the complaining major customer are stress carriers.

6. *Physical environment.* Noise, lighting, uncomfortable furniture, and temperature are examples of physical surroundings that can produce stress.

Verspeji (1989) researched several American organizations to determine the kinds of stressors that impact organizations' personnel, externally as well as internally. Verspeji found the following as the frequent causes of stress:

1. High Technology Helpers. The rapid change of computer/information technology initially initiate the stressor of change and doubts as to whether one would be able to functionally operate the technology, computer breakdown, jammed fax machines, new systems, etc. all contribute to this factor.

2. Supervisory Problems dealing with Alcohol or Drug Abuse by employees. The "bizarre" behaviors and rapid mood changes of drug abusers pose managerial understanding and control difficulties in the workplace.

3. Supervisory Malfunction. It is common in these modern times for supervisors to have undergraduate and/or graduate degrees. Yet, many supervisors have no insight into their proper behavior and have difficulty in supervising, causing frustration, sabotage, de-motivation, and job change.

4. Quotas, Deadlines and Reduced Staff Levels to Complete Job. Downsizing appears to have had more negative affects on organizations especially in job insecurity, non-loyalty and morale.

5. Work Environment. Social diversity issues, temperature, obsolete equipment, noise, toxic chemicals, etc.

6. Limited Workplace Privacy. The lack of adequate personal space gives rise to claustrophobia, monitoring of phone calls, contents of letters, and confidentiality.
7. Job Insecurity. Increasing mergers and takeovers; acquisitions; downsizing.
8. Corporate Policies on Smoking, AIDS, Drug Testing. All of the above are prominent stressors.
9. Overload. Lots of work and not enough time to do it. The fears of not keeping up, and having to take work home are stressor factors.
10. "Two Places at Once" Syndrome. The ability of trying to balance work and family appears to affect women more than men. It is reasonable to assume that many frustrations are displaced in either of these two environments (intimate and workplace) and can also negatively affect one's leisure environment as well, especially with alcohol or drug abuse as compensatory factors.

According to experts, "The distinction between work and non-work is blurred, overlaps, and is significant in any decision's analysis of stress" (Gibson, Invancekich, Donelly, Konopaske, 2005). Job and work stress have widespread implications as well as having to pinpoint the specific stressors and analyze individual characteristics. The work environment itself, may pose difficulties with toxic chemicals, dust, social density issues temperature variations, dangerous tasks, high noise levels, poor lighting, and unpleasant odors. All of these can lead to emotional as well as physical difficulties. Group and organizational stressors may include organizational politics, organizational culture, and intra and inter group relationships, downsizing, lack of performance feedback, sexual harassment, promotion challenges, and inadequate career development difficulties. Non-Job stressors are those caused by factors outside of the organization that have impact on the individuals' performance and productivity. Some practical observations and advice for managers and supervisors are as follows:

1. Realize that what is a stressor for one employee may not be a stressor for another.
2. Be on the lookout for burnout. Employees who are over zealous, workaholic and are always helping others as part of their job may exhibit signs of frequent depressive bouts, constant self-denigration, being emotionally exhausted, frequent visits to doctors, and perfectionist behavior.

3. When "out of character" employees are having interpersonal problems with fellow employees, customers, clients and management may be increasing levels of distress.
4. Management should have in place employee assistance programs that are readily available with the highest standards of confidentiality.
5. The organizations' physical plant should be as "stressor free" as possible with areas for relaxation, adequate temperature control, quick reaction-time to technological/physical problems, and attention to noise levels.
6. Individuals should try to be consistently positive in the three environments in which they function. A good balance between intimate, workplace and leisure environments cause less negative displacement consistency and equilibrium.
7. Practice effective interpersonal skills especially communication and problem-solving.
8. Learn how to set limits which prevents overload. Also learn how to say "No"!
9. Watch your emotional pressure points.
10. Don't waste time feeling guilty about what doesn't get done.
11. Try to enjoy whatever you are doing.
12. Don't sweat the small stuff. Change the way you evaluate situations. Remember it is how we analyze, evaluate or perceive situations that initiate our emotional responses.
13. Work smarter rather than harder.
14. Don't get involved in routine detail that should be delegated.
15. Attempt to "clean up your act." Avoid a general lack of self-discipline, personal disorganization, cluttered environments (desk, rooms, etc.).
16. Practice being an optimist and build on successes.

According to Greenberg, the ideal goal is to quantitatively reduce the amount of distress that we experience and to qualitatively change it into eustress. An optimal amount of stress is healthy and growth promoting.

Time Management Suggestions

The suggestions on managing activities in the allotted time are extremely valuable regarding the age-old business issue of time management. This section provides a few suggestions for time management, but the next chapter provides a comprehensive coverage of time management principles and goal prioritization based on one's mission and purpose in life. More than ever, application of such fundamental techniques during critical times at organizations will drive one's success and increase value for one's department and colleagues. Without steps to cultivate and maintain good work habits, time-management efforts will be defeated. The following tips may help one stay on track:

Conquer the clutter. Schedule 10 to 15 minutes each week to clear your work area of junk mail, old papers, and other accumulated clutter. Keep cleaning supplies handy so you can take advantage of the odd free moment to police your workspace.

Defuse distractions. Little distractions can add up to a major drain on productivity. If you are spending too much time on the phone, keep an egg timer at your desk and hold calls to a reasonable limit. Learn how to terminate calls politely. If co-workers often drop in to chat, close your door. If you are constantly walking around obstacles, consider a change of floor plan. Take steps to reduce distracting noise.

Know thyself. Rivers cannot be forced to flow uphill; nor should you try to work against your inner nature. Schedule the toughest work for your circadian period of peak productivity. Minimize the impact of sub-optimal climate control with a fan or small heater. Perhaps better or different lighting would boost your efficiency.

Eliminate redundancy. Analyze every process you use to determine if any steps can be eliminated. Common problems include multiple signatures for approval, extra steps designed to circumvent systems or correct problems that could be addressed more directly, and generating multiple copies that are no longer required.

Group and separate. Tedious or redundant tasks can be grouped for increased efficiency: file all at once, bill all at once, order all at once. Large, multifaceted tasks, on the other hand, may be best tackled in small pieces. For example, sort that large stack of paperwork on Monday, process some on Tuesday, some on Wednesday, and so forth until it's done. Using this approach, even the most daunting tasks become manageable.

Share the burden. As any quilter knows, many hands make light work, especially when tackling tedious or large tasks. Performance of dreaded chores like the annual inventory can take on a party atmosphere when many are involved and frequent breaks are scheduled. So, ask for help when you need it.

Seize the moment. Most individuals have a tendency to put off minor, less important tasks, and also spend significant chunks of time holding on the phone or waiting in line. Can you see an opportunity here? Make a list of tasks that take 5, 10, or 20 minutes, and keep the materials you need to do these tasks handy. That way, when you are put on hold or stuck in line, you can pull out that small job and finish it up.

Emulate others. Do not try to reinvent the wheel. If someone else always seems to be ahead of the game, watch and learn. If someone else has a speedier way of doing something, copy it. If you are having trouble getting specific jobs done, ask others how they organize and execute the task; perhaps you have overlooked some short cuts.

Make work fun. Introducing a bit of fun into your work will make the day easier for you and your customers. Challenge yourself to process one hundred pieces of paper every day for five days. Have a friendly contest with a co-worker to see who can process the most billing statements in an hour with no mistakes. If possible, flip your morning and afternoon schedules for a change of pace.

The average person spends too much time on many mundane things on daily basis because their urgency-driven world works that way. While that may be true for many of us in different stages of our lives, it is important that we take time to appreciate others and be thankful for what we have in our life. Yesterday is the past; tomorrow is the future and neither of these times can be of much use to one at the present time. However, the time right now is a gift called "present" and we should make the best use of it while we have it because once it is gone, it is gone forever and it becomes part of the past. By focusing on one's priorities and incorporating simple time management strategies, one will be efficient, organized, productive, and less likely to let tasks build up to a crisis level.

Taking Charge of Your Time

Time management skills are important for the reduction of stress in one's professional and personal life. Furthermore, besides experiencing less stress, effective time management can lead to more productivity and better financial returns. Experts continue to state that one's level of stress is, to a large extent, affected by one's priorities, expectations, and coping mechanisms with change. To assess some aspect of your day-to-day activities, answer a "yes" or "no" for the following questions (The Stress Management Handbook, 1995).

1. Are you constantly doing more than one thing at a time?
   Yes___, No___.
2. When traveling, do you feel the travel time is wasted?
   Yes___, No___.

3. Do you get angry when things don't run smoothly?
   Yes___, No___.
4. Do you feel you never get to really finish one thing before moving on to the next?
   Yes___, No___.
5. Are you constantly being told you work too hard?
   Yes___, No___.
6. Do you work more than 10 hours on a work day?
   Yes___, No___.
7. Are you too busy to develop a creative outlet, such as gardening or needlework?
   Yes___, No___.
8. Do you take less than a half-hour for meals or skip them?
   Yes___, No___.
9. Are you too busy to go outside each day for at least a half-hour?
   Yes___, No___.
10. Do you get less than seven hours of sleep at night?
    Yes___, No___.

Add the number of "yes" and "no" answers. If your answers are mostly "yes" to the above questions posed in the Stress Management Handbook, then it is best to closely evaluate and consider some of the time management principles. According to the Stress Management Handbook (1995), if you have mostly "yes" answers, then it is very possible that lack of effective time management and not setting priorities could be a cause for much of your stress. So, begin to focus on what is important and say "no" to what is not important.

Staying Lean and Healthy

Effective time managers will be less stressed because they proactively manage their activities and themselves based on their predetermined and worthwhile goals. Nonetheless, due to deadlines and the fact that sometimes we all take on (or are delegated to by our superiors) more functions than can be handled at one time, stress management techniques can be helpful in maintaining productivity. Enclosed are simple suggestions that can dramatically effect how you operate as an individual or as a team member during hectic (stressful) times in your organization.

Diet. Make an effort to eat more fruit, vegetables, and whole grains as a replacement for some of the high fat snacks and meals. Where you can, avoid the high fat products. It is tough work for your body to process, and it always pulls the energy from your body rather than driving energy into it. Always eat a healthy breakfast. Drink sufficient glasses of water, or only water, and avoid soda. Something else...if needed, drink very little caffeine. If you do drink caffeinated beverages, do so only in the morning. For many, this is one of the toughest goals and you may need to focus on it for a month to create a new habit to a point where it's working. Remember, in order to make a new habit or break a current habit, you must consciously do things differently for about 21 to 30 days consistently. Then the new habit will be formed. Caffeine is a stimulant, so it raises blood pressure, effects thinking, and can stay in the body for about 48 hours. If you are heavy coffee drinker, then get it down to only one or two cups of coffee a day, and try to be done with coffee drinking by about 10:00 a.m.

Sleep. The above suggestion on diet (especially the caffeine part) will definitely impact your ability to be successful with sleeping. During periods of physical, mental, or emotional stress, you must have recovery time, or you'll quickly begin to burn out and become groggy, sluggish, grumpy, and ineffective. For those with kids, especially small children, this can be challenging... but you can develop strategies to work around it, and you will see real results. Ben Franklin was right on..."Early to bed, early to rise, makes us all healthy, wealthy, and wise!"

Exercise. This does not necessarily mean running, aerobics, or weightlifting. Get up and move after sitting for more than two hours. Stretch, breath deeply, take a short walk, use the stairs... but take a few minutes every two hours or so and move to keep the blood flowing and your mind sharp. A friend has been running regularly lately, and it has made a big impact on his attitude and ability to get things done. If you can do it, experts recommend taking a 15-minute walk during lunch hour. If you want to avoid the heat and getting too much sun, then get up early and walk for 30-minutes in the morning. Trust the process on this one...it really does make a huge difference.

Think positively. Have the attitude of "We are almost there... and we have our goals directly in sight." Flush negative or useless things out of your mind, and replace it with positive, forward-looking feelings. The team is in this together, and together everyone will achieve more. Be a believer. It often takes hard work too, but a dedicated believer will always be victorious!

Think teams and team members. Ask for help and help your colleagues as they attempt to become stress-balanced and healthy. Finally, it is no secret that all of these work very closely together as a sure-fire package for success. Look closely... diet, sleep, exercise, a positive attitude... it's so simple, and it's so within your reach to do! Again, trust the process as the experts would not suggest anything to you that they would not do themselves. During busy workdays, these suggestions require that you commit to believing in yourself and what you stand for and what you want from your day. Remember, only you can ultimately drive yourself across the finish line.

Weekly Meeting Considerations

Successful problem solvers tend to plan on continuously communicating with their colleagues and team members to keep them informed. Effective communication and keeping everyone informed can greatly reduce the level of stress and uncertainly in the department and within the team. As an example, let us assume that successful problem solvers hold weekly team meetings with their employees and/or management team. In order to have effective weekly team meetings (employee or management meetings), one must first answer this question; what is team management? These ideas and suggestions can work for management and non-management teams alike.

Team management is a process that requires total involvement of all management people (team members) involved in the operation. In order to have this total involvement it is imperative that the management team operates as one cohesive unit. Granted we all, as management people, have our own specialty area, but in terms of team management we must look beyond specialization to the total operation. When one says, look at the total operation, it means take off the "blinders." Many people in management today are guilty of having tunnel vision and are missing some of the things that are going on around them. What we as management people must strive to do is to look at the total picture, take an overview, so to speak, and make our ideas and decisions based on what effect they could have on the total operation and the people involved, not just our own specialization, look at and see the whole picture.

As team managers, change agents must also be open minded to new and different ideas, they must be willing to give and take constructive criticism that will enhance the total operation. Change agents must also be honest with the entire management team as well as with themselves. When you are a team player you cannot be timid or hold back. Your thoughts could be just what the team needs or could be the catalyst to some unsolved opportunity in another area. At the same time, change agents must also realize that their thoughts and ideas may be rejected, so they do not allow hurt feelings to squelch their thought process.

As team players, change agents must also support the rest of the team. Do not be afraid to get involved or ask questions. Always remember that there is no one winner on a team. Either the whole team wins or the whole team loses, and everyone wants to win. This is the reason it is so important that everyone does his or her part to pull together as one and make a productive (management) team. The only way that all this can be achieved is by setting aside time each week for a scheduled (management) team meeting. Having a (management) team meeting will keep every person involved and on track. Use these meetings as tools to give you the winning edge.

Effective weekly (management) team meetings are an absolute necessity in any ongoing operation. As a team manager/leader, one must constantly be in touch with everything that is going on in and around the operation. It is imperative that team leaders are involved and knowledgeable in all areas. Good effective weekly (management) team meetings require everyone to inspect and constantly make adjustments, to always try to improve upon what was done the previous week. Do not become complacent with what has been achieved, know that you can always do better if you give it some time and thought. If we do not look at our performance weekly, how can we be effective? Things could become sloppy and standards could slip. By looking at performance on a weekly basis, the team will stay sharp, strive to improve and will progressively become more effective. Each week, it is imperative to have goals that will relate to an annual or ongoing vision. By having weekly objectives and milestones, it will undoubtedly make it much more realistic to achieve annual goals.

The bottom-line is to be involved, be knowledgeable, and be on top of the operation. Have the facts, know the figures, set short-term goals and objectives, know the long-term goals, plan your work and work your plan, set the example and walk the talk. Then your group will become the team that puts to use and practices effective weekly (management) team meetings in order for the total operation to win! Points to consider for the improvement of your (management) team meetings:

1. Set goals, without them there is no direction.
2. "Ice-breaker" exercises and social gatherings are great ways to introduce new members or new ideas to the team for the first time and to get everyone excited.
3. Invite other management people to your weekly team meetings.
4. Discuss special ongoing projects and draw ideas from your team members' strengths. Ask what they have done in the past and what they have observed throughout their years of employment.

5. Ask each member to discuss or run by with a "non-core" team member the team's ideas and to brainstorm and get new ideas from them about the project and its acceptance/implementation.
6. Management should share their individual strengths with team members (and management). Always be willing to ask team members and managers: is their some way I can help to strengthen your project/operation?

Now is the time to look and make the needed changes jointly with everyone on the team to achieve synergistic results.

Managing Change

The real test of an effective manager, especially these days, is how well he or she copes with personal, professional and cultural change. The rate of change has been increasing rapidly over the last three decades. In 1975, Alvin Toffler wrote a famous book, *Future Shock* which spoke about the ever-increasing rate of change and how the need to cope with so much change actually makes people ill. The father of social psychology, Kurt Lewin, described change as a three step process:

1. *Unfreezing* the old way of doing things. Unless you can show people the benefit of changing, it will be hard to convince them to invest the time and effort required.
2. *Moving* toward the change by introducing new behavior.
3. *Refreezing* new behavior. Unless you stabilize and monitor the changed behavior, people will drift back to the old way of doing things.

Perhaps a fourth step would be to institutionalize the new change, when needed. But why are people so resistant to change anyway? The hardest thing about implementing change is to get through the natural resistance that people have to change. There are several reasons for this phenomenon and habit is one of them.

Habit. It is very easy to just keep doing things the way you've always done them, especially if there seems to be nothing wrong with the results of the old habit. This is the "if it is not broke, why fix it" mentality.

Fear of the unknown. Habit and tradition are comfortable. When people are not sure what will happen if they change the way they do things, resistance sets in.

Fear of losing something. When employees are afraid they may lose a benefit or even a perquisite, they get anxious and dig in their heels against change.

Investment of past resources. When people or even organizations have invested time and resources in the old way of doing things, they are reluctant to change.

Fear of inadequacy. Sometimes employees feel that they are not capable of learning to do things a new way-this is particularly true in matters concerning technology. If they fear they will not be successful, they will try hard not to change.

These are a few of the primary reasons people resist change. How can managers overcome this resistance? Managers should begin by understanding that when they ignore the factors that affect the people involved in the change, the resistance usually accelerates. The traditional methods of dealing with resistance to change are not always effective. These include suppressing resistance through threats, reasoning, or selling the merits of the change; avoiding resistance by ignoring its existence; or lessening resistance by asserting its relative unimportance in comparison to the unanimity of the group. The common denominator of all these strategies is a basic neglect of the resistor's point of view. This is the wrong way to handle change. A positive approach is needed in which the resistor is listened to and dealt with respectfully. First, the need for change should be fully explained to the employees. The manager should not take for granted that the personnel already understand why the change is being introduced. Secondly, employees should be encouraged to participate in this planning-for-change process. By consulting with employees and soliciting their advice and opinions, the manager can encourage and earn their commitment to the change. If this is a major change, it should be introduced in planned, announced stages; this approach minimizes the disruptive potential of change. Third, management should show that it supports the change and talk about its merits, especially those of most interest to the employees. In sum, the key to successfully implementing change is effective communication and involvement of all persons affected by the change.

Creating Value through Effective Relationships

Creating value, through customer and supplier relationships, forms the foundation of relationship management. Recognizing that there have been shifts from traditional modes of marketing towards strategies that are more customer-focused is known as relationship marketing. Strong relationships with customers and suppliers can mean less stress for everyone and better sales. Whereas the traditional marketing role is focused on the product and the transaction, relationship marketing focuses on the customer. Moving

202 | Bahaudin Mujtaba

from an adversarial posture to one of cooperation is emphasized. At core, customers like to buy things – not to be sold things! Relationship marketing involves attracting, maintaining, and expanding relationships with the customer. The idea is to understand the customer and the requirements of the target market so well that the product sells itself.

Peter Drucker, author of many management books in the last sixty years, stated that the basic reason for business is to create and keep customers. Understanding this assumption, relationship marketing usually explores the interplay between the role of the customer and the opportunity costs involved in value oriented retention efforts. Simply stated, it is less costly to keep a customer than to cultivate a new one. There must be effort to keep the existing customers happy while pursuing new opportunities. Customers have been known to be more than critical, and less than appreciative of salespeople that only show up when the leases expire! The cultivation of good relationships leads to cooperation, trust and commitment amongst the stakeholders involved. In any relationship and/or change, all parties must have something to gain, and if any involved party loses, perceived value suffers.

Relationship management for the long term follows nicely, the observations of value driven processes that emphasize the effect any decision has over time. This is true for any relationship with any customer or supplier. The relationship management processes are influenced by many factors, including evolving technology, which can effect and speed communication between customers, vendors, and suppliers. Well-informed parties have much more to offer the relationship…gone are the days of the "information dump" perpetrated by traditional sales strategies (Johnson and Weinstein, 2004). Constant communications and feedback as components of a quality process encourage a better understanding of the needs of the parties involved. Effective communication also tends to level the field a bit evenly and take away perceived bias and advantage to one party.

The available literature on relationship marketing provides a wealth of information on the criteria that go into the determination of quality supplier relationships. The literature covers the synergies that can be derived from quality relationships between vendors and suppliers, and shows that value-oriented choices can pay huge dividends if well planned. Supply chain management is another key topic and is shown to be a strong influence in the development of long-term relationships that occur with customers after the transaction. Of interest are the concepts that illustrate the accommodation and involvement suppliers can have in streamlining the overall process. The end-user customer can benefit in any number of ways including pricing, flexibility, customization, and availability.

As trends drive a more relationship-oriented marketing climate, understanding the customer at all levels is the key. Supplier-vendor relationships as well as vendor-customer relationships must be fully assessed and understood. As business moves to deliver goods and services in a one-on-one mode to the customer, customization and flexibilities need to be considered as part of relationship marketing. Ensuring that outputs from the marketing process not only exceed, but also anticipate customer requirements will drive customer satisfaction and retention. When goods or services are not in line with expectations and the brand and value proposition are not honored; the relationship suffers; thereby causing stress for customers and employees.

Sometimes things do not go very well, and customers' expectations are not met by the organization or its employees. In such moments of truth, employees can use the CALM (Cool, Apologize, Listen, and Make it right) approach to make sure the customer is taken care of effectively for retention purposes:

- Stay Cool.
- Apologize for things not going the way they should have as promised.
- Listen to the customer with empathy.
- Make it right.

The CALM approach is a common tool that is used for Customer Service training and role-playing. This author has used the CALM strategy with managers and employees at Fortune 100 firms during workshops that focused on customer service and treating customers like guests. Many organizations today use such relevant tools to bring about positive changes in the organizational environment and they adapt relevant content and role-plays to the specifics of their organization and philosophies.

Having Fun- The Pike Place Fish Market

The book titled *"Fish,"* authored by Lundin, Paul, and Christensen (2000), introduces the principles that have been applied to the Pike Place Fish Market in Seattle Washington. Pike Place Fish Market is a nationally known tourist attraction known for its creativeness, friendly employees, and upbeat atmosphere. Based on personal observations in 2004, the fishmongers (employees) at the Pike Place Fish Market seem to engage customers in conversations and lively performances, while executing their daily responsibilities of selling fish and creating raving fans. Lundin, Paul and Christensen believe that if an organization applies the same principles as those of the fish market it will result in or change toward a more creative and productive work environment. This new environment will benefit the employees as well as their internal and external customers.

The book is a fictional tale of a manager that incorporates the *Fish* principles into her department at First Guarantee Financial. The manager, Mary Jane Ramirez, takes a position managing the dreaded department on the third floor. The department has a reputation as being unresponsive, slow, and "zombie" like personality. Top management at the organization has labeled the department a toxic energy dump that is negatively impacting the entire organization. Mary Jane is tasked with turning the department around quickly. A visit to the Pike Place Fish Market has such a positive impact on Mary Jane that she is inspired to learn more about the driving forces behind the market's success.

As observed in 2004, Pike's market regularly attracts crowds of people, both customers and onlookers. As part of their distinctive style, the fishmongers throw the fish to their co-workers for wrapping. The fishmongers engage the customer in conversation and one-on-one attention. It is not uncommon for the fishmongers to invite a customer to participate in the action by trying to catch a fish. The market exudes energy, and is an example of focused teamwork. One of the fishmongers at Pike's market befriends Mary Jane, listens to her work challenge and agrees to explain the principles behind Pike's success. The authors term these principles the *Fish Philosophy*. After learning the Fish Philosophy, Mary Jane implements the principles in her department. The principles are able to transform Mary Jane's department from a toxic energy dump to a great place to work. The Fish Philosophy is comprised of the four basic principles of (1): Choose Your Attitude, (2): Play, (3): Make Their Day, and (4): Be Present. When all four principles are applied they have a positive impact on an organization. The principles create an environment open to creativity and innovation. This change in the environment often leads to productivity gains and a more team-centered atmosphere.

The first principle of the Fish Philosophy is *"Choose Your Attitude."* Each person can actively choose the attitude she or he has in life. A person, let us say a male, cannot choose how others behave but he can control how he behaves. In the work environment a person may not be able to choose his work but he can choose how he approaches it. This principle of choice empowers the individual to control the things he can control beginning with himself and his attitude. In the tale, the employees on the third floor found the work to be tedious and boring and they let this dictate their attitude. Conversely, at Pikes Place Fish Market the employees choose to have a good attitude and that choice influenced the way that they approached their work.

The second principle of the Fish Philosophy is "*Play.*" Play involves introducing fun into the work day. When fun and play are introduced into the workplace they create energy and spark creativity. Even if the work is serious, an element of play and light-heartedness can be added. The fishmongers added play to their work by throwing the fish, calling out silly phrases and creating a fun working atmosphere. Play made it easier for them to do a job that may otherwise have been boring and tedious.

The third principle of the Fish Philosophy is "*Make Their Day.*" This principle involves creating memories for internal and external customers by focusing on them and making their day. The fishmongers focus their efforts on engaging the customers and including them in the fun. These efforts may include inviting a customer to catch a fish or encouraging customers to join in verbally on the banter between the fishmongers. By engaging the customers, the fishmongers create positive memories for the customers that they can then share with others. Serving the customer is the driving force behind making the customer's day. This service may include performing a function, listening or offering kind words.

The final principle of the Fish Philosophy is "*Be Present.*" To be present is to be focused on the customer or the task at hand wholeheartedly. All the employees' attention should be focused on one thing or person at a time so that they are completely dedicated to that thing or person. The fishmongers accomplish this by looking directly at the customer and making the customer feel like they are receiving all the fishmongers' attention at that time. When implemented together the principles can change or transform the work environment. The work environment becomes one where serving others is the focus. The incorporation of fun cultivates creativity, positive energy and teamwork. The employees in this environment improve their work life by choosing to bring good attitudes to work. These attitudes allow the employees to influence the work instead of letting the work influence them. By incorporating these principles, Pike Place Fish Market and its employees turned what could be considered boring and unpleasant work into exciting and memorable work. The daily attendance of many tourists and repeat customers at the market attests to its success.

The Fish Philosophy is relevant for twenty-first century's global management and cross-cultural change agents since its application can lead to building a competitive advantage through efficiency, innovation, responsiveness to customers, and quality service. A work environment that focuses on serving the customer and making the customer's day will increase customer satisfaction and reduce stress. If each contact with the customer leaves a positive impression then the organization's value to the customer will increase. This type of value creation will also contribute to customer loyalty. In addition to creating customer value, the principles help cultivate creativity which is important to innovation. When problems arise that deviate from the norm, the employees must be able to think of new efficient solutions. Environments that promote fun and positive energy make it easier for the employee to think of new ideas. The Fish Philosophy lays the ground work for positive change in the organization, but the employees of the organization are ultimately responsible for making it successful. The Fish Philosophy promotes concepts rather than strict rules and procedures. Management will have to educate and motivate their employees to embrace the principles and appropriately implement them. Management for instance cannot require that each employee choose to have a good attitude each day. Each employee must willingly make the decision about his or her attitude. Pike Place Fish Market and companies like Publix, Wal-Mart and Target show that the Fish Philosophy can successfully be applied to any organization. The book entitled *Fish* provides insight on how to transform an organization through common-sense principles. It provides the following four ingredients to success (Lundin, Paul, and Christensen, 2000, pg. 85-99):

1. Attitude - There is always a choice about the attitude that employees bring to the job. We can choose the way we do our work.
2. Play - Make the routine enjoyable. This creates the energy required to motivate people.
3. Make Their Day - Direct attention towards the customer. Involve and engage them in action to create a sense of endearment.
4. Be Present - We must be fully engaged in our work. Attentive and focused behavior produces results in the most efficient manner.

The book also shows how these principles transformed Pike Place Fish Market to World Famous Pike Place Fish Market (Lundin, Paul, & Christensen, 2000). The principles can be applied to the organization as well as to every day life of national or international employees, managers, and entrepreneurs. Besides making the communication and conflict resolution process easier, the application of these principles results in increased energy, reduced resistance to change, creativity, employee satisfaction, increased commitment, and bottom-line profits. Some of the suggestions for implementing the key four ingredients are listed below:

1. *Attitude* – Initiate a training program for employees on motivational topics.
2. *Make Their Day* – Offer extended coverage to customers by introducing flexible work hours for employees.
3. *Play* – Develop a creativity area for employees to express their talent.
4. *Be Present* – Practice listening skills and establish habits of not answering emails while talking on the phone.

The combined energies of employees and their belief in themselves make a tremendous difference. By sheer commitment of making a choice to change their attitude, together teams are able to mold their department into a satisfying and rewarding place to work.

Summary

The work environment of the twenty-first century should not have change agents and managers that are focused only on exceeding the weekly, monthly, or quarterly financial goals of the department or organization. These types of management approaches can lead to disastrous results, such as unethical decisions, and undue stress on employees. Unfortunately, many of today's managers are usually busy focusing on meeting the quarterly and weekly goals rather than taking the time to relax and focus on the big picture with their employees. They don't seem to have sufficient time to sit back and reflect on their purpose, mission, where they have been, what they have accomplished, and what is truly important in their personal and professional lives. Many managers seem to move from one problem to the next, being focused on urgent challenges which are not necessarily always important. If they were to proactively work on important goals, rather only those that appear urgent, then they would have less "urgent" issues to deal with in their daily operations. Overall, there seems to be little to no time for reflection and relaxation in the life of today's managers in the United States. Of course, this type of a hectic lifestyle can be stressful for managers, their family members, and their employees. Since one cannot be totally stress-free, managers, change agents and workers should focus on effectively managing their level of stress.

The only persons without any real stress are probably those who have "departed" this world or a person who has a mental illness or disability. Otherwise, everyone seems to have some type of stress in his/her life. Change can bring and cause both good and bad stress. *Eustress* is good stress and *distress* is bad stress. Major and continuous change can create a strong culture, where a high level of stress is the norm. Today's rate of change has been much greater than the past; yet, this is perhaps an initial start compared to the changes for tomorrow. In order to effectively deal with stress that is caused by major changes, experts suggest that in today's rate of change, sometimes one just has to "give up" or surrender to the change; another option would be to simply "toughen up" by developing higher levels of tolerance for adapting to change; and yet at other times, one has to "wise up" by not allowing self induced stress to take over one's life. The future promises greater rates of change with higher levels of complexity which can bring about more stress, when not managed properly. In many cases, the rate of change cannot be changed, but one's behavior can be managed appropriately to effectively deal with unforeseen events, thereby reducing stress. Stress, the invisible pandemic, is neither good nor bad by itself when balanced. There is good stress, such as the tension caused by marriage or graduation; and there is bad stress, such as those that are brought upon one by organizational politics, inconsistent or unrealistic demands, and the abuse of one's power or status. Too much stress can make one unproductive or sick, at best, and it can cause death at worst.

Stress occurs at all levels in organizations as a result of many factors including time pressures, personnel conflicts, and the quantity of work expected to be completed at a given time. *Stress* is an interactive condition where people are confronted with either an opportunity, constraint, or a demand for which the outcome is perceived to be uncertain and important. These dynamic conditions, when not managed effectively, can lead to physiological, psychological, and behavioral symptoms. Overall, stress is the wear and tear on the body that occurs in daily life. However, there are many things that can be done proactively to effectively balance one's activities in order to deal with the stressors of twenty-first century life. The Stress Management Handbook (1995) and experts suggest that one can combat stress by acting proactively (instead of reacting), taking control of one's time and major priorities, learning to effectively communicate with others, creating effective means of combating too much work as well as boredom, and taking the time to reflect on the positive aspects of one's job and contributions. The Stress Management Handbook and other experts offer the following commandments for stress management:

1. Don't let minor aggravations get to you.
2. Don't succumb to guilt.
3. Develop adaptation and coping strategies for new tasks and changes.
4. Learn to accept and adapt to change and new circumstances.
5. Change the way you look at stress by looking at it from several angles.
6. Develop a support system and social clique where trustworthy individuals can act as a sounding board to your concerns.
7. Separate things that are under your control from those that you can't control.
8. Learn to accept the things you can't change.
9. Focus on what is important as per your professional mission and purpose in life.
10. Develop a personal anti-stress regimen.
11. Don't take it personally, stay objective and focused on resolving the issue at hand.
12. Believe in yourself. Have enough self-confidence to find the necessary means of handling life's challenges and convert them to opportunities for yourself, your family members, and your colleagues.

Jeff Davidson (1997), author and stress management expert, states that most of what transpires in your life is the result of your personal choices with occasional interferences from the "left field." Overall, you make the choices that impact your life either positively or negatively. Davidson states that "Being true to yourself means having inner directedness," in life and understanding social changes helps you prepare for them while reducing some of the stress that are caused by the rapid change. So, pace yourself in a balanced way by focusing on all of your major goals (not just the professional ones). Being true to yourself, as well as honestly communicating your needs and desires both to yourself and others can help in keeping the level of stress in control.

Glazer-Stress Control Life Style Questionnaire

The Glazer test was designed by Dr. Howard L. Glazer and it is provided in the *Executive Stress* by Philip Goldberg and many stress management workshops. Each scale, in the set of twenty items, is composed of a pair of adjectives or phrases separated by a series of horizontal lines. Each pair has been chosen to represent two kinds of contrasting behaviors. Each person belongs somewhere along the line between the two extremes. Put a circle where you think you belong between the two extremes.

1.	Doesn't mind leaving things temporarily unfinished.	1 2 3 4 5 6 7	Must get things finished once started.
2.	Calm and unhurried about appointments.	1 2 3 4 5 6 7	Never late for appointments.
3.	Not competitive.	1 2 3 4 5 6 7	Highly competitive.
4.	Listens well, lets other finish talking.	1 2 3 4 5 6 7	Anticipates others in conversation (nods, interrupts, finishes sentences for others).
5.	Never in a hurry, even when pressured.	1 2 3 4 5 6 7	Always in a hurry.
6.	Able to wait calmly.	1 2 3 4 5 6 7	Uneasy when waiting.
7.	Easygoing.	1 2 3 4 5 6 7	Always going full speed ahead.
8.	Takes one thing at a time.	1 2 3 4 5 6 7	Tries to do more than one thing at a time, thinks about what to do next.
9.	Slow and deliberate.	1 2 3 4 5 6 7	Vigorous and forceful in speech (uses a lot of gestures).
10.	Concerned with satisfying himself, not others.	1 2 3 4 5 6 7	Wants recognition by others for a job well done.
11.	Slow doing things.	1 2 3 4 5 6 7	Fast doing things (eating, walking, etc.).
12.	Easygoing.	1 2 3 4 5 6 7	Hard driving.
13.	Expresses feelings openly.	1 2 3 4 5 6 7	Holds feelings in.
14.	Has large number of interests.	1 2 3 4 5 6 7	Few interests outside of work.
15.	Satisfied with job.	1 2 3 4 5 6 7	Ambitious, wants quick advancement on job.
16.	Never sets own deadlines.	1 2 3 4 5 6 7	Often sets own deadlines.
17.	Feels limited responsibility.	1 2 3 4 5 6 7	Always feels responsible.
18.	Never judges things in terms of numbers.	1 2 3 4 5 6 7	Often judges performance in terms of numbers (how many, how much).
19.	Casual about work.	1 2 3 4 5 6 7	Takes work very seriously (works weekends, brings work home).
20.	Not very precise.	1 2 3 4 5 6 7	Very precise (careful about detail).
	Subtotals	_ _ _ _ _ _ _	
	Total Score		

Now, add the scores for each area to get the subtotals and then total them up to get a total score. This test can give you some idea of where you stand in the discussion of Type A behavior. The higher your score, the more cardiac prone you tend to be. Remember though, even Type B persons occasionally slip into Type A behavior, and any of these patterns can change over time. The following are some general classification and analysis of the Glazer-Stress Control Life Style Questionnaire.

Total score	Type	
Total score = 110 – 140	Type A1	If you are in this category, and especially if you are over 40 and smoke, you are likely to have a high risk of developing cardiac illness.
Total score = 80 – 109	Type A2	You are in the direction of being cardiac prone, but your risk is not as high as the A1. You should, nevertheless, pay careful attention to the advice given to all Type A's.
Total score = 60 – 79	Type AB	You are a mixture of A and B patterns. This is a healthier pattern than either A1 or A2, but you have the potential for slipping into A behavior and you should recognize this.
Total score = 30 - 59	Type B2	Your behavior is on the less-cardiac-prone end of the spectrum. You are generally relaxed and cope adequately with stress.
Total score = 0 – 29	Type B	You tend to the extreme of non-cardiac traits. Your behavior expresses few of the reactions associated with cardiac disease.

Chapter Eight

TIME AND GOAL MANAGEMENT

Time management is a very critical skill to acquire for all local and global employees. Experts have yet to meet anyone at any culture who has time management truly figured out. However, it is a fact that effective time management requires personal reflection about one's life and one's priorities in life. George Bernard Shaw said that "Life is no brief candle to me. It is sort of a splendid torch which I have got hold of for a moment, and I want to make it burn as brightly as possible before handing it on to future generations." Making this torch as bright as possible requires managing one's activities so important actions are taken toward great causes that are personally and professionally valuable. Determining which actions are important and scheduling them into one's day, week, month, and year require time management skills. Albert Einstein commented that "Out of clutter, find simplicity. From discord, find harmony. And, in the middle of difficulty lies opportunity." Regardless of how busy one's time may be or appear, at least at a personal level, one can manage it effectively while capitalizing on the opportunities that lie ahead.

One of the most impressive programs seems to be Stephen R. Covey's approach to leadership, life, value-based decision-making, and time management. Covey, author of the *Seven Habits of Highly Effective People* (1989), discusses "big rocks" and "small rocks" in his analogy for managing activities in the allotted times. The "big rocks" are a person's most important life roles and relationships. For example, one's job can be a big rock as can be one's status as a parent, son, daughter, mother, uncle, neighbor, or father. Each person must determine his/her important life goals and continuously do what is needed to nourish and develop the relevant relationships and competencies in each role.

Critical Thinking and Decision-Making

Throughout life, human beings have been asked to learn by reading and listening critically, while responding with a systematic assessment of what is read and heard. However, many adults have not been taught the skills and the attitude required to think critically about their choices and decisions. Learning to read, listen, and think critically are the most important elements of people's adult lives. When you think about it, you are today where your thoughts have brought you due to its consistent conditioning power over time; and, you will be tomorrow where your current and future thoughts take you. You do not have much control over your past thinking, but have an incredible amount of control over your current and future thinking. By making a study of it, you can consciously change the pattern of your thinking as well the conditioning of your past thoughts over your behavior today. This is why "critical thinking" skills are so important for each individual.

Critical thinking is about developing an awareness of the assumptions under which people think, act, and systematically question assumptions prior to making a decision. In order to understand critical thinking, one needs to dissect the two terms and understand each to form a comprehensive understanding of its concept. According to the dictionary, *critical* means tending to find fault, characterized by careful analysis, a sound estimate of the problem, decisive, and dangerous or risky. *Thinking*, on the other hand, means to form or have in the mind; to conceive; or to believe, surmise, or expect; to determine, resolve, or work out; and to bring to mind or recollect. Critical thinking and decision-making are valuable tools. When skillfully applied they benefit businesses, individual existences, a country's existence, and the world at large. *Merriam-Webster OnLine Dictionary* (February, 2002) listed the following definitions:

◊ *Critical*: exercising or involving careful judgment or judicious evaluation.

◊ *Thinking*: the action of using one's mind to produce thoughts; marked by use of the intellect.

◊ *Decision*: a determination arrived at after consideration; a report of a conclusion.

◊ *Make*: to lay out and construct; to frame or formulate in the mind; to put together from components; to execute in an appropriate manner; to conclude as to the nature or meaning of something; to carry out.

Critical thinking can also refer to the awareness of a set of interrelated critical questions, ability to ask and answer critical questions at appropriate times, and desire to actively use the critical questions. Both decision-making and problem-solving are interwoven management practices that require critical thinking skills. Critical thinkers learn to see their own actions through the eyes of others by effectively questioning the basis of their assumptions and judgments.

Think about it. How many decisions do *you* make each day? Do you consider yourself to be a good decision-maker? When these questions are asked of participants, the answers fall into several categories. The most common answers to the first question are the realistic, "Too many" or, "They don't let me think at my job." When asked about the quality of one's decision-making skills the response is often mixed-almost everyone agrees that they could improve in this area. It is difficult to find anyone who is completely satisfied with his or her decision-making skills. Fortunately, better critical thinking and decision-making skills can be developed. You are not limited to your existing patterns of thinking and you can make significant improvement-*if* you are willing to try some new tools, techniques, and strategies. So, *critical thinking* can be seen as the event in which we are unprejudiced and judicious in reflection or consideration of the data collected through observation or learning. In ideal case, the critical thinking process happens in all mental activities.

The most surprising revelation to some individuals, reading about critical thinking, can be the major role critical thinking plays in life. At the jobsite, you expect to handle issues in a rational manner, weighing the possibilities and selecting the best course of action. Critical thinking has the same importance in personal matters. Do you send your child to a private or public school? Should you purchase term or whole life insurance? You must consider the advantages and disadvantages while remaining cognizant of your financial position and become aware of possible sacrifices necessary to achieve the desired result. Also, there is a relationship between one's professional and personal lives as one impacts the other. Through independent thinking and believing that we are all (in away) self-employed, we can maintain a positive attitude toward our personal and professional lives regardless of the challenges in each area. Getting fired, retiring, leaving a job, downsizing, reengineering, etc. are all examples of current events that we hear about every day and they impact our lives' as they require critical thinking skills. Current events and issues demand the use of critical thinking to accurately comprehend their impact on our lives. How will the present world situation affect you personally? Do you have a son old enough to join the war on terrorism? Did you balance your retirement fund or risk losing it all due to doubtful business practices of firms such as WorldCom, Tyco, and Enron? Is your job dependent on the airline industry and should you consider a career move? Asking such critical questions and making educated decisions can assist in protecting yourself and your family. Of course, it can also lead to great personal wisdom. "Practical wisdom is only to be learned in the school of experience…Precepts and instructions are useful so far as they go, but without the discipline of real life, they remain of the nature of theory only," said Samuel Smiles, author and reformer. With proper knowledge and wisdom, you can always bet on yourself. "We must have courage to bet on our ideas, to take the calculated risk, and to act" (Maxwell Maltz, author). It has been said that the secret of joy in work is contained in one word - *excellence*. To have the wisdom to know how to do something well is to enjoy it due to quicker and better decision-making ability. As Brian Tracey, speaker and author, said "Every great leap forward in your life comes after you have made a clear decision of some kind." The Chinese proverb states "Be not afraid of growing slowly; be afraid only of standing still."

One of my mentors named Leo Buscaglia, the beloved author and professor of "*Love,*" in the 1970s had received a poem from one of his students that can make a person think and ask critical questions about the purpose and meaning of life as well as actions and attitudes toward the things we do. The unnamed college student titled the poem, "*Things You Didn't Do,*" and the following is what she wrote.

◊ Remember the day I borrowed your car and I dented it; I thought you would kill me but you didn't.

◊ Remember the day I dragged you to the beach and you said it would rain and it did; I thought you would say "I told you so" but you didn't.

◊ And the time when I flirted with all the guys to make you jealous and you were; I thought you would leave me but you didn't.

◊ And the time I spilled blueberry pie all over your brand new car rug; I thought you would drop me for sure but you didn't.

◊ And the time I forgot to tell you the dance was formal and you showed up in jeans; I thought you would smack me but you didn't.

◊ Yes there were lots of things you didn't do; but you put up with me, loved me and protected me. And there were many things that I wanted to make up for when you returned from Vietnam but you didn't.

So, please take the time to think about your life, your attitude toward others and, most importantly, determine how you want to live your life and how you want to be remembered by family members, friends and colleagues. In other words, take the time to determine your life's purpose which is really the secret to the fountain of youth and that can be the beginning of your journey to living purposefully. According to Sophia Loren, actress, "There is a fountain of youth: it is your mind, your talents, the creativity you bring to your life and the lives of the people you love. When you learn to tap this source, you will have truly defeated age."

Determine Your Values

According to the Values Theory, people's values drive their behavior. Values can be at the conscious or subconscious levels. So, be your own friend and determine your personal values to make life decisions easier. When it comes to being a friend, the science fiction writer author Octavia Butler, states "Sometimes being a friend means mastering the art of timing. There is a time for silence. A time to let go and allow people to hurl themselves into their own destiny…And a time to prepare to pick up the pieces when it's all over." Of course, there is always time for you to reflect upon your values and consciously make them a part of your daily life by demonstrating them through daily and weekly behaviors.

The clearer your values are to you then the more proactive you can be in responses to stimuli and situational variables. For example, some people value "assertiveness" while others may value "aggressiveness" due to their cultural background and conditioning. Sharon Anthony Bower, an author, differentiated between the two terms (assertive versus aggressive) by saying "The basic difference between being assertive and being aggressive is how our words and behaviors affect the rights and well being of others." Also, such concepts as "rights", "freedom", "autonomy", "life", etc. can be strong drivers of behavior depending on the extent to which one values them. Internalizing one's values both consciously and subconsciously can lead to proactive and more informed decisions. So, it is best to take the time and reflect upon what one values. For example, if *one truly values life in all of its forms*" then this deeply held value can drive one's behavior in terms of teamwork, conflict, fighting, killing, and hurting others. Mahatma Gandhi valued life in all of its forms. He made his values clear by saying that he was willing to die for his causes, but was not willing to kill for any cause. In this case, Gandhi referred to people due to the colonialism and oppression which existed at the time but valuing life extends beyond people to plants, animals and all living things. Valuing life means being kind to cats, mice, dogs, and plants in the environment. Mother Teresa had similar values as Gandhi and dedicated her life to assisting others who were less fortunate. The examples of Mother Teresa and Mahatma Gandhi show that clarifying one's values also can point one to the right direction with one's mission and purpose in life.

Clarifying values can help a person fall in love again and again with his/her spouse due to seeing things from a different paradigm. For example, you may value family unity, being together, celebrating the achievement of worthwhile milestones with kids and extended family members. One day, you may discover that you are falling in love with the most unlikely person because you both value similar things and have similar goals. As such, you both may listen to the "*Falling in Love*" song by Elvis Presley. In one part of the song, Elvis sings "...as the river flows, gently to the sea, darling so it goes, some things are meant to be..." Well, if it was meant to be then it was meant to be and you just have to cherish and nourish what faith has provided. Think differently and examine the quality of your thoughts to see whether they match what you value in life. Also, don't take what you have for granted which is what happens to many people who often see that their neighbor's yards are greener. So, see the true value of what you have in life and then start searching for what you still want. This will clarify your values and the quality of your thoughts about what you have. Always remember what Marcus Aurelius Antoninus, Roman ruler and philosopher, said that "The happiness of your life depends on the quality of your thoughts."

Determine Your Life's Mission

As you may know, life is not a challenge, an issue, or a complex problem to be solved nor a question to be answered by philosophers. Life is rather a mystery to be experienced consistently, joyfully and systematically before it ends. Experiencing life consistently, joyfully and systematically requires understanding one's likes and dislikes while living toward some long-lasting purpose or cause which can be seen as life's mission. "This is an exciting world. It is cram packed with opportunities. Great moments await around every corner" said Richard M. DeVos, co founder of Amway. Determining one's mission can answer why one is in his or her chosen profession. Sometimes, professions are chosen simply because they offer similar fulfillments for all those who are attracted to it. As such, one can adopt the industry's mission or philosophy for the aspect of one's life. For example, my chiropractor, Dr. Robert Leshaw is a great doctor (Davie, Florida); and he has a sign in his office which represents his vision as a professional and, perhaps, the vision of his colleagues in the healthcare industry. The sign entitled *"Why Am I a Doctor of Chiropractic?"* provides the following answers:

- Because I honor the inborn potential of everyone to be truly healthy;
- Because I chose to care for the patient with the disease, not the disease itself;
- Because I wish to assist rather than intrude and to free rather than to control;
- Because I seek to correct the cause, not its effect;
- Because I know doctors do not heal, only the body can heal itself;
- Because I have been called to serve others;
- Because I want to make a difference;
- Because every day I get to witness miracles;
- Because I know its right!

While the professional aspirations of one's dreams are an important aspect of the personal mission statement, there are several other important aspects as well. Determining one's life mission or purpose requires much self-reflection about "right" and "wrong" as well as one's own personal values and beliefs. Self-assessment is a good way to start the intra-personal dialogue about a personal mission statement for one's life. However, having a mission statement is much deeper than just self-assessment. Your mission statement would only motivate you, and not anyone else, due to its content and your purpose in life. People like Stephen Covey, Mahatma Gandhi, Abraham Lincoln, and many others have always been very clear in their purpose in life. This clarity due to their mission in life helped get them past the difficult stages of their lives. So, a mission statement requires much more soul searching than just assessing oneself once every few years. Self-assessment is a starting point. There have been many top executives (after attending the workshops and creating a draft of their mission statement) who actually quit or changed their jobs because they discovered that their life is not about money, and they wanted to spend more time with their family members. So, creating a meaningful personal mission statement can be very powerful and life changing. It has been said that Stephen Covey's mission statement is made up of five words as a result of years of clarifying his purpose in life. Those five words motivate him to go to work and to do what is right based on his moral convictions. The philanthropist John D. Rockefeller III, said "The road to happiness lies in two simple principles: find what it is that interests you and that you can do well, and when you find it, put your whole soul into it -- every bit of energy and ambition and natural ability you have." Such clarity must link well and integrate with one's life purpose and competencies. Henry Ward Beecher, US abolitionist and clergyman, said "Do not look back on happiness or dream of it in the future. You are only sure of today; do not let yourself be cheated out of it." The key is to enjoy the moment and set your goals for the future you want to create for yourself and others around you. Orville Wright, co-inventor of the airplane, said "Will and I could hardly wait for the morning to come to get at something that interested us. That's happiness." So, having the goals of creating something interesting, contributing something for a worthwhile cause, and making this world a bit better than we found it is the road to personal happiness.

Tom Justin, an author and trainer, said "The only job we have been given when we came to earth was to create. Everything we do is a creation, from a job, to children, to thoughts. We all create all the time, it is all we do." Stephen Covey said the best way to predict the future is to create it; first mentally and then physically. The mental creation can start with reflection about one's life and its purpose, which can eventually be converted into written words in a mission statement.

This is a good time to begin writing a personal mission statement for your own life (that is if you don't already have one). This can be a very powerful document for better decision-making at changing times and effective time management. Read and reflect upon the following story in order to begin thinking about your purpose in life.

Once upon a time, there were two brothers named Alfred and Ludwig. Alfred had made his fame and fortune in the dynamite business while Ludwig made his money in oil and gas exploration. As it happened, Ludwig passed away. In their country, when they wrote an obituary, they really wrote an obituary. They interviewed people and basically wrote the story of his life. The paper made a mistake and wrote the obituary about Alfred. What people said about him was that he had made his fame and fortune by maiming and killing people. Alfred didn't like this and he dedicated the rest of his life to the promotion of worthwhile causes for humanity and world peace. Alfred was Alfred Nobel of the *Nobel Prizes*. Basically, this story is an example of re-scripting. It took a traumatic event that caused a paradigm shift, which made Alfred deeply reflect upon his life. There is another way for such reflections that is not nearly as painful and it is much easier. It is through the writing of a Personal Mission Statement. Very few individuals ever take the time to create a personal mission statement, which can be very powerful and life changing. Why not begin the process today.

Guidelines for Meditation and Reflection

Find a quiet room and relax for introspective reflection. Michel de Montaigne, the French Essayist, wrote "A man must keep a little back shop where he can be himself without reserve. In solitude alone can he know true freedom." Now, think of a person (maybe more than one) whom you really admire and who affected your life in a significant way for good. It does not matter if this person is living or dead or even if you knew them personally or even never met them. Think about who this person is and what s/he meant (means) to you. Begin to form a clear picture of this person and his/her life in your mind's eye. Who comes to mind? Perhaps your Mom, Dad, a friend from the past (or present), a community role model, country or world leader, or a figure from history. Think Deeply. You should be starting to get an image. Now, write the name of this influential person.

Mentally, consider the qualities you most admire in this person. You know the things you like about this person. Perhaps, they were honest, they kept their word, they were good listeners, hard workers, etc. *Think!* Start making a mental list and then write them down. When finished writing this list, put them into sentences answering the following question: what do you want to be, have, do, and gain in life when you are 100 years of age?

Now, write the answers to the above question in a way that is comprehensive and representative of your goals in life. Once it feels somewhat complete to you, then this is your first draft. After a few days or weeks, you can begin editing the document by changing, deleting, or adding to it until it represents you and your purpose in life. Once this mission statement is a document that motivates you everyday and during difficult moments then you know you have a good, purposeful mission statement. The final step is to focus on doing those things that help you accomplish your mission each day. This is what Stephen R. Covey calls "*Beginning with the End in Mind*" which happens to be one of the habits of highly effective individuals.

Initially, the draft of your mission statement might take about two to three hours of individual time (no interruptions) to think about your life and what it is about. During these two-three hours, you can create a draft that you can build upon during the coming months. Or, you can create this draft (for the time being) from a personal ethics statement, your list of personal values, and other self-reflection material/exercises about your life that you (may) have completed thus far. Consider your social, psychological, mental, economical, as well as your physical needs and desires and gain the needed knowledge of your inner internal motivation. Julian Simon, an economist, stated that "The main fuel to speed the world's progress is our stock of knowledge, and the brake is our lack of imagination." So, let your imagination go wild and beyond its normal limitations in order to explore your deepest wants, needs, and desires as you progress toward creating your life's mission statement and eventually your future. Robert Duvall, actor, said "If you don't daydream and kind of plan things out in your imagination you never get there. You have to start someplace." As such, mental creation should precede the physical creation of worthwhile dreams.

For a quick exercise on mission statement creation, you can check out the Franklin-Covey website at the Covey Franklin Leadership Center. It can help you get started on an initial draft for going to Franklin Covey's website (franklincovey.com/missionbuilder/). It takes "guts" to get it started and to look in the mirror each morning and ask: "Have I lived up to my goals and expectations?" This question can make one think and at times force one to change jobs, start new hobbies, spend more time with family members, etc. The key is to begin and, as Nike's slogan states, to "Just Do It." Make sure it covers your overall objectives and needs in life personally, professionally, mentally, socially, and physically.

You see that no one ever prepares for failure in life because failure cannot be a part of one's mission. On the other hand, avoiding failure is not part of the mission either, because failures can serve as a good learning opportunities toward one's mission in life. The key is understanding what went wrong, why it went wrong, what is the right process, and what can we do to make it right in the future. The following are examples of personal mission statements:

1. Serve yourself, but do no harm to others. Serve humanity, but do no harm to yourself. Grow and prosper yourself and humanity. Through balance, patience and critical thinking, evaluate when and if you will need to service one over the other.

2. To find happiness, fulfillment, and value in living I will:
   ◊ LEAD a life centered around the principles of growth, honesty, potential, and empowerment.
   ◊ REMEMBER what's important in life is happiness, health, financial security, family, and friends.

◊ REVERE admirable characteristics in others, such as being fun, tolerant, compassionate, creative, forgiving, and trustworthy, and attempt to implement similar characteristics in my own life.

◊ RECOGNIZE my strengths and develop talents as a person who is generous, hard-working, athletic, open-minded, a leader, and a teacher.

◊ HUMBLE myself by acknowledging that I can be excessive, obsessive, and introverted and by constantly striving to transform my weaknesses into strengths.

◊ ENVISION myself becoming a person who Lisa thinks is dependable, fun, and enthusiastic; Mustafa thinks is educated, giving, and responsible. Dad thinks is dependable, enthusiastic, and loyal. Mom thinks is caring, responsible, and fun.

So, finalize your personal mission first and the rest will be much easier as Greek Proverb states, "The beginning is the half of every action." Once your mission is clear, then focus on what is truly important (based on your mission statement) and say no to activities that are not important. Remember, things that matter most must never be at the mercy of things that matter least. Another concept to keep in mind is that what is important to another person must be as important to you as the other person is to you. These concepts will assist in evaluating which activities add value to one's mission in life and which ones do not. Furthermore, working on these activities will be much more enjoyable because they contribute to one's purpose in life. Therefore, one completes them with a sense of joy and pleasure. Aristotle said it well over 2,000 years ago when he wrote that "Pleasure in the job puts perfection in the work."

Also, don't forget to reflect upon the mission, its direction and progress periodically. Remember that "Questions focus our thinking. Ask empowering questions like: What's good about this? What's not perfect about it yet? What am I going to do next time? How can I do this and have fun doing it?" (Charles Connolly, Psychologist). Upon the completion of your personal mission statement, you also will need to determine your important roles in life and each week balance your activities in such a way that you regularly enhance those roles and nourish their progress in a balanced way. You also have to take time for your own development (physically, mentally, socially, spiritually, etc.) each week as well.

Personal Mission Statements

A personal mission statement can provide the basis for a new beginning just as the New Year's Day provides a new beginning for another year. Kevin Eikenberry, speaker and author, explains that "New Year's Day is special only as a symbol of a new beginning. The reality is that every day is a new beginning, a new chance to create the life that we desire." Human beings are given a new twenty-four hour period every morning and how this new day is used depends on one's goals and vision. So, "Hold yourself responsible for a higher standard than anybody else expects of you. Never excuse yourself. Never pity yourself. Be a hard master to yourself - and be lenient to everybody else" (Henry Ward Beecher, US abolitionist & clergyman). You can and should create your own mission in life by formally documenting it and constantly reviewing it. Ayn Rand, philosopher and author, said the following about creation:

> Men have been taught that it is a virtue to agree with others. But the creator is the man who disagrees. Men have been taught that it is a virtue to swim with the current. But the creator is the man who goes against the current. Men have been taught that it is a virtue to stand together. But the creator is the man who stands alone.

You have the talent to create your own future (first mentally and then physically through action). Author Thomas Wolfe tells us that "If a man has talent and cannot use it, he has failed. If he has talent and only uses half of it, he has partly failed. If he has a talent and learns somehow to use the whole of it, he has gloriously succeeded and has a satisfaction and a triumph few men ever know." A mission and vision of your future must be first created mentally before it can be created physically through action.

Just "Because You Can" Syndrome

Beware of the *"because you can"* syndrome, as it can rob valuable time away from your day, week, month, and years. Many people become victims of the "because you can" syndrome because either they cannot say no to people or they do not have anything else to do that is worthwhile or purposeful. For example, let us say that your job is to manage the activities and efforts of 300 people (faculty and staff) to provide "quality education and excellent operational service" to 2,200 students. You are a very busy individual and this huge responsibility keeps you very busy. However, you also have ten years of corporate training experience in diversity and time management workshops for executives. Your "peer" colleague at the institution asks if you would be able to take some time to prepare and facilitate several training sessions for faculty members and a few for outside members of the community. You and your peers know that currently you are the best person at this institution for this type of a project due to your experience and this project must be a success. However, you do not have to take on this extra responsibility since this is not part of your job and your "peer" has no direct impact on your success at the institution. You enjoy training but also understand that preparing this material and facilitating them will take many valuable hours away from working with your own departmental tasks and colleagues to provide "quality education and excellent operational service." Furthermore, being involved in the preparation and facilitation of this training will not assist in your professional endeavor with this institution in any way, regardless of the success rate for the program. You also know that you will enjoy this project and the facilitation while pleasing another colleague by doing this huge favor for him/her; but you are also fully enjoying your own current responsibilities and the purposeful interaction with people in your department as well. Even though you can take on extra projects, you should say "no" since it will take much valuable time away from your important professional role in life. It would be nice to be involved if you had "free" time, but your priority is not in training anymore and it does not advance your professional role. "Just because you can," due to your past experiences with it, does not obligate you to be the person to take on this challenge. The same is true of "babysitting" for family members, driving friends to the airport, picking up nephews and nieces from soccer, going to the late night parties with friends simply because you don't want them to go alone, etc. when you don't have the time to do so. Remember, "Just because you can" does not obligate you to do so. Bill Gates, one of the richest men on earth, can probably eliminate poverty and hunger in many small countries, at least temporarily, by donating a few billion dollars for resources. However, "just because he can" does not mean that he should if such a cause does not match his purpose in life. Mother Teresa, on the other side, devoted her life to assisting the elderly, poor and disadvantaged individuals in India because that was part of her mission in life. So, do not become a victim of "just because you can" syndrome by only taking on activities that add to your life's mission and important roles. Other examples of "just because you can" syndrome may include the following, and you can come up with your own as you think about it.

◊ Stealing is wrong and many know and agree with this concept. Yet, many individuals have opportunities to steal without anyone ever noticing but they do not steal. Just because they can does not mean they should.

◊ Many people have the opportunity to drive really fast, faster than the speed limit, on the roads to get home or to work. However, just because they can does not mean they actually do or that they should. Many individuals drive according to the speed limit because they know it is designed for the safety of everyone.

◊ A manager at one of the workshops commented that he has been married five times in the last fifteen years. Someone asked him why? He said "because he could." Why was he divorced so many times? He said because his wives did not want him hanging around with his "ex-girlfriends." Then he was asked "why did he hang around with them if he knew it would cause problems with his wife" and his response was "because he could." The reality is that he probably enjoyed being around friends and made time for it. Having the courage to resist such temptations during moments of truth are critical. There are individuals who have many opportunities to be involved in extra-marital affairs; however, they also understand that just because they can does not mean they should when such actions go against their values or if these activities bring pain to their loved ones.

◊ There was a manager who said that her teenage son makes her so mad at times that sometimes she wants to beat the daylights out of him. Then she said, "Just because I can does not mean I actually should." She is a good example of a person who controls her temper and exercises maturity and courage in such "moments of truth."

The moral of these examples is that "just because one has the opportunity to do something does not mean one should do it." Instead, one should do only those things that match his/her mission in life. It is OK to help someone who needs assistance temporarily, and it is perfectly OK to volunteer as a coach or a mentor every now and then; but one should not do things that do not match one's values and purpose in life. Creating a mission statement for your life, identifying your five to six important current roles, identifying activities that help you progress toward your life's mission and important roles each week, and scheduling as well as implementing those activities each day will be the key to effective time management and avoiding the "just because you can" syndrome. Of-course, one must use politically correct means of effectively avoiding it as to not hurt others' feelings while not becoming a victim oneself either. Harriet Woods, the American Politician, once said that "You can stand tall without standing on someone. You can be a victor without having victims."

Time Management Model: Important and Urgent

Generally speaking, "there are two days in the week about which and upon which I never worry. Two carefree days, kept sacredly free from fear and apprehension. One of these days is Yesterday... And the other... is Tomorrow" said Robert Jones Burdette, author. Many individuals spend a large percentage of the days and nights worrying about either the past or the future and achieve very little in the present. The past is gone but it can offer learning when one reflects upon it consciously for a limited amount of time. The future has not come but one can plan for it accordingly. However, actions must be taken in the present and these actions should be geared toward what is important in one's life.

In effective time management, activities can be categorized and understood as important, urgent, not important, and not urgent. The following definitions and concept are foundational in time management and effective decision-making.

◊ *Urgent* – Urgent is defined as activities that have the appearance of needing immediate attention.

◊ *Important* – Important is defined as all those activities that contribute to life's goals and mission.

Activities that are important will always produce better outcomes in the long-term. However, some activities are both important and urgent so they must be completed first. Activities that are neither important nor urgent can be left alone if they do not hinder your mission in life. The German philosopher, Johann Goethe, said "every man has only enough strength to complete those activities that he is fully convinced are important." So, discover your important activities in order not to waste time on the unimportant things. Some discipline is required when it comes to time management. When it comes to discipline Jim Rohn, motivational speaker and author, states "We must all suffer one of two things: the pain of discipline or the pain of regret or disappointment." Properly planning for doing what is important leaves no excuses for not achieving them. With regard to excuses Bob Burg, author and speaker, said "One trademark of successful people is that they don't let excuses deter them. They determine what it is they need to do - and then do it." So, focus on what is important by going in that direction one step at a time.

Jackson W. Robinson, President of Winslow Management Company, said that "Defying conventional ideas can yield unconventional returns." Defying the status quo and creating new ideas takes energy, vision, hard work, and at times temporary setbacks. So, "Never allow your energy or enthusiasm to be dampened by the discouragements that must inevitably come" (James Whitcomb Riley, poet Positive Words.) Unfortunately, often people allow such temporary setbacks to impact their enthusiasm and sometimes even speak ill of others as a result. Will Durant, historian and author, summarized it well when he said "To speak ill of others is a dishonest way of praising ourselves." Consequently, one should be very cautious, and always think and speak based on one's values.

Focus on the Important

It has been said that a person who does not make a choice actually makes a choice. Hopefully, choices are directed toward actions that lead one in the direction of what is important in one's life. Jawaharlal Nehru, Indian statesman, once said that "Action to be effective must be directed to clearly conceived ends." So, one must be focused toward end-results that are important. With regard to focusing Washington Gladden, writer and lecturer, said "It is better to say, 'This one thing I do' than to say, 'These forty things I dabble in.'" A mission statement can keep one focused on what is important and it provides the reasons for going toward a specific direction. Friedrich Nietzsche, philosopher, said "He who has a why can bear almost any how." A burning "why" will almost always find an efficient "how" in order to get to the predetermined destination. In the business perspective, the "why" deals with leadership while the "how" aspect deals with management tasks. One must know where and why before determining how to get there because going in the wrong direction will waste time, resources, and kill one's morale.

While focusing on the "big rocks" during one of his seminars, Dr. Covey, set up a bucket and asked a volunteer from the audience to take a smaller bucket of small rocks and several large rocks labeled things like - self-improvement, big project at work, vacation time, family, etc. The small rocks represented the small fires or emergencies that we are hit with everyday at home and at work. The instructions for the volunteers are clear and simple - you must fit all of the large rocks and all of the small rocks in the large bucket. Several volunteers attempted the task, each time placing some small rocks in the bottom of the bucket and then carefully selecting the most important large rocks, cramming, shoving, and pushing, trying to fit all of the rocks. Most participants tend to miss the key concept of the exercise which is really the moral of the presentations: You will accomplish a lot more in your day, your week and your life if you start with the "big rocks" first and leave the remaining empty space for the "small rocks." As expected and planned, all of the rocks fit into the large bucket when you place the large ones in first and pour the small rocks into the gaps and holes between them.

The same exercise can be conducted a little differently using the same concept of "small rocks" and "big rocks." A professor stood before his "Principles of Change Management" class and had some items in front of him to demonstrate effective time management. When the class began, wordlessly, he picked up a very large and empty glass jar and proceeded to fill it with *"colorful golf balls."* He then asked the students if the jar was full? They agreed that it was. So the professor then picked up a box of pebbles and poured them into the jar. He shook the jar lightly. The pebbles, of course, rolled into the open spaces between the colorful golf balls. He then asked the students again if the jar was full. They agreed it was. The professor picked up a box of sand and poured it into the jar. Of course, the sand filled up everything else. He then asked once more if the jar was full. The students agreed with a unanimous --yes! The professor then produced two bottles of water from under the table and proceeded to pour the entire contents into the jar effectively filling the empty space between the sand. The students laughed.

Now, the professor said, as the laughter subsided, I want you to recognize that this jar represents your life.

◊ The *colorful golf balls* are the important things -- your family, partner, health, children, friends, and your favorite passions such as your job/profession--things that if everything else was lost and only they remained, your life would still be full.

◊ The *pebbles* are the other things that matter like your hobbies, your house, and your car.

◊ The sand is everything else -- the small stuff! If you put the sand into the jar first, then there is no room for the pebbles or the golf balls. The same goes for your life. If you spend all your time and energy on the small stuff, you will never have room for the things that are important to you. Pay attention to the things that are critical to your happiness. Play with your children. Take time to get medical checkups. Take your partner out dancing.

Play another 18 holes of golf and a game of tennis or racquetball every now and then. There will always be time to work, clean the house, give a dinner party, and fix the disposal. Take care of the golf balls first -- the things that really matter. Set your priorities. The rest is just sand. One of the students raised her hand and inquired what the water represented. The professor smiled and said, I'm glad you asked.

◊ The *water* is a symbol and a reminder for enjoying, relaxing and taking time for you and for nourishing all of your roles in a balanced way. It just goes to show you that no matter how full your life may seem, there's always room for enjoying a couple glasses of cool water with your friends to satisfy your thirst and cleanse your system!

Water is the symbol of flexibility, and it makes a powerful statement as an ending to this quick demonstration of making sure that one's big rocks are clarified, planned and scheduled. Actually water is both flexible as well as adaptable to its surroundings as it can be fluid, solid ice, or it can become moisture and simply evaporate in thin air. All mission-oriented individuals need to remain flexible as well as adaptable in their daily activities by taking advantage of the wonderful opportunities life brings their way each and every day. With regard to important life moments, Susan B. Anthony, Women's Rights Advocate, states:

Sooner or later we all discover that the important moments in life are not the advertised ones, not the birthdays, the graduations, the weddings, not the great goals achieved. The real milestones are less prepossessing. They come to the door of memory unannounced, stray dogs that amble in, sniff around a bit and simply never leave. Our lives are measured by these.

In other words, some unexpected events or opportunities that come your way may not be as attractive as others (that are stated in your goals), but they do make life fun, fulfilling and enjoyable if you can cease the opportunity and live in the moment.

Many time management experts use this philosophy when setting goals, writing an action plan, and prioritizing tasks. If needed, we should force ourselves to remember to work on the "big rocks" a little bit each day - otherwise we would become bogged down with small emergencies and never feel as though we have accomplished anything. Education is usually a "big rock" when we are trying to gain competency in our professions, and many competent professionals continue to hone their time management skills because they don't want important "small rocks" like some of the "big rocks" to get pushed aside from time to time. What is important is that you don't ignore "big rocks" for very long. Just like trees, "big rocks" such as your relationships need constant nourishment and development if they are to sustain and grow. As you know, after all is said and done, no matter how famous or important a person might be, the size of his/her funeral is going to depend a lot on the weather. Nonetheless, it is important that you focus on the "big rocks" before inviting others to your funeral!

Conscious thinking, deep reflection, prioritizing according to one's mission, and planning improves time management skills which is all about managing the needed activities in the allotted time. Most of us have experienced the difficulties of balancing available time with the many commitments and opportunities we would like to fulfill. Each day, managers are bombarded by a multitude of tasks and demands in a setting of frequent interruptions, crisis and unexpected events. It can be easy to lose track of objectives and fall prey to what experts identify as "time wasters." For many of us, time is probably dominated by other people and/or by nonessential activities rather our own "big rocks." Through the personal benefits of improved focus, flexibility, coordination, control, and planning everyone can become better time managers. The following are quick tips on how to better manage scarce time:

◊ Do say "No" when others' requests will divert you from more important work toward your "big rocks" that you should be doing.

◊ Don't get bogged down in details and routines that should be left to others.

◊ Do establish a system for screening your telephone calls.

◊ Don't let "drop in" or unannounced visitors use too much of your time.

◊ Do prioritize work tasks in order of their importance and urgency.

◊ Don't become "calendar bound" by losing control of your schedule or other important opportunities that surface. Need to adapt daily.

◊ Do work tasks in their order of priority by focusing on the important first.

◊ Do take the time to laugh often with your friends and family members. Valerie Bell, author, says "Shared laughter is like family glue. It is the stuff of family well-being and all-is-well thoughts. It brings us together as few other things can."

Time management is important because more time for research on complex problems may equal better decisions. In some cases, having more time for proper research can prevent problems and disasters from taking place. Think of *Exxon Oil Valdez, The Chernobyl Disaster* in Russia, the *Space Shuttle Challenger*, and other examples where perhaps more time for research, reflection, and better decision-making may have led to different choices and results.

The organizational culture of most competitive firms tends to be fast paced and they usually require immediate solutions to problems. However, thinking of good ideas and creative solutions requires time. This is also true of our own lives. We need to take the time and see what makes sense for our purpose in life and how many hours we should devote to important tasks (big rocks) each week. Many of us might be wasting valuable time because we have a hard time determining what is important and eventually stop trying. Think, for a minute about meetings. How much time do professionals spend or waste in meetings? How many times have you thought to yourself after an hour-long meeting, we could have accomplished everything covered in a total of 15 minutes. The same is true for bureaucratic rules and regulations. How many hoops do we have to jump through in any given day? If these bureaucratic rules aren't followed to the letter, will it really make a difference? What happens sometimes is that we confuse what is important with what is urgent. Think about the busy lives of famous people who have accomplished great things. Did they have more time than other individuals or were they devoted to a cause that was important to them? If you are working toward a cause that is important, then it doesn't matter how many hours you work on it because it should be enjoyable to you!

When Albert Einstein was working on his theory of relativity, he used to stare out of windows and just daydream. Leonardo DaVinci used to sit and stare at cracks in the wall. F. Neitzsche could not write unless he took long walks. Mahatma Gandhi used to have "silence days" where he would sit and meditate for an entire day. If these individuals could make time in their schedules, then certainly all of us can make time for the most important objectives, tasks, and people in our lives. You may need to use some of your internal courage to get a start on the right direction. Oprah Winfrey, the popular talk show host, said "The only courage you will need is the courage to live the life you are meant to." Our time in this world is limited and it goes very fast. Our time in this world is like a dream that can be scary and last a long time or it can be exciting and fun which goes very quickly. You see, a dream is only a dream while you are still dreaming and sleeping; as soon as you wake up it is no longer a dream because reality hits you. Our time in this world is just like having a dream and it will be over before we know it. The difference between a dream and our time in this world is that we have more control over our time and can turn our noble and worthwhile dreams into worthwhile goals that can become a reality if we use our time appropriately toward predetermined and worthwhile goals.

Some people live a healthy life, and some people live a prosperous life. While others live a short life, a life full of suffering and hardships, and a life that is not so prosperous. It is a factual perception that we may not be able to change our destinies or things that happen to us in life, but we can change our actions and response to what happens to us in life. Success is not what you get in life, it is what you do with what you have and what you receive that makes you successful. So, all of us need to ask ourselves what am I becoming if I keep doing what I am doing right now? We need to ask ourselves, what do I need to become in order to get what I want in life? If you are not willing to become that person then you better change your "wants." Answering this question also helps create strong reasons for one's goals in life. Having strong goals are great motivators and knowing the reasons for wanting those goals are even more powerful motivators for action and eliminating procrastination.

The average person spends too much time on many mundane things on a daily basis because their urgency-driven world works that way. While that may be true for most of us in different stages of our lives, it is important that we take time to appreciate others and be thankful for what we have in life. As stated before, it is best to remember that yesterday is the past; tomorrow is the future; and neither of these times can be of much use to us at the present time. However, our time right now is a gift called "present" and we should make the best use of it while we have it because once it is gone, it is gone forever and it becomes part of the past. Many teachers, mentors, and other writers have suggested the following guidelines with regard to time to help us focus on what is truly important in life:

1. Take time to think, for it is the source of growth, knowledge and power;
2. Take time to play, for it is the cistern (holding tank) of perpetual youth;
3. Take time to read, for it is the foundation of wisdom and understanding;
4. Take time to pray, for it is the greatest power on earth both psychologically and spiritually;
5. Take time to love and be loved, for it is what brings joy;

6. Take time to be friendly, for it is the road to happiness;
7. Take time to laugh, for it is the best lubricant;
8. Take time to give, for life is too short to be selfish; (We leave everything materialistic behind when we depart this world but our *faith*.) The only things that we take with us are things that we give away to help others who are less fortunate than us.
9. Take time to work, for it is the source and price of happiness and contribution to the society; however
10. Never take time to waste, for it is the road to failure and depression.

There is a wise statement about misuse of social time and it says: "great minds discuss ideas, average minds discuss events, small minds discuss people, and very small minds discuss themselves." There is no reason for anyone to waste time complaining about others. For busy managers, understanding the concepts behind the following terms is important in effective time management.

◊ *Murphy's Law*: What can happen, will happen. Take the time to plan and provide plenty of opportunities for activities that you want to happen in your life. Invite those activities and tasks that will drive your purpose of life and your mission in the right direction.

◊ *Pareto Law*: It states that 80% of the results flow from 20% of the activities. So, some activities have much more impact than others and we can call them "High leverage activities" or "big rocks."

◊ *Parkinson's Law*: It states that work expands to fill the time available to complete the job. The safeguard for this is to set realistic deadlines, to train people appropriately and trust them to do their jobs the right way and to be ethical about its completion.

◊ *True North*: The North Star at night helps pilots see the north direction. Faith, thinking, hope, and education are our true north star, our yardstick, our ruler, our inspector, and our guide, which can measure our effectiveness to see whether we are on the right path or not. So, organize your life and execute your actions around your priorities according to the mission and purpose of your life and that becomes the essence of time management.

Overall, remember that life is full of many special gifts and valued treasures that should be put first and must never be ignored as stated in the following little poem by Larry S. Chengges.

> When we count our many blessings, it isn't hard to see
> That life's most valued treasures are the treasures that are free.
> For it isn't what we own or buy that signifies our wealth....
> It's the special gifts that have no price... our family, friends, and health.

First, one must understand his or her beliefs and values. There's nothing that can help you understand your beliefs more than trying to explain them to an inquisitive child...so try it. If you can explain it to children then you are probably pretty clear on your beliefs, values and goals in life. When it comes to the clarity of ones goals, values, vision, and what inspires a person, Pete Goss (a sailor who successfully sailed around the world - alone) said "My parents taught me that I could do anything I wanted and I have always believed it to be true. Add a clear idea of what inspires you, dedicate your energies to its pursuit and there is no knowing what you can achieve, particularly if others are inspired by your dream and offer their help." So, make every day an inspiring day. Overall, remember that "The purpose of life is not to win. The purpose of life is to grow and to share. When you come to look back on all that you have done in life, you will get more satisfaction from the pleasure you have brought into other people's lives than you will from the times that you outdid and defeated them" said Harold Kushner, Rabbi and author.

Taking Calculated Risks Based on Priorities

Taking calculated risk based on clearly defined values and priorities means one is moving in the right direction toward achieving the goals and learning. Charles Handy, author of "*The Age of Unreason*" said the following with regard to change and learning: "Those who learn best and most, and change most comfortably, are those who:
   ◊   Take responsibility for themselves and for their future;
   ◊   Have a clear view of what they want that future to be;
   ◊   Want to make sure that they get it; and
   ◊   Believe that they can."

William Sessions, a former FBI Director, said "Looking back on my life, I wish I'd stepped forward and made a fool of myself more often when

I was younger because when you do, you find out you can do it." Samuel Johnson, writer, said "The world is not yet exhausted; let me see something tomorrow which I never saw before." Of-course, prior to taking calculated risks, it is incumbent upon each person to explore his/her values, mission in life and possibilities by watching and asking others for their suggestions. Furthermore, one needs to really listen to what others say and learn from them. With regard to listening Oliver Wendell Holmes, physician and poet, said "It is the province of knowledge to speak, and it is the privilege of wisdom to listen."

Managing Priorities and Time[5]

Henry Ford said "The whole secret of a successful life is to find out what it is one's destiny to do, and then do it." One's destiny should be the motivation in itself. Somebody once said that a motivational speech is like a cup of ice cream on a hot summer day or a nice cup of coffee early in the morning to wake you up—satisfying at the moment, but the effects wear off quickly. Another favorite saying about motivation is that it energizes incompetence, as it has been with wars where individuals have given their lives due to motivational and charismatic leaders and the leader's cause. At best, there are limitations with only motivational pep talks. They tend to create immediate peaks and long valleys. Even though people get motivated when they are watching Jane Fonda do her workouts, simply watching doesn't necessarily help one lose the extra pounds. That's why one should plan to be more instructional with the presentation (including self-talk) than purely motivational. This is not meant to leave you the impression that motivation isn't important. For example, even though the effects quickly wear off, we do take showers every day; and even though motivational quickies wear off, we need them for energy, vision, reflection, and goal setting. Sometimes, we just need to "jumpstart" and energize our can-do spirit. Personal success has to be personally imagined and believed before it can be achieved and this is certainly true in effective time management since you are the driver of your time. So, you need to constantly use positive self-talk that you will be able to manage your time around your priorities and that you will be able to achieve your goals. Most people do much negative self-talk which reinforces their fears and stands in the way of their progress. So, practice telling yourself that you will achieve your goals and do this consciously every day. Remember, if

---

[5] - Some of this material has been used in the author's speeches over the past fifteen years, and parts of it in the remaining portion of this chapter come from Dianna Booher (1991) who has prepared quality speeches, to be used by managers, in her book entitled "*Executive's Portfolio of Model Speeches for All Occasions*" by Prentice Hall.

you had a colleague or friend who talked to you, like you talk to yourself in terms of fear and negative self-talk, would you continue to hang around with that person? Probably not! Remember, negativity is contagious.

The objective here is to offer you something more than motivation. The purpose is to leave you thinking about some concrete techniques you can use tomorrow morning. To remain focused, let us concentrate on success in sales as an example but the concepts can be applied to any profession. We're beyond hit-and-run selling. It used to be that all you had to worry about was finding a map of your territory and then make calls. But being state of the art in sales means that you have to take ownership and become your own general manager. Competitive companies are now asking that you be responsible not just for sales volume, but also for seeing that the volume makes the organization profitable. You are expected to sell *internally,* get the support you need, work with the delivery people, the installers, the service people, and others in the value chain. You are also expected to negotiate effectively with the customer within the ranges outlined. Often, you are expected to develop your own marketing plan. Today, it takes much more time to earn the same dollars as it used to take thirty years ago. That means that no matter how new the "state of the art" in selling, we are still back to the basics of selling: *Time is your best tool; you have to use it to your advantage.* "If we all did the things we are capable of doing, we would literally astound ourselves" said Thomas Edison, scientist and inventor. Although time-management tools aren't new to you, they can get lost in the garage on occasions. A quick review and summary can be beneficial.

First, set priorities. Experts will keep telling you to add value to the products or do the little extra things that can enhance the quality of your product. Experts also tell you to be there when customers need answers to their problems—to offer more and more consulting services. But you may be feeling frustration. "If my day is already full," you may be wondering, "how am I going to add value?" Focus on the 80/20 rule again. Eighty percent of your results come from 20 percent of your activity, from 20 percent of your clients. So, list all your activities and set some priorities. What activities bring in the most revenue? What things could an assistant do to free you up for those top-selling activities? Could you pay $20,000 to an assistant to increase your commissions by $50,000? What activities could you *stop* doing to give you more time to concentrate on those profit-making priorities? You've heard it said: "You win some; you lose some, but you have to get dressed for them all." Some sales efforts call for blue jeans. These might be little things, but they can make a big difference. "He who waits to do a great deal of good at once will never do anything. Life is made up of little things. True greatness consists of being great in little things" said Samuel Johnson, Writer, compiler of an early English Dictionary.

Second, determine the right mixes between reach and frequency. You always have to balance these two: Do I spend my time and budget reaching more people with our message? Or spend my time contacting the people who buy more frequently? Generally, it's more important for potential customers to get your message more often…than for a large base who may or may not be potential customers to hear your message sporadically.

Third, learn to give CPR by phone. Consult…Personalize…Recommend. Consult by asking questions of the customer about his or her needs. Personalize by explaining the benefits of your product in terms of the needs the customer has just expressed to you. Recommend what the customer needs to buy from you. With the cost of the average sales call being very high, we've got to get off the plane and on the phone. Nobody said the telephone has to be impersonal. Just remember, not the same pitch to everyone: Use the CPR method – Consult, Personalize, and Recommend.

Fourth, use letter writing as a pro-active sales strategy. Instead of those three-hour, goodwill-building visits, write a "thinking-of-you" letter or note. Letter writing, once you get a collection of models for your customers, can be a sales strategy unto itself. A side benefit is that it builds goodwill in less time than a half-hour phone conversation or two-hour trip to the customer site.

Fifth, stop putting everything in writing. Get rid of those ubiquitous transmittal letters that say, "Here it is." That habit ties up your sales correspondence in the word-processing pool for days. Just put your business card or a handwritten note on the literature, the price list, the specs and put them in the mail. Underline the answers to their questions in the sales literature. A handwritten note says to the customer that you're personalizing your pitch, that you listened to their needs, that you preferred a speedy response to a formal typewritten transmittal. Decide how formal the paperwork has to be. If a note will get the job done, why send a 20-page report or proposal?

Sixth, get rid of the clutter. Clutter is not the sign of hard work. It's the hallmark of the disorganized and the inefficient. Get organized.

Abraham Lincoln quipped: "Things may come to those who wait, but only the things left by those who hustle." Ask yourself at the end of the day tomorrow, or at the end of next week, are you *using* your time or *losing* your time? If you're losing it, set priorities. Determine the right mix between reach and frequency. Give CPR by phone. Adopt a pro-active letter-writing strategy. Stop the unnecessary paperwork. Get rid of the clutter. In sales and marketing, well done is better than well said. Mary Francis Berry, former Chair of U.S. Commission on Civil Rights said "The time when you need to do something is when no one else is willing to do it; when people are saying it can't be done."

Set Personal and Professional Goals

The person determined to achieve success in his/her life soon learns the principle that progress is made one step at a time toward predetermined goals. Soccer, football, or basketball games are won one play at a time and the team with one more point usually wins. Similarly, a business grows bigger one customer at a time and a person grows and achieves his/her wildest dreams one goal at a time. In other words, every big accomplishment is a series of little achievements toward a bigger purpose in life. Such life purpose must be converted into realistic and practical actions that can be taken each day. Otherwise, the life purpose without realistic actions may only become a good intention that is never implemented. Do not become a "Mr. Meant To" as expressed in the following little (anonymous) poem.

> Mr. "Meant To" has a comrade
> And his name is *"Didn't Do,"*
> Have you ever chanced to meet them?
> Did they ever call on you?
> These two fellows live together
> In the house of never win,
> And I am told that it is haunted
> By the ghost of *"might have been."*

Meaning to do something worthwhile and doing it in a timely manner can produce good results and happiness. Actions alone may not bring happiness, but there is no happiness without action. It has been said that the road to hell is paved with good intentions (Mr. Meant To). Let us twist this a bit and say, "The road to *achievement* is paved with good intentions." We call good intentions "goals." You have heard it before that if you don't know where you're going, any road will get you there. So it's not enough just to "start out" in your career; you have to know where *you're* going as an individual and as an organization. Dr. Ken Blanchard, author of the *"One Minute Manager"* and *"Situational Leadership"* said "Set goals big enough that God will be proud." You need to have a purpose and you need to have a mission that can be converted into specific goals. For example, in soccer, there's no point in carrying the ball forward until you know where the goal is so you can score. At many of the organizations, they usually tell new hires right from the beginning that they have to let their managers know what their career aspirations are. Do they want to stay in a technical field? Do they want to be a specialist or do they want to be a generalist? Do they want to get into management and formal leadership positions? Managers must know where their goal line is—and they have to know their employees' goal lines—so that they know who to give the ball to, when to pass the ball and with what type of further training.

Yet talk is cheap. Everybody talks about goal setting. Most firms have corporate mission statements and objectives, department goals, and sales quotas; what is their value if they are not put into good use? An old proverb from India sums it up like this: "No one was ever lost on a straight path"; and you'll have to admit it, some companies have gotten lost in the global race for quality products because they are looking for short gains or perhaps their "goal line" is not clear to everyone on the team.

About 90 percent of all new products launched in the U.S. are failures. However, such experiments with new products lead to understanding and learning what to do and what not to do. An Indian Philosopher by the name of J. Krishnamurti said "You must understand the whole of life, not just one little part of it. That is why you must read, that is why you must look at the skies that is why you must sing and dance, and write poems, and suffer, and understand, for all that is life." The same is true for our professional lives and one must keep attempting to set new goals toward higher goals. Our success rate as an individual and as an organization can be enhanced if we're always looking for ways to improve those odds by determining the "goal line." So why don't *people* set goals as frequently as corporations? One answer to this question is "fear." Not having goals covers up for failure. We don't have to face failure if we have no yardstick. If we don't do much, nobody—including ourselves—knows. People without goals drift to the sidelines and eventually disappear. The most important thing about a goal is to have one. Effective goals focus one's attention toward his/her purpose and mission in life. A major element of being or becoming an effective goal setter involves understanding how adults learn best and what makes them stay focused. Dr. W. Edwards Deming, business consultant and author, said "Learning is not compulsory. Neither is survival." Adults understand this concept and learn about their professions because they want to use the learning to achieve their personal and professional goals.

You too may like the story about an older man who was trying to lead a contrary donkey down the road. A passer-by stopped him and commented on the way the donkey was behaving. "Oh, I can make him do anything I want him to with just a kind word," the owner said. "Doesn't look like it to me," the other sneered. "Sure, I can," the owner said. Whereupon he climbed off the donkey, picked up a two-by-four beside the road, and clobbered the animal on the head, then explained to the onlooker. "I simply have to get his attention first." While abusing an animal is never a good thing, "clobbering" (ourselves or animals) may not be necessary if we proactively determine our mission in life so we can have appropriate goals to achieve them. Goals get our attention. Losers stay busy doing things. Winners and successful people concentrate on planning before they ever make a move. For people who don't give attention to long-term goals, the future is any time after tomorrow; but the future has a habit of suddenly becoming the present. Twenty years from now, you don't want to be trying to determine what you want to be when you grow up. To repeat: Goals make one focus. So, what are the characteristics of effective goals?

Well, *first*, good goals are set by choice, not default. Good goals require planning as Ben Franklin said "Proper planning, early to bed, early to rise - Makes a man healthy, wealthy and wise." Proper planning requires that you set the long-term goal at the outset of any project. Have you ever started out for an evening or afternoon drive with a friend without a particular destination in mind? After a mile or two the conversation began to go like this:

◊ "Where do you want to go?"
◊ "I don't know—where do you want to go?"
◊ "How about to the Afghani restaurant for an afternoon snack or even dinner?"
◊ "Well, we already passed that highway."
◊ "Okay, how about a game of basketball?"
◊ "The best basketball court is all the way across town."
◊ "Well, then how about a movie?"
◊ "Hmmm. It is 2:45—everything's already started now."

Perhaps, you have had some of these experiences. John R. Noe, in his book *Peak Performance Principles for High Achievers,* sums up the experience like this: "By the time we are ready to make the big decisions, the options have been narrowed by our little choices along the way. If we do not clarify our goals, our lives will be controlled by haphazard decisions." As you can reason, "not deciding…is deciding." In goal setting, the same is true.

The *second* characteristic of a good goal is that it's a big goal—one worthy of your efforts. If you intend to succeed beyond your wildest expectations, you have to have some wild expectations. A few people wake up every day to go out and slay dragons but most are satisfied to chase lizards day after day. If you're an "average" performer, don't set your sights on "above average." Look at "excellent." Whatever the average might be, look at what your colleagues would term a "reasonable" goal, and then double it. That would be worth working for and worth achieving. Consciously or unconsciously, you always get what you expect. So the secret to success, at least for some individuals, is to raise your expectations and to set goals worthy of your personal time and effort. Don't let the "fear" that you won't reach big goals keep you from setting them. Just keep in mind that FEAR is an acronym that stands for False Evidence Appearing Real (FEAR). The author and management consultant Peter Drucker says the following about goals and objectives: "Objectives are not fate; they're direction. They are not commands; they are commitments. They do not determine the future; they are means to mobilize the resources and energies of the business for making of the future." Oliver Wendell Holmes agreed: "The greatest thing in this world is not so much where we are, but in what direction we are moving." Unless you set big and worthwhile goals, you'll never move beyond your current abilities.

The *third* characteristic of a good goal is that it has a completion date. Goals are dreams with deadlines. Always put a deadline on your goals, because deadlines wake you from your dreams to bring you to the reality of achieving them. Sleepwalkers don't get around very well—at least not without bumps on the shins. One of the authors of the bestseller *Thriving on Chaos,* Fred Brooks, a System 360 Chief Designer at IBM, had this to say about the lack of setting corporate goals: "How does a project get to be a year behind schedule? One day at a time." So, set five-year goals, ten-year goals, six-month goals, and so on. Without deadlines for their achievements, goals are simply good intentions and "pie-in-the-sky" plans.

A *fourth* characteristic of a good goal is that it is followed up by a plan of action or a strategy. Someone once said that "Even if you're on the right track, you'll get run over if you just sit there." You have to put the "how-to" to the goal. If you plan to switch careers, what new training will you need? Where can you get it? What college or corporate course? If you plan to raise funds for a civic memorial, how? Which contributors do you want to reach—individuals or corporations? Do you want to use a direct-mail campaign or a fund-raising dinner? Or both? Goals do very little good without plans of action to bring them into reality. Successful companies have elaborate plans. You wouldn't dare to go to work for them if they didn't. "Buy low, sell high. Collect early, and pay late," are all general strategies. Sounds good in theory, but we'd be in trouble if we depended on a paycheck from companies that didn't have a more complete game plan than that. Without plans, the only way businesses run are downhill. The same is true for individuals and organizations. We need specifics to be successful.

A *fifth* characteristic of a good goal is that it can be broken into specific short-term steps and completion dates. Maximum achievements are the result of minimum steps. A big house is built with one little brick and nail at a time. A suit is sewn one seam at a time. A business is built one employee at a time. Similarly, high school is completed one year (short-term goal) and one course at a time (current goal).

Sixth, good goals are written goals. Committing them to writing makes them real. You can review them, modify them, and commit their accomplishment quality levels and dates to others. They're constant reminders of where you've decided you want to be at what point in your life.

Finally, good goals generate excitement. The late Malcolm Forbes said, "Men who never get carried away should be." Don't be afraid to show your commitment—some might even call it fanaticism—about reaching a goal. If you're kicking and screaming about reaching or not reaching a goal, at least we all know you're alive. Let us summarize good goals. How to set good goals:

◊   Set them by choice, not default.
◊   Set big goals.
◊   Add a completion date.
◊   Develop a plan of action.
◊   Set short-term steps and interim completion dates.
◊   Write goals down.
◊   Get excited about the stated goals.

Norman Vincent Peale may have oversimplified it, but probably not, as he said "Plan your work for today and every day; then work your plan." If you don't start, it is certain you will not arrive. The author Tyrone Edwards said "People never improve unless they look to some standard or example higher or better than themselves." If you do not set higher goals and standards, then effective and efficient improvement may not be possible.

Gary Ryan Blair, author, said "The best opportunities in life are the ones we create. Goal setting provides for you the opportunity to create an extraordinary life." Remember, you can create your future by setting goals and achieving them; and by realizing the following:

◊ The best way to determine your limitations is to go too far.

◊ The best way to find out how far you can go is to go too far.

◊ To find out "how far", you need to go too far.

◊ When you have gone "too far", stop and examine your goals realistically to see how much further you may want to go!

Set Goals with Specific Timelines

Managers and change agents have goals but so do teachers, musicians, retirees, children, and people of all cultures. Regardless of the position, each person is a salesperson and should have specific goals. When it comes to selling, we need to keep in mind that everybody is selling something- an idea, a dream, or a point of view. So, determine what you are selling and then set realistic goals to achieve it.

The best way to predict the future is to create it, first mentally and then physically. You can create your future by deciding where you want to set the goal posts…and then develop a specific plan to get there. As you know, the difference between a goal and a dream is the written words and documentation. Your immediate goals should be successfully achieving a few important activities today and this week. However, short-term goals should focus on specific important objectives and activities for this month, next month and this year. Long-term goals should focus on major achievements and objectives in the next five years in the progression toward your mission in life.

Both short and long-range goals can be applied to any profession; however, the following paragraphs will continue the example of sales. The need for an overall marketing plan is acute; and that plan has to have three parts: Research your market…Position yourself against your competitors...Then develop a promotional plan to tell about your uniqueness. Like any road map, the plan needs to be on paper to take you through important decisions to your destination. That's management's part—as leaders. They have designed the overall marketing plan, but employees have to have their own map to come along. That means as employees and future leaders, you need goals. You also need a detailed map to get you to your predetermined destination and mission. You're familiar with those maps you get at the rental car agencies. They have a blow-up of the immediate area and the rental car agency is marked with a

"You are here" arrow. The problem with those maps is that they don't tell you "how to get there from here." You may know the finish line, the destination, but if you're driving from Los Angeles to New York, you'll need a few other state maps before you pull out the little blow-up of the local area.

You need both kinds for the complete trip; so you need both big goals and little, intermediate goals. Screenwriter Mark Caine said it this way: "There are those who travel... and those who are going somewhere." You've seen the difference in the airport traveler's face. That big-picture direction—or lack of it—in a salesperson's face is a dead giveaway to customers. The blow-up of the end destination will help you travel. But the intermediate road maps will get you where you want to be. The point is simply this: If you want to become the top salesperson, you have to set intermediate goals for making those daily sales calls and you have to put a time frame around those goals. When will you finish the market research on those five new companies in your area? By when will you develop a standard proposal as a model? By when will you send out that direct-mail piece to 16 new prospects?

Some people *fear* to set such specific goals with actions and deadlines, because then they're committed. What's even scarier is to commit those specific goals to someone who can check up on you. So, some people just never get specific about their plans. Don't let yourself get away with that. Sure, if you set such specific goals you'll run into obstacles. The manufacturer may keep the price that you wanted to include in your direct-mail piece in limbo for two months; or, you get caught up on the lengthy proposal for the big sale and make only ten of your 22 planned calls. Never mind those exceptions or "interruptions." Obstacles are always part of the picture. If you find a path with no obstacles, then it probably doesn't lead anywhere. Don't be afraid to be specific with your goals and timetables, and don't hesitate to commit those specifics to yourself and to others. Don't be afraid to think big. Just keep in mind that nobody really succeeds beyond his or her wildest expectations...unless he or she begins with some wild expectations first.

So, set your goals high. Imagine the results you want. Then make it happen for yourself through short and intermediate goals. Never wait on "the big opportunity," the big once-in-a-lifetime chance. That's another reason sales reps fail to get anywhere—waiting for luck. Rather than going out to look for customers, they're out in the backyard, looking for four-leaf clovers. So, set specific goals—commit yourself with specific activities and deadlines. Accept obstacles when they come. Think big. Make your own opportunities.

Here's a final consideration for goal setting: Set risky goals. Your goals this year may be more than simply selling $X worth of product. Experienced, exceptional salespeople eventually get their egos out of the way and work to make the business *as a whole* more profitable. That is, they're not afraid to try something new. To risk, to bring back to management an unfavorable customer comment on a product or service, to encourage an improvement in the product. In other words, they even take risks in their selling. They're not just satisfied to turn in acceptable numbers. They set goals to go after the hard sell. In short, they act like management and owners.

These salespeople see selling as a creative experience. They learn from failure. They're true team players and understand business success from the whole team's point of view. Whatever your long-term goal—whether it's in terms of volume or in terms of creativity with high-risk customers—you *will* fail on occasion. Challenging, specific goals always dictate a few failures. But so what? What if you misjudged a customer's walk-away point? What if you're wrong from time to time? When all is said and done, nobody is going to march you out to the parking lot and shoot you, *since that is illegal in most places*. Selling isn't only a numbers game; it's an intellectual game: Shutting your competitors out and locking your customers in. The surest way *not* to fail is to determine to succeed—with specific goals ahead. Purposeful and predetermined goals that are aligned with your deeply held values are your best tools to achieve your long-term vision. If not goals; then what? If not you; then who? If not now; then when? Envision the target destination. Plan how you'll get there—every day, little by little. Then strike out on a steady, straight path.

Managing Procrastination

With regard to procrastination Peter McWilliams, author, said "When we put things off until some future -- probably mythical -- Laterland, we drag the past into the future. The burden of yesterday's 'incompletions' is a heavy load to carry. Don't carry it." Eliminate the mindset of "why do today what you can put off till tomorrow" by replacing it with the mindset that important activities must get done since they are critical to the achievement of your life's mission. Do not become a "Mr. Meant To" since that does not lead to achievement of worthwhile goals since Mr. "Meant To" has a comrade and his name is "*Didn't Do*."

Oftentimes when one's goals and purposes are not clear, the motivation to achieve things goes away. Extreme cases may lead to boredom and depression. Try to clarify your purpose in life by reviewing your mission and if it does not excite you, then take the time reflect upon your dreams and change your mission so it can get you motivated about your life. Denis Waitley, author and speaker, says "Get excited and enthusiastic about your own dream. This excitement is like a forest fire -- you can smell it, taste it, and see it from a mile away." Clarity of purpose can eliminate the "Mr. Meant To" syndrome.

One way to complete large "important" tasks that cause procrastination is to break it down into small chunks of manageable tasks that can be completed in a short period of time by one person and/or with other's assistance. Also, the small tasks can be linked to specific rewards to provide physical motivation and energy to get things done. Jon Erickson, scientist and author, said "I found that I could find the energy... that I could find the determination to keep on going. I learned that your mind can amaze your body, if you just keep telling yourself, I can do it...I can do it...I can do it!" Eileen Caddy, author and co-founder of the Findhorn Community encourages everyone to "Stop sitting there with your hands folded, looking on, doing nothing: Get into action and live this full and glorious life NOW. You have to do it." Believe in your goals and purpose by continuously reminding yourself of their importance.

Kahil Gibran, author and philosopher, said that "Believing is a fine thing but placing those beliefs into execution is a test of strength." Luckily, each day, people are given new opportunities to test their strengths regardless of what problems one may encounter. According to E.F. Schumacher, an economist, "It is never very clever to solve problems. It is far cleverer not to have them." However, sometimes one encounters them in the process of trying to find out what one can and can't achieve. "Sometimes it is more important to discover what one cannot do, than what one can do," said writer Lin Yu-t'ang. In practicing the habit of seeing what one cannot do, a person may discover new possibilities, and thus build a new image and purpose for oneself. "Our self-image and our habits tend to go together. Change one and you will automatically change the other" said author Maxwell Maltz.

Plan on Persistency to Achieve Your Mission

Enthusiasm is a critical variable for persistency in achieving one's worthwhile and predetermined goals. Dale Carnegie said "Flaming enthusiasm, backed up by horse sense and persistence, is the quality that most frequently makes for success." Enthusiasm accompanied by the vision of value creation will always be an unbeatable pair. Once upon a time, there was a well-known "tribe leader" who started off the yearly meeting with his people by holding up a $50 bill. In the room of 200, he asked, "Who would like this $50 bill?" Hands started going up. He said, "I am going to give this $50 to one of you but first, let me do this. He proceeded to crumple the $50 dollar bill up. He then asked, "Who still wants it?" Still the hands were up in the air. Well, he replied, "What if I do this?" And he dropped it on the ground and started to grind it into the floor with his shoe. He picked it up, now crumpled and dirty. "Now, who still wants it?" Still the hands went into the air. My friends, we have all learned a very valuable lesson. No matter what I did to the money, you still wanted it because it did not decrease in value. It was still worth $50. Many times in our lives, we are dropped, crumpled, and ground into the dirt by the decisions we make and the circumstances that come our way. We feel as though we are worthless; but no matter what has happened or what will happen, you will never lose your value. Dirty or clean, crumpled or finely creased, you are still priceless to those who DO LOVE you. The worth of our lives comes not in what we do or who we know, but by WHO WE ARE. You are special - Don't EVER forget it! If you do not add value by serving others due to the challenges one faces while doing so, you may never know the lives your services touch, the hurting hearts it speaks to, or the hope that it can bring. Count your blessings, not your problems; and remember: amateurs built the ark, professionals built the Titanic. If your faith brings you to it - your faith will bring you through it as well. With regard to understanding faith, once a person asked a Prophet, "What is true faith?" The Prophet replied, "When your good endeavors bring you pleasure and your transgressions cause you anguish, you know that you are a person of faith."

So, regardless of the challenges one may be facing or may face, it is always best to have faith and show great enthusiasm about worthwhile goals. Mark Victor Hansen, author and speaker, is quoted as saying "Doing what we were meant to do creates fun, excitement and contentment in our lives, and invariably, in the lives of the people around us. When you're excited about something it's contagious." Always value yourself and your worthwhile dreams; eventually, others will join you. Remember, who you are, as a human being, and where you are headed will always make you unique in this world of billions! The key is to stay true to your dreams and plans.

Mahatma Gandhi said "If I believe I cannot do something, it makes me incapable of doing it. But when I believe I can, then I acquire the ability to do it, even if I did not have the ability in the beginning." As such, you shouldn't close your eyes to prospective problems or obstacles; you should be realistic in resolving them, but, at the same time look for ways to win toward progress rather than excuses for lack of progress (or losing)! When it comes to progress, George Bernard Shaw said "A man learns to skate by staggering about and making a fool of himself; indeed, he progresses in all things by making a fool of himself." Sometimes, there are temporary setbacks either because one is not fully prepared or due to other situational variables. Nonetheless, they do provide opportunities for reflection, improvement and better strategies toward the stated objectives and goals.

Whenever you're in conflict with someone or a decision, there is one factor that can make the difference between damaging your relationship and deepening it. That factor is "attitude." Have the attitude of doing good things "anyway" as did Mother Teresa, Gandhi, Dr. Martin Luther King, and many other effective leaders of society. Mother Teresa had many great suggestions for every human being, and through being a role model she basically pointed many areas that everyone can and should be persistent as this is the way she lived her life. She stated the following which relates to many areas of everyone's life that requires persistency:

◊ People are often unreasonable, illogical, and self-centered; Forgive them, anyway.
◊ If you are kind, people may accuse you of selfish, ulterior motives; Be kind anyway.
◊ If you are successful, you will win some false friends and some true enemies. Succeed anyway.
◊ If you are honest and frank, people may cheat you; Be honest and frank anyway.
◊ What you spend years building, someone could destroy overnight; Build anyway.
◊ If you find serenity and happiness, they may be jealous; Be happy anyway.
◊ The good you do today, people will often forget tomorrow; Do good anyway.
◊ Give the world the best you have, and it may never be enough; Give the world the best you've got anyway.
◊ You see, in the final analysis, it is between you and God; It was never between you and them anyway.

Persistency is what makes the impossible possible, the possible likely, and the likely definite. Common terminology aside, there's no such thing as "hard sell" and "soft sell." According to CEO Charles Brower, there's only "smart sell" and "stupid sell." The goal is to make an effective sell to the person who needs your product or service. *Pig-headed* persistence is not productive nor effective when the customer has no need for your product or service. *Planned* persistence is and can be very effective and a great time saving device. Now, this not to suggest the method of the bachelor who suddenly decided he wanted to get married. He proposed to his current sweetheart, and she turned him down. Disheartened, he was sharing his frustration with a friend who advised him not to despair, but to be persistent in his dream of getting married. Thinking that there are "plenty of fish in the sea", the next day, he stood on the street corner and proposed to every woman who passed. You'll agree that that was a "stupid sell" at the wrong time. Persistency requires effective thinking with the right goals in mind first as Knute Rockne, Football Coach, explains that, "Football is a game played with arms, legs and shoulders but mostly from the neck up." In football, the goal of winning is clear yet the players must think and adjust accordingly in each moment in order to achieve their objectives. Similarly, with regards to bad moments and negativity, George Foreman, Championship Boxer, states: "That's my gift. I let that negativity roll off me like water off a duck's back. If it's not positive, I didn't hear it. If you can overcome that, fights are easy."

Persistence involves being persistent for the right things at the right time, and making appropriate adjustments to get there. It involves identifying those prospects and current customers who need your products and then keeping your face...or phone number...or fax number...or friendly letter in front of them consistently and persistently even when they send mixed messages. There was a man who checked in for a flight at the airport and purchased a million dollars of life insurance from the automatic machine in August 2005. Then being one to play with gadgets, while waiting for his flight, he wandered over to one of those scales that give out a fortune card. His card read, "A recent investment is going to pay a big dividend." Like he was, you may feel a little ambivalent and disheartened from time to time with customers who string you along. When they ask you to "drop by" and you have to invest a little more time with them, you may not always be sure that's good news.

Planned persistence, can lead to positive results in the long-term. It simply takes patience. In fishermen's way of thinking, nothing takes more persistence than sitting in a boat out in the middle of the water for hours on end with nothing to stare at but that little bobbing on the surface or tug on the line. Like fishermen, persistent salespeople need at least five qualities:

◊   *Trust* - You have to trust that your persistent effort will pay off. The vacation-only fishermen often have the fish or cut-bait philosophy, but those who do it for a living trust their skill and know-how to pay the bills.

◊ *Vision* - Persistent salespeople have to envision the pay-off. You can't keep taking snapshots of the day-to-day still life. You have to take movies of the whole party—the long-term plan. You as successful salespersons have to motivate yourselves by envisioning the reality of reeling in the big one. You envision the kind of fish you want to catch, then you choose the appropriate place and lure.

◊ *Commitment* - Persistent salespeople commit to their long-term plan. You can't get the big fish if you row out only so far, decide the fish aren't biting, and then head back for shore. Staying in the deep water takes commitment to the whole trip. Once in the appropriate, promising fishing hole, you as successful salespersons develop a network inside your client's organization. You look for new internal clients if your first contact isn't biting, and when someone bites and you make the sale, persistence means a call back. You ask for referrals and personal recommendations. You always think leverage. How can I use this open door? Who else can benefit here if I get the word to them? Once you get the door open, keep it open. Studies show that within 10 years, 81 of every 100 customers just drift away. Persistence means keeping them on the line - for good- through relationship marketing.

◊ *Courage* - Persistent salespeople have to have courage when motorboats and skiers dash around them. The tendency is to look for a new fishing hole. If you do your homework up front and know the prospect has a need, why change fishing holes? Keep your line in the water. You may even have to add another pole or two to discourage the skiers from coming too close and getting tangled up in your business.

◊ *Accountability* - Finally, like fishermen, persistent salespeople are accountable. People who fish for a living don't return to shore after half an hour with, "The lake is too big and the fish aren't biting." They figure out how to make them bite. Successful sales persons know that progress comes from a detailed plan. You are accountable. You feel responsible for the plan, you will be responsible for the results, and you deserve the credit.

About persistence and consistency, Vince Lombardi said: "Winning is not a sometime thing; it's an all time thing. You don't win once in a while, you don't do things right once in a while, you do them right all the time. Winning is a habit...unfortunately, so is losing."

Success is getting up before dawn one more time. Just like a fisherman, success is about trusting your skill and your reel. Success is an insight about where the fish will most likely bite. Success is commitment to stay in the boat, the courage to reel in the big one, and the accountability for the results when returning to shore. To the salespeople likewise, success is long hours...Trust in your skills and knowledge...Vision to prospect...Commitment to persist...Courage to leverage for other sales, higher volume, better referrals...Accountability to the organization, your families, and yourself for your success.

Also, the secret to a successful and rich life is to have more worthwhile beginnings than endings. So, stay persistent and get right back up each time you fall as worthwhile beginnings provide new opportunities. Do not forget that the present life in this world is merely a sport and a pastime; a time when people may play foolish games, competing against one another for greater wealth and/or larger families. The present life is like a plant that flourishes after rain: the gardener is glad to see it grow; but soon it will wither, turning yellow, and become worthless stubble. Success in this world counts for nothing if it is not helping others and you both currently and eternally. Success may speed up one's hair color conversion to white, but then again that may be a small price to pay for achieving your goals. In 1986, I once had a chance to attend a performance at the Edison Community College Performance Hall by Phyllis Diller, the famous American comedienne, as she told the audience that "If you don't have wrinkles, you haven't laughed enough." So, enjoy life and stay persistent, even if you get a few wrinkles. Persistency often accompanies and/or results in enthusiasm. With regard to enthusiasm, the artist Edward B. Butler said "One man has enthusiasm for 30 minutes, another for 30 days, but it is the man who has it for 30 years who makes a success of his life." So, be persistent and enthusiastic about your life goals and success will be the natural and ultimate corollary regardless of the challenges. Carol Burnett, actress, said "I have always grown from my problems and challenges, from the things that don't work out, that's when I've really learned."

Know "the Customer"

Most people tend to only think of "end-users" as their customer and, thus, spend much of their time attempting to please them. In the mean time, they totally ignore their employees and colleagues, or the internal customers, who also assist in offering good value and service to the "end-users." In many cases, it is only the frontline employees that come in contact with the customer. In other words, some change agents, managers, and leaders forget the concept of the "value chain" continuum where almost everyone in the organization, including vendors and suppliers, adds to the overall operation and the total value received by the "end-users." So, the term customer can apply to anyone who receives a benefit from you or anyone who depends on you in order to get the work completed. As such, for managers, all employees, vendors, and suppliers become customers. Similarly, for workers, one's boss, colleagues, and others that one depend on become his or her customers. The good thing is that the same principles of treating them with respect and dignity can apply to both groups of external and internal customers. Therefore, one must always attempt to understand them through the continuous gathering of relevant information by keeping one's finger on their "pulse," by making their jobs easier, and by fulfilling their demands as quickly as possible. In terms of acquiring information, someone once said that "There are three principal means of acquiring knowledge…observation of nature, reflection, and experimentation. Observation collects facts; reflection combines them; experimentation verifies the result of that combination." The key is to make sure these employees, colleagues, and vendors verify the quality of the service as they are the recipients and customers. It is their perception of the service and quality of the product that should be used as a "yardstick" for measuring one's level of success. Someone has said that "The true delight is in the finding out rather than in the knowing." So, know as much as possible about the customers' needs, desires, and demands and then work on efficiently fulfilling them in a timely manner.

All individuals can think of themselves as private institutions that have personal and professional responsibilities to their internal and external customers. The personal customers can be inclusive of the people in our personal lives, (parents, children, uncles, aunts, grandparents, relatives, etc.) and professional customers can be colleagues, co-workers, suppliers, bosses, and everyone in the value chain including the final beneficiary of one's efforts, expertise, service, and/or product. The responsibility of fulfilling such needs should be met strategically in a balanced way based on priorities. Christopher Morley, author, once said that "If we all discovered that we had only five minutes left to say all that we wanted to say, every telephone booth would be occupied by people calling other people to tell them that they loved them." Luckily, we all have more than five minutes to covey this message, but it must be done in a strategic and planned manner to both our personal and professional customers. One's mission should focus on all such important roles in one's life.

Professional customers in one's place of employment can be internal or external. Most people tend to focus only on the end-user (the person who pays for the service or product) and not necessarily on the internal customer who serves the end-user. Your number one customer should be the people who help you serve the end-user. For managers, their number customer should be their employees and colleagues. The same is true for salespeople as their number customer could also be their colleagues and the support staff. These internal customers must be treated as the number one customer since they are a very important part of the value chain and how they treat the end-user impacts the long-term relationship. Often times, the support staff are the first point of contact with end-users and these first impressions as well as the follow-up interactions are extremely critical in acquiring and retaining the final customer. The days of the one-night stand are over. Today's selling relationship are analogous to a marriage; both partners (owners and leaders) must commit to it and the families (supporting staff, suppliers and vendors) should help and support them in this unity. However, many so called "less-effective salespeople" are still selling products while customers are buying relationships. Second, the days of "mass marketing" are dead but many retailers and salespeople are still stuck spending valuable time in such efforts rather than focusing on meeting the specific needs of their customers. Everyone needs a custom solution. Nothing fails like success that often encourages complacency...success that has become stagnant. To stay in the market today, we have to listen to customers, keep our finger on their pulse, and make changes as needed. Not one-time changes, but monthly and daily changes. So, what this means to you is this: Get to know your customer as well as you do your marriage partner. Develop intimacy with your customers; of-course, develop this relationship with customers along with and through your employees as well as supporting people in the value chain. If the way a (sales) job or prospect is progressing is too complex or time consuming and you believe there might be a better way of successfully achieving it but do not have the time to follow up with it personally, then delegate the task to the laziest person in your department and soon you may discover the easiest way of getting it done.

In marriage, that intimacy is developed by talking and by sharing self-knowledge. It's the same with your customers; they want intimacy. They want to hear what you know about your company's service, technology, products, and future plans. What can you do for them specifically now? What plans do you have to meet their needs tomorrow and during the next decade? Educate your prospects. Given a choice between a low-priced, no frills, what-you-see-is-what-you-get product and a higher-priced product that comes complete with a knowledgeable salesperson to act as a consultant, today's customer is choosing the knowledge base. The more your customers know about your products, the more likely they are to buy. If you don't know your product, you're being irresponsible in the relationship; but intimacy requires more than self-talk.

To get intimate with your customers, you have to help them disclose self-knowledge. Never stop asking questions. It's amazing what a few minutes spent with your customers will tell you about what needs they have. Know what benefits motivate them. Charles Revlon once said about his marketing of Revlon products: "In the factory, we make cosmetics. In the store we sell hope." Find out what motivates your customers and the benefits they want, not just the features they desire in a product. That's valuable knowledge to effective sales and management. To stay competitive, you have to turn the customer's wants-and-needs list into next year's products and services. Lead your customer to disclose self-knowledge. Then deliver it with better quality faster than others. This is where the marriage analogy breaks down. The advice is *not* to disclose your spouse's snoring or spending habits to friends or neighbors, but such customer knowledge is valuable. Selling, like marriage, also involves changing. The newlywed husband who expects to have a gourmet meal set before him every night promptly at seven is in for a surprise. His expectations are going to need to change. The same is true with your customers. You may have to change their expectations to build volume. Under normal conditions, customers call a real estate agent, expecting to buy a house, but what if they learned that most customers buy two houses—one to live in and one to rent out as an investment? You'd have to change their expectations if you wanted to sell them two houses. If your customers expect to order only six-months' supply from you, you have to lead them to expect to need a two-year supply. If they expect only a product—one your competitor also offers—you have to lead them to expect that they will need training to use that product and guess who is the only provider of that now-expecting training?

Another facet of the marriage relationship is protection. Happily married people protect each other physically—or at least try to. They protect each other's health by the right kind of diet and insistence on more rest and less stress. They protect each other's reputation. They protect each other's best interests in general. The same should be true with the sales relationship. You have to protect your prospects. Big-ticket items represent a risk—customers have to risk their money on something you claim is worth the price. You have to reduce their perception of risk by offering guarantees. By making it easy for them to believe you. By encouraging them to talk to satisfied users. Let them taste it, feel it, see it. Tell them about the buy-back policies, if you don't see one, create it. Assure them you'll be there to hold their hand through the birth. What would marriage be if partners couldn't count on each other to "be there" for them? That's your role, too, with your customer. When there's a problem, be there to add value. If you're present, ready to help when problems surface, customers will remember you forever. They will fall in love with the product, your enthusiasm, and your firm.

As in all marriages, there are the all-night sessions, the arguments, the tears, and the truth telling. You need that—especially with prospects and with customers you lose and must win back. Ask prospects why you failed—sincerely. Was the product not suited to them? Did you really not understand their needs? Is the customer afraid the value won't be perceived by the rest of the work family, especially higher-ups? Did you just not communicate well? Was your proposal off target? Were you unresponsive when they had questions and wanted answers? At worst, with such specific questions, you may get some good feedback. At best, the prospect might change her or his mind.

The challenge is to look for a marriage relationship out there with your customers. Make a date and tell customers about your offerings and find out their needs. Encourage them to tell you about their wildest dreams. Protect them; reduce their risk so they can make that buying decision. Add value by "being there" for them when there's a problem. Act with integrity, shape the future, deliver results, care about people, act as one team, and have a winning attitude. Most importantly, make sure your employees and teammates are happy with their jobs and goals.

There is a 2005 article published in the *Wall Street Journal,* entitled *"Happy Workers Are the Best Workers,"* by Steven Kent, which discussed the importance of treating employees with respect and paying them fairly and the positive outcomes will follow. It is essential for all leaders, managers, and change agents to remember this point with regard to keeping employees happy, especially during change implementation, as they are the most critical part of almost all organizations. Kent (2005) states that "It has been conventional wisdom that reducing wages and benefits improves profit margins, earnings, and even stock price because, generally, investors reward companies that cut these expenses. In reality it's not that simple." Kent continues to state that many investors have not asked the more important question: Can companies be even more successful by focusing on optimizing each employee's contribution, rather than simply looking for ways to reduce the cost of employing them? Kent encourages that customers, stakeholders, and investors should be more conscious of how employees who clean hotel rooms, do other chores, and cook meals are treated and paid, rather than simply looking to see whether the expense can be reduced to the lowest point. Kent states that "Staff motivation, although difficult to quantify, should be part of the investment analysis." Many executives and managers claim that they are treating employees with respect and paying them fair wages, which should go a long way toward establishing an efficient and creative organization. However, a good number of companies and their managers do not live up to the claim of treating employees fairly and equitably. Kent states that "service companies that go that extra mile often derive tangible benefits, such as lower staff turnover and reduced training expenses." Adapting such practices can produce a higher quality of customer service, which becomes a competitive advantage for the twenty first century organization. Kent (2005) believes that "investors should look beyond cost cutting initiatives and ask whether the company is getting the very best out of its people. In other words, is it being well managed?"

Summary

Effective time management and goal-setting are important for twenty first century professionals and managers that often juggle many important issues simultaneously. The creation of a mission is a great start for one's management of time based on priorities. The priorities can then be linked with one's daily, weekly and monthly activities. One can focus on those "high leverage activities" or "big rocks" in order to achieve one's life-long goals. Professional achievement of goals and sales or revenue targets can be planned since they fit into the category of big rocks. However, one must be clear about the importance of various roles, and thus should never allow high priority tasks to be at the mercy of tasks that add no value to one's purpose in life. The creation of a personal mission statement and value clarification can greatly assist in such a prioritization process.

Chapter Nine

CHANGE AND GENDER DISPARITIES IN INFORMATION TECHNOLOGY[6]

C hange can take place and impact a person at the individual, interpersonal, organizational, and/or environmental levels. Similarly, change and cultural conditioning can impact people as well as industries and professions. Such is the case with the field of information technology which has a unique culture and its own challenges with regard to gender concerns which should be changed for the better. Gender concerns in information technology have impacted organizations, interpersonal relationships, and individuals in school and within the field. This chapter presents literature that identifies factors which are affecting the role women are playing throughout the field of information technology and how technology can be used fairly to educate autistic children. Two key structural factors are identified-women's life stages and institutional/organizational structure and change. Additional elements which play a key role include cultural biases, experience levels and mentoring. No single factor can explain the disparity between males and females educationally, and regarding issues of equity in pay and promotion. However, the integrative model as a whole provides a view of the interactive nature of these factors and the cumulative affect that they have on women's careers.

Statistically, inequality can be identified yet this inequality cannot solely be, or even primarily be explained by discrimination. Since current remedies to inequality are aimed at discrimination, it is crucial to identify other elements which are producing this outcome so they may be more clearly recognized and perhaps addressed through policy and/or structural changes. These goals underlie a belief that women have a critical and necessary role to play in the field of information technology in the U.S. for reasons of

[6] - This chapter is co-authored with Susan K. Key, Philip F. Musa, and LeJon Poole from the University of Alabama at Birmingham; and Margarida Karahalios, The John Hopkins University.

competitiveness, as well as parity. Efficient resource allocation and utilization of human capital can be improved by increasing equality in the field, both in industry and in academia.

Introduction to Women in Information Technology

It has been popularly assumed that women in the field of Information Technology (IT) would not face the same barriers to hiring and advancement that women have encountered in other more traditional and established fields, such as business, law and medicine (Northrup, 1988). This notion was based on some real, as well as some imagined, differences between IT and other fields, as well as some encouraging statistics from the 1970's which suggested that women were entering the sciences at the university level in increasing numbers, and were successfully making the transition to industry and higher levels of the academe. These developments spurred both academics and the popular press to take a look at the important role that women have to play both as scientists and policy makers at the managerial level in a field which is critical to the continued economic growth and competitiveness of the US.

While this topic has been addressed from a variety of directions no definitive work has presented a model which explains what the role of women currently is in Information Technology, what the future may hold, and how or if IT differs from other professional endeavors in offering opportunities to women. Grappling with this complex issue has been difficult as a number of interactive, dependent factors appear to be at work. These factors, while identifiable, impact women in different ways and at different critical stages in their development, professionally and academically (Sheinin, 1989; Trauth, 2004). It is no small part of the problem that there has been little coordinated data collection or sufficient empirical studies to paint a completely accurate picture of this complex, and changing area.

While data is available on current job classifications in terms of gender, definitional problems make much of it difficult to accurately assess. Terms such as administrative, executive or managerial which are used by the U.S. Department of Labor Bureau of Statistics for example, may not be narrowly drawn enough to provide a clear picture of the role of women in management. When these terms are not clearly defined, as they are often not, it is difficult to assess if women are moving into policy-making, leadership roles or not. Additionally, longitudinal studies or other statistics that might provide the clearest picture over time in terms of promotional paths which women are taking are simply not available in any meaningful way.

Current Status of Professional Women

While the role of women in the labor market is not a new phenomenon, a perspective on the change in the role of women professionally provides a backdrop for an analysis of what is currently occurring in IT and the related sciences. Women age 16 and over currently participate in the labor force at a rate of 59.5% and make up 47% of the labor force (U.S. Dept. of Labor, 2003). This represents an increase of over 20% for women in the last four decades and a decline in participation by men of 10% in the same period. In education there have been similar gains, women account for 56% of the estimated 1.14 million students getting degrees on U.S. campuses. In comparison, the number of men getting degrees has begun to fall (Challenger, 1999). Women in 2003 received 54% of all bachelor degrees and 52.5% of all masters degrees in the US compared to 43.4% of bachelors degrees received in 1971, and 40.1% of masters degrees conferred in 1971 (Hacker 2003). The same increases have not been seen in computer science where women received only 28% of computer science and IS degrees were granted to women in 2000 down from a high of 37% in 1984 and back to the levels seen in the 1970's (Evans, 2000). At the doctoral level women's achievements across all fields have been impressive--in 1971 they received 13.3% of earned doctorates, this number nearly tripled to 48.9% in 2000 (U.S. National Center for Educational Statistics, 2000). However, the field of computer science in general and IS in particular closely resembles the 1970's with only 13% of doctoral degrees earned by women (Evans, 2000). Hacker (2003) provides a useful snapshot of the professional degrees currently pursued (Hacker 2003).

As a result of educational attainments, women are increasingly represented in the political and professional world. Women now comprise 13.8% of the U.S. House of Representatives and 14% of all U.S. Senators (Canavor, 2004). Approximately 32% of all physicians are women in contrast to 13% in 1975; 32% of lawyers and 21% of judges are women in contrast to 7.1% and 6%, respectively, in 1975 (U.S. Department of Labor, 1975, 2003). During the period from 1976 to 2003, the percentage of female psychologists increased from 31.6% to 67%, the percentage of female scientists increased from 18.6% to 41%, and the number of engineers increased from 1.6% to 20.4% (U.S. Department of Labor, 1975, 2003). Not surprisingly, women's achievements in the professional realm are reflections of their increased presence in professional schools. In 1973, approximately 20% of entering medical students were women; by 2003 about 50% of all entering medical students were women. In the realm of professional schools there have been similar increases with women making up 40% of MBA students and 46% of law students in 2000, compared to 3.6% and 5.4%, respectively, in 1970 (Parks, 2000).

At the upper echelons of industry women are not as well represented as they are in the professions and professional schools. Of the Fortune 500, women hold 14% of board directorships, and 16% of officerships, and only 1.2% of CEO positions compared to 1987 when women held only 3-4% of the directorships and 2% of the officerships, and only 4% of the Fortune 1000 were headed by women in 1987. Despite some increases in board participation, the percentage of women holding one of the 5 most highly compensated positions within companies included on the database is a mere 3% despite the fact the men and women aspire equally to be chief executive officers (Buress, 2004; Smith, 1989; Canavor, 2004).

While many women have yet to attain the position of CEO, their ranks have increased at lower and middle levels. There were more than 7.1 million women in full-time executive, administrative, or managerial positions in 2000 – a 29% jump from 1993. Men experienced only a 19% increase over the same timeframe (Armas, 2000). In 2000, there were 514,000 more women in executive positions than in 1997, compared to only 392,000 more males over the same timeframe (Armas, 2000). These statistics demonstrate that clearly women have a greater role in the professional world today than they did two decades ago; however, what they don't reveal is the level of influence that women are or are not attaining in individual fields.

Current Status of Women in Informational Technology

In tandem with women's rising involvement in the professions, their participation professionally throughout the information technology field has grown as well but not without difficulties. In 1990, about 35.7% of all mathematical and computer scientists were women; by 2003, this number had dropped to 28% (U.S. Department of Labor, 2003). In the computer science and IS professions there were minor gains in some areas but they were less dramatic than in other professions. In 2003, women comprised 27% of computer programmers which was virtually unchanged from the 26% in 1975 and down from a high of 32% in 1988. However, at the lowest ranks of the field--data entry--women's participation was decreasing slightly, from 92.8% in 1975 to 81% in 2003. This phenomenon is indicative of the fact that some positions traditionally held by women are being garnered by men (Hacker 2003).

Again the entrance of women into industry in informational technology mirrored strides that were made by women educationally throughout the

1970's, 80's, and 90's in computer and information sciences. In 1970-1971, women received only 13.6% of the bachelor degrees which were conferred in these fields; by 2001 this figure had grown to 30.3%. Also encouraging was the increased number of Masters and Doctoral degrees which were conferred to women during this same period. In 1970-71, only 2.3% of the Ph.D.s given in computer and information sciences went to women; by 2001 this figure had slowly increased to 19% (U.S. National Center for Educational Statistics, 2003.). The increase in some higher level positions being held by women is remarkable in some aspects.

The median age of these women who hold high-status positions in computer programming occupations is 30 years. Many employers believe that being young is an advantage to learning new skills (Ecevit, 2003). In another study of 2 sets of data collected over 20 years apart from the two populations that differed in age, education, and work experience showed similar results. Women and men who described themselves as possessing a greater amount of masculine characteristics were more likely to aspire to top management (Powell, 2003). Also, differences in aspirations to top management have not changed in the last 20-year span between personality testing. This is different than the results that would have been expected (Powell, 2003). Despite these facts, it is still noteworthy that the Department of Trade and Industry shows that 80% of employees, male and female, would like to spend more time outside of work (O'Keefe, 2004).

It has been thought that since IT is a relatively young field, impediments to the advancement of women long existent in other fields, such as an established "good old boy's network," a large pool of more qualified and experienced male professionals, the lack of female role models and mentors, and established discriminatory practices, would not present the same barriers to women. However, currently 95% of computer industry management at the upper level is male, with, interestingly enough, 30% of management positions being held by women. These figures for women are below the levels in other industries. Despite this, observers have continued to suggest that the industry is "blind to sex and race." Rather, it has been suggested that the small number of women currently in top management in this industry (5%) represents a unique opportunity for advancement as women cannot help but be "noticed and remembered" (Berney, 1988). Additionally, it has been claimed that since most of the men in this industry are young and were ostensibly raised in two decades of the feminist movement, they embrace egalitarian views and would thus be less likely to engage in discriminatory behaviors (Berney, 1988). While these views represent an encouraging and optimistic viewpoint, they do not adequately take into account the variety of structural and social factors that inescapably and inevitably shape women's careers in Information Technology throughout industry and academia (von Hellens, et al., 2001).

As this study suggests, there are a combination of factors which interact to affect the path that women take both specifically in Information Technology, as well as in industry in general. While discrimination is certainly one variable of interest, the absence of mentoring, the work-family dichotomy that women are engaged in, and the structure of organizations and institutions also contribute to an observable lack of equality at all levels (Blum and Smith, 1988). While all current data demonstrates progress in the representation of women across fields, the income differentials which reflect the economic reality for most women have remained impervious to these other changes. These statistics are disturbing because they reflect the lack of upward mobility of women, the clustering of women in entry-level, lower paying positions across industry and the academe, and the mysterious salary gaps which appear over time between men and women of equal tenure.

Rhode (1990) has outlined the issues of gender equality and employment policy. She points out that while an unprecedented equality in formal treatment has been seen as a result of changes in ideological, economic, demographic and legal patterns, the difference in the 'actual status' of women and men is still quite significant. Women made a median of 60.7% of men's median wages in 1960 (Hacker 2003). In the decades to follow, women's share of earnings declined to a low of 60.2% in 1980 until they regained a 71.6% share in 1990, and soared to a record 73.3% in 2000 (Hacker 2003). Thus, in about 50 years women's earning power has increased a paltry 10% in comparison to men's. The statistics for women in computer science and IT tend to be less disparate than other professions where women earn on average 85% of what men do, and at the entry level are 91% of male salaries (U.S. Department of Labor, 2003). Another recent study that controlled its data based on the number of years in the workforce, showed that women in engineering earn approximately 97 cents for every dollar earned by male engineers (Parks, 2000).

Traditional Barriers to Employment Opportunities for Women

While certain occupations are male dominated, others are clearly female dominated. Unfortunately, the female dominated occupations are consistently lower paying regardless of the intellectual or experience level required by the type of work. It has been claimed that approximately half of the female workforce is in areas which are at least 80% female (Reskin and Hartmann 1986). In American society, the typically 'female' work force such as school teachers and nurses, require much more academic preparation but pay less than typically 'male' jobs such as carpentry, auto repair and plumbing. In addition to the occupational stratification, within the same occupations women hold different jobs. Typically, they are concentrated at the lower part of the ladder, displaying vertical segregation, i.e., the higher the level, the lower the proportion of women at that level. Less than a quarter of IT workers are women, representing about 1.5% of the entire Canadian labor force. Yet overall, women comprise just over half of the total labor force. There is some evidence that women computer programmers are more thorough in their development strategies than the men. The men tend to be more interested in the latest technology (Greiner, 2004). Also, women are more likely to use relationship-building strategies than men, by seeking high-visibility assignments and networking within the organization (Canavor, 2004).

Rhode (1990) has explained these differences in a variety of ways which make them impervious to legal remedies, such as continued occupational segregation by gender, continuing salary and promotion differentials between men and women in less gender-segregated occupations, insufficient attention and solutions to remedying continued structural factors that contribute to women's disadvantaged status, and other more complex issues which create barriers not addressed by current equal opportunity legislation. Like other work in this area, these observations are essentially descriptive rather than normative. While they attempt to point to the complex set of factors and structural elements that have led to women's current status, they do not fully identify the predictive indicators.

Factors Which Impact Women's Professional Careers

Sheinin (1989) has proposed a model which compares the stages of women's personal lives to their academic and scientific careers. In order to provide a fuller predictive and explanatory power in assessing the impact of a variety of factors on women's progress professionally, and specifically in information technology, we present an extension of the Sheinin model. Before presenting the model, the authors first discuss some of the factors that come to bear.

Sheinin and others (Barinaga, 1992; Gazso 2004) have suggested that one factor that explains differentials in salary and promotions between men and women is the variety of roles that women assume-- wife, mother, parental/caretaker--during peak periods of their professional and academic careers. This factor along with several others help to explain both the "leaks," that is women either dropping out or not achieving tenure or higher level positions, that occur throughout women's careers in academe and industry. "Women's life roles" can in some sense be termed a structural factor, in that they are in some measure determined both by biological factors as well as ingrained social institutional factors. The other major structural factor that affects the career progression of women is organizational and institutional structure and organizational change (Blum and Smith, 1988). The notion that the structure of institutions work to limit opportunities is not a new one. This was first written about extensively by Rosabeth Moss Kanter (1977) in *Men and Women of the Corporation*. These two factors interact throughout women's lives and have different impacts at different stages of women's lives and careers. Within these essentially institutional factors, a number of processes interact to have important impacts. These are cultural biases which incorporate both the internal view that women have of themselves (self-expectations), and the external view of women (stereotyping, for example) that is held by society in general; the role of mentoring; and the levels of experience that women bring to academe and the marketplace.

Women's Life Stages: Early Educational Experiences

While this model can be applied in all professions across industries to produce a variety of results, here it will be specifically applied to the sciences and the resulting affects on women's careers. Educational institutions begin to impact boys and girls early in their education; this is particularly true in the sciences and in computer learning. Early on both boys and girls are socialized to associate computers use with the sciences-- particularly mathematics (Cooper, *et al.*, 1990).

Cooper *et al.* studied computer learning in middle schools with boy and girls aged 11 to 13. They found that the software most popularly used to teach math, spelling, language and other subject matter has a "predominately male orientation," that is, it uses symbols such as guns, space missiles, warships which are engaged in aggressive action and competition. They found that these programs were preferred by boys, and that boys experienced less stress using them in public situations. By contrast, girls experienced more stress when learning with the male-oriented aggressive computer software in a public setting and reported that "blasting asteroids out of the sky" was boring while the boys' stress increased and the girls' stress decreased when word-oriented software was used (Beyers, 1984). Stress levels for both groups lowered in private contexts for all software used. It can be argued that computer science's culture has been built around male preferences. For example, introductory courses in computer science hone in on the very technical aspects of the field. Women in general are less interested in technical details as much as they are to making the technology fit into a need. Perhaps this gives insight as to why women comprise less than 20% of the nation's computer science research graduates (Sarkar, 2002).

Cooper et al.'s (1990) findings suggest that early on boys and girls begin relating to information technology in different fashions. The work found that women experience higher levels of stress in a public setting. This fact is particularly interesting as most computer learning takes place in public settings--most educational institutions have computer facilities which house large numbers of computer terminals. Equally interesting is their finding that much of the extant educational software has a "male-orientation." Both of these factors, the work suggests, create performance anxiety and decreased success levels in girls at this age; adolescence is perhaps the genesis of the process of women leaking out of the pipeline in information technology.

Cultural Biases: The External View

Other studies which have been done in this area support the conclusion that the process of disenfranchisement from computers begins early on in women's educational experiences. Collis (1985) found that sex differences in attitudes in computers are strongly established in grade school and that teachers in middle and high schools had a positive attitude with respect to computer abilities of males and negative attitude for females. Additionally, while females expressed a belief in equality in ability for computer learning and usage, both males and females reported much less confidence in women's ability to actually perform individually on a computer (Collis, 1985).

The nature of science itself, or at least how "science" has been defined in our culture, also may play a role in how suitable women are perceived to be to the role of scientist. The hard sciences are based on the assumption that the subject and object are radically separate. The more traditionally masculine view of life, in which there is a separate objective world external to the subject, is reflected in the objective nature of the sciences in the western world. Computer science, like other sciences, is built on the notion of a 'single truth'. There is little room for a multiplicity of truths in any hard science. In fact, computer science goes one step further by dividing the world into binary digits. This becomes evident to the user of computer technology in the way that most software is written; that is it allows one to perform the tasks only in the language used for labeling the commands and operations.

The Internal View of Self

Contrary to this binary view of the world, girls and women do not reduce their world into black and while, zeros and ones, or into yes and no, according to Turkle (1984). Turkle suggests that women are more likely to operate on the notion of multiplicity of truths and grey areas--she calls them "soft masters" in contrast to boys and men who she calls "hard masters." "Hard masters" reduce their world into two clearly distinct divisions without room for doubt, indecision and conflict. It is not surprising to note that computer terminology--"hard drives", "megabytes", "rams"--seems to reflect this more male, "hard master," orientation identified by Turkle. She suggests that the masculine culture which endorses decomposition, decisiveness, imposition of will, analysis of concepts with a top-down approach, is in complete synchronization with the world of computer systems; the feminine culture, which is empathetic, caring and non-domineering, on the other hand, is inherently at odds with it.

Studies like Turkle's (1988) suggest that it is not just an external or stereotypical view of women that affects their continuing involvement with computers. Adolescent girls, according to her, tend to see computers and related objects as sensuous and tactile with the system providing a language for communicating and negotiating with a psychological entity while boys see computer systems as sets of formal rules. Thus, it seems difficult to separate even at early stages in women's lives which of the factors impact women most strongly--external or internal. It would appear to be the interaction of a combination of cultural and institutional factors which put men and women on different paths.

Kolata (1984) has reiterated the notion that girls and boys are given different signals in a variety of ways throughout their formative years. Girls are given overt as well as covert signals that they should be interested in dolls and not in mechanical tools, for example. They are taught the 'feminine' virtues of patience, cooperation, empathy, non-competitiveness and non-aggression. The lack of these virtues in boys is not considered as objectionable as it is in girls. They are also steered toward softer subjects like liberal arts and literature, and away from math and sciences. This notion prevails even though it has been demonstrated repeatedly that girls score higher grades than boys in most subjects including math and sciences (Campbell and McGabe 1984). However, determining to what extent gender-differentiating behavior which appears in adulthood is due to childhood experiences and to what extent it is genetic still remains unanswered. Regardless of the debate on the extent of its effect, the role of social expectations on confidence levels and performance is well documented (Collis, 1985).

As Collis's (1985) study revealed, these expectations have a two-pronged effect: first, human beings tend to respond to other people's expectations and, second, the person can be subsequently conditioned into believing that the expectations represent their real ability. Thus it was not surprising that she found pronounced differences in the self-confidence of males and females in regard to computer usage. The remarkable finding was that when asked to respond to the statement, "females have as much ability when learning to use a computer" females showed strong agreement while the males tended to doubt the statement. However, in spite of demonstration of general confidence in female abilities with regard to computers, when asked the same question about themselves as individuals, females did not display the same confidence in their own abilities.

A Model of Gender Disparity in IT

From the foregoing discussions of the various factors that contribute to the gender disparities in the IT profession, we now present the model of gender disparities in IT from a global perspective. As discussed above, the model takes into merges ideas espoused by Kanter, Blum and Smith, and Sheinin. In this model, as shown below, inertia in institutional and organizational structure as well as women's life cycle stages tend to have unique set of variables that lead to gender disparities in information technology.

<table>
<tr><th>A
Inertia in Institutional and
Organizational structure</th><th>B
Women's Life Cycle Stages</th></tr>
<tr>
<td>

⇒ Limited terminal Degrees in IT
⇒ Limited mentoring and networking
⇒ Good Ole boy network
⇒ Unequal pay for same work
⇒ Cultural biases
⇒ Expectations
⇒ Glass ceiling

</td>
<td>

⇒ Education delivery method favors boys (sciences, IT, etc.)
⇒ Mariiage effects
⇒ Motherhood
⇒ Chilrd rearing and nurturing
⇒ Cultural biases
⇒ Expectations (internal and external

</td>
</tr>
</table>

Both A and B Lead to Gender Disparities in Information Technology

Women's Life Stages: Entrance into the University and Industry

As women enter both educational institutions and industry, other factors begin to play larger roles in their careers. Along with cultural biases and gender conditioning which affect women's childhood and adolescence, additional factors beyond culture such as mentoring, attainable experience, additional life roles, and organizational structure, which were present earlier, begin to play an even more important role. One aspect that continues to play an important role is the specific culture in the world of information technology. This has been documented by Rasmussen and Hapnes (1991), and identified as the "hacker culture" from which women they studied in a university setting were completely excluded. Rasmussen and Hapnes suggest that "the culture of computer science is important in producing and reproducing male domination in higher education in CS." Thus, it influences the integration of women and their position within the field of computing (Rasmussen and Hapnes, 1991). They suggest that this culture creates shared values between the faculty and the students and that the hackers who are male are seen as being 'bright and creative' while women remain on the periphery in isolation from the dominant culture within the university. The result of this is that contact between faculty members who view females as lacking in the "instrumental attitude" of the culture, and women students is decreased (Rasmussen and Hapnes, 1991). This coupled with the very few numbers of women on the faculty leaves women students with little guidance for their careers.

The Role of Mentoring

Studies like that of Rasmussen and Hapnes (1991) demonstrate the tie in between culture and other important factors which affect women's careers such as mentoring and the availability of role models. Mentoring has been found to be critical in the advancement of professional careers (Kram, 1985; Burke, 1984). Researchers have claimed that in general women face more gender-related interpersonal and organizational barriers in their obtaining a mentor than men (Kram, 1985; Ragins, 1989). Reportedly, women have less access to informal settings necessary for initiating and building mentor relationships (Hunt and Michael, 1983). It has also been said that men and women find it more comfortable to mentor proteges of the same gender (Kram, 1985). Among the reasons given for this is that it is perceived to be potentially less scandalous (Bowen, 1985). The traditional expectation for women to take a passive role in initiating relationships forms another barrier for women seeking mentors (Hill, et al., 1989).

Ragins and Cotton's study (1991) which examined mentoring barriers for women, found that after controlling for experience as a protege, age, rank, and tenure, women perceived the presence of more barriers than men in gaining a mentor. The decreased availability of mentors for women may explain their paucity at higher levels in information technology both in industry and in academia. Statistics might suggest that this problem may be even more acute for the women in this field where women hold only 5% of upper management slots, and constitute 8% of tenured faculty (Barinaga, 1992). The average female manager or professional does not have the role models and/or the same-sex mentors available to her which are considered critical in the advancement of professional careers (Kram, 1983; Burke, 1984).

This situation presents a self-defeating cycle for women. Without the support of a mentor who can help women in selecting the right research problems, provide encouragement, serve as a liason to important contacts in the field, women may be less prepared for key positions as their careers progress (Barinaga, 1992). Lack of experience in proteges with upper-level mentors is reported to result in a higher perception of barriers than those who have had such experience (Ragins and Cotton, 1991).

The failure of women to achieve upper-level positions or gain access to those in those positions then tend to perpetuate the informal network structures which are an effective tool for male advancement and which had been established before women started climbing the professional ladders. Some of this network, often referred to as the "good old boy's club," is based on masculine activities, which reflect traditional social and cultural roles, such as sports talk, golf tournaments, etc. and other shared experiences as a means for building camaraderie. As these studies on mentoring suggest, women are often left out of these informal networks of 'power sharing and dissemination' across industry and academia. Three out of five women with high-tech jobs say they would choose another profession if they were starting out today because of a perceived glass ceiling, according to a survey by Deloitte and Touche' (Vuong, 2001). Sixty-two percent of men said women are faced with additional struggles to reach top ranks, while 62% of women surveyed said they believe that they face a glass ceiling (Vuong, 2001).

The Role of Experience

Another common explanation for women's lack of advancement is that most men holding the top positions entered their respective professions at least twenty years ago. At that time, not many women were earning bachelors and masters' degrees in business and technical fields, and entering the workforce. As a result, not many of them are at the top today. In the 1980's, it was believed that these factors were not at work in information technology as a profession. IT was labeled 'gender-blind'. The industry was thought to be too young to have established industry-wide norms, expectations and images, and perhaps women were less likely to be perceived as outsiders. Starting in the 1980's women had entered the workforce in more comparable numbers as men with roughly equivalent educational attainments and work experience, unlike other professions where women were at a disadvantage educationally, and in terms of work experience, and thus had to catch up with men's accomplishments. Also, the fact that women tend to shy away from technical degrees may not be the reason why they are absent from the IT's executive ranks. Fewer than half of the recent IT executives surveyed in a recent study had math, computer science, or engineering degrees (Melymuka, 2003). However, about 60% of the women surveyed thought that women hit a glass ceiling in technology jobs. They said barriers to advancement include gender bias, sex discrimination, and a lack of female role models (Mincer, 2001).

However, Pfaffin (1984) reports that while the number of women in sciences and technologies has increased along with improvements in entry-level opportunities and reduced entry-level salary differentials, career advancement opportunities have not gone through a comparable change. Ahern and Scott (1981) demonstrated that women and men who started out with similar credentials did not achieve similar success in career advancements. Women had significantly lower salaries than men, obtained tenure at a later age and were less likely to obtain it at all. This was true regardless of their marital status and of whether they had children or not. Regardless of their degree, women are more likely to work in administrative or clerical roles. In just 3 years after graduating from their universities, female graduates' earnings are 76% of those of male graduates (O'Keefe 2004).

A 1990 study by the Association of Computing Machinery predicted that the trend observed in the 1970's and 1980's of women working in the computer industry may be "short-lived" because of pervasive gender bias which could be found at every educational level (Frenkel, 1990). This bias appears to be directing women away from the industry, as well as away from academic careers in information technology (Frenkel, 1990). The study concluded that "There is mounting evidence that many women opting for careers in computing either drop out of the academic pipeline or choose not to get advanced degrees and enter industry instead.... consequently, there are disproportionately low numbers of women in academic computer science and the computer industry," (Frenkel, 1990). In 1984 women comprised 40% of computer science and engineering degrees. In 1996 it fell to 28.5% of these degrees. Today, these areas of study are being gender-comprised by just 15-20% of women (Evans, 2000).

While the number of computer science Ph.D.'s fluctuates yearly, it continues to remain at a relatively low level--approximately 15%, and there is growing evidence that women who do get these degrees are not pursuing careers in academics (Frenkel, 1990). For example in computer science, the percentage of females entering the academic market is consistent with the percentage of females graduating with doctorates in the field (Gries and Marsh, 1992). Since 1970, the female population of the computer science graduates has remained at a constant level of 10-14%, which is consistent with their share of associate professorships during the same period. However, only 4% of full professorships are held by women. This would suggest that female faculty members are not being retained at the same level as male faculty members, that is, they are not achieving tenure, and are for some reason leaking out of this part of the pipeline. Also, women comprise only 40.8% of the post-secondary teachers in the U.S. and they earn a median weekly pay that is 79% that of their male colleagues.

The outlook in industry also suggests that forces are at work, preventing women from gaining the critical levels of experience which they need. As stated before, women are a rarity at upper levels of management (Myers, 1990). Studies of self-reports by women indicate that the majority (70%) feel that they must work harder than men on the job, and 58% reported that harassment in the workplace was prevalent. Some 78% stated that while starting pay was comparable, promotions were not (Frenkel, 1990). Fewer women than men believe that opportunities have advanced for them in the last 5 years (30% versus 41%). Twenty-four percent of women still see their working culture as "inhospitable" versus 13% of men (Canavor, 2004). Numbers like these can perhaps be attributed to the same reoccurring problems which women have encountered in other fields--it would seem difficult to account for these findings in terms of real experience differentials, though. However, more empirical work is needed in this area.

The Impact of Critical Life Stages on Women's Careers

Another "leak" which affects the progress of women's careers is real and perceived conflicts between work and family. Women's early career experience generally coincides with the stage in a woman's life when she is marrying and starting a family. At this stage in their lives, professional women are faced with trying to manage a career, a home and child care. For some women, marriage itself places limits on promotional possibilities as they may restrict themselves geographically due to their spouse's career. Interestingly, equal percentages of women aspire to become CEOs, whether they have children living with them or not (Canavor, 2004). Additionally, women who have full personal lives may be viewed by the organization--be it a university or a corporation--as lacking a strong commitment to their work or not being as serious about their careers as their male colleagues (Barinaga, 1992).

It has been suggested that it is at this point that women begin to lag behind men in terms of promotions (Higgins et al., 2000; Higgins et al., 1994). Higgins et al. (1994) suggests that this result is in response to real conflict felt by women; their work suggests that women who put their careers first or on par with their husbands' careers face more conflict at home than women who put their careers second. This study examined how the lives of women and men are affected by taking work home, specifically using an "electronic briefcase" (working at home on the computer for work). Three hundred and fifty-nine dual-career couples with children were analyzed. Seventy-three percent of the men chose the electronic briefcase work style in contrast to only 49% of the women. The findings were that men and women who do not use the electronic briefcase experience similar levels of work-family conflict while the women who used the electronic briefcase experienced significantly more conflict than the men who did and women who didn't. The study concluded that men are able to work longer hours without increasing conflict at home.

Since Felice Schwartz (1989) first introduced the concept of the "mommy track," some of the blame for women's failure to achieve greater equity in promotions and pay has been placed on a lack of commitment which results from the conflicts of having a family. Interestingly enough, Konrad and Cannings' (1990) study suggests that this dilemma of career commitment may not be gender specific. Their study found that men who had a higher level of family commitment, "career-family men" tended to work shorter hours, had lower pay, less training, fewer years of service and less preparation for top management than did men who were "career-primary" yet they were similar to "career-family" women. Discouragingly, it would appear that regardless of reality, women were uniformly perceived to be more family-committed--women who were found to be "career-primary" worked longer hours but still were in lower paying jobs, and received less training and preparation for top management (Konrad and Cannings, 1990). Thus, both real and perceived commitment to other life roles would appear to create career barriers for women.

The Role of Organizational/Institutional Structure and Change in Women's Careers

The final factor that has a life long affect on women's professional careers is the structural forces at work within organizations. Traditionally, the entry-level jobs which were open to women did not have paths which provided upward mobility (Kanter, 1977). Current competitive forces--both globalization and down-sizing--have resulted in decreased opportunities for women in information technology and across industry (Buress, 2004). Many organizations have flattened their structure by eliminating many middle management positions which represented promotional opportunities for professional women who entered many organizations during the 1970's and 1980's (Blum and Smith, 1988). Universities have also been affected by economic factors which have led to a decrease in tenured positions, and an increase in "temporary" positions such as lecturers where women are concentrated (Barinaga, 1992).

Additionally as many firms become global, promotional paths require an international assignment--assignment for which many women are not considered (Adler, 1984). Women currently represent only 3% of expatriate managers, and Adler's (1984a) work suggests that this is due to the perception of male managers that women will not be accepted in this role rather than women's refusal of international assignments. In fact, once women are given international assignments they perform as well as males (Jelinek and Adler, 1988). These kinds of organizational changes have added to the barriers that the traditional hierarchies already presented.

A Case Study of Women in Information Technology

While this discussion only reflects women's status in IT in the US, international data suggests that the problems which women face in the US are shared universally. Since this industry is increasingly global, and is in some respects at the heart of the reason for the globalization of many firms, this is particularly discouraging. Women in IT in the United Kingdom, for example, appear to be even worse off than women professionals in the US. As in the US, the computer industry in Britain is male-dominated, and women who work in it are paid less than their male counterparts, let go more frequently, and promoted less often and less rapidly. Much like it did in the US, the computer industry in the early 1980's in Britain promised women job opportunities in an atmosphere of equality and non-traditionalism. In Canada, the number of women employed in technical jobs remains fairly static at just 28% (Evans, 2000).

However, this promise has not been fulfilled. In 1990, only 20% of the computer industry in Britain were female (Whyte, 1990); this is in contrast to US Bureau of Labor Statistics which estimates that approximately 30% of computer specialists, computer system analysts, and computer programmers in the U.S. are women. The same reasons cited for inequalities in the US are also cited in Britain--the absence of female mentors in industry and academics, and unwritten discriminatory practices (Ryan, 1990) which prevents women from advancement. As in Britain and the US, women in Japan and France also complain of the inescapable "glass ceiling".

Interestingly enough, an example from Singapore presents a picture of how equality can be achieved in a developing economy where both industry and the academe are strongly motivated to increase the skill level of the profession for economic reasons, regardless of gender. In 1987, approximately 55% of the graduates of the four main centers for computer studies were women, and 41% of the workforce in computer industry is female with 58% of the analyst programmers and 52% of the systems analysts/designers being held by women (Kheng, 1990). Professional women's presence in computer programming is high in Turkey compared to the USA or The Netherlands. In Turkey, women constitute 39% of system analysts and 44% of computer programmers. The same figures for The Netherlands are 20% and 15% respectively. Even in the USA where women are encouraged to choose computer sciences through scholarships and affirmative action programs, the percentage of women system analysts and computer programmers is 36% and 27% respectively (Ecevit, 2003). While family commitments are a concern, the role of women in IT in Singapore has been characterized as equal and discrimination free (Kheng, 1990).

Women, Technology and Economic Developments in Afghanistan

Information Technology (IT) is a key determinant in transforming the economies of developing nations as well as nations in transition and, thereby, ensuring their place in a global economy. As IT affects these changes, nations are also transformed socially and politically. Negotiating this transformation within cultures that have existed for thousands of years requires balancing traditional values with Westernized values that accompany IT and interacting in a global economy. The inclusion of women in IT appears to be one of the most controversial issues in the transformation of these nations because this transformation appears to require women to assume more Westernized roles that may violate established cultural roles. Yet, a closer examination of the lessons learned from women in IT in Western society shows that women can effectively be included in IT and support traditional existing cultural mores. Gender needs transcend cultural needs.

Women represent some of the poorest and least educated population group within developing nations, and IT has the potential to overcome their poverty and marginalization. As such, it is important to leverage the uses of

IT in addressing the needs of these women—not only to improve their status, but also to improve each nation's overall economic status. When a nation's development is hindered by the ravages of war, women's state and a nation's state suffer even more. Many providers of families, as well as workers and leaders of a nation are lost. Many women, society, and the nation are left to care for these families. Under these conditions, it is even more imperative to create an IT enabling environment that includes women socially, politically, and economically so that they can take care of their families and help to reconstruct their war-torn nation. Afghanistan finds itself in such a position. In order to create a nation of citizens that contribute to reconstruction, it is important for Afghanistan to define educational policies that embrace the female population in IT. The result is not only a generation of women that are IT literate and positive contributors to the growth and development of Afghanistan, but a generation that can serve as IT intermediaries for older women to help the latter become economically empowered through IT as well.

Beyond including women, Afghanistan needs to consider including individuals with disabilities as part of their reconstruction effort. Disabilities are increasing across the globe, with some disabilities such as autism, reaching epidemic trends. Rather than including this population in the development of nations, societies across the globe, in general, seem to dismiss the potential of such individuals to positively contribute to the economies of nations. Women with disabilities are an especially marginalized group who face even greater poverty and alienation. IT, especially computer-aided instruction, has the potential to remediate or mitigate the symptoms of disabilities. In doing so, it has the potential to train individuals with disabilities to perform skills that can be part of the reconstruction of Afghanistan and for which they are most appropriately suited.

A characteristic of individuals with autism, for example, is that they like routines. As such, they are perfectly suited for repetitive work whereas the typical population would become bored and not wish to perform such work. This section addresses a gendered as well as a disabilities approach to IT education. It focuses on autism as a specific disability because it is the most pervasive developmental disability. It affects every aspect of a person's life and does so throughout a lifetime. All this is provided in the context of American education as it provides decades of lessons learned. Interestingly, it also shows, how across the globe, people face the same issues and challenges when attempting to integrate women and individuals with disabilities in education, especially IT education, and society. We have a long way to go towards full inclusion of all populations within our societies, economies, and politics. IT can serve as a vehicle for accomplishing these goals, and Afghanistan can become a participant in the effort to do so.

Autism, Gender, and Technology

Autism is a neurobiological syndrome—a collection of characteristics—with heterogeneous and impaired behavioral expressions in three interrelated areas: (a) social interaction, (b) communication, and (c) activities and interests that result in disordered development. The fundamental basis for the success of computer aids in helping individuals with autism seems to rely on a complementarity of worlds: the world of the computer and the world of the individual with autism appear to be complementary. The world of the computer either shares the same characteristics as the world of the person with autism or satisfies some of the same needs. The world of the computer is objective, two-dimensional, lacking in social contact and cues, non-threatening, logical, repetitive, consistent, predictable, focused, infinitely patient, filled with an extraordinary depth and breadth of visuo-spatial cues, and requiring sensorimotor interaction (Panyan, 1984). Furthermore, the computer world affords the individual with autism total control; the user determines when and how to interact with the computer (Nimmo, 1994; Swettenham, 1996). The computer world seems to mirror and complete the solitary world of the person with autism. The computer and the individual with autism seem to speak the same language.

Educational programs for learners with autism must be systematically developed to be (a) engaging and to provide (b) explicit instruction that is (c) organized in manageable chunks of information and (d) explicitly shows the connections between the chunks of information to create a gestalt. Insofar as a large portion of learners with autism are visual learners, this information must also be (e) presented in visual form. Furthermore, since learners with autism require (f) intensive, (g) repetitive, (h) individually paced intervention, the format of the educational program must meet these needs. Essentially, learners with autism require a well-designed explicit, structured, intensive, consistent, individually-paced instructional program (Karahalios, 2005). Interestingly, these are the same requirements for any population group—women, men, rich, poor—wishing to learn new skills, especially ones with low literacy.

Communicative and social deficits are at the core of the diagnosis and treatment of autism. Various factors such as attention and motivational deficits, stereotypic behaviors, resistance to change, and language delays impede the development of individuals with autism. Computer-aided instruction (CAI) appears as a viable tool to provide this type of education. It can be used to engage students in learning, increase attention and motivation, encourage language development, and effect positive behavioral changes (Panyan, 1984). Since their first use in the 1970s, computers have been seen as useful tools in attempting to overcome communicative and social deficits of individuals with autism: "Increasingly sophisticated computer technology can meet the needs of children with disabilities in ways that were only dreams until the advent of personal computers" (Hutinger, 1996, p. 105).

The promise of computers to help individuals with autism is, however, being compromised. Regardless of the reason for computer use; e.g., educational, social, or rehabilitative, the format of the interaction is generally based on an inherently male gender-based play motif. Since play is increasingly gender-differentiated as children grow up, computers increasingly discriminate against their needs and wants of female children and, thereby, alienate them. As such, children of the female gender, including those with autism, are deprived of optimal opportunities to overcome the symptoms of their disorders as well as opportunities for potential skill development that could result in greater empowerment and autonomy. The female population with disabilities is subjected to double discrimination: sexism and disability bias (WEEA, November 1999).

Eradicating Gender and Disability Bias

In 1972, the US Department of Education passed Title IX as an effort to reform gender inequality in schools. This amendment required that 'no person in the US shall, on the basis of sex be excluded from participation in, or denied the benefits of, or be subjected to discrimination under any program or benefits of, or be subjected to discrimination under any program or activity receiving federal aid' (GREAT, "What's been done," 1998). The following year, 1973, Section 504 of the Rehabilitation Act made it illegal to discriminate against anyone with disabilities seeking employment with federal contractors and grantees. In 1975, the Individuals with Disabilities Education Act (IDEA) mandated that all children with disabilities be educated in a least restrictive environment—placing them in regular classrooms as much as possible. In 1980, the Science and Engineering Equal Opportunities Act was passed. This legislation proclaimed that:

> It is the policy of the United States to encourage men and women, equally, of all ethnic, racial, and economic backgrounds to acquire skills in science, engineering and mathematics, to have equal opportunity in education, training, and employment in scientific and

engineering fields, and thereby to promote scientific and engineering literacy and the full use of the human resources of the Nation in science and engineering (SEEOA, 1980).

As recent as 1990, The Americans with Disabilities Act (ADA) was passed to ensure equal opportunities to individuals with disabilities in the areas of employment, public accommodations, state and local government, transportation, and telecommunications (WEEA, November 1999). Regardless of all this legislation, gender bias and disability bias still persist—in society, at large, as well as the educational system, in particular. Insofar as technology integration has been emphasized in K-12 in the last decade, these biases have materialized in a technology gender gap and gender bias. The "Title IX at 30: Report Card on Gender Equity" which reviews the progress we have made in gender equity in the thirty years after the passage of Title IX, reveals the different marks in different areas of gender equity, with technology and career education being the worst offenders (NCWGE, 2002).

Considering that gender and disability bias are acknowledged and that the federal government has passed legislation to address these biases, then why do these biases persist? The following sections explore how and why females are discriminated and alienated by the computer field as well as what steps we can take to reverse this discrimination and alienation in the hope of providing fair access to what appears to be a promising tool for ameliorating the symptoms of disabilities as well as providing empowering self-management opportunities.

Gendered Play and Preferences

Psychologists have defined four genders: male, female, undifferentiated, and androgynous. Each gender shares certain stereotypic characteristics. The male gender is defined by such characteristics as analytical and aggression. The female gender is defined as nurturing and emotional. The undifferentiated gender possesses few male or female stereotypic characteristics while the androgynous gender possesses some of both. Koch writes that "Although men and women can display characteristics of any of these four genders, in our society women are socialized to be of the female gender" (1994, p. 14). Research indicates that this socialization has the greatest impact on children's play preferences, learning abilities, and temperament; we teach children how to "act" like girls and boys (Swanson, 2000).

The primary differences between the gendered play of boys and girls appear to be based on the genders' interactions with their environment, each gender's self-image, and society's gendered expectations. Boys are more aggressive than girls; they play competitively. Girls play cooperatively. Boys are more concerned with justice, following the rules, competition, autonomy, objectivity, and control. Generally, as stated by researchers, "men are not expected to become involved with people, but to be involved with things" (Kieran-Greenbush, 1991, pp. 171-2). Girls tend to follow a care approach where they are concerned with being fair, being supportive, nurturing, working together, being emotive, using their intuition, and personal experience. They like to work together collaboratively and cooperatively. They are socialized to be less aggressive and assertive. Young boys often choose to spend their "free time" running around, exploring, and experimenting, and these activities help them prepare for the world of science and mathematics. Young girls are not specifically encouraged to participate in these "boy" activities, and are more often encouraged to "be careful." When boys and girls play together, boys' play preferences tend to prevail. In a 1990 study, both performed roughly equally in math. However, self-perceptions of skill and competence differed. Twenty-two percent of the boys and only 14 percent of the girls strongly agreed with the statement, "I am very good at mathematics." This self-image reinforces for girls that they do not belong in the "boys'" domain. Young children tend to choose colors, toys, and activities that they feel are meant for their sex, and like to play with other children of the same sex. Children get approval from their peers when their play is appropriate to their sex. Those who play in cross-sexed activities tend to be criticized by their peers or left to play alone (Kieran-Greenbush, 1991).

Implications for the Information Technology Industry

Despite the existence of real barriers, women in information technology have been urged--as women routinely have been in more traditional fields--to use so-called "male" career strategies, such as networking and game playing to achieve success in this male-dominated field (Johnson, 1990a). Such advice presupposes that such skills will be effective in overcoming the very real barriers which are in place. Johnson (1990) suggests that women are more balanced than men, that they are more rational and calmer than men, that they are more naturally helpful than men, that they possess stronger negotiating skills than men do, and that by using and displaying these skills they can achieve success in upper management. It has even been suggested that these skills alone give women an advantage over men, and through achieving greater visibility, women will be able to obtain managerial success (Molloy, 1991). Such advice once again casts women in the role of "helpmate," and inappropriately blames the victim for not relying on personal skills to overcome hurdles to equality in pay and promotion which are due to structural and cultural factors.

The reality is that fewer women are opting for computer related majors in schools, a trend which promises a shortage of labor force in the industry during the next decade (Barinaga, 1992; Trauth, 2002). This is occurring at a time when the U.S. is not educating enough of its own scientists, and is relying heavily on foreign born males to fill the gap. Currently, for example over 50% of the Ph.D. candidates under the age of 35 in engineering are foreign born. This does not bode well the industry or academia as a whole if the U.S. is to remain competitive in the sciences. While "hero" stories are often reported as examples and incentives for women who are struggling at lower and middle level positions, they are anecdotal and do not reflect the empirical reality. Examples such as Kathy Hudson's appointment to vice president of corporate information systems for Eastman Kodak Co. in 1987, and the success and acclaim she has achieved in this position should operate to encourage women (Krass, 1990). This example as well as those of IBM's enlightened policies for child-care and parental leave are encouraging and should set the standard for the industry. However, IBM and Eastman Kodak are the leaders in the industry, and by no means represent the norm within it. The average or even above-average woman in the industry can rarely see herself reflected in examples such as Hudson's, nor are IBM's ideal family policies part of her working life.

It is also interesting to note that Kathy Hudson's appointment was much opposed because she was a woman, and it was claimed--too inexperienced. However, it was a move by Eastman Kodak to improve the representation of women in upper management. Additionally, she had to prove herself with extraordinary performance that won her Information Week's Chief of the Year in 1990 in order to be considered a "success." Other stories such as Sandra Kurtzig's successful tenure as chief executive officer and co-founder of Ask Computer Systems, Inc. are puzzling and less encouraging. There are no other women in Ask's top management, other than Kurtzig, and Kurtzig herself inexplicably claims that she "does not see boards of directors as a path toward accomplishment" and would never place women's issues before stock holders issues (Savage, 1989). It is important to note that when a woman executive leaves an executive position voluntarily (example Brenda C. Barnes as chief executive of Pepsi-Cola North America), it unleashed a vast public debate about women's conflicting ambitions for achievement at work and time at home (Stanley, 2002). Women are under much more scrutiny as executives simply because there are so few of them (Stanley, 2002).

While such examples may be interesting or noteworthy, they do not represent the average woman's position in the IT industry and may offer false hope, rather than realistic attainable goals. Current evidence discussed earlier in this article suggests that gross inequalities in both pay and promotion between men and women continue to be the norm throughout most of the IT industry. This coupled with other data which suggests that IT organizations are restructuring to accommodate more part-time employees, and to provide training for women at low level entry positions does not paint an optimistic picture for female workers in this field (Whyte, 1990). Women with up to 5 years experience are paid almost exactly the same as their male counterparts in most technology jobs, but women with 10 or more years of experience earned an average of 9% less than males with equivalent experience and skills. Overall female techies earn an average of 92 cents for every dollar their male counterparts earn, and thus averaging $5,071 less in annual pay than men (Hacker 2003).

The fact that IT appears to be following the path of all other professional fields wherein the disparity between the genders is obvious, has taken away the optimism shown in the initial stages of the development of the IT field. The promise of IT being the industry where women were welcome, where the only thing that counted was competence has evolved into a reiteration of the barriers which continue to be present across the professions to continued equality and upward mobility for women. Sixty percent of women currently in IT would choose another profession if starting their careers today, and 62% of them point to the glass ceiling as being one of the reasons (Vuong, 2001). In terms of overall satisfaction with compensation, 54% of women say they are unhappy with pay compared to 49% of men. The desire to be better compensated may be why 63% of women and 57% of men say they are unwilling to accept a pay cut, even if it was in exchange for a more satisfying job (Vuong, 2001).

Summary and Implications

In order to better understand the reasons why girls and women are not playing a more equal role in computing, a workshop was held at the National Educational Computing Conference in the June of 1990. The Communications of the ACM reported extensively on this workshop in their special report "Women and Computing" (Frenkel, 1990). Suggestions were made to improve access to computers for women throughout the educational system, to improve parental education, to provide more child care options for working couples, to create more formal mentoring relationships in educational institutions and in industry, and to provide reentry options for female computer scientists as needed. These suggestions all address some of the leaks which were identified in the model presented here.

Research needs to be done to understand further the role that each of these factors play. A valuable contribution of the NECC workshop was in emphasizing the need for qualitative methodologies for studying the issues. It is important to look beyond the 'excuses' provided for the lack of women's participation in this leading-edge industry while the industry is still in a formative stage. A failure to do so before it is too late would perpetuate the problem, and make for an even more complex situation. Changing attitudes is the key to any fundamental change in social practices. Subtle discrimination which creates some of the observable leaks is difficult to detect and deal with, yet it has lasting and cumulative effects. It is the lack of recognition of the forces at work coupled with an unwillingness and failure to alter the complex mix of attitudes, norms, values, expectations, and organizational structure which has traditionally kept women at the lower half of the social pyramid (Rhode, 1990).

The consequences for the IT industry are more immediate. The decline in the number of women entering the IT industry may spell crisis for the industry soon. There is evidence of a trend indicating a decline in the number of white males entering college, which happens to be the population forming a major segment of the IT industry. It has been predicted that with more and more women moving away from this industry and fewer white males preparing for their traditional foothold too, a labor shortage in the IT industry is expected and the advancement of the field in the U.S. is likely to be hindered (Frenkel, 1990; O'Keefe 2004). The loss of the potential contributions from women who were discouraged from joining the industry and/or who have not made it to decision making positions is not trivial. It is for this reason, if not for ethical or moral reasons, that the issue of gender parity needs to be addressed. It is hoped that by a clearer picture of the factors at work these issues can be addressed.

All of these recommendations, as well as the issues discussed throughout this chapter, will have a critical impact on the role which women will play throughout the information technology industry in the future. Some changes are necessary and must be proactively pursued in order to create synergistic results from the talents of both genders in a fair and equitable manner. Most critical to this role will be the advances that women are able to make within management in this industry. It is crucial to understand that the place women will create for themselves within management in information technology will be shaped by the experiences that they have throughout their educational life and their early years in the industry. It is for these reasons that continued qualitative and quantitative research must be aimed at the identifiable factors which are hindering women's progress throughout the field.

"BAIT AND SWITCH" IN ADVERTISING[7]

As mentioned in previous chapters, change can take place and impact people individually, interpersonally, organizationally, and/or environmentally. Similarly, change and cultural conditioning can impact people in marketing industries and advertising professions. The world of business and global competition has impacted and changed how marketers advertise their products to attract customers. Some marketers have even resorted to inappropriate or misleading ads, which is a change for the worse, to lure clients to their places of business. The Western style of advertising has been bombarded by criticism for using inappropriate tactics which need to be changed in order to restore consumer trust in business and large corporations. The advertising industry has been accused of encouraging materialism, consumption, and stereotyping. Advertising causes people to purchase items for which they may not have an immediate need. Western advertising, in some cases, takes advantage of children, manipulates behavior, and uses sex to sell products or services. Barely a week goes by without some advertisement or campaign, or the ad industry, being the focal point of some controversy. Advertisement is often defined as a sponsored-identified message regarding a product or organization that can be verbal and or visual and can be disseminated through one or more forms of media. Using Afghanistan and the United States as examples, this chapter discusses advertisement practices that are not only unethical, but may also be illegal. Unethical forms of advertising have serious legal implications on the business, organization, as well as for the consumer. One form of advertisements that poses an ethical dilemma is called the "bait and switch" approach. Furthermore, this chapter

---

[7] - This chapter is co-authored with Kendrick D. Traylor, University of Phoenix-Online.

examines the impact of using such an approach with regard to value creation for stakeholders and makes appropriate recommendations for individuals, consumers and organizations as they bring about effective changes toward moral or ethical behaviors. A value theory framework is offered to assess controversial or deceitful advertising and its role in stakeholder value maximization.

Ethical Challenges and Deception in Advertising

Over the past few decades, there has been an increase in advertisements that have proved to be unethical. Unethical ads, some of which have proven to be deceitful, are reaching and influencing individuals each and every day. The current methods of ad evaluation may be inadequate for many of the controversial or innovative ads, including the ads, which are intentionally designed to be deceitful. Bruce Barton, chairman of BBDO, stated that "Advertising is of the very essence of democracy…an election goes on every minute of the business day across the counters of hundreds of thousands of stores and shops where the customers state their preferences and determine which manufacturer and which product shall be the leader today and which shall lead tomorrow." This is a good example of how companies think in regards to advertising and selling a product or service.

Many organizations and consumers have fell victim to the effects of "Bait and Switch" tactics for products and services in some shape, form or fashion. The Federal Trade Commission, various governmental agencies, and numerous associations have developed strict guidelines for governing the advertisement of products and services. Within the United States these policies exist and huge fines can be levied for those that are not in compliance. The next issue is how do these policies affect advertising in the global arena? With the mass globalization of products and services going abroad, do the same principles apply in foreign markets?

With the introduction of the Internet, many principles that apply to traditional means of advertising such as television, radio, newspaper and direct mail in the United States of America will have to be addressed. For example, Afghanistan is beginning the rebuilding efforts after being under the control of the Taliban regime and prior to that being controlled by the Russians for nearly ten years. While the author this book was born and raised in Afghanistan and can relate to the past as he looks toward to the future, the co-author of this chapter was deployed to Afghanistan serving as a part of Operation Enduring Freedom to assist and rebuild the Afghanistan National Army (ANA) and has witnessed the first democratic presidential election this country has ever had. During the first democratic presidential election in Afghanistan, the candidates embarked in public relations campaigns to get their respective messages out to the Afghan people. As a result an $80,000 agreement was developed to carry election advertising (Afghanistan, 2005). One must note that Afghanistan is a country that has a very high rate of illiteracy, vast rural areas, and in some parts of the country, there is no electricity. So, how are advertising campaigns possible? The answer is through the use of radio and local word-of-mouth networks. In many parts of Afghanistan, one can listen to the radio to obtain the basic information, similar to people who use television in developed nations. With this being the first real major advertising campaign to reach the entire country, the candidates had to ensure that their messages were realistic. For many, this was the first time that they were able to hear what was going on in other parts of the country. In the past, the various warlords in the respective areas controlled the media. This means that the people could hear only what the warlords wanted them to hear. So the warlords could use "bait and switch" tactics as they saw fit. With no regulations regarding the messages, they could utilize false propaganda and make it seem realistic. With these election-advertising campaigns, other messages will naturally follow, such as Public Service Announcement targeting safe water that was launched during the Ministry of Health Diarrhea Prevention Week (Afghanistan, 2005).

One can see that the future of advertising in Afghanistan will be greatly influenced by the effects of the election advertising campaigns that have been conducted. If the people feel that these campaign ads are totally false, then this will have a huge impact on future advertising in this country. One has to truly understand the situations that Afghanistan has been under to get a full effect and appreciation of the media and the current advertising situation. It will be extremely important for the government to ensure and set guidelines for the huge impact advertising will have on this country in the near future and long-term outlook. As Kendrick (second author) has traveled throughout Afghanistan in 2004 and 2005, he has seen billboards in the large urban areas advertising by the only two cell phone carriers currently in this country, Roshan and Afghan Wireless Communications Company (AWCC). Since Afghanistan is vastly rural, radio has the greatest advantage to reach the largest portions of this country.

There are many countries in the global environment that do not currently have any rules, guidelines or regulations regarding advertising.

As such, the effects of "bait and switch" will not enter into the consumer decision-making process. In such a case the buyers can easily be persuaded into purchases that do not actually deliver what the message promises. Consumers in Afghanistan could easily fall victim to companies attempting to locate business operations that didn't exist before. It will be up to the government to quickly step in and develop appropriate rules that will protect the consumers and provide them avenues to seek recourse for adverse actions of these businesses advertising their products and services. The proceeding pages describe this form of misleading advertisement and other challenges related to the "bait and switch" strategy impacting consumers throughout the world with specific examples from the United States of America.

The "Bait & Switch" Approach to Advertising

People throughout the world are concerned about recent studies and observations that have documented the decline in ethical / moral behavior of corporate leaders in business and non-business responsibilities. There are even Broadway shows demonstrating the bottom-line mentality / orientation of business leaders. A colleague had gone to see a Broadway show titled "*How to Succeed in Business without Really Trying*" and Ralph Macchio (star of The Karate Kid movies) played the leading role (Mujtaba and Traylor, 2003). Not only are there such shows that encourage people to make a quick buck, but also hundreds of textbooks showing the short cuts without much consideration for long-term leadership and thinking. There is no long-term value in shortcuts, but that is what seems to be driving this urge toward short-term profitability and at times unethical behaviors. Executives and managers, for example, are reporting incorrect figures (see any publication on Enron, Xerox, WorldCom, and other major firms getting caught into this trap) about company performance or they are pressuring their employees to lie, cheat, and rob people of their belongings to make higher bonuses and profits for themselves. Business researchers and ethicists report that contact lens managers, in order to beat sales targets, shipped products to distributors, which were not ordered by them or the doctors. The Sears Automotive employees were caught on videotape for lying about their work and overcharging people to earn a higher bonus (Mujtaba, 1997). There are also serious ethical concerns about people who cannot distinguish between a simple "right" and "wrong" choice. Of course, today there are many decisions that need to be made between many "right" choices. The traditional "right" goal of the firm has been to maximize shareholders' wealth; and thus the conventional financial economist currently is viewing moral issues as a constraint on "profitable" behavior. Many researchers suggest that this view could cause people to act immorally. Perhaps, the main purpose of a company should not be just to make a profit, but, it should be to make a profit ethically in order to continue its business and to do so even better and more "abundantly."

Ethics must be brought back into the culture of the organization and its planning process in order to build trust among all members of the firm. Ethical behaviors lead to high morale and high levels of trust among employees and customers. Trust generates commitment; commitment ensures effort; and efforts that are strategically positioned are necessary in today's competitive global economy. According to researchers, ethics should be central, not peripheral, to the overall management of the firm. According to DeGeorge (1993), the point of business ethics is not to change peoples' moral convictions, but to build on them. DeGeorge states that morality should be at the core of the business because morality is the oil as well as the glue of society and, therefore, of business. Despite the fact that much has been written about the decline of ethical behavior, and how to prevent immorality in firms, researchers see new approaches where the ethical lines are being crossed. "Bait and switch" strategy is one of many that some advertisers have used to take advantage of consumers. According to the market-based management theory, this will become a value-destroyer if continued in the long-term. According to Charles Koch (1993),

> A business firm is not just a piece of society, but a mini-society in its own right. Like societies that adopt market-based rules and cultures, organizations can vastly increase their effectiveness by using the market system as a guide for redesigning their own systems. In fact, during the past several decades, many of the most forward-looking management thinkers have de-emphasized hierarchy, authority, and other 'command-oriented' management techniques that became common during the first half of this century.

So, if the "mini society" uses strategies that are contrary to the "laws of the harvest" then eventually the "mini society" will fail. During the late 1800's and the beginning of the 1900's, management thinkers tended to follow the command-oriented "*scientific* management" school of thought championed by Frederick Taylor. The similarities between the Taylorist approach to management and Soviet-style "economic planning" are not many. According to Koch, "both approaches arise from the same framework: a framework that can understand order and coordination only as the deliberate product of some planner's design...as a result, both Taylorism and centralized economic planning depend on the ability of a central authority, whether economy-wide or organization-wide, to accumulate, process, and act on vast amounts of knowledge." However, Koch goes on to say that "more and more organizations are realizing that, regardless of what businesses they are in, they must also be in the 'knowledge business'... They must focus on generating and mobilizing the knowledge of their employees...To survive and thrive in today's business environment, an organization must be able to learn, adapt, and improve itself continuously...If it does not, its competitors will soon leave it far behind." So, organizations must devise structures and processes that allow them to learn and adapt "value adding strategies" in the changing world of advertising as consumers are becoming less tolerant of firms that use deceitful advertising strategies.

Factors Causing "Bait and Switching"

Amidst the increased competition in today's marketplace, many organizations have lost sales and revenues, which they traditionally have relied upon. As a result, many organizations find themselves in an economic crisis. The bottom lines are hurting, and customers are going elsewhere. So, in a move to generate additional traffic, and gain some short-term revenues, many organizations feel that they need a gimmick or hook to lure customers back into their doors to increase sales. As a result, many will advertise and heavily promote a lower priced item that will appeal to the consumer's interest. Once customers come, they hopefully will look at and purchase other items as well. The real factor here is whether or not the lower priced item actually intended to be the featured item or was it just a bait to lure in customers?

"Bait and Switched" Defined

So what exactly is meant by the term "Bait and Switch"? In simple terms this is using something to attract consumers or an audience into creating an action among a large population of people to take action on a particular product or service and then change the product or service. According to the Dictionary of Business Terms (2000), "bait and switch" in advertising is when a retailer offers something for sale at bargain prices with no intention of selling the advertised products or deals. The "bait and switch" scheme lures consumers into businesses with attractive offers, only to influence them through various techniques so they can make more expensive purchases. To accomplish this, "bait and switch" sellers downplay the quality of the advertised "specials." The salesperson may also speak against the guarantee, claim a lack of availability, or state that the best credit terms don't relate to the advertised product or service. In some cases the advertised specials will not even be available for sale, or salespersons may refuse to show the special to interested buyers. For example, in 1998, Bahaudin and his wife went to a major retail chain in Lakeland, Florida to buy a television advertised for $250. Instead, they bought another television for $380 because this model would "match the new government requirements for all televisions and would be adaptable with the new DVD players when they come out." The salesperson explained that the television that is advertised (on special) is basically out of date and not a very good deal.

Some "bait and switch" sellers have been known to go as far as to penalize those salespersons that do sell the advertised special to consumers. Sometimes businesses can actually sell out of the product that is being advertised. Most businesses will offer a "rain check" on the item if they run out. The "bait and switch" approach doesn't always have to do with advertising because other professions can use it as well. A politician can introduce a bill for one attractive issue and then switch the contents to reflect a hidden agenda. Politics are filled with "bait and switch" tactics, otherwise few to no legislation would ever pass.

Deceptive Advertising Tactics

In advertising, the "bait and switch" tactic is deceptive, unethical, immoral and illegal, which brings up another term to illustrate. The term Deceptive Advertising is defined (Dictionary of Business Terms, 2000) as advertising that makes false claims or misleading statements, as well as advertising that creates a false impression. One could argue that deceptive advertising is the same as the "bait and switch" strategy. There are definitely some similarities, but they are totally different topics. To illustrate both points, one can look at real world examples of deceptive ads occupying the airwaves. Let us see an actual case involving deceptive issues in advertising and it also brings out some legal implications. The Federal Trade Commission (FTC) authorities charged "Miss Cleo" promoters with deceptive advertising: meaning that there were billing and collection practices where the advertised "Free Readings" result in large phone bill charges. "Miss Cleo," the purportedly "renowned Jamaican psychic," whose ads promote "free" readings to callers seeking advice was the subject of a federal district court complaint. The complaint charged two Florida corporations, Access Resource Services, Inc. (ARS), and Psychic Readers Network (PRN), with deceptive advertising, billing and collection practices. According to the complaint, the defendants misrepresented the cost of services both in advertising and during the provision of the services; bills for services that were never purchased; and engaging in deceptive collection practices. The defendants also harassed consumers with repeated, unwanted, and unavoidable telemarketing calls that consumers cannot stop (FTC, 2002). So, based upon this example there clearly was deception. There also existed a bait to lure consumers to call to obtain more information. The deception exists by advertising one service and actually performing a variety of different services with high charges. So, in a sense a switch existed. A particular question that must be asked is why didn't the media catch on to this manipulation when the ad was being developed? Surely, someone knew or at least should have thought about the truth of the advertisement. Herein lies the problem: there is the First Amendment to the United States Constitution, which guarantees the right to free speech and expression.

Consider this example, look at most fast food chains today. Many of them, at least throughout Florida, are offering combo meals, extra value meals, etc. These meals are pre-priced according to the type of sandwich one wants. How many times have you been told, "Do you want to super size, biggie size, or for just 39 cents you can get a large drink and fries"? The actual profit in these combo packages can be the drinks. One wouldn't go into McDonald's or Wendy's just to purchase a soft drink alone. The soft drinks alone have no value, but add a sandwich and some fries then the value turns into profit when the combo is upgraded. Is this considered a "bait and switch" tactic? The answer can be both yes and no, but they are offering the product or service at the advertised price and they are honoring it according to the guidelines. So does this qualify as being deceptive? Perhaps not since people are getting value for their money.

Essential Elements of Advertisements

According to the American Advertising Federation Board of Directors, each advertisement must contain the following in their ads:
1. *Truth.* Advertising shall tell the truth, and shall reveal significant facts, the omission of which would mislead the public.
2. *Substantiation.* Advertising claims shall be substantiated by evidence in possession of the advertiser and advertising agency, prior to making such claims.

3. *Comparisons.* Advertising shall refrain from making false, misleading, or unsubstantiated statements or claims about competitors or their products or services.
4. *Bait Advertising.* Advertising shall not offer products or services for sale unless such offer constitutes a bona fide effort to sell the advertised products or services and is not a device to switch consumers to other goods or services, usually higher priced.
5. *Guarantees and Warranties.* Advertising of guarantees and warranties shall be explicit, with sufficient information to apprise consumers of their principal terms and limitations or, when space or time restrictions preclude such disclosures, the advertisement should clearly reveal where the full text of the guarantee or warranty can be examined before purchase.
6. *Price Claims.* Advertising shall avoid price claims, which are false, or misleading, or savings claims which do not offer provable savings.
7. *Testimonials.* Advertising containing testimonials shall be limited to those of competent witnesses who are reflecting a real and honest opinion or experience.
8. *Taste and Decency.* Advertising shall be free of statements, illustrations or implications, which are offensive to good taste or public decency (Adopted by the American Advertising Federation Board of Directors, March 2, 1984, San Antonio, Texas.).

So, if all advertisements should adhere to these standards then why are twenty-first century businesses still engaging in practices that are either illegal and/or unethical? Think of all the deception associated with nutritional products that promote quick weight loss. Are they violating these rules? In many cases one can say, "Yes, they are violating many of these rules." Why is this advertising method illegal? For two reasons: 1) It relies on false information, and 2) It works way too well at deceiving people.

One of the main problems is that, oftentimes, these underhanded techniques work all too well. They are often based on deception, misdirection and other highly refined but sharply unethical techniques. The goals, aims, and objectives of advertising are to reach the largest audience at the right times. This closely relates to the utilitarian view of ethics as proposed by John Stuart Mill, which seeks as its end the greatest good (or utility) for the greatest number. Because many advertisements are attempting to reach many of the same audiences, there must be some way to differentiate themselves from others perhaps by differentiating their products or services. In order to gain the attention of the audience, the message must be unique - totally different from the others. So, it is very easy to see why some advertisers employ captivating messages in order to gain the consumer's attention. As one can see the opportunity to deceive customers is great.

Deceptive tactics can bring much negative publicity for the advertising industry. Deceiving consumers into a business falsely to persuade them to purchase a higher priced item goes against moral values of the average individual. Individuals, who currently work in the advertising industry, need to take personal responsibility to protect and monitor their profession's public image.

Effects of the "Bait & Switch" Strategy

The "bait and switch" occurs in every facet of modern twenty-first century living. Advertising is the most common practice for this "bait and switch" strategy simply because of the media that it represents. If a particular business has to rely on this tactic to sell products then something is wrong with this picture of the "Entrepreneurship or American Dream." It might as well be called the "American Scream," since consumers are thinking they are getting something at a great price, when in reality they are getting scammed. Ouch! The next time you see an ad for a product, take the time to actually look at the ad itself. Many individuals do not read the fine print or fail to adequately perform and research before making a purchase. People are so consumed with "getting a deal" without actually realizing that they may not be getting the deal they thought they would. All individuals, as consumers, need to be aware of the Latin terms "*caveat emptor*," which means "let the buyer beware."

There are times in which the seller is actually using deception to gain an unfair competitive advantage. However, such sellers fail to realize that true competitive advantage as stated by Michael Porter (1985) grows fundamentally out of value a firm is able to create for its buyers that exceeds the firm's cost of creating it. So, is advertising through the "bait and switch" approach wrong? Until something is done about it or it is challenged, then how can it be wrong? Yes, it is morally wrong; but as long as no one questions it then to the business or organization it might appear right due to the increased profits in the short-term. So, is the advertising strategy of "bait and switch" seen today as truthful, deceptive or just a lie? While the average consumer will see it as deceptive and unreliable, the legal answer to this question will often be an uphill journey, over numerous hills and valleys. Hopefully, questioning such tactics and approaches to advertising will challenge many thoughts, provoke numerous debates, and create new control measures. Overall, consumers must beware since some marketing efforts and ads are simply designed to attract, but not necessarily to deliver (Mujtaba, 1999).

Protecting against False Advertising to Deliver Long-Term Value

The following, taken from a publication titled False Advertising (2002), are things you as a consumer can do individually to protect yourself from deceitful and misleading strategies:

- Shop around for your own price comparisons.
- Check all advertising claims before buying.
- Ask for a "rain check" when advertised products are not available.
- Ask to see a permit for going out of business sales.
- Be on guard when you see anything for free.
- Don't let yourself be moved from a low-priced "bait" to an expensive "switch."
- Report false advertising to the Department of Consumer Affairs.

The individual media genres such as television, radio, newspaper, and magazines have a responsibility to ensure that the ads they are developing and running are not in violation of the "bait and switch" rule. This comes down to the account executives, the production departments, and the management of each media property. There are many things to consider when developing an advertising campaign. The campaign has to be truthful and not misleading to the consumer. If an advertisement is found to be misleading and false, there are remedies in which the consumer can pursue in obtaining judgments. The Federal Trade Commission (FTC) has the authority to bar advertisements under the FTC trade act and the Lanham Act. The FTC also has the power to order corrective ads (FTC, 2001). Corrective advertising requires a business to run ads that alert future consumers to certain unfavorable facts about a product not revealed in past advertising campaigns. A famous example involved Listerine mouthwash. For years, Listerine was touted as a cold and sore throat remedy. The FTC forced the manufacturer to run ads stating that Listerine would not cure colds or relieve sore throats. Surely, this is not part of a desirable marketing strategy (Ponzak, 2002).

The bottom-line is that when the "bait and switch" strategy is used an organization's relevant stakeholders can suffer in the long run. The businesses will be subject to lost revenues, customers will become unhappy while seeking more government regulations, and there will be increasing legal costs / lawsuits. The media that allows the ad to run in the first place can be subject to FTC regulations and could possibly lose their license. The consumer loses faith in future advertising as a whole and will question any ads used by the media that ran the false ad in the first place. Paying close attention to contents and details will separate the honest businesses and media from ones that are looking to gain instant success through increased revenue and traffic through deception.

Organizational responsibility. Since the main purpose of an organization is to fulfill one or more needs of their customers, then their agents (managers and leaders) must use strategies and effective selling techniques that are value-adders in the long-term. Using the "bait and switch" strategy is a value-destroyer since it hurts the customers, the organization, the advertising industry, the owners, and the employees of the firm in the long-term. So, since this approach does not maximize Value Over Time (Pohlman & Gardiner, 2000) for the relevant stakeholders of the organization, then it must be avoided at all costs. In his book, Peter Block (1993) explains, "Having a group of people whose job is to watch and monitor steals accountability and responsibility from those doing the work…We can neither legislate nor engineer accountability." So, organizations must take responsibility for truthful advertisements and train their people to ensure they are being truthful because it will determine their long-term survival. Delivering superior customer value is and should be the responsibility of every person in the organization and decisions should be made from a long-term perspective in order for the firm to maximize their value over time (Pohlman and Gardiner, 2000).

According to Charles Koch (1993), author of Introduction to Market-Based Management, the notion of profitability is a factor that drives companies to provide maximum value to all customers for the least cost. Customers reward companies' efforts by their purchases. Some criticize this view stating that companies tend to focus more on the short-term profit based goals (such as using "bait and switch" strategies to boost sales) rather than long-term ones; however, this does not account for those companies that devote capital to the production of future profits. Their vision is to increase the value of assets. In a market-based system, "transferable property rights create powerful incentives to conserve and care for valuable resources" (Koch, p.26). This philosophy motivates the entrepreneur to pledge for future returns and to take into consideration that today's decisions will affect future outcomes. To illustrate this point, compare a homeowner with a home renter. A homeowner has a vested interest to contribute resources towards the property. This is considered an investment in which the homeowner is rewarded through increased property value. On the other hand, a renter is not rewarded for his or her contributions and thus has no incentive to contribute resources in the property. Moreover, if a renter does invest money and resources, it is a loss because if the renter moves s/he does not regain those resources. These differences can be seen when comparing a market-based system to a socialist system. A socialist system does not take future outcomes into account. Companies within this system do not have the incentive of future profits and thus experience more destruction than production.

Market-based management is an incentive system that companies should incorporate into existing systems as an enhancer and this might deter wrongdoing and encourage effective long-term decision-making. Effective systems of motivation affect individual employees who in turn contribute to the outcomes of the company. A profit and loss operation affords "rewards, conveys information, and redistributes control over resources" (Koch, p.27). Using defined roles and responsibilities should reinforce a market-based system. Clear standards add to the best interest of a company's goals. Individual contributions should benefit not only the company, but also the individuals. Employee evaluations and feedback place importance on an individual's behavior, putting it in context with the expectations and goals of the company. Different means of monitoring individuals allow room for expansion of employees' performance.

The success of a company depends on how a company distributes its resources toward the long-term orientation and success of the organization. Capable and ethically fit employees who successfully contribute to the increased profits of the company in the long-term should be given more responsibility to make decisions about how the company will use its resources. In such cases, they will be less likely to tolerate the use of "bait and switch" strategies in their firms.

Individual responsibility. In today's society, there are many alternatives to actually perform research on a particular item prior to purchase. The consumer today has access to a variety of sources to make a logical decision before making a purchase. So, individuals must take personal responsibility and do their homework prior to each new purchase. If the individual fails to research the firm, service or product, then the buyer should accept the consequences for making a bad decision.

Success is based on responsibly fulfilling consumers' needs without using deceitful strategies to attract and retain customers. Capital One

Financial Corporation is an industry leader in customer service in this area and they became one of the top firms in the industry not by using "bait and switch" tactics, but good common sense strategies of knowing their customers and fulfilling their needs. They use innovative ads to attract consumers and then they use good strategies to understand the customer's needs and to effectively fulfill those needs better than their competitors. The company's success is attributed to its extensive use of high tech computers. Computers house information in one out of seven households across the United States and perhaps other developed nations. This information also reveals customer behavior. When a customer calls the computers are able to identify who is calling, predict a reason for the phone call, and after reviewing 50 options of who should take the call, the computer chooses the best option. The steps mentioned tend to occur in just 100 milliseconds. Nigel Morris and Rich Fairbank, two friends with no prior experience in the banking industry founded the company. They were able to successfully win customers away from established companies. Capital One's success is built on the premise of testing and learning. The company tests everything, from product offerings to every procedural change to every job applicant. It runs experiment after experiment. The result of this testing is Capital One's ability to deliver the right product on a timely basis to the right customer. The focus is not a credit-card strategy, but a marketing tool that any organization can use. By studying the reasons why customers call, the company also has perfected the art of minimizing the wait time that the customer experiences when trying to connect him/her to the appropriate service personnel. The search for the correct department costs the company in more ways than one. Not only does this frustrate the customer, but also the company incurs costs by the second for the call. This calling system has become a competitive advantage for Capital One. Capital One creates value for customers by investing in technology that makes their life easier. In a world of automated voice messaging systems, it is very easy to get caught up and frustrated after sitting on the phone for a long time, just waiting to hear a human voice. The company has designed a data collection system that is relevant and suits the customers' needs. The result is a happy individual who can readily access account information, and in some cases, even bargain the interest rate that he/she pays on credit card purchases. Capital One is one of the innovative selective few that uses innovative ads to attract customers and retains them by offering superior service.

The Walt Disney Company, as it is known today, was founded in 1923. Although it has evolved through many changes in how and where it does business, it is one of America's great success stories, using innovative ads and delivering what it promises. The Disney Company has embraced technology to its advantage and branched out from animated cartoons to every avenue of entertainment. Since the conception of the Disney Brothers Studios, Disney has diversified into two major movie studios and has an alliance with a third. It also owns its own distribution company, ten theme parks worldwide, a television network, broadcast television and radio stations, six cable stations, two sports franchises, and has the fourth largest presence on the Internet. Disney is the second largest media conglomerate worldwide behind AOL Time Warner. Disney's success is largely due to the foresight of its owners, the use of technological advances, and staying true to its mission and values over the past seven decades. They create innovative themes in their ads to attract audiences from around the globe and deliver what they promise once customers enter their premises. This is their way of creating "raving fans" and maximizing value for their stakeholders over time. Disney has always been a lead character in the entertainment industry when it comes to quality service, adhering to customer values, and the use of the latest technology to fulfill the needs of their audience. This, in part, is what has made them so successful and will keep them on course far into the future. As Walt Disney once said, "If you can dream it, it can come true." At Disney, the mission is to "...make dreams come true, create magical memories, [while] developing lifetime friendships with each guest." This is done by creating an organizational culture that thrives on giving superior service in all aspects of their business.

Publix Supermarkets is another success story with innovative ads, clean stores, and impeccable service in their industry. George W. Jenkins in Winter Haven, Florida founded Publix in 1930 and eventually their main offices moved to Lakeland, Florida. It is one of the ten largest-volume supermarket chains in the U. S. and is also the largest employee-owned supermarket chain in the country. They use innovative ads, especially during the Holidays, to attract customers and they keep them coming back by offering great value and an environment "where shopping is a pleasure." Publix's dedication to superior customer service and quality products has made it a recognized leader in the grocery business, most recently by an American Customer Satisfaction Index survey published in Fortune magazine. The company has also been named one of America's top 10 in the book, "*The 100 Best Companies to Work for in America*," as well as one of the top companies in Fortune's recent list of best workplaces. The company prides itself on its community involvement and environmental awareness. In fact, Publix was awarded the United Way of America National Spirit of America® Award in 1997 and the United States Environmental Protection Agency's Environmental Merit Award in 2000. While most businesses have been suffering because of the bad economy and high unemployment rates in the United States during the last few years, Publix's stocks increased. As a wholly employee-owned company, Publix stock is not publicly traded and is made available for sale only to current Publix associates. Since Bahaudin Mujtaba, the author, worked at Publix for about sixteen years, he likes to think he had a small part in their success along with his colleagues throughout the various states. While Disney makes "dreams come true," Publix makes "shopping a pleasure" for its customers and "working a pleasure" for its employees. Publix's most recent venture was PublixDirect, a wholly owned subsidiary of Publix Super Markets, Inc. that provided online grocery shopping and home delivery. Their trucks could be seen throughout Fort Lauderdale, Florida delivering food to online customers. However, after several years of operation, PublixDirect was discontinued perhaps because this service was mainly competing with Publix stores throughout South Florida since this company dominates the food market as the number one retailer in the state. While they decided to close PublixDirect so they can focus on the main competency, which is being the best food retailer, the company has acquired and opened new stores throughout Florida and other states as they focus on progressively growing into the existing and new markets around the United States. How does Publix do it? How can the company be profitable when the economy has been slow during the past few years (especially in these tough economic times when American military forces have fought in Afghanistan and occupied Iraq) and yet provide such a good work environment for its employees and be socially responsible? The key to Publix's success is living the principles of Value Driven Management to maximize stakeholders' value in the long-term while offering superior customer service; and another key is not using deceitful tactics to attract customers. By using honest and creative ads, using Value Driven Management principles and delivering what is promised, any firm can successfully deliver good value, as has been the case with Publix, Disney World, and Capital One.

Maximizing long-term stakeholder value. It is obvious that corporate America has become increasingly criticized for perceptions of unethical practices and intentions. Recent high-profile cases of exploitative corporate brutalism are well-documented in the popular press as large companies such as WorldCom, Enron, and Arthur Andersen (among others) have been portrayed as breaking trust with public faith (Ampofo, Mujtaba, Cavico, and Tindall, 2004) through deceptive practices and unsavory agendas that compromised the espoused values they had communicated to investors, employees, customers, regulators, and other stakeholders (Pohlman, 2004). Pohlman stated that all too often, managers and employees are pressured to improve the bottom line in the short term at all costs; and this can result in situations where the lack of focus on long-term value creation generates difficulties for the organization as observed with Enron and other firms in the last five years. In efforts to pursue more profit, boost stock performance, or enhance competitiveness, these firms engaged in either obscuring the facts, intentionally reporting inaccurate financials, and crafting messages intended to manipulate public perceptions of reality (Ampofo *et al*, 2004). The moral dilemmas in corporate advertising abound, and decision-making among multiple ethical alternatives and models often remain unclear, even with robust ethical policies in place (Badaracco, 1997). Given this complexity, another ethical approach might involve linking decision-making by advertising leaders to natural law or virtue ethics (LaZara, 2001) where responsibility rests in the exercise of societal consciousness and a sense of stewardship (Block, 1996; Kotler & Armstrong, 1990; Hosmer, 1996). This approach would tend to appeal to principle-centered (Covey, 1995) and/or values-based ethical strategies (O'Toole, 1996).

Pohlman and Gardiner (2000) introduced Value Driven Management (VDM) as a holistic ethical decision-making framework for determining true value adders and value destroyers. VDM is based upon values theory, which maintains that internal values drive individual actions and behaviors (Pohlman & Gardiner, 2000; O'Toole, 1996). The underlying theme of VDM is to make decisions that maximize value over time for all relevant stakeholders (Cavico & Mujtaba, 2005) through an examination of values drivers similar to Kantian universalism (Hosmer, 1996). In other words, deciding on ethical direction is accomplished by examining the sets of values held by an organization's relevant constituents or stakeholder groups. The framework extends not only to organizational owners but also to global, national, or regional cultures and subcultures as well as micro-organizational climates and/or the values of employees, suppliers, customers, competitors, and third party entities such as unions and regulators. In determining ethical actions based on values theory, principled advertisers would contemplate questions as to what actions, people and/or processes either add or destroy long-term value for all stakeholders--and in what ways. It would then become the responsibility of both leaders and followers within firms to maximize value-creation through a collective understanding of these values drivers rather than based on pure economic profit motives.

In the Pohlman and Gardiner (2000) VDM system, eight critical facets are emphasized that form Value Driven Management: (1) external culture or the social context in which decision-making occurs; (2) internal culture or the unique context in which intra-organizational decisions are made; (3) employee values, which must align with inter- and intra-organizational values in ways that maximize total value; (4) supplier values, which usually involve fair treatment of partners in channel partnerships; (5) customer values with regard to quality expectations and moral considerations, for example; (6) third party values that may include rule-based ethics centered in compliance; (7) competitor values, which tend to drive their strategies and tactics; and, (8) owner values, which include the shareholder's values whether tied to economic value maximization, societal conscious goals, or other objectives. Although practical and simple to articulate, the VDM method may still suffer from some of the same difficulties posed by postmodern complexification (Hage & Powers, 1992) that encumber utilitarian ethical strategies. That is, values tend to exist as diverse, divergent, subjective, and frequently changing phenomena. Many practitioners and scholars have noted the difficulty of prioritizing competing values and ethical principles (Badarraco, 1997; Kotler & Armstrong, 1990, Jue, 2004). Kotler and Armstrong said that "Managers need a set of principles that will help them analyze the moral importance of each situation…, but what principles should guide companies and marketing managers on issues of ethics and social responsibility?"

Consequently, one emerging ethical framework that may assist in the prioritization of values and principles during the process of assessing deceptive advertising is spirit-centered leadership (Jue, 2004; Jue & Mujtaba, 2004a, 2004b). An increasing subset of avant-garde practitioners and thinkers have begun to call for a radical shift to spiritual entrepreneurship, which accepts the supremacy of transcendent principles over all others: "What makes the shift to spiritual entrepreneurship so critical is that it removes our reliance on outside measures to guide our business decisions" (Sfeir-Younis, 2002, pp 9). This mode of ethical decision-making places a greater focus on appeals to transcendent principles, which may be aligned with Jung's collective consciousness as manifested through conscience (Madsen, 2001; Jue, 2004). Spirit-centered leadership creates a balancing fulcrum that utilizes virtue ethics, principles of stewardship/servant-leadership, and emotional intelligence in governing all other values that emerge in leadership decision-making. Using spirit-centered leadership to prioritize VDM could create a robust method of assessing both the role of specific advertisements in maximizing value as well as increasing awareness of the potential adverse consumer and social effects arising from negative forms of deceptive advertising approaches such as the "bait and switch" approach. Regardless of the ethical framework or combination selected, the increasing incidence of deceptive advertising in the postmodern milieu definitely necessitates an equally urgent focus on both understanding the nature and bounds of its ethical use as well as ensuring that value is maximized rather than destroyed for consumers, organizations, nations, and society at large.

Summary

Creating specific guidelines should be a start to eliminating deceptive advertising such as the "bait and switch" approach which has been used throughout the world and innocent victims in developing countries such as Afghanistan can easily fall prey to such ads. The government in developing nations must prepare appropriate strategies to protect consumers from the "giant arms" of multinational corporations that often "dump" unwanted or inferior products in developing countries. The American Marketing Association (AMA) has guidelines in their Codes of Ethics which states "the basic rule of professional ethics: not knowingly to do harm." Yet, many firms seem to harm others knowingly because it is advantageous to them. With regard to "honesty and fairness," AMA mentions that "Marketers shall uphold and advance the integrity, honor, and dignity of the marketing profession by being honest in serving consumers, clients, employees, suppliers, distributors, and the public." AMA also encourages "avoidance of false and misleading advertisings" as well as "avoidance of sales promotions that use deception or manipulation." They further mention, "any AMA member found in violation of any provision of this Code of Ethics may have his or her Association membership suspended or revoked." While suspending and revoking membership to the association is a good start, the industry needs to do more in conjunction with government authorities to enforce the rules by imposing tougher standards to all advertisers (not just members of certain associations).

On the other hand, since ethical actions must be above and beyond the laws, both individuals and their organizations could follow Kant's

Categorical Imperatives. Kant's concept is called the "supreme principle of morals" (Mujtaba, 1999). It is the universal moral rule in which people command themselves to obey them. It states "act only on the maxim that you can at the same time will that it should become a universal law." According to Immanuel Kant (1785), an action is moral if:

1. It can be suggested to being made consistently universal;
2. It derives and respects the autonomy of human beings; and
3. It respects rational beings as ends in themselves.

People can make ethical decisions that are truly universal but it requires using universal principles and critically thinking about their decisions. As human beings and as leaders, each individual must use his or her critical thinking apparatus to make advancements and contributions to the society by working ethically. The human brain, which helps differentiate between right and wrong, as well as good and bad. It can send a signal to the big toe and back of an average sized adult 177,000 times a second. Consider that the average brain has so many nerve cells that if they were laid end to end they would circle the globe 20,000 times. Tapping into this potential is a whole other issue. It takes training and effort to put the brain to good use by thinking critically. While these are important skills to possess, they do not always come passively as they require critical, active, and conscious involvement.

According to the dictionary, the term critical means tending to find fault, characterized by careful analysis, a sound estimate of the problem, decisive, dangerous, and risky. The term thinking, on the other hand, means to form or have in the mind; to conceive; or to believe, surmise, or expect; to determine, resolve, or work out; and to bring to mind or recollect. Critical thinking and decision-making are valuable tools that can assist in eliminating unethical behaviors such as using "bait and switch" approach to take advantage of unsuspecting consumers. When skillfully applied, such critical thinking skills can greatly benefit businesses, individuals, organizations, and the world at large toward effective change. So, be a critical thinker when it comes to your firm's selling strategies. Take responsibility to insure ads are truthful, honest, and objective in all communications. Ethical ads and delivering what the ads promise generate trust, and trust leads to loyal and caring customers. Remember, "Only one life that soon will pass; and only what is advertised truthfully will last."

Chapter Eleven

PROGRESSING AMID CHANGE: WAL-MART'S MANAGEMENT PRACTICES

Many companies and their personnel have been dramatically successful amid major changes which impact them at the individual, interpersonal, organizational, and/or environmental levels. The Wal-Mart Corporation is one of those companies that have been impacted by change at all these levels as they conduct business and expand their operations throughout the globe. Wal-Mart has also greatly benefited from deeply-held universal values, philosophies, and management practices which have made them successful in diverse countries. With Sam Walton's philosophy of proactive change, continuous development, and leadership, Wal-Mart has become a national success due to effective application of management concepts in its day-to-day operations. In a short span of about forty years, this company has become the envy of any and every major corporation in the world. This chapter presents how Wal-Mart has achieved this enormous success, the concepts of scientific management and Theory Y of motivation practiced by many of the managers at Wal-Mart to effectively deal with various forces causing major changes in today's work environments.

Introduction to Wal-Mart Corporation

By maintaining its promise to customers of "everyday low prices," Wal-Mart has injured many of its competitors. Although Wal-Mart, like any other firm, experiences problems and challenges in the workforce, it continues to thrive because they learn from their experiences and change or adapt accordingly. Wal-Mart, in 1962, opened its first Wal-Mart

Discount City and now it sells more toys than Toys "R" Us, more clothes than the Gap and Limited, and more food than Kroger and a few other supermarkets combined (Upbin, 2004). If Wal-Mart was its own economy, it would rank 30th right next to Saudi Arabia while growing at the rate of about 11% each year. The Wal-Martization of the world is bringing about good and bad changes to commerce around the globe. Wal-Mart is expected to be the first trillion dollar retailer in the world. In 2004, total sales at Wal-Mart were $256 billion with 68% from Wal-Mart Stores, 19% from its international operations, and 13% coming from its Sam's Club. Wal-Mart's annual profits are about $9 billion and they have a market value of $244 with assets worth over $105 billion during 2004. As of April 2004, in addition to its approximately 4,000 stores in the United States, Wal-Mart had over 640 stores in Mexico, 404 stores in Japan, 267 stores in United Kingdom, 236 stores in Canada, 92 stores in Germany, 53 in Puerto Rico, 34 in China, 25 in Brazil, 15 in South Korea, and 11 stores in Argentina while expanding into these countries on a continuous basis. Currently, it employs over one million people in the United States and nearly half a million individuals internationally. Furthermore, it ranked 10th on Forbes Leading 2000 Companies in the World based on composite scores for sales, profits, assets, and overall market value (Upbin, 2004). As a matter-of-fact, Wal-Mart ranked first in sales, ranked sixth in total market value, and they ranked eight in overall profits through Forbes ranking of World's 2000 Leading Companies in Forbes April 12, 2004 issue.

Traditional Management Practices at Wal-Mart

The four functions of planning, organizing, leading, and controlling are all part of management's responsibilities at Wal-Mart in their day-to-day operation as they serve thousands of customers every day. Wal-Mart managers use some of the administrative management theories in their organizational structure that has helped them to be efficient. Examples are the widespread use of cross-departmental teams and empowerment concepts to decentralize some of the decision making to the lowest levels. Wal-Mart practices the concept of empowering employees and, similar to Nordstrom, it uses an inverted paradigm approach in their organizational chart whereby employees are on top and often participate in decisions that impact them and their customers. Senior managers understand that the persons who are in direct contact with customers on a day-to-day basis are the frontline employees, and they hear the positive and negative feedback from customers and, therefore, are best equipped to serve them well.

Managers also practice the behavioral management theories as they seek to promote each employee's desire to be innovative and create a team-oriented atmosphere that leads to high morale, cooperation and synergy. At Wal-Mart, like most other successful organizations, the relationship between managers and employees is more of a partnership rather than an "us and them" mentality. The managers inspire employee loyalty and reap the rewards of paying attention to the people at the front lines as they have grown into a giant. A strategy used at Wal-Mart for employee motivation is offering employees an opportunity to participate in the profit sharing. By sharing profits with employees, Wal-Mart instills loyalty and inspires them to do well as they join in the success and failures of the store. Sam Walton believed that the more you share profits with associates – whether it is in salaries, incentives, bonuses, or stock discounts – the more profit will accrue to the company as everyone treats the organization like their own personal business thereby becoming intrapreneurs. Similar to the Publix philosophy, the way management treats their associates is how the associates will treat customers. So, if managers treat employees well then the associates treat customers well and the customers will return. This is relationship-based marketing, and it is where the real profit lies – not in trying to always recruit new customers for one-time purchases. Satisfied, loyal, and repeat customers are at the heart of Wal-Mart's success. This is emphasized in the principle that "the most important contact ever made at Wal-Mart is between the associate in the store and the customer" (Walton, 1992). As such, employees are expected and motivated to treat their customers like kings and queens.

There are many traditional management and motivation theorists that have paved the way for organizational success, of which a few are discussed here to show how accurately their concepts reflect the current methods used at Wal-Mart Stores. There are many motivation strategies used by Wal-Mart managers and Theory Y is one of them. The management historians discussed are Douglas McGregor's motivation theory, Frederick W. Taylor's insightful and structured method of scientific management, and the revised principles of management simulated by The Gilbreth's are some of the strategies utilized in this successful corporation. Douglas McGregor did considerable research on behavioral management and is credited for developing Theory X and Theory Y which are applied by many of today's managers.

Motivation of the Workforce: Theory X and Theory Y

Douglas McGregor, born in 1906, was a social psychologist who studied the behavior of human beings in the workplace, served as a management consultant, and as a management theorist. He initially worked as a social psychologist at the Chief Executive College and eventually became a Professor of Management at the Massachusetts Institute of Technology (MIT). In 1960, McGregor wrote a book titled *"The Human Side of Enterprise"* that examined behavior of individuals at work and formulated what has been popularized as Theory X and Theory Y. For many decades, Theory Y principles were utilized for management training workshops that influenced organizations to implement and design personnel policies and practices that build trust between employees and management. Theory Y is based on Maslow's higher level needs: belonging, esteem, and self-actualization. As a result of research, he believes that workers prefer not to be directed and controlled externally, but rather they prefer to be empowered in order to exercise self control and self direction as they see appropriate. Theory X concept is rooted in the idea that people need to be directed in a quid pro quo format. It essentially states that the organization relies on money in order to satisfy the employee's lower level needs, and once these needs are satisfied then the motivation to work productively is lost. Theory X has a negative set of beliefs following the assumptions that people inherently dislike work and they avoid work whenever possible. The main thought behind Theory X is that people are not disciplined, ignore responsibility, they have no ambition to work on their own, and they seek only security to fulfill their basic needs. So, Theory X states that managers have to control, coerce, direct, and threaten employees with punishment in order to get people to work productively.

On the other hand, Theory Y is an optimistic view which assumes that people are disciplined, prefer to be empowered, enjoy working, and want to take personal responsibility. The main thought behind Theory Y is that people exercise self discipline; they have self control, and are committed to the mission once they buy into it. McGregor referred to these assumptions as *"cosmologies,"* denoting a comprehensive conception of the world. According to McGregor's initial thoughts, these two theories were not particularly in relation to work and organizational life nor a "cookbook" for managing the workforce. Nevertheless, some managers view Theory X as traditional management toward the workforce, while Theory Y represents an ideal view of human behavior. McGregor, with regard to Theory Y, claims that not all individuals are psychologically mature and, as such, work can be considered a burden for them. Their passive and dependent behavior has to be directed and controlled by external variables. He further claims that these people are not immature by nature; it is either the influence of earlier socialization or their experiences in the organization that has forced this type of behavior and expectations. So, managers have an active obligation in changing this type of behavior, but the conditions of the organization must lead individuals to use their creativity or it will not gain the commitment or involvement to change. Basic definitions of Theory X allow for very little to no flexibility in management style, while Theory Y has a wide range of styles available depending on the workforce and the situational variables at hand. McGregor believed that managing people requires specific skills and expertise from managers because their success depends on the effective utilization of their people's talents, minds, abilities, and efforts to have a successful organization.

Sam Walton's management style and Wal-Mart's organizational culture depict some assumptions of the Theory Y style of management. Walton used a very unique style and became a very popular leader with employees and customers. He believed that a happy employee meant happy customers which would eventually lead to more sales and bottom line profitability. Thus, Wal-Mart associates tend to have fun in the workplace and often start out with the Wal-Mart cheer throughout the store. Sam Walton once said, "My feeling is that just because we work so hard, we don't have to go around with long faces all the time – while we're doing all of this work, we like to have a good time. It is sort of a *whistle while you work philosophy*,' and we not only have a heck of good time, we work better because of it."

Besides Walton's philosophy, there are other key factors that contribute to the motivation of employees and the success of Wal-Mart: profit sharing, treating associates like partners, creating a motivational environment, communicating everything to partners, appreciating and recognizing associates' work, celebrating individual and departmental successes, and listening to everyone in the company. For the most part, Wal-Mart employees are average employees with exceptional passion to the company and commitment to giving good service, whether it is merely a smiling greeter at the front of the store, helping customers find what they need, or an associate interacting with a customer and making a special attempt to remember the customer's name. Because of empowerment, employees are usually willing to do more for their customers and store. Sam Walton created a participative management atmosphere which also parallels McGregor's Theory Y. Theory Y makes the following general assumptions:

- People are self-directed and want to meet their work objectives if they are committed to them.

- People are generally committed to the stated objectives if appropriate rewards are in place to address higher order needs.
- People usually accept and often seek personal responsibility.
- Most people can handle responsibility because creativity and ingenuity are common in the population.
- Effort in work is as natural as work and play. All individuals enjoy playing.

Aligned with these assumptions and Theory Y principle, there were ten of Sam's rules for building a successful business that have been practiced by Wal-Mart's management. The following are Sam's ten values presented to Wal-Mart employees which are helpful for everyone in today's changing work environment:

- *Rule 1.* Commit to your business. Believe in it more than anybody else. I think I overcame every single one of my personal shortcomings by the sheer passion I brought to my work. I don't know if you're born with this kind of passion, or if you can learn it. But I do know you need it. If you love your work, you'll be out there every day trying to do it the best you possibly can, and pretty soon everybody around will catch the passion from you – like a fever.
- *Rule 2.* Share your profits with all your Associates, and treat them as partners. In turn, they will treat you as a partner, and together you will all perform beyond your wildest expectations. Remain a corporation and retain control if you like, but behave as a servant leader in a partnership. Encourage your Associates to hold a stake in the company. Offer discounted stock, and grant them stock for their retirement. It's the single best thing we ever did.
- *Rule 3.* Motivate your partners. Money and ownership alone aren't enough. Constantly, day-by-day, think of new and more interesting ways to motivate and challenge your partners. Set high goals, encourage competition, and then keep score. Make bets with outrageous payoffs. If things get stale, cross-pollinate; have managers switch jobs with one another to stay challenged. Keep everybody guessing as to what your next trick is going to be. Don't become too predictable.
- *Rule 4.* Communicate everything you possibly can to your partners. The more they know, the more they'll understand. The

more they understand, the more they'll care. Once they care, there's no stopping them. If you don't trust your Associates to know what's going on, they'll know you don't really consider them partners. Information is power, and the gain you get from empowering your Associates more than offsets the risk of informing your competitors.

- *Rule 5.* Appreciate everything your Associates do for the business. A paycheck and a stock option will buy one kind of loyalty. But all of us like to be told how much somebody appreciates what we do for them. We like to hear it often, and especially when we have done something we're really proud of. Nothing else can substitute for a few well-chosen, well-timed, sincere words of praise. They're absolutely free – and worth a fortune.

- *Rule 6.* Celebrate your successes. Find some humor in your failures. Don't take yourself so seriously. Loosen up, and everybody around you will loosen up. Have fun. Show enthusiasm – always. When all else fails, put on a costume and sing a silly song. Then make everybody else sing with you. Don't do a hula on Wall Street. It's been done. Think up your own stunt. All of this is more important, and more fun, than you think, and it really fools the competition. "Why should we take those cornballs at Wal-Mart seriously?"

- *Rule 7.* Listen to everyone in your company. And figure out ways to get them talking. The folks on the front lines – the ones who actually talk to the customer – are the only ones who really know what's going on out there. You'd better find out what they know. This really is what total quality is all about. To push responsibility down in your organization, and to force good ideas to bubble up within it, you must listen to what your Associates are trying to tell you.

- *Rule 8.* Exceed your customers' expectations. If you do, they'll come back over and over. Give them what they want – and a little more. Let them know you appreciate them. Make good on all your mistakes, and don't make excuses – apologize. Stand behind everything you do. The two most important words I ever wrote were on that first Wal-Mart sign, "Satisfaction Guaranteed." They're still up there, and they have made all the difference.

- *Rule 9.* Control your expenses better than your competition. This is where you can always find the competitive advantage. For 25 years running – long before Wal-Mart was known as the nation's largest retailer – we ranked No. 1 in our industry for the lowest ratio of expenses to sales. You can make a lot of different mistakes and still recover if you run an efficient operation. Or you can be brilliant and still go out of business if you're too inefficient.
- *Rule 10.* Swim upstream. Go the other way. Ignore the conventional wisdom. If everybody else is doing it one way, there's a good chance you can find your niche by going in exactly the opposite direction. But be prepared for a lot of folks to wave you down and tell you you're headed the wrong way. I guess in all my years, what I heard more often than anything was: a town of less than 50,000 population cannot support a discount store for very long.

Scientific Management Practices at Wal-Mart

Frederick W. Taylor is the founder and father of scientific management. His model included four management objectives which are: 1) studying the ways in which tasks are performed on the job to identify methods of improvement; 2) determination of the standards of operation needed to train employees properly through the creation of rules and regulations manual; 3) selecting appropriate employees in the hiring process to perform specific tasks based on the knowledge, skills and abilities they possess using the aforementioned training procedures; and, 4) develop an incentive program and reward based system for those who exceed the acceptable performance level to encourage high performance. The logic behind guiding employees towards specialized task oriented positions lead to efficient use of talent and time.

Frank and Lillian Gilbreth, who are known for their contributions to motion studies and the original movie *"Cheaper by the Dozen,"* have had significant impact on the study of productivity. They are associated with an amended version of Taylor's scientific management, focused more heavily on the actual procedures involved in accomplishing each specific task. Their intention was to create a more efficient and effective way of meeting objectives without expending unnecessary energy or wasting time. They also wanted to create a way for employees so they could be working smarter as opposed to harder through their work on motion studies. Taping the actions of workers and studying the movements to determine which motions could be eliminated to perform optimally was the methodology utilized in search of finding the best way to perform tasks. While Wal-Mart does not literally tape events to enhance the process, they do offer training sessions to new employees to ensure they are taught the best practices by existing employees on how to interact with customers and do specific jobs to the best of their ability.

Wal-Mart relies heavily on customer satisfaction through variety and low prices of their goods. Sam Walton challenged associates to exceed customer expectations by using their best judgment to go out of their way to satisfy consumers at every opportunity. In doing so, every associate in each locale becomes empowered to take appropriate steps to accomplish this goal. While Wal-Mart has a formal organizational structure which consists of a management hierarchy (i.e. President and CEO, Vice Presidents, Store Managers, Sales Associates), members of the sales associate staff are respected and encouraged to offer valuable insights into company practices for review and integration in the day-to-day operation. Wal-Mart does not have one standard mission statement, but Sam Walton developed 10 rules for building a business, which were discussed earlier. As these rules relate to the management theory put forth by Frederick Taylor, several of these fundamental business building blocks directly coincide with Wal-Mart's strategic plan. Wal-Mart representatives are assigned specific types of jobs which require them to focus on small portions of tasks in the grand scale of business; however, the stock people are stakeholders as well as the cashiers. They all have interaction with customers which requires them to not only know their particular job well but those of others as well. For instance, a cashier still needs to know how to guide a customer to the appropriate area of the store to find the item of choice with a pleasant demeanor instead of just pointing them into that direction. Commitment to their jobs keeps associates motivated to put forth their best behavior as a store representative.

Money is typically associated with being the primary reward distributed to those who perform most favorably; however, Wal-Mart's founder and subsequent executives recognize that it is further essential to motivate associates through alternate avenues. Some of these techniques are through open communication of strategies and changes to impart knowledge on all partners, through discounted stock options as a profit sharing effort, immediate praise and recognition for a job well done and even singing a theme song to energize staff on shift (Wal-Mart, 2004). An employee supposedly stated that "Management knows that we feel appreciated when they listen to us. We deal with the customers directly on a daily basis and have the best perspective on what they want" (Avila *et al*, 2004). Pushing responsibility down in the organization and expecting good suggestions to come up through the associate channels requires listening to everyone which is firmly stated in Rule 7. Displaying appreciation in this manner reflects highly on the positive rapport this company maintains with its internal representatives. Wal-Mart associates generally seem content with the management practices in their organization despite the fact that unionized labor bodies may say otherwise. The prices remain low, the work environment is pleasant, associates are treated as stakeholders with a voice; and Sam Walton's goal continues to be met with a successful team of partners that exceed his performance expectations.

Today, it is more than obvious that Wal-Mart has been using scientific management and Theory Y concepts as they strongly believe in their empowered employees working as a team towards planned and future goals. Wal-Mart follows the four objectives of Taylor as related to scientific management. For example:

1. Wal-Mart managers utilize everything around them to make their organization more technology efficient as they spend millions of dollars each year on computers and hire computer technicians, or analysts to deal with networking systems all over the world.
2. In terms of scientific selection, the organization holds various training seminars for the development of their workers, newly promoted and current managers, truck drivers, cashiers, and the employees who restock the shelves with merchandise. Wal-Mart not only hires outsiders with a qualified background, but they try to hire people from within their company in various positions as can be seen from the usage of their employees in their commercials on televisions and paper catalogs.
3. On the development of employees, Wal-Mart encourages managers to build a healthy relationship with each employee as this allows for a more comfortable working environment.
4. The division of work is almost equally shared among managers and employees, as each group is responsible for what best suits them to do in the company.

Although scientific management has been one of the most influential management theories, Frederick Taylor gained much criticism for it since it can create a machine from human beings for routine jobs that require no thinking. In his own words, Taylor explained: "The old fashioned dictator does not exist under scientific management. The man at the head of the business under Scientific Management is governed by rules and laws which have been developed through hundreds of experiments just as much as the workman is, and the standards developed are equitable." Strict application of scientific management theories in routine jobs can and do lead to boredom due to the continuous repetition of tasks that require little to no thinking. As such, job enrichment strategies can assist in the elimination of boredom and the creation of high employee morale in workplaces that use scientific management concepts.

Management Principles in Business Environments

Wal-Mart has made good use of various management science theories that provide rigorous quantitative techniques, and thus enable appropriate individuals more control over Wal-Mart's use of resources to produce, acquire and sell goods and services. The management science approach to management focuses on the use of rigorous quantitative techniques to help managers make maximum use of organizational resources to produce goods and services in a timely manner. Management sciences deal with a specific set of concerns which include: quantitative management, operations management, reengineering, total quality management, and management information systems. Wal-Mart has applied quantitative management through its supply chain system for the past three decades and this supply chain application has differentiated them from their competitors to make them a world leader. Wal-Mart employs a sophisticated technology which allows efficient operations, sales tracking, and reduces inventory turnaround by making their suppliers partners as they get the needed information in real time. This supply chain system helps managers and suppliers keep track of goods that are selling, determine how much inventory to have in stock, and identify what products sell the most depending on the season, resulting in better decision making by managers. The operations management systems used by Wal-Mart provide managers the tools needed to perform their job efficiently and to assist managers in making the best decisions. Managers also systematically receive input from their employees to respond to customers' needs and their changing desires. They also oversee the acquisition of inputs, control of conversion processes, and disposal of goods and services to determine where there is a need for improvement. For Wal-Mart owners, this means making sure their decisions will produce the desired goals with minimum labor, expense, and materials. Successful implementation of this system is perhaps one reason why Wal-Mart is able to offer customers good variety at affordable prices.

   Total Quality Management (TQM) is a concept rooted in the idea of continuous improvement in the operation to reduce cost, increase quality and to serve the needs of customers in the shortest period of time. TQM tools employ and rely on participative management principles centered on empowerment, education of employees, and the needs of customers. TQM focuses on improving the quality of an organization's products and services and stresses that all of an organization's value-added activities should be directed toward this goal. The core concept behind TQM and quality secret is that there is always a better way to get the job done by eliminating the waste associated with the way jobs get done. Wal-Mart has put into practice TQM in various ways within the organization which is seen through the hospitality employees provide to customers as they come into their stores. Wal-Mart also implements TQM by continuously seeking the best products and the lowest prices from national and international suppliers around the globe. In keeping with their promise that the customer is number one, Wal-Mart continues to find ways to exceed the customer's expectations by offering product variety and low prices. By continuing to improve the quality of goods, variety, and the way they are sold, Wal-Mart ensures that their standards remain competitive and their customers remain satisfied. Wal-Mart works closely with partners and suppliers to achieve this and has adapted standards for all of its suppliers to ensure they understand their responsibilities in remaining competitive. Jointly with suppliers in the value chain, they scan and monitor the task and the general environments to stay aware of their customers' changing needs and of their competitors' strategies. For example, a task environment at Wal-Mart is composed of forces which stem directly from distributors, suppliers, competitors, and customers. These forces affect the means in which an organization acquires input and its ability to extract outputs. These forces affect managers on a day-to-day basis and therefore have the most direct consequences upon short-term decision making.

   Customers. Customers are and will always be an important force for any organization that directly deals with them since they buy the goods and services produced by an organization thus ensuring its survival. Wal-Mart fills the needs of each population, for example, by identifying and focusing on their needs (Avila *et al*, 2004). One example can be observed by seeing and identifying an increase in customer demand for plus-size clothing, Wal-Mart was able to add an additional outlet to attract new customers while offering them what they wanted at low prices. Wal-Mart's strategy for addressing this force was to create a plus-size division increasing its apparel sales nationally and internationally. Its mission was to create a plus-size department which was neither demeaning nor insensitive to the customer's feelings. Wal-Mart was able to accomplish this by thoughtfully calling its plus size department "Women's" as well as developing its own sizing category which includes sizes phrased as 14W to 28W (Avila *et al*, 2004).

Competitors. A driving force for Wal-Mart is competition and in the large scale discount stores industry, Target and Kmart are its closest competitors in the United States. Competitors can create many obstacles, such as lower prices, product monopolies, and loss of market share. Integral to its survival is Wal-Mart's awareness of what other competitors are doing to either identify or satisfy customer needs. A surging retail trend which Target identified is the consumer attraction to signature lines sporting either national or private labels such as their Isaac Mizrahi clothing line or the Todd Oldham home furnishings. In order to remain competitive, for example, one of Wal-Mart's strategies has been to eliminate old worn-out brands such as Kathy Lee and Bobbie Brooks brands and push its new stylish label known as George. The George brand of clothing also has a cost/benefit option because there are no intermediaries that allow margins on the clothing to be significantly lower than other national brands guaranteeing the Wal-Mart business strategy of "Always Low Prices, Always." According to analysts, Wal-Mart apparel for 2004 comprised 20% of its total sales, making this strategy an effective decision to deal with the competitor force. Overall, competitive comparisons show that Wal-Mart has been out-performing their competitors for many factors detailed in Table 10 (prepared as a team by Anayansi Avila, Anita Edwards, Theresa Fitzpatrick, Charlette Williams, and Jennifer Wohl, 2004). Also, other relevant reasons for Wal-Mart's high performance and Kmart's low performance are summarized as well.

The general environment at Wal-Mart, similar to other large organizations, includes forces stemming from technological, socio-cultural, demographic, economic, political, legal and global forces which greatly impact the task environment. These forces tend to be more elusive and more challenging to identify and resolve than the direct forces in the task environment.

Demographics. Demographic forces are the results of changes either in perceptions, or characteristics of a population such as age, ethnic group, and social class. As the economy becomes more open to globalization, the diversity of customers will also become an important force for this giant retailer's selection of employees, location, products, and marketing strategies. The result of this impact is that Wal-Mart is building stores in more diverse, ethnically dense neighborhoods. In order to attract a variety of local customers, Wal-Mart used the business strategy known as "Store of the Community." This led to the creation of a marketing campaign using commercials with ethnically diverse employees and shoppers, speaking about their personal experiences dubbed in their native tongues. An example where this strategy has been successful is the Wal-Mart Canadian market, at least in Vancouver, which has a multitude of commercials in several languages such as Italian, South Asian, and Cantonese in order to match the native tongue of the local prospects.

Table 10 - Comparisons among Wal-Mart and Kmart

Factors	Wal-Mart	Kmart
Employee Empowerment	Uses an inverted paradigm approach whereby employees are on top and participate in company decisions.	Uses normal hierarchical structure which does not empower employees to make changes.
Supply Chain Technology	Employs sophisticated technology which allows efficient operations, sales tracking and reduced inventory turn.	Technology avoidance and complacency resulted in depressed margins, sagging prices, and stagnant inventory turn.
Profit Sharing	Offers employee profit sharing programs which instill loyalty and inspires its employees to do well.	Offers typical employee benefits with no profit sharing options.
Customer Service	Takes care of its internal and external customers ("Taking Care of People").	Has lost pulse of its customers.
Prices	Strives to bring customers highest value at lowest prices and a warm welcome.	Prices are normally higher than those offered by its competitors
Market Strategy	Leader in creating new industry trends and uses effective advertising campaigns.	Exercises attitude that if "it is not broken, don't fix it."
Customer Convenience	Offers shopping convenience 24/7 throughout its multiple locations (rural and urban) as well as through the Internet.	Store locations limited to U.S., Puerto Rico, and U.S. Virgin Islands and provide limited hours of shopping convenience.
Products	Offers wide product selection.	Offers limited product selection due to store size limitations
Global Expansion	Operates over 3,000 stores in the U.S. and over 1,000 stores internationally.	Operates stores in the U.S., Puerto Rico, Guam, and U.S. Virgin Islands only.
Retail Divisions	Operates neighborhood markets, supercenters, general merchandise stores, foreign operations.	Operates discount stores and supercenters only.

Technology. Another example of an indirect force which has had a tremendous effect on Wal-Mart is the effective use of the latest in information technology. Wal-Mart used information technology to modernize its stores in the 1970's by integrating bar-code scanners at its registers and involving suppliers in the sharing of information. Logged sales data was then sent to management giving them exact data on purchasing and current stock. This strategy, as a result of effectively using technology, is the Just-In-Time inventory Management system used at Wal-Mart. The Just-In-Time system allows them to store products that are needed and order according to demand which reduces the high cost of inventory storage and purchasing. Wal-Mart is also introducing the new radio frequency identification RFID technology into its supply operations. The new technology will replace bar codes, help deter theft, and cut costs (Kaiser, 2004). RFID uses radio frequencies to transmit data about the merchandise. RFID tags will hold more data than the existing bar codes and unlike bar codes they will not need to be scanned by hand. The technology has not been perfected yet, so Wal-Mart is taking a bit of risk to be one of the first retailers implementing it. As evidence of Wal-Mart's commitment to the RFID technology, Wal-Mart is requiring its top 100 suppliers to begin using it as of January 2005 (Kaiser, 2004).

Value Delivery Practices in Wal-Mart

With Sam Walton's philosophy on delivering value, Wal-Mart has become a national and international success in less than four decades from its inception because they deliver value for all of their relevant stakeholders. The strides that Wal-Mart has taken in the retail and grocery industries and the fast pace at which it has excelled has never been seen before by any other retail corporation on such a massive scale. In a short span of about forty years, this company has become the envy of many major corporations in the world. By maintaining its promise to customers of "everyday low prices," it provides unbeatable value for current and prospective customers. Wal-Mart, a Delaware corporation, has its principal offices in Bentonville, Arkansas. In 1962, the first Wal-Mart Discount City store was opened. In 1984, the Company opened its first three Sam's Clubs, and in 1988, its first Wal-Mart Super Center (combination full-line supermarket and discount store).

In 1992, the Company began its first international initiative in order to provide the same value and low prices on a global scale. The Company's international presence has continued to expand, and is growing faster than ever across the globe. Jointly, the sales from the countries of Canada,

Mexico, and the United Kingdom make up about 80% of its international revenues. Wal-Mart, with $47.5 billion in international sales making up one-fifth of its overall revenues in 2004, has enjoyed an enormous success and does not seem to be losing momentum nationally or internationally, despite some temporary challenges and setbacks. As mentioned before, Wal-Mart has been the fastest growing and largest private employer in the United States. According to Upbin (2004), the Wal-Martization of the world is bringing about good and bad changes to commerce around the globe. Due to its relentless vision for low prices, more and more manufacturing jobs are moving to developing economies, such as China, leaving United States workers unemployed. On the other hand, international commerce through Wal-Mart will create "over 800,000 jobs worldwide over the next several years, not to mention the labor needed to build the stores, parking lots and distribution centers" (Upbin, 2004). Wal-Mart is expected to be the first trillion dollar retailer in the world. Wal-Mart has become what it is due to its national and international operations which show an organization that is both effective and efficient in pursuit of providing low prices for customers. Wal-Mart has been consistently rated as the number one efficient retailer in the world (Biesada, 2004). The application and realization of their slogan "Always Low Prices, Always" is perhaps one of the main reasons for its success at home and abroad. Wal-Mart partners with efficient suppliers to provide consumers with quality goods at affordable prices in their stores.

Wal-Mart's founding philosophy and the implementation of successful leadership skills and management strategies have led to its global success. One can easily expand on some of the strategies that have brought them enormous success and opportunities in today's competitive world of retail business. Some of Wal-Mart's highlights are the following:

- Total sales at Wal-Mart were $256 billion with 68% from Wal-Mart Stores, 19% from its international operations, and 13% coming from its Sam's Club. Wal-Mart's annual profits are about $9 billion and they have a market value of $244 with assets worth over $105 billion during 2004.
- As of April 2004, in addition to its 3,550 stores in the United States, Wal-Mart had 640 stores in Mexico, 404 stores in Japan, 267 stores in United Kingdom, 236 stores in Canada, 92 stores in Germany, 53 in Puerto Rico, 34 in China, 25 in Brazil, 15 in South Korea, and 11 stores in Argentina while expanding into these countries on a continuous basis.

- Wal-Mart employs over one million people in the United States and nearly half million individuals internationally.
- It ranked 10th on Forbes Leading 2000 Companies in the World based on a composite scores for sales, profits, assets, and overall market value. As a matter-of-fact, Wal-Mart ranked first in sales, ranked sixth in total market value, and they ranked eight in overall profits through Forbes ranking of World's 2000 Leading Companies in Forbes April 12th issue.
- Wal-Mart is recognized as one of the leading employers of individuals with disabilities in the United States. In the 2002 annual poll by CAREERS FOR THE DISABLED magazine, named Wal-Mart first among all U.S. companies in providing opportunities and a positive work environment for people with disabilities.
- Wal-Mart is one of the leading employers of senior citizens in the United States, employing more than 170,000 associates who are 55 years of age and older.
- Wal-Mart received the Hispanic National Bar Association (HNBA) 2002 Corporate Partner of the Year Award for its consistent support and best practices in the area of diversity.
- Wal-Mart is the leading private employer of emerging groups in the United States. More than 160,000 African American associates and more than 105,000 Hispanic associates work for Wal-Mart.
- Wal-Mart received the 2002 Ron Brown Award, the highest Presidential Award recognizing outstanding achievement in employee relations and community initiatives.
- The National Action Network (NAN) presented Wal-Mart with the 2002 Community Commitment Corporate Award in recognition of community involvement and diversity practices.

Organizational Management Practices

Organizational management theory is based on the set of forces and conditions that operate beyond an organization's boundaries, but affect a manager's ability to acquire and utilize resources (Jones & George, 2003). Wal-Mart has used organizational management principles to help improve the way they utilize organizational resources and compete successfully in the global environment. As previously discussed, strategic management and Total Quality Management are two approaches which have helped

Wal-Mart leaders make better use of organizational resources. Wal-Mart's senior managers have been able to strategically build stores throughout the country and establish appropriate mechanisms to deal effectively with contingencies. By planning for every possible challenge that is not within its control, Wal-Mart has been able to continue operations and provide continuous service under diverse and uncertain conditions. Wal-Mart has established distribution centers in strategic locations to ensure continuous and timely services to its customers and to reduce the risk associated with unexpected disasters. Consequently, if an unfortunate incident (such as a tornado, hurricane, or earthquake) were to occur in the Midwest this should not negatively impact the delivery of products to stores it has in the west, east, or south sides of the country along with the international divisions.

Wal-Mart has used the "Every Day Low Prices" (EDLP) value proposition consistently in all of its communication in its quest to become the world's largest retailer through conquest and relationship marketing strategies. They also use an aggressive acquisition strategy that allows customers from different countries to benefit from its EDLP. Wal-Mart as a company has grown considerably in the past two decades, and now forms almost two percent of the U.S. economy. Each week, over 100 million customers, in search of EDLP at Wal-Mart, pass through the super stores where they can get diverse products and services, do their banking, get their eyes checked, or have the oil changed in their car – truly a one-stop shopping experience (Kalakota and Robinson, 2003).

Wal-Mart employs many programs designed to meet the competitive pressures within the industry including: Every Day Low Prices, Always Low Prices – Always, Item Merchandising, Store-Within-a-Store, Price Rollbacks, and Store of the Community concepts (Kalakota and Robinson, 2003). Successful strategies implemented by Wal-Mart to support these programs are centered on its focus on communities, use of advanced technology, and establishment of a sophisticated supply chain management system with its partners. Although Wal-Mart stores are ubiquitous in most United States regions, each store is tailored for the needs of the community as popularized by "Store of the Community" concept. Decentralized store management is extremely important given Wal-Mart's size and their aim of meeting each community's demands. Wal-Mart's philosophy is that managers and employees who are closest to the customers know what is important in their locale. They are also encouraged to use technology to assist them in making factual decisions about the local community through the available data. Effective use of technology has enabled Wal-Mart to create efficiencies in the value chain with diverse partners that are unmatched by leading companies in other industries. Using technology to simplify processes, eliminate waste, analyze and effectively respond to factual data has been the main strategy at Wal-Mart. Thus far, technology has aided Wal-Mart in reducing its operating expenses as a percentage of sales to less than 15 percent (Kalakota and Robinson, 2003). Wal-Mart was the first major retailer to implement Just-In-Time (JIT) Inventory Management and build a Retail Link System which provides sales data by item, store, and day to partners in the supply chain. This information saves suppliers time and expense in planning their production and distribution, which translates to lower merchandise costs in the long-term. As a result, synergy among everyone in the value chain, Wal-Mart shelves are hardly ever empty, thus satisfying the needs of most customers.

The Concept of Value Driven Management

A valuable resource for all retail managers and leaders to read is the textbook written by Pohlman and Gardiner (2000) in order to get a comprehensive introduction to *Value Driven Management* (VDM). As mentioned before, VDM provides a decision-making framework that can be used in a variety of situations. VDM is based upon Values Theory which claims that what people truly value drives their actions and behaviors. The underlying theme is to make decisions that maximize value over time for stakeholders in the long-term. Value Driven Management is a practical model that managers can use in their daily work life in a variety of decision-making scenarios. The authors explore the underlying assumptions of VDM including (1) what is valued drives action; (2) the creation of knowledge and its appropriate use leads to value creation; (3) there are value adders and value destroyers; (4) values can compete or be complementary; and, last but certainly not least, (5) all employees are employees – emphasizing that everyone's input and actions are critically important to the success of the organization!

Pohlman and Gardiner also offer several cases and examples—good and bad, of how companies reveal their values, or relative lack of values, in their decision making. Pohlman makes use of his time as Director of Human Resources at Koch and provides inside information about the philosophy and value system of Koch. One of the best lessons one can learn from his Koch experiences is that developing a value based management system (and/or market-based management at Koch) takes years and top management support. It is not a quick-fix, nor an easily implemented system. VDM is system-wide, an important part of an organization's culture, and as with anything having to do with organizational culture, it takes time and reinforcement to implement. The authors use the Johnson & Johnson Tylenol case, well-known to many by now, as an example of how easy it is for a company to make a really good, customer-friendly decision which leads to good will and profit for the company if the values are clear. J&J's CEO did not have to figure out what to do when Tylenol was tampered with—the ethical value system of J&J made only one choice possible—pull the product. The resulting benefits to the public and to J&J as it reaped huge public relations (PR) rewards are well documented. The negative example to this, however, is the Exxon Valdez case. Here, the "too little too late" scenarios, caused an outraged public and billions of dollars in punitive damages. Exxon's CEO didn't seem to have a systematic value system to help him decide how to handle the crisis or the resultant confusion, and then the half-hearted attempt to do "something," caused a PR disaster for Exxon. Similar examples are provided for all the value drivers (the above examples relating to external customer values). The ideal situation, of course, is congruence between organizational values and the employee's values. This leads to inevitable job satisfaction and an environment within which both the organization and the employee can prosper.

The basic purpose of Values Driven Management (VDM) is to motivate managers and employees, when contemplating making decisions or taking actions, to consider the impact of these decisions and actions on the value of the organization over time. This determination can be accomplished only by an examination of the sets of values held by the relevant constituents (or "stakeholder" groups) of the organization. These encompass world, national, societal cultures and subcultures, organizational culture, the values of employees, suppliers, customers, competitors, and third parties (such as unions and government regulators), and most importantly, but not exclusively, the values of the "owners" of the organization (Cavico & Mujtaba, 2005).

Maximizing value over time. A significant goal of VDM is to maximize value over time. "Value" is a subjective term referring to something that possesses worth, intrinsically or instrumentally. In the business context, value typically is regarded in a monetary sense; but value also encompasses such notions as happiness and security as well as morality, ethics, honesty, and integrity. The goal of VDM is to maximize the value of the organization over time, especially in the sense of maximizing its long-term profitability, by creating "win-win" scenarios whereby the value of the organization and its constituent groups are maximized. A long-term perspective is taken, but not so long as to prevent the prediction of the reasonably foreseeable consequences of a decision or action on the organization and its "stakeholders," and then the resultant impact on value maximization over time for the organization. The subjectivity and diversity of value, the long-term view, and the necessity of foreseeing consequences make VDM decisions quite complex; and thus will require the VDM decision-maker to engage in careful determinations, accurate predictions, equitable balancing and weighing to use wise judgment.

What is valued drives action. A vital underlying assumption of VDM is that what causes individuals and groups to take actions are their values. If values, therefore, are not understood clearly, there will be no way to define, predict, satisfy, or even compete with value driven actions.

There are value adders and value destroyers. There are people, processes, and systems within organizations that add and destroy value. There are, for example, employees within organizations who destroy more value than they create, perhaps as a result of being in the wrong position with the wrong types of skills and abilities, or perhaps they are totally incompatible with their organization's means or ends. It is every employee's responsibility to seek out a role that adds value and ensures success; and the organization's responsibility to eliminate value destroyers by placing people in the proper jobs and instituting proper processes and systems. According to Cavico and Mujtaba (2005), "The VDM model and method is a philosophical as well as a practical approach, which is simple to state and discuss, but arduous to implement." If VDM is learned well and administered thoughtfully and consistently, the ultimate goals of achieving, creating, and sustaining long-term growth, surplus, wealth, and value maximization will be attained in any organization and Wal-Mart is a good example of its application. Wall-Mart provides value for its customers through low prices. There are many value drivers that have an effect on Wal-Mart's operations, progress, and success. An assessment of the most relevant value drivers can be seen by looking at their customers, employees, external cultures, suppliers, and competitor values. The following paragraphs explore a few of the relevant stakeholders and their values.

Customer values. Customer values require managers to keep their finger on the pulse of customers since their needs and desires may change often and since customer service is important to create customer value. At the heart of Wal-Mart's success and growth is the unique culture that Sam

Walton built. His business philosophy was based on the simple idea of making the customer feel that s/he is number one. He believed that by serving the customer's needs first, his business would also serve its associates, shareholders, communities, and other stakeholders. Wal-Mart's culture has always stressed the importance of customer service. Its associate base across the nation is as diverse as the communities in which they work. This allows Wal-Mart to provide the service expected from each individual customer that walks into their stores expecting low prices. Thus, creating value for customers is Wal-Mart's strongest value-adder. Wal-Mart's commitment to providing customer value is inherent in one of its core beliefs of "Service to Our Customers" passed on to employees as they become oriented to the culture of each store. As part of this commitment, Wal-Mart has set a goal of exceeding customer's expectations with what Sam Walton coined "aggressive hospitality." Wal-Mart wants its Associates to exceed customer expectations with friendly attitudes and an eagerness to assist customers. As part of exceeding customer expectations, Wal-Mart has also instituted the Ten Foot Rule which has been practiced by many retailers in the past two decades including Publix in the state of Florida. *The Ten Foot Rule* encourages associates to greet customers and offer assistance whenever customers are within ten feet of the associate. Furthermore, Wal-Mart provides value to its customers through its pricing philosophies. The slogan: "*Always Low Prices. Always*" that appears on its ads alludes to this goal. Wal-Mart provides consumers with quality goods at an affordable price. Wal-Mart's pricing philosophies include the Everyday Low Price (EDLP), Rollback and Special Buys philosophies. Wal-Mart's goal is to pass its savings onto the customer and achieve a profit through the volume of sales generated as a result of lower prices and repeat customers.

External cultural values. External cultural values include all those values outside the organization that may have an impact upon it, beginning with the values of the local community. Wal-Mart's commitment to people means that it also takes its responsibility as a corporate neighbor seriously. Local Wal-Mart stores have made a difference in their communities by:

a) Educating the public about recycling and other environmental concerns via a "Green Coordinator," a specially trained associate who coordinates efforts to make each store environmentally responsible.

b) Raising funds for local children's hospitals via the Children's Miracle Network Telethon.

c) Sponsoring a Community Matching Grant program that involves fund-raising efforts by a nonprofit organization with the participation of Wal-Mart associates.
d) Underwriting college scholarships for high school seniors.

Wal-Mart's community involvement approach is unique and it is guided by associates who live in the local area and understand its needs. Wal-Mart associates combine financial and volunteer support to assist organizations that make a positive difference in local communities. In addition, Wal-Mart has launched several national efforts to help the larger, U.S. community.

Some neighborhoods do not welcome Wal-Mart into their communities due to its negative impact on the local merchants and the diversity of available local businesses. For example, some local residents opposed a proposal to open a new Wal-Mart store in Inner Grove Heights (Bonner, 2004). In addition to the impact on local businesses, Wal-Mart's low wages and large building design were questioned. Some of the local residents believed that Wal-Mart's presence would change the rural suburban nature of the community and drive out smaller businesses. In Minnesota, Wal-Mart agreed to change its building design to alleviate concerns about the look and size of the building. Before Wal-Mart can fulfill its commitment of giving back to the community it must have the support of the community. Thus, when picking new locations for stores, Wal-Mart considers the wants and needs of that community.

Supplier values. Suppliers in Wal-Mart reflect many of the sensitivities of the global community, and meets its suppliers', customers', and shareholders' expectations about how they conduct business. The three pillars of Wal-Mart's foundation – respect for the individual, striving for excellence, and customer service – constantly challenge Wal-Mart to deliver best practices and require the same from its suppliers. The way Wal-Mart conducts its business, as well as the manner in which its suppliers conduct their business, impacts Wal-Mart's reputation among its customers and shareholders. Wal-Mart has created standards for suppliers that want to conduct business with them. Based on these standards, suppliers, their contractors, and their subcontractors must conform to the ethical standards and business practices stated in the contract. Wal-Mart regularly monitors the factory base of its suppliers to ensure compliance with the legal requirements and standards in the jurisdictions in which they conduct business. This includes labor and compensation laws, health and safety laws, and environmental laws. If the jurisdiction's legal requirements exceed industry standards, Wal-Mart requires its suppliers to conform to the laws of the jurisdiction in which it is operating. Wal-Mart depends on its suppliers to provide goods and services in a timely manner at a low cost. Doing business with Wal-Mart provides suppliers with an opportunity to increase sales and market share (Fishman, 2003). Wal-Mart is also known for improving the efficiency of its suppliers by insisting that suppliers match Wal-Mart's ability to move and track goods. As an example, in January 2005, Wal-Mart required its top 100 suppliers to implement radio frequency identification (RFID) tags on its merchandise. This new technology is an inventory tracking system that tracks merchandise from the supplier to the store. Wal-Mart has been accused of applying major pressure on its suppliers to reduce costs or risk losing Wal-Mart's business. This criticism is a potential value-destroyer for Wal-Mart and the suppliers. Some suppliers must increase efficiency as well as reduce jobs to meet the cost cutting demands of Wal-Mart (Fishman, 2003). Even through sales increase, the suppliers experience a loss in profits due to the price cutting. In some cases, claim the critics of Wal-Mart, the reduced profits and job loss may negatively impact the suppliers and reduce the benefits of the increased sales and market share. Wal-Mart must also consider how their relationships with their suppliers may impact customer's perception from a public relation's perspective.

Individual employee values. These values involve the employee's personal values, and are very important since it could have a major impact on the organization's continued success. Careful selection of employees whose personal values closely match those of the organization is essential to an organization's success (Pohlman & Gardiner, 2000). Wal-Mart depends on its employees to achieve its goal of exceeding customer expectations with high levels of service. According to Pohlman and Gardiner, an organization's value over time is maximized when the individual employee's values match those of the organization. Wal-Mart hires employees with values congruent to the organization so that Wal-Mart, the customer, and the employees can jointly create value for everyone involved. The associates play an important role in Wal-Mart's success as they maximize value over time for relevant stakeholders. Wal-Mart associates know it is not good enough to simply be grateful to their customers for shopping at their stores – they demonstrate their gratitude in every way they can. They understand that doing so is what keeps their customers coming back to Wal-Mart. This philosophy was noted by Sam Walton who believed that if the organization expected the employees to take care of the customers, then the organization would have to take care of the employees (Gale Group, 1999), representing a reciprocal relationship. As stated before, he believed in an inverted pyramid structure with the associates on top, and the "back office support" personnel on the bottom. Wal-Mart has an open door policy where associates are encouraged to bring suggestions to their supervisors on how to make the organization more successful. Wal-Mart also provides its employees with benefits such as profit sharing, 401K plans, medical and health benefits. Since the inception of Wal-Mart's profit sharing plan in 1972 and the inception of Wal-Mart's 401(k) plan in 1997, Wal-Mart has contributed over $3 billion toward the retirement funds of its associates.

Competitor values. This facet of the stakeholder and value theories relates to the rivalry among sellers and the attempt by competitors to win customers to gain a competitive edge. Despite its enormous success, Wal-Mart remains vigilant to its competition and stays ahead to maintain its competitive advantage. Some of Wal-Mart's biggest competitors in the United States have been Kmart and Target. For several years now, Wal-Mart has gained a considerable lead over Kmart because it can and does offer lower prices on many of its products. Wal-Mart is an example of a high performing organization and Kmart is an example of a low performing organization that has struggled to effectively compete with Wal-Mart in the past few decades. Wal-Mart is the largest retailer in the world with billions in profits each year while Kmart lost $2.44 billion in 2001 and $3.22 billion in 2002 (Griest, 2004). The performance levels of the two organizations differ because Wal-Mart has been able to successfully build a competitive advantage through efficiency, innovation, quality, responsiveness to customers, and other factors while Kmart has lagged behind in these areas possibly due to complacency and avoidance of integrating technology in a timely manner into their work processes. Wal-Mart has also hired a diverse workforce into its organization to keep pace with the changing consumer demographics. Lastly, it has expanded its operations globally and increased its presence in the U.S. with the addition of new stores as well as through non-traditional advertising on the World Wide Web.

Summary

Upbin (2004) stated that, for Wal-Mart, "Europe has proven at times adept, at times inept, at acquiring. In China, it struggles with a dauntingly primitive supply chain. In Japan it is taking rice-grain-size steps so as not to damage a powerful but backward retail ecosystem...it...stumbled among stronger competitors in the huge markets of Brazil and Argentina."

Wal-Mart entered Hong Kong and two years later in 1996 left due to mistakes in merchandise selection and location. It left Indonesia in less than two years after its entry in 1996 because one of their stores in Jakarta was looted during the riots. Furthermore, Wal-Mart made mistakes in Germany, South Korea, Brazil, and other international locations, but due to its distaste for repeating mistakes, Wal-Mart managers learn and adjust quickly to changing circumstance. Certainly, Wal-Mart has limitations and learning curves as they compete with local, national and international competitors that are small and large. Yes, they too can learn from others as they adjust to bring about low prices to more consumers around the globe. Yet, many smaller competitors, focused on uniquely delivering better overall value, are successfully growing despite Wal-Mart's success with their customers. Wal-Mart is so massive now that it has a market capitalization as large as the gross domestic product of many developed countries. The company said at its 2003 annual meeting that it expected to hire 800,000 people over the next several years, and it had plans to build about 278 stores in the United States and 113 in international locations in 2004.

Modern organizations are in a constant state of flux as they reshape themselves to meet the demands of investors, employees, owners, and customers simultaneously. The companies that are built to last and grow are those that change on all fronts nationally and internationally as they increase value for all relevant stakeholders such as customers, employees, owners, and third parties by providing everyone great value. Wal-Mart has shown that it is keeping its momentum for creating superior value by offering an organizational culture that is passionate about reducing cost and offering lower prices.

The successful and effective application of scientific management and motivational theories has led many managers in the retail environment to be very successful with their employees and customers. The companies that are built to last and grow are those that change appropriately as they increase customers, revenues, market value, and bottom-line profits by providing everyone great total value. Wal-Mart has shown that it is keeping its momentum for creating great value by offering low prices and diverse products in a changing retail world.

Chapter Twelve

INTERNATIONALIZATION, RISK AND REPATRIATION[8]

Global change, a reality of life, impacts workers individually in both national and international organizations, interpersonally as they interact with colleagues from cross-cultural backgrounds, organizationally as new rules and policies are set to accommodate diverse vendors, and environmentally as they deal with the demands of new climates, topographies, and governments. While there are many risks, for most firms, international assignments are a way to share and gain global competence, knowledge and skills all over the world. Internationalization is a reality for today's corporations and their leaders, managers and workers. Employees, known as expatriates, are sent on international assignments to fill a position in a foreign subsidiary; develop their managerial talent; spread corporate values; and implant organizational objectives to subsidiaries of the entire organization.

Firms consider many elements when staffing employees for these assignments; from technical ability to cross-cultural and emotional maturity. The perfect candidate, however, does not exist and judging the candidate's ability has no effect on creating a smooth transition back home (Baruch, Steel & Quantrill, 2002). The repatriation process consists of many steps and depending on how they are handled, can affect repatriates' re-adjustment, their commitment to the firm, and can reduce the benefits of the assignment to the firm. Consequently, companies do not pay nearly as much attention to the process of repatriation as they do the expatriation process (Jassawalla, Connelly & Slojkowski, 2004). As reported in the *European Business Forum* (2004), the most common issue faced by organizations in the repatriation process is how to deal with the high

---

[8] - The chapter is co-authored with Elizabeth Danon-Leva and Erica Franklin. Nova Southeastern University.

expectations of repatriates after they return home in the context of what actually happens (p. 73). Most organizations feel repatriating employees is a "no-brainer," and they treat workers as if they are returning home from a business trip. There are four stages in the repatriation process that affect how workers adjust to life at home. The first step is preparation, the second step is the physical relocation, the third step is the transition, and the fourth step is the re-adjustment stage (Dowling & Welch, 2005, p. 161). The readjustment phase, which includes dealing mentally and emotionally with the changes and realities of being at home, is the source of most problems in repatriates' lives; as work, personal, and social changes can often result in reverse "culture shock" and maladjustment. Many companies do not understand this phase sufficiently and therefore cannot handle it effectively. One goal of this chapter is to highlight the elements of repatriation that led to maladjustment of the workers and to develop a comprehensive repatriation program that minimizes the effects of maladjustment on the worker and the organization.

A colleague who recently attended a seminar titled "*Adapting to Change*," described how people generally react to change. First there is a culture shock and it is hard to accept the change; later, one starts to accept the new environment, then the expatriate is accustomed to it and now the person has made this part of his or her day-to-day activities. Perhaps this process also applies to expatriates going to new and different cultures. At first it is difficult, because one may miss his or her family and friends; the expatriate is in a different environment, affected by different customs, different language, as well as different norms and regulations. As time passes, one starts to accept more things from the new culture such as the local customs and the people. Later in time, one is often so accustomed to the new place and culture that he or she is, in a way, also part of that environment because s/he has adapted to it, is following the local rules, speaking the language, watching the same sports as the local citizens, and so on. Of-course, the actual process can be challenging since individuals are different and react to cultural change differently.

Internationalization: Influences and Challenges

This section discusses international management in the context of the theory of internationalization. Does the theory of internationalization reflect the current managerial decision-making process companies face when going abroad? First, a brief overview of the literature is presented, followed by a presentation of some criticism, concerns, and limitations on the theory of internationalization. Then understanding relationships and influences internationalization has on international managerial decisions is discussed. Finally, some practical recommendations for management and international manager's on internationalization are presented. Overall, this section on internationalization seeks to examine some of the complex challenges and influences that international management and multinationals face when deciding to internationalize their operations.

Introduction and Literature Review

The purpose of this research is to explore the internationalization theory and its relationship with management and international management. Discussion about internationalization and its impact on business, relationships, public, and private policy is commonplace. However, despite numerous journal articles and research about internationalization and regardless of industry, international businesses and management are constantly being influenced and challenged. This area has garnered more attention as the globalization process moves forward. While there is no consensus on how to measure a firm's degree of internationalization, many valid attempts have been made.

It is understood that the portrayal of regional economic integration has struggled to bring regions together geographically and/or economically by way of eliminating or lowering trade tax and tariff barriers. Eliminating or lowering trade taxes and tariffs facilitates the flow of monies and in some cases merges labor with monetary policy and fiscal systems. Traditionally, this portrayal was presented more as an economic obstacle excluding and in competition with other countries and regions. Nevertheless, economic globalization is understood as the internationalization of the production process and the means by which it is financed. The world today can be described as an enormous marketplace that is not static but dynamic and fast paced, marked by tremendous technological advances (Culpan, 2002; Danon-Leva, 2005). Technological advances have helped propel the world toward breaking down previous cultural, communication, and trade barriers (Senge, 1998).

International business is augmented with technology advances and the economic transformations seen in various countries, in addition to the economic transformation in the former socialist economies (e.g. Russia) and other eastern European countries (e.g. Croatia and Slovakia), and emerging economies such as Southeast Asia (e.g. South Korea and Taiwan) and Latin America (e.g. Chile). Multinational corporations (MNCs) have responded to these changes in the globalization process by searching to internationalize by means of forging alliances among regions and industries.

Reinicke (1997) states that "globalization has been asserted but not defined" (Reinicke, 1997, p.127). It is being defined more and more as cross-border integration and relationships, and cross-border movement of trade, finance, technology, and information. Researchers have used the traditional definition of internationalization, which maintains that this is a process in which a firm increases its involvement abroad consequently crossing borders (Peyrefitte, Fadil, & Thomas, 2002; Welch & Luostarinen, 1988; Johanson & Vahlne, 1977; Doz & Prahalad, 1991). Welch and Luostarinen (1988) insist on the difficulty of defining the internationalization theory, used only to describe outward movements and decisions, because it lacks clarity. Furthermore, based on Welch and Luostarinen's research and the dimensions of internationalization in their model, a company has many potential directions from which to choose.

Welch and Luostarinen (1988) observed a gradual pattern in the internationalization process; Johanson and Wiedersheim-Paul (1975) confirm an internationalization pattern emerged in their research using a sample of four large Swedish MNCs. Luostarinen (1979) also confirms in a study that a pattern emerged as well as an evolutionary process in the development in the entry modes, product offered, and market penetration using three-quarters of the Finnish industrial company's population, regardless of the type of foreign operations. An investment pattern is revealed in Yoshihara's (1978) research with Japanese firms. An Australian study (1984) argues that there is not a consistent pattern in its study of 228 foreign investment cases (Welch and Luostarinen, 1988).

Johanson and Vahlne (1977) observed that a firm's internationalization is based on economic and business aspects that influence the level of international involvement, thus illustrating a firm's internationalization pattern. Johanson and Vahlne (1977) developed a dynamic internationalization model "one cycle event." They assume that lacking knowledge is an obstacle for international expansion and development and yet this can be acquired abroad; thus leading them to distinguish between a) a firm's involvement abroad as an extension of its operation, and b) a firm's continual establishment of operations abroad. The focus of the model by Johanson and Vahlne (1977) is to study a firm's involvement abroad as it pertains to an extension of its operation. This model seeks to incorporate previous empirical research and their empirical research of Swedish firms, as well as a firm's behavioral theory by Cyert and March (1963). Their research demonstrates Swedish firms develop an internationalization process at a slow pace (Johanson & Vahlne, 1977).

Consequently, Johanson and Vahlne (1977, p. 23) posit that the internationalization process is a direct result of a "series of incremental decisions." The focus of their internationalization model is to identify shared characteristics in the internationalization process rather than decision-making styles. Furthermore, observations have shown the timing of newly established operations abroad is related to the psychic distance between the home and host country; this could also contribute towards limiting a firm's internationalization. *Psychic distance*, according to Johanson and Vahlne (1977), is defined as "the sum of factors preventing the flows of information from and to the market." Some examples can include "differences in language, education, business practices, culture, and industrial development" (Johanson & Vahlne, 1977, p. 24). The main structure of the model suggests a continuous cycle: the results or output of one decision will comprise the input for another decision. What's more, fueled by a firm's long-term profitability and growth strategy, all decision-making is influenced directly by market knowledge and market commitment and a firm's ability to identify risk, perceive opportunities, and evaluate alternatives, as well as consider the existing economic and business environments (Johanson & Vahlne, 1977).

Criticism, Concern, and Limitation with the Theory

In early academic research, the internationalization process was analyzed, documented, and explained from a foreign investment perspective. Welch and Luostarinen (1988) suggest that while this was a "starting point," left unanswered were questions of the process before, during, and after. They assert the internationalization theory analysis was static and consequently lacked any dynamic aspect; long-term perspective was given little importance or consideration. To address the lack of long-term approach, Welch and Luostarinen (1988) point out that in the early 1970s research (Aharoni, 1966; Wilkins, 1970 & 1974) was shifting towards a longitudinal approach and the identification of steps or patterns of foreign investment decision-making processes. Wilkins' (1970 & 1974) research based on Nordic companies was able to identify significant dynamic elements that assisted in determining a blueprint or "patterns of internationalization" (Welch & Luostarinen, 1988, p. 35). To further illustrate the importance of broadening the definition of the theory of internationalization, Welch and Luostarinen (1988) point out the growth many companies have experienced through internationalization by subcontracting. Hence, one can observe the connectivity and interdependence between a company's outward growth, inward growth and expansion that can be experienced.

The internationalization process implies a market process and not a management process. Buckley (1993) considers this ironic, since this process relies on human resources to be successful. Nonetheless, Buckley (1993) puts forward the following criticism of the theory of internationalization "as a means for putting management back in" (p. 200). First, the theory neglects that the growth process a firm encounters is considered dynamic and ongoing and not static. Second, the theory addresses a firm's growth relative to the market and not to another firm. The theory falls short in addressing "why one firm is more successful than another" (p. 201). Third, international competition is not part of the model. Fourth, the theory does not address the relationship between a firm and its environment. Lastly and fifth, the theory does not address the implication of relationships within a firm (Buckley, 1993).

The simplest form considered to measure and assess the degree of internationalization (DOI) that has been used is a company's foreign sales as a percentage to total sales (FSTF). Sullivan (1994) suggests that using foreign sales as a percentage of total sales as the only indicator for determining the degree of internationalization is risky for the firm. This in part is due to a given moment in time in which the numbers obtained could be "artificially inflated or deflated" with a phenomenon that has no bearing on a firm's internationalization, e.g. foreign currency (Sullivan, 1994, p. 337).

Welch and Luostarinen (1988) contend while this may be a simple numerical equation it has drawbacks; mainly, the lack of any other information that pertains to how the international venture was conducted and how decisions were made. In response, they suggest a broader framework is necessary to encompass the different dimensions of internationalization. Their model suggests that as a consequence of diversity of international operations, organizations must take into consideration and answer: how to go abroad, what goods are to be sold, what are the sales objectives, where should the expansion be located, what organizational structure is required to go abroad, what financing should be used, and what personnel and skill requirements are needed. Furthermore, there exists "dynamic factors" that can make a company feel constrained, limit their level of commitment and exposure, and/or influence a "forward momentum": first, the availability of the resources (financial means and personnel) to carry out an international expansion; second, market knowledge; third, communications structure and existing networks; fourth, identification of risks and uncertainty aspects; fifth, controlling aspects based on the level of commitment and stage of internationalization; and, sixth, management's commitment to an internationalization strategy (Welch & Luostarinen, 1988, p. 51-54).

Researchers (Johanson & Vahlne, 1977; Welch & Luostarinen, 1988) concur that some of the main concerns that are not addressed in the internationalization theory are the lack of market knowledge, including how to do business in a foreign country, and international operations, all of which are part of a firm's internationalization process. This lack of knowledge directly influences any decision-making process management must make in connection with taking operations internationally.

In recent years, concern about the environment has increased and prompted some researchers (Hart & Ahuja, 1996; Klassen & McLaughlin, 1997; Nehr, 1996; Dowell, Hart & Yeung, 1998) to study the relationship between and on the impact of various financial aspects such as performance and growth by MNCs in the internationalization process. Concern over the lack of empirical research on the relationship between a firm's degree of internationalization and MNCs environmental performance prompted Kennelly and Lewis (2002) to research and focus on this apparent gap.

Kennelly and Lewis's (2002) research consisted of performing cross-sectional and longitudinal studies on 138 U.S. based S&P 500 MNCs. They used 1993-1998 environmental performance data obtained from Kinder, Lyndenberg and Domini, a social rating and investment service, and a variation of Sullivan's (1994) degree of internationalization measures which includes Ronen and Shenkar's (1985) psychic zones. The authors incorporate two variables: environmental performance and sales as a control variable. Cross-sectional results demonstrated support for the hypothesis; i.e., there is a positive relationship between the degree of internationalization of a firm and its environmental performance. Longitudinal results demonstrated that "none of the correlations show a relationship between variables…correlations are positive in every case…statistically significant." Based on these observations, there is support for the hypothesis (Kennelly & Lewis 2002, p. 485).

The theory of internationalization does not discuss the role of management in a firm's internationalization process. Leadership must have some influence in the decision-making process to internationalize. In strategic leadership literature, the upper echelon theory (Hambrick & Mason, 1984) posits that the role of managers can reflect experience (Peyrefitte, Fadil, & Thomas, 2002). This limitation in the internationalization theory prompts Peyrefitte, Fadil, and Thomas (2002) to explore in their study the relationship between management experience and levels of internationalization. Additionally, the study puts forward that the level of internationalization is positively related to a manager's experience, both functional and organizational, as well as the functional background heterogeneity. A sample of 87 Fortune 500 largest U.S. firms in four industries was used. Firm-specific data from 1992 was obtained from the Compustat database and all executive data was obtained from Dun and Bradstreet's Reference Book of Corporate Managements. Using a hierarchical regression analysis, the results demonstrated a positive relationship between a mean level of internationalization for both functional and organizational experience and "no statistical relationship between functional background heterogeneity and level of internationalization" (Peyrefitte et al., 2002, p. 499). This outcome further concludes that managerial experience plays a significant role in the decision-making process and commitment level a firm undertakes to internationalize. However, diversity could be used to explain why there is no correlation linking functional background heterogeneity and level of internationalization. On the other hand, diversity may well prove to be a double-edged sword for management's decision-making process by either motivating or hindering creativity (Peyrefitte, Fadil, & Thomas, 2002).

It is important to point out that amid studies (Johanson & Vahlne, 1977; Kennelly & Lewis, 2002; Peyrefitte, Fadil, & Thomas, 2002; Welch & Luostarinen, 1988) that assert the various ways to measure the degree of internationalization by examining the evolution and relationships with a firm's organizational structure, top management and managerial experience, as well as the market, environmental performance, and international operations, Sullivan (1994) sustains "the reliability of measuring the degree of internationalization of a firm remains speculative" (p. 325). Considering the frameworks that have been used previously, Sullivan (1994) points out that it is easy to replicate the study of a relationship between one independent variable and dependent variables. Furthermore, Sullivan (1994) states that "the medley of measures has neither helped establish a standard criterion nor clarified the content validity of measurement" (p. 326). Determined to offer another approach that addresses what he considers DOI measurement shortcomings, Sullivan (1994) developed an aggregate index (DOIINTS)[9].

In their article, Ramaswamy, Kroeck, and Renforth (1996) analyze the internationalization construct put forward by Sullivan (1994). To accomplish this, the study replicates Sullivan's analysis by using the same firms and database to create the index. After reviewing the results

---

[9] - Five variables used to measure the degree of internationalization: DOIINTS = FSTS (Foreign Sales as a percentage of Total Sales) + FATA (Foreign Assets as a percentage of Total Assets) + OSTS (Overseas Subsidiaries as a percentage of Total + Subsidiaries) + PDIO (Psychic Dispersion of International Operations) + TMIE (Top Managers International Experience).

Ramaswamy, Kroeck, and Renforth (1996) raise concern over the dimensionality, variable substitutability, "lack of standardization and marginal evidence of reliability" (p. 176) of this internationalization construct and conclude that this "multi-item aggregate index" (p. 167) approach does not capture the complexities of internationalization thus limiting its use (Ramaswamy, Kroeck, & Renforth, 1996).

Influence and Challenges in Managerial Decisions

Johanson and Vahlne (1977) view internationalization as "the product of a series of incremental decisions" (p.23). Welch and Luostarinen (1988) found evidence in their Nordic studies of a pattern where there is a positive and direct relationship between level of internationalization and the method used to internationalize. That is, as internationalization increases, a firm's commitment also increases. For example, they suggest that a non-exporting company that desires expansion abroad will start gradually by enlisting an agent, and then will progress to a sales subsidiary, finally ending with a production subsidiary. Market diversity will influence the degree of operational diversity.

From a market point of view, management will need to determine the location for expansion. Frequently, for newcomers in the internationalization process, this means selecting a location that seems easier to penetrate because of familiarity with the culture, proximity, and lower costs; as the company matures it will shift its activities further (Welch & Luostarinen, 1988).

Much of the success companies obtain abroad is due to the management team in place, both domestic and internationally. The level of skills, capacities, and type of individuals that make up the management team as well as the personnel policy contribute to a company's effective implementation of the internationalization process. While Welch and Luostarinen (1988) point out the difficulty of measuring the human factor effectively, they affirm that "international personnel development….remains as a prime indication of the internal extent to which a company has effectively become internationalized" (Welch & Luostarinen, 1988, p. 42).

Financially speaking, management looks for creative and sophisticated mechanisms and techniques that enable them to expand abroad, often taking full advantage of both international or local financial policies and systems. For the most part, acquisitions allow companies immediate expansion, which includes, additionally, a developed local network (Welch & Luostarinen, 1988).

Kennelly and Lewis' (2002) research results illustrate the challenge and responsibility MNCs have towards environmental issues as they continue down the path of internationalization; their expansion, performance, and corporate success will be based in part on their ability to positively affect the environment. Management plays an important role in the decision-making process. The identification of opportunities, determining a firm's vision, and direction for growth influence the level of internationalization; that is, the scale and scope a firm hopes to achieve (Buckley, 1993 & 1996; Peyrefitte, Fadil, & Thomas, 2002). Managerial decisions are typically based on a company's strategic long-term view, a point in time, and the overall environmental influences considered both local and international. Consequently, it is logical and practical to think that patterns of internationalization will be different from company to company and from country to country; these too may change according to the environment. Welch and Luostarinen (1988) are quick to point out that those sequential steps and patterns do not equate to smooth paths of international expansion. Environmental influences and "general on-going influential factors" can present themselves as opportunities or as threats, and companies will accordingly adapt their paths to maintain the "forward momentum" which can affect a company's level of commitment to internationalize and make the internationalization process a bumpy one (Welch and Luostarinen, 1988, p. 50). Another important influence according to Welch and Luostarinen (1988, p. 48) that affects managerial decisions are the individuals that form the management team: their "evolution" and "perception" on internationalization.

Managerial decisions include determining the scale and scope of all company business that is international (Buckley, 1993 & 1996). Traditional internationalization theory gives MNCs' management a minor role in all decision making; yet management functions are a major component in international business theory. Buckley (1993) suggests in his research on internationalization that managerial decisions driven by external circumstances are characterized by: first, management's skills, as shown by the ability to communicate and coordinate a variety of the firm's products which facilitates economies of scale and scope as well as horizontal and vertical integration; second, knowledge of markets which assists managers in determining areas of opportunities, recommending direction of growth and promoting cost efficiencies; third, managers seek growth opportunities and exercise external influences so as to "play a proactive role in contriving market imperfections" (p.199); and fourth, the use of internationalization as a "strategy weapon" (p. 200) that increases the competition's transaction costs (Buckley, 1993).

Recommendations for International Managers

The dynamics of management in the managerial decision-making process to internationalize is influenced by internal and external factors. As presented in Figure 10, managers must contend with many factors. To the extent management and international managers are aware of these internal and external forces, better decision-making will be achieved, overall risks will decrease, and overall probability of success is increased.

Figure 10 - Managerial decision-making dynamics

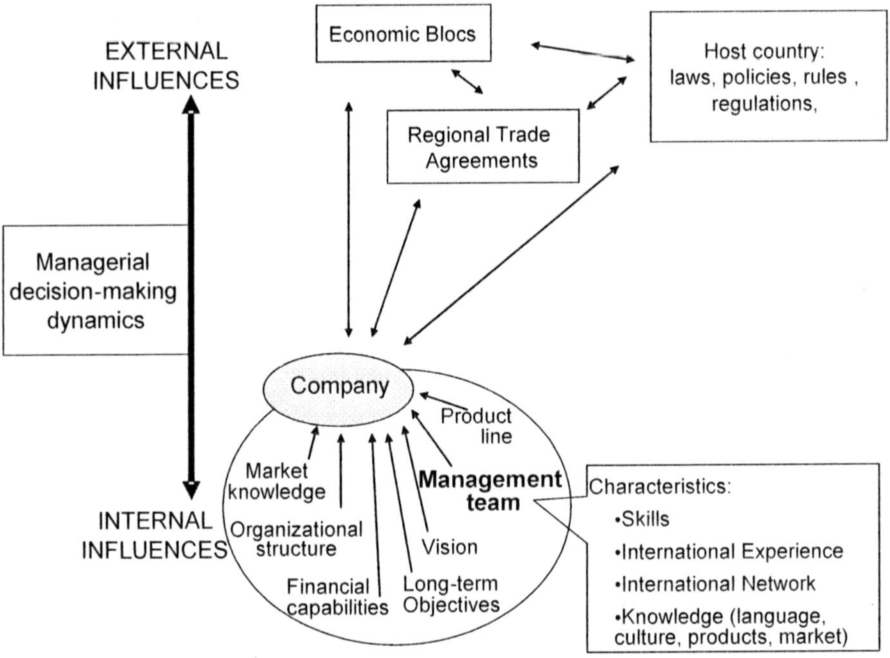

Internal Influences

To the extent a manager and all top management personnel have knowledge and understanding of a company's vision and long-term objectives, its organizational structure and financial capabilities will assist in shaping and establishing a product strategy and company level of commitment to put forth. Additionally, knowledge of the market where the company's products and the competition co-exist will assist in: first, ascertaining whether to commit resources (people and money) to launch a product internationally; second, determining whether to increase the existing level of commitment of a company abroad with the same product or introduce a new product(s); third, settling on the location(s) to internationalize; and fourth, the entry form into a new market.

A capable management team that understands the complexities and dynamics of internationalization would benefit from ensuring its team members have international experience, an international network, knowledge, and skill.

International experience. The more a person has international exposure or experience the broader his or her knowledge base and ability to assist in strategy, planning, and the decision-making process to internationalize. Many times, the number of years in the international arena, the ability to handle diversity i.e. culture, projects, in different world regions and industry are what is highly valued by companies. Different organizational structures define management differently, which can be a reflection of a culture. For example, the organizational structure for many American businesses is hierarchal (Ramaswamy, Kroeck & Renforth, 1996).

An international network. An international manager is expected to have a network of relationships in different parts of the world. This network of relationships may include suppliers, contractors, brokers, competitors, and other professionals in many industries all over the world. The ability to nurture and maintain these relationships will prove invaluable to the international manager in the decision-making process.

Knowledge. An international manager acquires knowledge through doing business in other countries. The awareness of how to conduct business in another country, operations, understanding and knowledge of another culture, as well as local customs and behaviors, foreign languages, local way of life, and ability to learn and adapt to other markets is invaluable.

Skill. An international manager that is most successful will have acquired or learned some combination of soft skills such as oral and written communications, leadership, critical thinking, work ethics, flexibility and adaptability, conflict resolution, negotiations, and team and relationship building. Understanding of the strengths and weaknesses of the market, products, the company and competition is a must.

External Influences

An international manager must be cognizant of the international forces, economic, political, and social variables that may shape or even determine how a company can internationalize. The knowledge of a host country's laws, policies, rules and regulations, business associations and organizations will assist in giving the manager a framework from which to start. Ascertaining the economic bloc to which host country belongs and all the regional trade agreements the host country participates in will uncover any trade tariffs or barriers, as well as trade incentives the company must pay attention to when planning and settling on a strategy to internationalize.

Internationalization Summary

Even though it has not been an uncommon practice for companies to internationalize, one can conclude that the number has increased enormously. This is a consequence of the increased ability to buy and sell their products in the global marketplace which has been enhanced by changes in technology. Technology directly influences internationalization by eliminating trade barriers. "Technology both enables and...requires globalization" (Kobrin, 2005, p. 51) thereby creating complex networks of information and knowledge. This is evidenced in the number of trade agreements and economic blocs developed that are observed in different regions of the world to assist in the facilitation of buying and selling of products. For example the North American Free Trade Agreement (NAFTA) between the United States, Canada and Mexico, the European Union (EU) with 15 European nations, Mercosur and the Andean Common Market both within South America, and the economic bloc the Association of Southeast Asia Nations (ASEAN) between 9 Asian countries (Hodgetts & Luthans, 2003).

This study agrees with past research (Buckley, 1993; Johanson & Vahlne, 1977; Kennelly & Lewis, 2002; Peyrefitte, Fadil, & Thomas, 2002; Ramaswamy, Kroeck, & Renforth, 1996) in that management's role is key to all decision-making activities of a company. Managerial decisions influenced heavily by constant changes in technology shape the company's vision, which includes whether to internationalize or increase the level of commitment to internationalize; thus, directly affecting trade regions and economic blocs as well as political, economical, and social environments.

Management must actively pursue the mindset of internationalism along with a management team of international managers in order to be successful. Thus, the role of international managers in the decision-making process to internationalize is essential. Buckley (1993) argues that international management is a two-way street, where business is a growing and learning experience for managers. International managers that are articulate, well-informed of events locally and internationally, active, and involved are capable of influencing a company's future. Their contribution, as Boddewyn, Toyne, and Martinez (2004) suggest, is to develop relationships with diverse groups of individuals from local and foreign communities, propose internationalization models to organizations, and participate and contribute to the different facets of global development e.g. social, cultural, ecological. Companies that do engage in international business increase their level of commitment and internationalization over time. Reviewing the history of these companies demonstrates their ability to influence the "nature of economic growth and development," and their contribution to 20th century history of global economics, while offering an explanation of "today's world economy" (Wilkins, 2005, p. 150).

International managers have in their hands the capability to shape paths for companies and set examples of ethical business practices, as well as create social and ecological awareness and wellbeing. International managers carry the responsibility to be envoys of the world, as this study would like to refer to them "corporate business diplomats," that promote not only their business products but also relationships through building trust and cultural understanding.

Cultural Change and Expatriates

Edgar Schein (1992) and many other researchers have seen culture as the assumptions, values, perceptions, and behaviors of an organization. This pattern and expectations of behavior are often passed on to new members of the organization through formal and informal means, thus providing a continual social structure. One can state that culture is a socialization process inherent to organizations of sizes. Culture is supported by the organization's values, norms, practices, policies, and structures. Some of the major elements of culture are as follows:

- Culture does condition people and drive behavior.
- Culture regularizes human behavior.
- Culture is an inherent part of any established organization.
- Change is evolutionary, and it can be revolutionary.
- Culture implies that organizations are established as social systems.
- The fields of anthropology, social psychology and organizational behavior can provide the base of knowledge for organizational culture.

A practical and working definition of culture can be used in today's global organizations to discuss cultural change, the elements of change, and the implications of change for expatriates in the repatriation process. There are three major elements of culture which are:

- *Artifacts.* This is the organizational history, and the value of holding on to all things that have made it great, and those that the organization is willing to carry forward.
- *Values.* Values are things that are important to the organization and facilitate decisions as well as drive behaviors.
- *Structure.* Structure is a view of the organization in terms of how it is positioned to support the organizational strategy and decision making processes.

Culture is at the heart of the social fabric of an organization; it drives specific behaviors based on the conditioning of the culture, and it can be defined "as the way we do things around here." An interesting phenomena associated with culture is the "external" perception of the organization that is positioned in the marketplace. Schein's definition of culture suggests an external integration which in many cases is the opportunity for the organization to associate itself with its market and the way that market perceives the organization.

Organizational cultures are created formally or informally...they are always created. Creating and establishing an effective organizational culture is the responsibility of the founder and senior leaders. Creation of organizational culture is a process of determining what is important to the organization based on its values and overall purpose. It is also about determining how, when and who will make decisions, and what the organization wants to communicate to the external stakeholders. Bolman and Deal (1997) developed and implemented four frames for implementing and sustaining organizational change. The four frames are:

- *Human Resources-* human resources personnel and functions are very important in an organizational change, and HR professionals are generally responsible for the people side and legal impact of initiating and executing organizational change.
- *Political-* when there is change, there is going to be winners and losers.
- *Structural-* structure generally defines the work processes, provides clarity as to what and who will get it done.
- *Operational-* given the change, what will be the impact on the organization's operations and who will be impacted by it?

Bolman and Deal provide a 'framework' for the change process, and in many ways their framework is a broad view of how issues associated with the change process can be integrated with other available methodologies.

Organizational change practitioners know that change is an evolutionary process and does not happen without support from top leaders, assessments, reviews, communications, and everyone's participation. Schein and Hatch suggest that organizational culture is a socialization process, and so is the process of bringing about a cultural change. Education about the change, participation of key stakeholders in the change process, and support for the change are three important elements involved in the change process. The organization's leadership must know and understand the drivers for change and create a strategy for implementing the initiative to effectively bring about cultural change. By acknowledging the need for change, the leadership must consider the following:

- The need for change.
- Who or what organization / department will own the change process. This is generally the HR function.
- Facilitate a design of what the change will mean for the business strategy, structure and operational procedures.
- The leader should design a communication plan that clarifies the need for change, and considers using employees as focus groups for feedback.

The leader and change agents should implement a broad-based communications plan that begins the process of education to all parties as to what is going to change, the reasons as to why and where the organization is going as a result of successfully implanting the change. There must be recognition that change causes anxiety for those impacted by it and the process has to be managed to reduce any potential anxiety. A key issue in organizational change is gaining the support of those that will be affected by the change. Often, there are steps that can be taken to facilitate transitions and change, and to gain support from those that may be negatively affected. Of-course, the implementation process should occur and must be supported by constant communication among all parties. Furthermore, there must be a follow-up and evaluation process to document learning for future change management initiatives.

Global Business Climate and Risks

While understanding organizational culture is important, global managers and leaders must also understand the business climate and risks in each environment. As business goes global, the decision of where and how to do business becomes a major consideration. Throughout the world, political and other forces impact a company's ability to successfully conduct business. Terrorism and natural disasters like the recent Asian tsunami pose challenges to companies that conduct business or consider conducting business in affected countries. The leaders should consider and discusses the following questions before initiating change: What are some of the organizational challenges or risks associated with doing business in a new environment or introducing new changes in existing markets, and how do they affect a company's decision of whether to do business in this market? Do the benefits outweigh the risks? Or is it better for a business to abandon a location due to consideration of the risks? Can companies be successful and profitable in the face of these types of threats? How do successful worldwide corporations deal with the threat of terrorism to their daily operations and how do they respond in a natural disaster?

Global business, or business in general, is a fundamentally risky endeavor, and those who are willing to take some risk in the global arena may be positioning themselves for tremendous rewards down the road. This road, however; is not free from other risks, such as natural disasters, wars, and terrorism. Many countries around the world are poor, have high unemployment rates, and lack the financial resources to uplift the living standards of their people. This presents an opportunity in the areas of foreign investment, foreign sales, economies of scale, etc. for entrepreneurs and multinational organizations. However, there are many challenges that will influence the decision process.

The World Development Report 2005 states that expanding opportunities for people in developing countries is a pressing concern for governments and the global community. Approximately half of the world's population lives on less than $2 a day and 1.1 billion people barely survive on less than $1 a day. Young people have more than double the average unemployment rate in all regions, and population growth can add another two billion human beings on earth (many to the developing countries) over the next 30 to 40 years. The good news is that more governments are creating the infrastructure and appropriate policies which are conducive to attracting foreign investments. Countries such as China, India, Afghanistan, and Malaysia are examples of developing nations that will continue to grow so long as they can maintain security. Investments in these countries have fueled phenomenal growth and at the same time have resulted in reducing poverty levels to historic proportions. The investment climate should benefit the community as a whole and not just the business. What is apparent is that appropriate and balanced policies and regulations are removing barriers to investments, protectionism, law enforcement, and corruption. Furthermore, factors pertaining to ethical business practices, worker safety standards, and taxation are all important ingredients for a good investment climate that benefits not only businesses but also the communities.

It is worth noting that while the immediate impact of 9/11 on many U.S. businesses was disastrous, the same is not true globally. After 9/11, many U.S. companies won contracts exceeding tens of billions of dollars in the most dangerous places in the world, namely Afghanistan and Iraq. Many U.S. companies have reacted quickly and adapted well to threats of terrorism and war. In addition, U.S. companies are importing more products than they are exporting, resulting in huge trade deficits for the United States. The U.S., being the largest consumption society in the world, has a good appetite for cheap foreign products. American companies in the United States have continued to outsource work to foreign countries, and this trend is increasing in spite of war and terrorist threats. National and international companies face many challenges in today's modern marketplace. Some of these challenges are the result of security issues and global terrorism. The reality of these challenges is captured in the following saying: "Those who today run businesses in the nastier parts of the world also face a bewildering range of threats to the safety and health of their employees. Indeed, there are many more disagreeable places to choose from than there were a generation ago" (Doing Business in Dangerous Places, 2004).

After the September 11, 2001 attacks on the United States, most companies decided to stay in their respective locations in New York City. Some companies temporarily relocated. A few, such as Citigroup, American Express, and RBC Financial Group moved to other locations (Tymkiw, 2002). Some companies chose not to be located in proximity to structures that could be considered a terrorist target. The fear of being close to such a structure became a reality for employees who "…saw the second plane pass their windows on the way to strike the second tower, just three short blocks away" (Wikler, 2001, p. 20). Businesses that are heavily dependent on the travel industry may also be reluctant to do business where terrorism is an eminent threat. Some companies are particularly vulnerable to the disruptions terrorism threats can cause. Chuvala (2001) discusses the impact of the September 11 attacks to the taxi and limousine service business by saying, "airports were closed for several days, and air travel has been depressed since the attack, resulting in a slump in demand for airport shuttle service" (p.19).

Czinkota and Knight (2005) suggest that companies tend to consider the indirect effects of terrorism more than the direct effects when deciding to participate in national and global economies. They state that many companies will consider the "potential role of terrorism" in the countries that they do business with. Governments of these countries often do their best to combat terrorism by imposing new regulations and policies that will ultimately affect the value of chain activities, which can cause major disruptions. Companies are now constantly on the look out for any drops in the continuity of the market. Company officials and managers need to take a good look at their business on both areas of supply and demand. A large consideration for companies deciding where to do business is the risk to their supply-chain. Supply lines can be the lifeblood of the company in today's competitive environment. Chopra and Sodhi (2004) write that the "Supply-chain problems result from natural disasters, labor disputes, supplier bankruptcy, acts of war and terrorism, and other causes. They can seriously disrupt or delay material, information and cash flows, any of which can damage sales, increase costs — or both" (p. 53).

Employers sending people to dangerous places need, first of all, to be honest about what they are doing. That means thinking early about the risks involved. Too many companies entering markets in third world countries, even those not at war, greatly underestimate the cost of security. Employers need to be concerned about and take the safety of their employees into consideration, especially when doing business in dangerous environments. Many companies tend to retreat at a serious threat to just one staff member (Doing Business in Dangerous Places, 2004).

Even in the face of threat, companies can be successful and profitable. Terrorists have grown bolder in recent years and communicate better. They are financed and armed better than in past years. There are key trends currently emerging among companies in response to terrorism. Two goals are prevalent. Limiting reliance on any single region or customer, can limit their exposure to unexpected interruptions in both sides of the business. The other goal is to develop markets to diversify the risk and balance the exposure to terrorism. Another approach to deal with inefficiencies is for companies to produce more of the essential inputs themselves as opposed to buying them from suppliers. They will tend to procure supplies from a broader supplier base from sources located in a broader range of locations or from more established sources that are considered safer to reduce their vulnerability.

National and international organizations also may need to increase their inventories of essential resources to reduce their risks by cushioning against the effects of natural or manmade disasters. This will minimize shipping delays and interruptions in the supply chain. Companies that already have subsidiaries in these locations are better positioned to deal with the impact of terrorism primarily due to better communication and access to local information. Establishing alliances and joint ventures offer effective strategies for gathering information that could allow for more effective measures in dealing with the threats.

Other manifestations of risk in the world include floods, hurricanes, Tsunamis, and earthquakes. The methods of reducing the risk involved with conducting business in areas where various calamities are prevalent, are just as valid for a company looking to be successful in the face of these dangers. Additionally, a formal documented backup plan is essential in enabling the company's resources to deal with any impact from these threats (Czinkota & Knight, 2005).

Companies cannot afford to sit back and let unforeseen events cripple their businesses. Besides being sensitive to employees during such troubling times, administration has to rebound from disasters and keep their businesses running. It has become much more crucial for companies to establish ways of not only protecting the business, but their employees as well from threats of terrorism and natural disasters. The best way to combat an event that cannot be predicted is to plan for the worst. Since the attacks of September 11 and the recent rash of natural disasters around the world, companies are forced to deal with the realities of how such events can be devastating to one's business.

The majority of businesses create a natural disaster task force, disaster recovery, business continuity or master emergency plan that goes into effect the moment a warning is issued. These plans are discussed and revised regularly to adapt to the rapidly changing world. This plan usually entails; the process in which employees are either evacuated or kept safe on the premises, the order in which major equipment is shut down and protected, how emergency supplies are distributed, which departments (or personnel) are required to remain and how long, etc. These plans are not only to protect the company's well-being, but also the well-being of employees and their families. According to *Disaster Management: Calm in a Crisis,* there are three reasons for developing such a plan to protect one's business: moral, physical and conceptual (2004). The development of a plan can be long and tedious. Companies that take time to complete and execute these plans have proven that the plans are beneficial and rewarding in most cases. *Disaster Management: Calm in a Crisis* gives the following important steps to developing one's own plan for disaster preparedness and recovery (2004):

- Understand your entire business and dependencies.
- Carry out a business impact assessment.
- Complete a 360-degree risk assessment.
- Develop a feasible, relevant and attractive response.
- Plan exercising, maintenance and auditing.

As soon as the immediate danger has passed, administration goes right into the task of recovery. These tasks include business functionality and employee care. Some of these include locating missing employees, providing emergency housing, day-care services, equipment repair / assessment, property repair / assessment, locating vital records, and utilities recovery (Kiger, 2004). Communication during this time can be extremely difficult due to the fact that companies may have lost all ability to make contact through email or phone. Although this is a major setback it is important for companies to find a way to communicate and deal with incoming problems by remaining patient and positive while providing quick and decisive decision-making (Disaster Management, 2004).

The ever-changing world has presented a risk to companies that it can no longer avoid. Companies and managers alike have to make a conscious effort to evaluate the possibilities of disasters and make changes to accommodate the prospective unexpected events. Although no natural disaster or terrorist attack is predictable the ability to understand its affects on one's company and how to deal with their results is important. It is critical to business survival and the effective management of a company's expatriates.

Retaining Expatriate Employees and Repatriation

When international employees, expatriates, return home from an international assignment, they often find that their jobs are gone, their newly learned skills are under-utilized, there is a lack of interest by others in the expatriate's previous assignment, and unhappiness with the new jobs. On a personal level, repatriates find that friends have left town, social relationships have changed, their city is different, and their extended family may have changed. Perhaps there are unrealistic or misinformed expectations of the life repatriates think of when returning home to the company (Mujtaba, 2006). This is extremely aggravated by some firms' lack of further development of the repatriates within the firm, which then leads to high turnover for key, experienced staff.

While on an international assignment and when getting ready to return home, expatriates formulate a set of expectations about their impending life. These expectations can range from compensation, job-opportunities, standards of their previous job, to acceptance by new and former coworkers. As a result of the insights offered into how employees view their repatriation process, it can be deduced that there is, in fact, a gap between the expectations employees have of their awaiting jobs, and what actually happens when they return back to headquarters; all of which affects the level of commitment of repatriates to the firm. Researchers tend to blame the companies for the expatriates' lack of commitment to the firm through misinforming expatriates about what to expect from the firm when they return from international assignments. The underlying idea is that firms should try to close the gap between what employees expect from the firm and what the firm actually offers to the returning expatriate. This needs to be done in order to lessen ill feelings towards the firm in an attempt to halt repatriate turnover.

Another factor that affects repatriates' commitment to the firm upon return from international assignment is the psychological contract. The *psychological contract* is a tool that expatriates use to relate how well an organization compensates and prepares them for an assignment abroad to how well they perform in the assignment and their satisfaction with the company. This contract also goes on to further determine, in the case of repatriates, how committed to the organization workers will be after the assignment is completed. In order to ensure expatriates' commitment to the firm after returning home, the company must satisfy such implied and explicit contracts. Once a breach between repatriates' expectations and what happens when they return home has been identified, then there are steps that businesses can take to try and close this gap to meet the expectations of employees; and, thus, mentoring can be part of the solution.

Issues Repatriates Face

Personal issues. When preparing for the return home repatriates often assume and think that little has changed back home, and they can just slip right back in with little problem. According to Andreason and Kinneer (2004), expatriates form good memories and myths of impending life at home, but these expectations are often shattered when they return (p. 14). Life at home is not as stagnant as many had thought as they find that friends have moved, and their extended family has changed as well as society at home. This causes a letdown that gives rise to reverse culture shock, which is simply "feelings of fear, helplessness, irritability, incompetency, and disorientation" of one's own culture (Griffith & Pustay, 2003, pp. 585-586). Social and personal issues faced by repatriates are the losses in their personal and professional living status. In the foreign country, expatriates usually receive higher compensation including domestic help, paid education for their children and increased status in the community. However, when repatriates come home these privileges are often revoked leading to depression and disillusionment (Andreason & Kinneer, 2004). Other readjustment issues normally not considered are personality or other changes in the expatriate caused by the foreign culture. Unknowingly, some expatriates pick up elements of the host country's culture, values and norms, and integrate these into their lives. Since repatriates do not see this in themselves as others do, this may turn them into outsiders of their own culture. Damage to self-esteem can occur when no one at the office seems to care about the expatriates' assignment. Surprisingly, people are not always interested in hearing what happened during the worker's assignment, which further leads to feelings of loneliness and isolation. Isolation can also be attributed to expatriates not being able to keep up with events in their hometown. The family is not able to get mail, listen to radio, or get local papers and magazines to catch up while away on assignment. If the spouse traveled on assignment with the expatriate, the spouse may have a difficult time adjusting to the fact there may be no jobs available when they return. If this occurs, there may be a strain on the personal relationship of the couple, leading to more personal problems in the readjustment stage (Dowling & Welch, 2005, p. 171). Not only do personal issues affect the readjustment phase, but work-related issues may play a greater role.

Professional issues. There are a variety of issues that repatriates face in the work environment. Some of the professional issues repatriates have to deal with are anxiety due to unsure career prospects; forgetfulness on behalf of the firm; devaluation of their international experience; and any negative effects of their new roles-constraints, demands, discretion, and lack of skill use. For example, repatriates have to get used to the structure of the home firm after being away for so long or may face lower decision-making power in their post-assignment jobs (Baruch, et al., 2002). After a foreign assignment, most expatriates hope to at least return to their former position. However, when they come home repatriates are often placed in a lower-level position that makes no use of their newly gained competencies or knowledge (Andreason & Kinnear, 2004, p. 16). These workers expect that their newly gained knowledge and experience will entitle them to a new job, either in another department or a promotion in their current area. However, this has been found not to be true, even in the twenty-first century. A 2002 GMAC Survey showed that more than half of corporate respondents offered no definitive guarantee of employment after expatriate assignments were over (Dowling & Welch, 2005, p. 162). This leads to another issue in repatriation: a phenomenon not foreseen by repatriates is the "out-of-sight-out-of-mind" syndrome (Oddou & Mendenhall, 1991, p. 26). Surprisingly, when expatriates go on assignment, the firm somehow forgets about them; so when they return home, people usually do not remember them and their jobs are gone as new hires are placed in the positions once held by the expatriates.

The effects of the personal and professional repatriation issues have a combined effect on the workers' commitment to the firm that results from expectations formed by the repatriates before they return home; all of which have an effect on the organization as a whole.

Effects of Expectations on Repatriate Turnover

Expectations. Many companies are so concerned with the cost of creating expatriates that they often forget the costs of losing these workers when they leave. Expectations formed by employees before they leave on an international assignment and before they return home have a large impact on their commitment to the firm. When repatriates come home with certain ideas of their life and are met with a reality that is quite negatively different from what they expected, they feel disgruntled and may leave the firm. The biggest gap in expectations that has the most influence on repatriates' readjustment is the difference in the expectations of their career life and the realities of what happens when they return home. According to Strob, Gregersen, and Stewart Black (1998), this mismatch in expectations and perceptions is related to job constraints, job discretion, and job demands in their new roles. Firms may present workers with less discretion in decision-making on their job. As a result, employees feel under-utilize, under-appreciated and are more likely to have maladjustment and leave the firm. The job demands of the new role may also be less than the worker hoped for in terms of using their new international knowledge. If repatriates expect more restrictions in their new jobs and are indeed met with more obstacles, they will be less satisfied and less likely to stay committed to the organization.

Value of the repatriate program. The type and value of a firm's repatriation program also affects repatriates commitment to the company. There is a gap between what firms claim they offer in terms of repatriate programs and what repatriates said these same firms provided in terms of repatriate programs (Napier & Peterson, 1991, p. 21). Dissatisfaction also occurs if employees are not given adequate support and are utilized improperly upon their return. Evidence shows that some repatriates leave their firms within two years of returning home due to ineffective utilization of their new talents by firms (Klaff, 2002, p. 40). In a study conducted by David Martin, Professor of management and human resource management at American University's Kegod School of Management, it was reported that less than 40 percent of repatriates get to use their new talent and skills they developed on the international assignment. If this trend continues, organizations may lose the international competencies that are the foundation for many of these international assignments (O'Sullivan, 2002). This circumstance leads to a personal question: Why would firms even send expatriates abroad and spend the money to train and sustain them if they do not want to capitalize on the new found skills and knowledge of the worker. The answer to this question is simple: firms simply do not gauge the benefits of international workers to see how they benefit the broader context of the organization.

Poaching. Another factor in expatriate turnover is head-hunting or poaching by other firms. Because firms are not widely known for their retention of international managers, there are many companies that seek out these workers once or even before they return home. The head-hunters offer better guarantees of employment at their companies and more compensation in order to gain the benefits from these talented workers (Brewster, 2004, p. 73). To ease the readjustment phase in repatriation, it is necessary to manage the expectations and perceptions these workers have about life at home. To effectively manage and form the expectations of repatriates, firms should build a comprehensive repatriate program that helps to form realistic expectations.

Designing a Repatriate Program

To overcome the problems faced by firms and workers during repatriation, an effective repatriation program should be developed that addresses relevant issues before departure, while the assignment is in effect, and when the assignment ends. The prescribed program is meant to deal with expectations related to work problems and personal readjustment to repatriation and to minimize turnover and use skills that benefit the firm. The first thing companies should address when evaluating repatriate issues is determining "what are these employees worth to the firm?" This question not only helps develop strategies for retention, but also encourages the firm to develop the best use of expatriates to enhance its competitiveness and global competencies. This question should be answered in terms of return on investment (ROI). According to *Personnel Today* (1994), Lance Richards calculates ROI by successfully placing the expatriate in the home firm, finding and using their new skills and competencies, and making sure these workers stay with the firm (p. 19). The company should look at the returning workers as an investment that needs to be capitalized upon. This view helps organizations to gauge the benefits of international workers to see how their work fits into the overall context of the firm. The Repatriation Program Model (presented in Figure 11) is a comprehensive visual that can initially assist managers in designing an effective repatriation program.

Figure 11- Repatriation Program Model

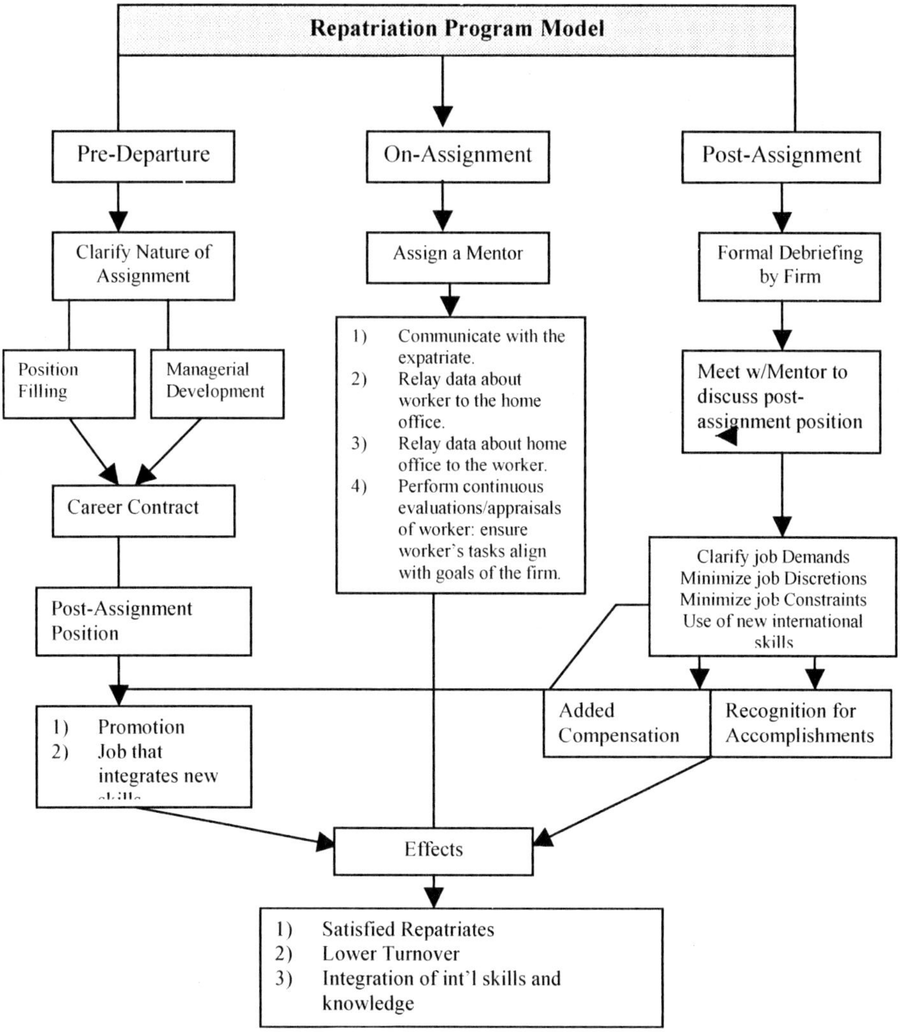

Pre-Departure Components

In order to plan a comprehensive program, the repatriation process must begin before workers leave on international assignments. The firm should consider creating assignments that link the goals at home with the goals for the assignment abroad that seek to fulfill and expand the goals and boundaries of the host country. Communication about expectations versus perceptions needs to be addressed first. There needs to be consistent and accurate data about how the expatriates feel the international assignment will affect their career development within the firm. Data analyzed from other expatriates shows that the area most needing improvement is in pre-departure discussions: task clarity and career counseling within formal guidelines for repatriation set forth by the firm (Jassawalla, et. al., 2004, p. 40). Before departing, task clarity involves explaining exactly what role the expatriate will be in during the assignment; what the firm expects of them and how evaluation is performed. This helps to shape the expatriates' expectations of their role overseas while emphasizing the accomplishment of the assignment. For instance, if the worker is simply going to fill a position, they should be told this and not expect to come back into an executive position. This helps to lessen anxiety and confusion about career development upon their return. Career counseling prior to departing for the overseas assignment involves telling how the assignment will fit into the goals of the firm, how the expatriate's contribution to the assignment benefited or will benefit the firm, and how knowledge and skills gained abroad will enhance the career development of the expatriates. The firm must include job options for the expatriate when she or he returns home, dependant on their international performance. This goes also back to the ROI concept of determining how valuable the employee is to the firm. By defining the specifics, the firm will be able to provide tailored career counseling on the front end to clarify expectations of workers for when the assignment ends. It is also wise for the expatriate to get a promotion or train for a new job before leaving on the assignment. If the expatriate candidate is in a management or upper-level position before departure, the firm should consider pre-promoting the expatriate because he or she already possesses the traits and experience necessary for upper-level positions (Gregerson, Strob, & Stewart Black, 1998). These agreements should be done in the context of a written agreement—a career contract. Verbal agreements have not been known to hold up well as managers often forget they exist when the worker returns; so a written, hard-copied employment contract may be deemed necessary (Lazarova

& Caligiuri, 2001). In the case of turnover at home, whoever the expatriate worked with before leaving may not have passed on any agreements or knowledge of the expatriate (Strob, et. al, 1998, para. 22). The written agreement, preferably filed away with a third party, perhaps the designated mentor, ensures that the expatriates' pre-departure expectations match their post-assignment expectations. This minimizes the miscommunication in the case of staff changes at home and spells out the details of the new job they will have when the international assignment is over. Part of the employment contract should be initiated by the assignee. Frazee (1997) feels that assignees should inquire about the nature of the assignment on a philosophical level to better their understanding of what to actually expect from the assignment. A representative of Deloitte and Touche proposes that workers ask (Frazee, 1997, para 16): Why is the assignment necessary; is it to fix a problem or staff an area in the host country; or is it to gain knowledge about the host culture's way of doing business to use in an assignment at home or the like? Asking these questions helps expatriates to refine and accurately shape their expectations of what will occur in repatriation. By promoting workers to new positions with more autonomy, defined work roles and shaping their expectations, companies can counteract the negative effects repatriates experience resulting from job changes (Gates & Budman, 1996, para. 11).

On-Assignment Components

The repatriation program must continue while the worker is on the foreign assignment. Action taken in this stage is meant to help alleviate the "out-of-sight, out-of-mind" syndrome, helps transfer repatriates' knowledge, and keeps the worker from suffering reverse culture shock. The main goal during this stage is for the office to maintain direct contact with the expatriate in the host country (Lazarova & Caligiuri, p. 5). This helps to ensure the worker is not lost and forgotten while away and further advances his/her career prospects upon return. This portion of the program should include visits not only for home to see family members, but more importantly, visits to the home office to stay connected and heighten the expatriates' visibility in the organization. To strengthen communication ties between home and host locations, the worker needs to be included in company emails from the home office, the firm's newsletters, and maintain personal contact with former co-workers at home. These steps also work to keep the employee abreast of changes in the home office such as staff rotations, structural changes, new projects, and the corporate culture. Maintaining effective communication counters the effects of loneliness and isolation felt by workers when they return from their international assignment (Jassawalla et al., 2004. p. 42). One best way to implement and maintain a course of action for repatriation during the assignment is to establish a mentor program. Expatriates often vocalize their desires for such a system (Klaff, 2002, p. 32). The proposed mentor program for repatriates is to prepare the worker for life back at home, but more importantly, to enforce visibility and track the accomplishments of the worker back in the home office. This mentor needs to be placed exclusively in the home country and can be either a former or future superior of the worker. Having a future manager as a mentor would entail the firm and the expatriate agreeing in advance on a new career move (Oddou & Mendenhall, 1991, p. 32). By having a manager as a mentor, the firms' goals of developing international skills, transferring knowledge, and promoting career development occurs on behalf of the worker. If the firm already has a mentorship program for new workers, it should be extended to help expatriates while on assignment. This mentor program needs to be independent of the foreign mentorship program that is in place to help the worker adjust to the host country. For example, AT&T's mentoring system for repatriates involves visits to the home office and a 'journeying home' program that occurs six months before returning home. This program provides a psychologist and a representative from human resources to actually visit the expatriate and their family in the host country to prepare them for the trip home (Klaff, 2002, p. 43). The mentor should also work to involve the tasks, skills, work of the absent worker into development programs at home (Dowling & Welch, 2005, p. 177). Performance evaluations of the expatriates and a regular review of the processes of the worker should also be done to ensure they fit into the goals of the home firm (Napier & Peterson, 1991).

On a personal level, expatriates and their families can take proactive measures to lessen the negative effects of repatriation while they are away. The worker should try to maintain as much contact as possible with the home office, make friends before leaving, and contact them just as they would if they were still at home. It would also be wise to subscribe to home newspapers, magazines and/or register with relevant online entities to keep up with what is going on not only in the home country, but also in their home town. The expatriate should choose to update the firm on their work and progress in the home country; especially if the firm is sporadic in keeping up with the employee in the host country. Such efforts will ensure that the worker is still seen, and gives the firm a chance to see how the accomplishments of the worker fit into the growth, competitiveness, and mission of the firm.

Post-Assignment Components

The repatriate programs suggested above is meant to be proactive and pre-emptive of the negative perceptions expatriates have when they return home. Doing the steps above correctly reduces the amount of distress experienced by repatriates upon their return home. However, there are still steps after the trip home that can be implemented to support the repatriate program.

First, the company should have a formal debriefing procedure. This debriefing should include getting back on track with the mentor, but first consist of interviews with managers to gain information on the nature of the assignment and discussions of the effects of their experience. A few things the worker and the firm should discuss include opportunities and any constraints the worker experienced, the practices of the subsidiary, business culture, and the social culture of the host country (Mead, 2005 pp. 410-411). After the debriefing stage, the firm should provide extra assistance to the family as a whole. This session should include a therapist or industrial psychologist to help the family cope with any leftover concerns after returning home and maybe even other repatriate families to share their experiences. If the firm uses this knowledge of the culture, politics, marketplace, it will be able to capitalize on the investment of sending the worker on the assignment.

The next stage in post-assignment repatriation program is to implement the job changes that were agreed upon before departure in the career contract. The expatriate should meet back with their assigned mentor to thoroughly discuss the details and aspects of the new job. The repatriates could possibly be used as learning nodes and placed in jobs accordingly. Another option is to develop an international team that uses a select group of repatriates for international business (Stahl & Mendenall, 2000, p. 263). This can be especially helpful in smaller firms where international functions are centralized. This should have been clarified under the career agreement signed before the departure. Although the firm is responsible for making sure these actions take place, the firm should encourage the mentor to stay with the worker as they move into the new position. To further ease the repatriation process, it is imperative that the expatriates be placed in jobs that put their new knowledge and skills to good use. Most employees feel they have gained a significant amount of experience and skills that should be used by the home firm, so it is not as if the expatriate has nothing to offer. If the purpose of conducting international business is to cross-plant ideas and practices that aid in business and strengthens a competitive advantage, why not use these expatriates to implement their new knowledge in processes that enhance the company (Dowling & Welch, 2005, p. 174). Firms may do this by broadening the scope of the new job for the workers. If the new job is a promotion this aspect is covered; if the job is only a new position on the workers' previous level, then it is imperative the workers feel that their new skills are actually being used (Gates & Budman, 1996, p. 58). Enabling workers to have more job discretion in their new positions allows the workers to use practices and habits that are comfortable to them to help reduce frustration and anxiety in performing their new task. The new job should preferably be one in which the worker will have a leadership position. This should not be that difficult, judging from the fact that most expatriates are ages 35-54 and are in managerial positions (Napier & Peterson, 1991, p. 22). Naturally these workers already possess the level of expertise necessary to have and maintain an upper-level position; the international experience has only made their case stronger. Employees should have more discretion and fewer constraints in their new roles if they are promoted or even demoted. In the case of any increased obstacles in their newly assigned roles, the firms should alert the worker to any constraints in the new job that may pose a problem to their new roles.

Expatriates also routinely cited a lack of fair compensation and recognition for their services while being overseas (Napier & Peterson, 1991). When they return home the workers do not have to be paid at the level of their international assignment pay, but should have some bonuses for their work overseas. The firm also should have simple actions to highlight the workers' accomplishments. This works to highlight the gain from the assignment and serves as an incentive to reduce turnover.

Summary

In conclusion, it is highly important that the firm acknowledge possible repatriation problems and develop strategies to resolve them to support workers. When the firm fails to design and implement effective re-entry strategies for their staff: 1) employees are more likely to leave the firm; 2) provide a negative view to future expatriates; and 3) skills gained by the worker are not fully used (Bolino & Feldman, 2000, p. 377). The new knowledge and competence is lost, and the firm is not able to sustain and spread its competitive advantage to new markets. A successful repatriate program should be one that works to minimize the above effects, helps workers gain a respective job that highlights a repatriate's new talent; has virtually little cross-cultural problems, and has low turnover intentions and outcomes (O'Sullivan, 2002, p.22). One overall aspect of the repatriation process is the mindset of the organization. The firm itself must integrate a global mindset into its values (Frazee, 1997, para. 40).

Doing this will put the firm in the habit of looking at things from a global perspective, which hopefully spills over into effective treatment of expatriates and repatriates. This approach ensures that the firm values expatriates' experience.

MAKING CHANGE STICK

Bringing about effective change is not an easy task as it involves people and people of creatures of habit. People often respond to change negatively as it can impact them and their colleagues or family members at the individual, interpersonal, organizational, and environmental levels. Therefore, making change stick is not an easy task, and this process becomes especially challenging when it is being initiated in a cross-cultural work environment. While the role of leaders and change agents are important throughout the process, it is especially critical in managing crisis and situations when people are uncertain about the future or new ways of doing things. Change agents and organizational leaders must recognize such events (crisis, shortage of required resources, etc.) and lead their teams and groups of individuals impacted by the change through this process. Leaders and change agents must become effective coaches and mentors to everyone involved in the change process. Monitoring and observation of such events requires constant involvement from all leaders (D'Eugenio, 2005).

David P. D'Eugenio, author and change specialist, states that in order for change to be successful and sustainable, leaders and their employees must use common sense, learn on a continuous basis, and adapt as per the current situational variables. D'Eugenio was a guest speaker at Nova Southeastern University on August 10, 2005 and spoke on the topic of *Transitional and Change Management: Assessment Application and Achievement*. For sustainable success, D'Eugenio's three main suggestions are:

1. *Sense.* Be attuned to what is going on around you. Proactively obtain data on a regular basis from your environment.
2. *Learn.* Explore the incoming data to decipher what is going on. What does the data have to say? What are the obvious and emergent themes, patterns, and trends?

3. *Adapt*. Change and evolve with your surroundings. Identify and consciously choose to change in the direction of that which serves your long-term health and success.

Dynamic change is a constant in today's work environment. As such, using good sense, learning the latest data, and adapting to the current facts are essential ingredients for sustainable cross-cultural change. In the twenty-first century environment, change keeps picking up speed in all industries and professions. Today's employees and customers are living in a constant period of transition, and the shelf life of solutions keeps getting shorter since what works today can become history a few months later (Pritchett, 1993). Pritchett asks "Where is all the change coming from?" He states that "If people create change –and obviously they do – then we should expect a rapid increase in the rate of change as the population doubles in the next few decades." This growing population is armed with new technology which feeds and sustains on itself. Pritchett (1993) stated that "about 80% of technological inventions have occurred since 1900." It is best to think of technological change as something that keeps multiplying on a continuous basis. Still another source of this rapid change is knowledge or information which seems to be doubling about every four to five years. Some of the commonly addressed sources of change for businesses can include changes in leadership, management, organizational structures, products, services, customers, customer demands, and location of where the firm produces or offers its products.

Because of rapid changes, new knowledge and doubling of information about every few years, the future promises more change than experienced thus far. What is interesting to know is that change has no conscience and it does not play favorites (Pritchett, 1993). Yes, it is also true that change can quickly or slowly destroy organizations that do not adapt to the new circumstances. Pritchett (1993) states that high-velocity change calls for major shifts in behavior: "More specifically, we must think differently. Reorder our priorities. Develop faster reflexes. Give the culture an entirely new set of responses. We can't afford to ignore change and just do what comes naturally. We must face and do what works."

Shakers, Movers, Housekeepers, and Lifers Making Change

A colleague and a very successful graduate of masters of business administration program by the name of Rick Pinelli once stated that he sees organizations having a diversity of people, change agents, and managers that can be categorized as shakers, movers, housekeepers, and lifers. Rick is the Director of Wholesale Financial Relations for Time Warner's Retail Sales and Marketing. Rick has worked for Time Warner in the past fifteen years, mostly in the Tampa areas of Florida but travels often to meet clients. According to Rick, such a categorization process can be logical, rational, and an efficient organizational structure. The following are a skeleton of Rick's initial thoughts and overall concept regarding shakers, movers, housekeepers, and lifers (in his words) which can be further developed and researched in the future (Personal Communication with Rick Pinelli on April 07, 2004).

Shakers. Shakers are high profile individuals with great vision, ability and desire to take risks in order to make effective and innovative organizational changes. About 10% of an organization should be Shakers and life expectancy is 3 to 5 years. Change is "created" as a result of new ideas and innovative ideas that are risky but have clear opportunity for the future improvement and growth. Shakers' priorities are directly tied into the established mission/vision statement. Shakers work "out of the box" and oftentimes require having the reigns pulled in to structure the drive. Chaos will result if a company is run by shakers but they are necessary in order to succeed and grow. There is no thinking "inside the box"; as a matter of fact, for shakers there is no box at all and the paradigms are few and far between.

Movers. Movers are the Upper Management Individuals that "organize" and control the ideas created by the Shakers. The organization of Shakers, sometimes radical ideas, is imperative to make them feasible and rational. Movers are more stable with the company and are considered long term employees. Change is "evaluated" and "organized" into a working set of processes and procedures while keeping sight of the Mission and Vision Statement of the organization. About 30% of an organization should be Movers and life expectancy is approximately 5 to 10 years. Movers are the strength and practical side of the organization, with the Shareholders and Stakeholders in mind at all times. Long term goals are first and foremost and the mission and vision statements are kept in check with the application of existing business practices of those that they manage, as well as the ideas that are presented by the Shakers. Change is "invited" and organized into a working manner for future success and growth.

Housekeepers. Housekeepers are Middle Managers and Staff. Middle managers who follow the directives set forth by the Movers or Upper Management. They offer ideas for process and procedure improvement but generally are the mainline company backbone of getting the job done. About 50% of an organization should be Housekeepers and life expectancy is 10 to 15 years. Change is "accepted" and the proper steps to enforce them is the main task. Innovation and more radical thought processes are left up to the Shakers - who are then "prioritized" by the Movers - who then establish guidelines for Middle Managers to follow, implement, and enforce with the staff. Housekeepers are very long term employees who manage the goals and directives, keep the processes in check, and enforce established procedures in order to meet the goals and objectives set by the Movers.

Lifers. Lifers are those individuals who are complacent and generally short-term to a great degree. They follow orders but are not receptive to change, nor do they recognize the long-term goals or objectives of the organization. They are "workers" who have limited input and in fact prefer not being involved in any risk. Approximately, around 10% of an organization should be Lifers and life expectancy can range from 1 to 3 years. Change is "not recognized" and oftentimes considered disruptive for Lifers. Change requires a retooling of existing processes and procedures, which take more effort than they are willing to make. There is an expected turnover that exceeds all other organizational levels but this is important to have. The exit and entry of these short-term employees or "lifers" is designed to introduce new entry level employees who can offer the organization new ideas and possibly move into the Housekeeper level and then on to the Movers level with guidance and direction from the movers who act as mentors.

The Impact of Change

Change can impact people personally, professionally, mentally, socially, economically, and spiritually. Change can impact individuals, cultures, economies, countries, regions, and societies. Change can impact people positively or negatively, and to some extent, the impact of changes is determined by one's response to it. As such, it is best to be proactive rather than reactive about responding to incremental and dynamic changes in the society. George W. Bush, President of the United States, mentioned that the American economy is moving, which is a sign of progress and development in the country. Jay Leno, late night television comedian, on August 2005 commented that "yes" the American economy is moving alright…it is moving to China, India, Indonesia, Mexico, and other such economies. Another name for this process of jobs moving to other economies is known as outsourcing.

Outsourcing of jobs is a phenomenon impacting millions of workers in the United States and around the world. Siegel (2005 mentions that "From 2001 until the present, U.S. industry fared remarkably well in dealing labor crises" by:

- Demanding and achieving higher levels of productivity from an overburdened workforce;
- Utilizing temporary labor and consultants;
- Outsourcing and offshoring some of its labor requirements; and
- Encouraging older workers to postpone retirement and/or return to the labor force.

Siegel mentions that the above solutions are very much temporary, similar to "band-aids," dealing with the symptoms. According to Siegel (2005), "there are, right now, five million more jobs than there are people to fill them. This imbalance will increase to over 10 million unfilled jobs by 2010." As such, one solution is outsourcing, which offers the following benefits (Siegel, 2005):

- Improve the quality of an organization's new hires;
- Improve the efficiency and effectiveness of its talent acquisition or hiring process;
- Provide talent acquisition and hiring process expertise that enables the client company to focus on its own core competencies;
- Decrease recruiting costs while simultaneously providing significant value;
- Providing flexibility and agility to the organization's staffing function;
- Ensure appropriate development and maximum utilization of human capital assets;
- Improve the flow of a divers slate of candidates; and
- Supply the technology necessary to provide appropriate metrics for business decisions and compliance, as well as customer or candidate satisfaction.

Regardless of how the jobs are being outsourced or where a country's economy is moving in the twenty-first century environment, it is certain to bring about changes that can impact some workers negatively, while providing opportunities for others. Of course, those who are feeling or seeing the negative impact of such transitions are likely to resist the change as they care about their family members, jobs, and their colleagues. Another area of resistance to change is political and spiritual ideologies among groups of people living in similar and diverse cultures due to the divisiveness of many decades coming from respected leaders. Thus, the dichotomies of you are either a "believer" or "nonbeliever," white or black, man or woman, "with us" or "against us," "terrorist" or "civilized," and other such concepts are widespread both in the western and eastern worlds. Such dichotomies not only cause tension among a diverse workforce when not managed effectively, it can also further nourish the cycle of reinforcing biases and stereotypes that can continually grow and drive human behavior. At times, managers who only use a Western style of managing change as traditionally implemented in the United States can have a hard time in foreign nations because the locals may not want to bend to the will of the west due to political ideologies and biases. What is important to remember is that global managers cannot purchase long-term loyalty and commitment to lessen resistance to change initiatives, and they cannot force change on others. Change must be initiated jointly with others both with and through them. Experts have mentioned that while third world and developing countries have their challenges and issues, the developed nations are also dealing with the widespread issues related to:

- Biases toward minorities,
- Discrimination toward older workers,
- Profiling other individuals based on their skin color or place of birth,
- Priests abusing children for their personal pleasures,
- Women marrying women,
- Men marrying men,
- Women dressing as men,
- Men dressing as women,
- Males changing their sex to become females,
- Females changing their sex to become men, and
- The fact that a rape takes place every 4 seconds in the United States.

While the stated changes are perhaps "normal" part of societal transitions, some people are strongly opposed to these changes in the society and they discourage their people from viewing such changes as normal. Yet, change agents must take such views into consideration as to lessen the level of resistance in bringing about professional advancements in the society, regardless of everyone's personal biases and beliefs. Despite the media's attention toward some of the abuses, especially as perceived by the Western world, countries like India, Turkey and Iran seem to have an excellent education system and their economies are incrementally moving forward. For example, countries like Afghanistan, Pakistan, Iran, Turkey, and many others have groups of individuals that are highly educated professionals and many of them take their spiritual beliefs seriously. Such devotion and commitment to personal ideologies of life and the belief in the hereafter must be considered by global managers as they initiate, promote, and execute change in a cross-cultural work environment. Furthermore, while respecting local beliefs and ideologies, global change agents must be persistent in selling the change by letting everyone know how it can benefit them both in the short term as well as in the long term. Calvin Coolidge has been quoted as saying, "Nothing can take the place of persistence. Talent will not; the world is full of unsuccessful people with talent. Genius will not; unrewarded genius is almost a proverb. Education alone will not; the world is full of educated derelicts. Persistence and determination alone are omnipotent." Of course, persistence accompanied by interactive effort and training to positively influence others is the key to bring about positive change. As such, formal training can be a useful tool in bringing about positive change. The Cross-Cultural Program Training Model presented in Figure 12 can be a starting point for initiating training.

Figure 12- Cross-Cultural Training Program Model

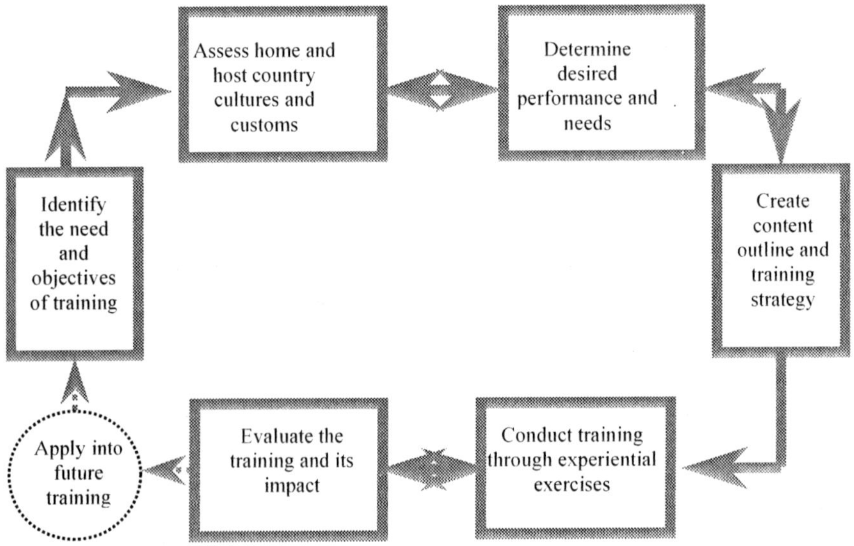

Organizational Culture Shift

Price Pritchett (1993), in his little valuable book, entitled *Culture Shift: the Employee Handbook for Changing Corporate Culture,* states the following about culture and change:

1. Leaders, managers and employees are architects of the corporate culture. These individuals shape it by how they behave. Every single thing a person with the company does serves as one more building block in the habit patterns that make up the personality and the culture of the organization.
2. In time the culture takes on a life of its own. It gains power and influence. And as the habits grow stronger, the culture begins to shape one's behavior more and more.
3. Culture can be controlling. But as powerful as it might be, the culture cannot change without permission from its people.
4. The problems come when the world changes but the culture can't… because people in the organization won't give it a chance.
5. Today –in a world of high-velocity change – the culture needs everyone to help in order to break its bad habits. Workers need to teach it better ways to behave. It relies on employees to give it a new set of responses that hold more promise for the future.

Pritchett (1993), as illustrated in Table 11, offers some excellent suggestions as cultural guidelines for changing the way managers and employees handle change:

Table 11 – Cultural Guidelines for Handling Change (Pritchett, 1993)

Stop doing what comes naturally…	and do what works
Slow Down	Speed Up
Panic	Stay Cool
Wait for Instructions	Take the Initiative
Get Ready	Get Going
Try Harder	Try Easier
Waste Time and Energy on Emotions	Spend Energy on Solutions
Play it Safe	Take More Risks
Rely More Heavily on Strengths	Don't Let Strengths Become Weaknesses
Try Not to Break Things	Welcome Destruction
Avoid Mistakes	Make More Mistakes
Shave Standards	Shoot for Total Quality
Protect Yourself	Protect What Can Protect You
Be Loyal to the Culture	Practice Aloyalty
Believe in the Problems	Have Faith in the Opportunities
Blame Others for What You Don't Like	Take Personal Responsibility for Fixing Things
Act Like an Adult	Act Like a Child

In their booklet, entitled *Business as Unusual,* Price Pritchett and Ron Pound (1993) offer the following suggestions for today's employees, managers, leaders, and change agents.

1. Be a change agent.
2. Don't give away your power.
3. Keep a positive attitude.
4. Give your troops clear-cut marching orders.
5. Focus on short-range objectives.
6. Establish clear priorities.
7. Nail down each person's job.
8. Promise change… and sell it (carefully).
9. Get resistance to change out in the open.
10. Raise the bar.
11. Motivate to the hilt.
12. Encourage risk-taking and initiative.
13. Don't try to cover all the bases yourself.
14. Create a supportive work environment.
15. "Ride close herd" on transition and change.
16. Rebuild morale.
17. Provide additional job know-how.
18. Pass out more "psychological paychecks."
19. "Beef up" communication efforts.
20. Go looking for bad news.
21. Protect quality and customer service.
22. Recruit your good people.
23. Take care of the "me" issues in a hurry.
24. Play the role of managerial therapist.
25. Reduce the level of job stress.
26. Be supportive of higher management.
27. Be more than a manager or supervisor… be a leader.

In their other booklet entitled *High-Velocity Culture Change,* Price Pritchett and Ron Pound (1993) offer yet even more perspectives and suggestions for employees, managers, leaders, and change agents that are dealing with such rapid changes. The authors state that "Changing corporate culture is a heavy-duty stuff" and everyone should take it seriously. Pritchett and Pound (1993) mention that "Most organizations don't have the foresight to change their culture before the world forces it on them." While some organizations proactively start to make the necessary changes, others don't have sufficient determination to sustain their efforts. While yet others totally lose control over their destiny and organizational culture because of the rapid and evolving changes.

Successful organizations and their leaders recognize that they cannot achieve a cultural transformation without pain, chaos, and strategic planning toward determined goals and objectives. These organizations and leaders also recognize that changing an established organizational culture is an agonizing process. Pritchett and Pound (1993) offer a number of great guidelines that help organizations achieve dramatic culture shifts efficiently while protecting their organization's future. The following are some of their suggestions (Pritchett and Pound, 1993):

1. Don't let the existing culture dictate your approach. "…you'll have trouble creating a new culture if you insist on doing it in ways that are consistent with the old one."
2. Focus on the future. "Analyzing your present culture is like going to history class, when you could learn more valuable stuff from studying the future."
3. Deliberately destabilize your group. "…you must hit with enough shock effect to immobilize the old culture at least temporarily."
4. Care harder. "It's time for 'tough love'; caring harder. Caring enough to take the company through the tough, unpopular struggle of culture change so it can survive."
5. Disarm the old culture. "You must seize control of the energy – turn it to your advantage- so it can't be used to fortify and perpetuate the old culture."
6. Change the reward system. "If you don't make significant changes in the reward system, you'll actually reward resistance."
7. Keep score. "Measure change, reward results, and you'll see the whole organization take a different attitude."
8. Promote the Vision. "The change effort needs to become a cause, a crusade, and your job is to champion the vision."
9. Free the people. "Free your people from bureaucracy, and you'll find it much easier to enlist their support for culture change."
10. Crank up the communication effort. "Standard communication procedures simply won't cut it."
11. Expect casualties. "If it does so happen that you hang on to all your people, it's either a near miracle or a sure sign of bad management."
12. Demonstrate unwavering commitment. "People have to believe you're dead serious about this endeavor and determined to see it through."
13. Involve everyone. "Your job is to give everyone in your group personal accountability for transforming the culture."

14. Make structural and administrative changes. "Breaking worn-out habits and fighting bureaucratic practices are empty acts if you don't offer employees something better."
15. Provide a living example. "You will find no better way to coach employees on what the new culture must look like than by how you carry yourself."
16. Achieve hard results in a hurry. "Ultimately, culture change lives or dies by dollar signs. It's a language everyone understands."
17. Bringing a new breed. "You want pistol, hot-blooded people bent on making their mark. Not mild mannered, conforming types who will succumb to the awesome power of the existing culture."
18. Don't trust loyalty. "Loyalty is a treacherous thing in a world of rapid change."
19. Build a power base. "… you can develop a reputation as public enemy # 1 and still prevail if you have a good supporting cast."
20. Encourage eccentricity. "You need radicals. Rebels. Revolutionaries. People who howl at the moon."
21. Orient, educate, and train. "If you're going to break the grip of the old culture, seize control of the schools. That's one of the basic rules followed by revolutionaries."
22. Go flat out. "Start out fast and keep trying to pick up speed. Leave skid marks."

Managing Conflict and Rumors toward Positive Change

Employees and managers are all going to experience conflict in their professional endeavors since conflict seems to be a natural part of everyday life. How the conflict is managed will determine whether it escalates to a higher level or whether it is solved responsibly at its root. According to Charles Beck, conflict covers a broad range of interactive behaviors usually carrying negative connotations. Conflict can range from minor differences of opinion to all out war about certain issues or resources. In examining conflict from a communication perspective, Charles Beck views three levels of conflict which include individual, organizational and societal. At the individual level, there is internal conflict or cognitive dissonance when dealing with incompatible demands. The dissonance, however, may come from the organization or society (Beck, 1999). Conflict, according to Beck (1999), is not all bad as every human interaction contains inherent conflict. Individuals differ from each other in terms of values, special interests, individual perceptions among other things. This situation can be the sources of many conflicts. Experts purport that individuals should learn how to have lively controversy rather than deadly quarrels. Researchers have identified a series of positive benefits that can be derived from conflict and they include preventing stagnation, stimulating interest, stimulating curiosity, serving as a medium to air problems, and serving as a medium for solving problems. Conflict can produce new ideas that can move an organization forward especially with teamwork and solutions to complex challenges. On the other side, conflict can lead to organizational problems and a huge waste of resources. Conflict can become destructive if the conflict remains unresolved.

According to Beck (1999), the traditional way of discussing conflict considers three main scenarios, namely win-lose, lose-lose, and win-win. The primary ways for responding to conflict seem to be dominance, compromise, and cooperation/negotiation. In a win-lose situation, *dominance* produces a clear winner, but lingering resentment will keep its controversy or contention alive at the covert level. *Compromise* on the other hand, provide, some positive benefits, but both participants feel a sense of loss, uneasiness, resentment, or a sense of betrayal may linger and participants may feel unhappy over the final results. *Cooperative negotiation*, however, can bring a positive benefit for both participants, thereby increasing the likelihood of a more lasting resolution.

Effective managers must focus more on negotiation rather than domination because the culturally diverse workforce today does not readily follow orders in comparison to previous generations. Negotiation involves both sides starting with extreme positions far more than either expects to get. Usually, before the negotiation begins, positions of participants harden as participants come to the table with a position to defend. With this type of negotiation, one party must win and one loses as an effective compromise is difficult to achieve (Beck, 1999). The negotiation should instead focus on specific issues rather than claims of either side. In this case, objectivity is displayed and the result is based on issues and not emotions and self-interests. Another important feature in negotiation is status, as it includes ones past experiences with conflict.

There is an assumption within the conflict communication concerning both self and the process. It is important to understand self-assumption, self-image and self-confidence in order to reflect the degree to which the individual believes s/he can succeed. A self-confident person will have more options within the process while believing that anything is possible (Beck, 1999). Successful resolution of conflict requires understanding the concerns of the other, also creativity in finding common ground between one's own goals and those of the other. Within organizations, negotiation and conflicting parties must trust each other in order to reach a workable solution. The method chosen to solve a given conflict is dependent on either the stage of the conflict or the relative position of the conflict. Conflict resolution between individuals and in organizations can take place through face-to-face meetings, phone conversations, memos, reports, and videoconferencing. Charles Beck (1999) states that from a conceptual perspective the process of conflict resolution includes the effective and the less effective approaches which individuals can select from in order to resolve the conflict. The effective include confrontation, changing perceptions and collaboration, while the less effective include the passive and ineffective approach of avoidance, inaction, withdrawal, accommodation, premature resolution, rigidification, dominance, and compromise (Beck, 1999). Negotiation and mediation are key aspects in conflict resolution. Very often, a mediator is used in an effort to solve or settle a conflict. The mediator is usually seen as a third party who cannot take sides, but is objective in order to resolve the conflict. A manager or trade union often plays the role of mediator in the workplace.

It is important for participants to be emotionally stable in the communication process so that the conflict will not escalate to the extent that people defend a position whether or not the position ultimately reaches their goals. Anger seems to disrupt information processing and goal orientation which can restrict an individual's ability to find mutually agreeable solutions. Effectively resolving conflict depends on the communication climate between the participants. Conflict resolution attempts to reach workable agreement with positive benefits for both sides; however, to effectively deal with conflict, cooperation is required.

Global managers, similar to local managers that deal with major changes, are likely to face conflict due to different personalities of their employees or limited resources. These managers must also be aware of various tactics for dealing with rumors and culturally insensitive comments. Philosopher Blaise Pascal once said, "never speak well of yourself." It is better to let one's actions, as a leader, do the talking. Philosophers encourage leaders to "Live a life that will earn you the kind of reputation you desire. People will notice; be humble and you will be lifted up; demanding respect and admiration is like chasing an elusive butterfly; chase it, and you'll probably never catch it; sit still, be quiet, be confident, and it may land right on your shoulder." Actions speak louder than words and a leader's overall behavior will certainly communicate much about his/her character to others than anything s/he says.

Global employees and managers should have a good understanding or knowledge of the business (the job), knowledge of the global markets, and knowledge of the local cultures (as demonstrated in Figure 13). Lack of such knowledge and understanding can lead to high amounts of stress, miscommunication, lack of trust with others, and conflict with other stakeholders. Also, without such competency, amid all of these conflicting cultural beliefs or practices one can get lost. Being competent about the job (task), the global market, and the local culture can certainly make sharing information easier and conflict management less time consuming.

Figure 13- Cross-Cultural Knowledge Management

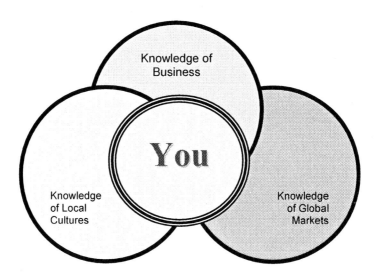

Sharing information with others is a fact of life and spreading misinformation with others is also a reality, especially when there seems to be years of animosity and distrust of corporate leaders due to job insecurity, layoffs, bribery, and other such actions caused by selfishness or corporate greed. It is necessary that educated individuals not spread misinformation about leaders, politicians, or one's colleagues in the workforce. Effective leaders can benefit from the facilitation skills and wisdom of Socrates about why rumors or certain messages should not be shared with others especially when the message has not been verified to see if it is true, important or even useful. Perhaps one can use this story to take a stand and hopefully influence others to "stop" and think about "the spoken words" and its impact on the person. People often wonder why some people have such great friends and manage to keep them. If one successfully applies the *"Triple Filter Test"* in one's conversations, the same could work for everyone. The following is the story behind the "Triple Filter Test" coming from Socrates as he saw an appropriate opportunity to teach a great lesson in the given situation.

In ancient Greece, Socrates was reputed to hold knowledge in high esteem. One day an acquaintance met the great philosopher and said, "Do you know what I just heard about your friend?" "Hold on a minute," Socrates, the great situational leader, replied. "Before telling me anything I'd like you to pass a little test. It's called the "Triple Filter Test." "Triple filter?" said the acquaintance. "That's right," Socrates continued. "Before you talk to me about my friend, it might be a good idea to take a moment and filter what you're going to say. That's why I call it the triple filter test."

1. *"The first filter is Truth.* Have you made absolutely sure that what you are about to tell me is true?" "No," the man said, "actually I just heard about it and..." "All right," said Socrates. "So you don't really know if it's true or not."

2. *"The second filter is Goodness.* Is what you are about to tell me about my friend something good?" "No, on the contrary..." "So," Socrates continued, "you want to tell me something bad about him, but you're not certain it's true. You may still pass the test though, because there's one more filter left."

3. *"The third is the filter of Usefulness.* Is what you want to tell me about my friend going to be useful to me?" "No, not really."

"Well," concluded Socrates, "if what you want to tell me is neither true, nor good, nor even useful, then why tell it to me at all?" This is why Socrates was a great philosopher and held in such high esteem. Rumors, which seem to flow often among people, should be stopped and corrected instead of spreading them when they have no reality but can damage an individual's reputation or morale in the department. So, one should always remember the application of the "Triple Filter Test" by passing ones' messages through the filters of "truth," "goodness," and "usefulness." It is a moral imperative for leaders to always make sure what is said is true, good, and useful before it is passed on to others. Leaders can certainly use similar strategies to influence their followers and hopefully stop people from passing on rumors and misinformation in their workforce.

During an interpersonal conflict with a team member or colleague, one can remain focused on stating the facts, their feelings and future expectations rather attacking the other person. For example, when hearing an offensive comment or joke about minorities or women in the workplace, one can immediately use the Four-F Model (facts, feelings, future expectations, and following up) by calmly saying: "When you make comments like that about women..., I feel angry and disappointed because…they are false and inappropriate in the workplace. Please don't make comments like that again." In most cases, repeating the facts of what was said by the person, one's feelings as a result of hearing what was said, and future expectations would take care of the situation as it brings this concern to the attention of the person making the comment. The person is likely to either clarify the misunderstanding, if that was the case, or change his or her behavior as a result of this awareness. As such, there may not be a need to place an official complaint with the human resources department or the company's lawyers since the goal is to have a healthy work environment. This is a very effective method used by skilled individuals to bring about positive changes in their departments one person at a time thereby eliminating the existence of a hostile work environment. Of course, if the candid discussion, based on the Four-F Model, does not work and there is a repetition of inappropriate comments then one must take appropriate actions to inform the organization. After all, the best way to resolve conflict is to seek cooperation from all parties involved and to create a win-win solution for everyone.

Principles of Attachment Amid Changes

Mr. Bill Vass, executive vice president of Publix Super Markets, shared his five principles of attachment in the closing session of the 1998 Publix Leadership Meeting in Orlando, Florida. The five principles, as presented in Table 12, are: surprise, honor, invitation, notice, and example. The principles are based on the underlying truth that "employee and customer retention requires attachment." This premise is true whether the attachment is healthy or unhealthy. The model used at Publix was based on Mr. George Jenkin's, founder of Publix, ability to develop healthy attachments with associates motivated by a deep concern for them as individuals.

According these principles of attachment, only spirit feeds spirit. One cannot SHINE unless one is attached personally. One must not trade his or her birthright for convenience. Depending on one's personality style, one may pass the organizational spirit to one or two individuals or to large groups of people, but a change agent must commit to passing it on. One must practice the principles until they become a habit. One must build the application into his or her daily routine, perhaps consciously at first. Mr. Bill Vass used the acronym SHINE to remember the five principles of attachment. Table 13 provides some of the examples associated with each principle and how it was applied in the organizational culture of Publix through management training seminars.

Table 12 – Principles of SHINE

Principle	Statement
Surprise	We attach to people and organizations to the degree they provide us positive surprises.
Honor	We attach to what we honor and what honors us.
Invitation	We attach where we are invited to participate in thinking.
Notice	We attach where our effort is noticed.
Example	We attach to work we consider significant. Our sense of significance depends on how people we respect feel about the work we do.

Table 13 – Application of SHINE Principles at Publix

Principle	Example of Application at Publix
Surprise	• Negative surprises break trust. Creating positive surprises for people is the commitment to keep "dating" even after the wedding takes place. • Create an environment where associates can say, "Things have turned out better than I ever expected." In that environment, people automatically share the Publix Spirit. They overcome the spirit of entitlement and feed a continual attitude of gratitude. • Managers and employees cannot surprise everyone everyday, but they personalize the surprises and keep them meaningful.
Honor	• Honor is a double bond. It applies to every person every day. • Honor's intention is to fill the person's spirit. • Honor is stronger than respect.
Invitation	• Managers and leaders must help others build their image of what they know and can do. Managers and leaders help others build confidence in themselves. • The company's strength is the management's influence on the self-esteem of associates. • Be careful not to exclude others because you know something they don't know.
Notice	• Human nature is to want to experience again what we have loved, where we have had success. • Practice noticing the 98% at- or above-standard performance, instead of focusing on the 2% exceptions and deviations.
Example	• People attach to you (and to their work) when you deeply respect and honor them and when you take interest in their work. • The work is significant because someone you deeply respect has selected it. You are willing to participate in the work to understand it and value the skill and commitment it requires.

The best way to implement change is to SHINE and be the role model for the expected outcomes. Leading by example has received much positive result for individuals like Mahatma Gandhi, Mother Teresa, Dr. Martin Luther King, and many others throughout the world. Accordingly, managers can use the same strategy to initiate and implement beneficial changes in their workplace by being a model, while involving everyone in the process.

Mentoring Employees Through Change

Senior leaders and managers can help those impacted by major change by becoming mentors to them. Mentoring is an art that can be used by top leaders, managers, employees, union members, government officials, customers, and suppliers to influence others toward positive change or direction. The October 2005 issue of South Florida's Smart Business Journal provided an article entitled "*The art of mentoring: characteristics needed for mentoring employees to increase performance.*" The article, written by this author, states that mentoring is a continuous process of sharing relevant information with selected people that can maximize the success of an institution, while guiding and supporting each person toward individual and collective achievement opportunities. Mentoring is a developmental, caring, sharing and helping relationship where the mentor helps the mentee. Being and effective mentor or mentee can be learned.

Mentoring relationships lead to effective learning organizations and they also relieve stress within the organization. A complete list of mentor and protégé characteristics found within the literature, as well as the factors assisting and detracting from successful mentoring relationships can be found in Table 14 (Mujtaba, 2006). It has been observed that the best mentors are also the best mentees (protégés). Once an individual has had a successful relationship as a protégé, he or she is much more likely to be a successful mentor. Mentors and protégés, however, bring different expectations into the relationship. Research has also been conducted on the difference in expectations mentors have and the role gender plays in the relationship. For women, a protégé's ability and potential are the most critical element in a mentor accepting a protégé, while for men a potential protégé's ability is not as important.

Table 14 - Taxonomy of Mentorship Characteristics

Characteristics of effective mentors	Characteristics of effective protégés	Factors assisting in effective mentoring	Factors detracting from effective mentoring
Trustworthy	Trustworthy	Organizational support	Time and other work demands
Previous experience	High self-efficacy	Company training programs	Organizational structure and large span of control
Knowledge, confidence, wisdom, and judgment	Open-mindedness	Mentor empowerment	Competitive work environments
High self-efficacy	Patience and persistency	Setting standards and expectations	Unclear expectations of mentoring from the company, distrust
Transformation leader	Commitment to the vision and mentee's success	Open communication between mentor and protégé	Mentor displaying Laissez-faire leadership
Approachable	Willingness to learn	Respect and sensitivity	Command and control leadership
Willingness to share personal knowledge and that of the organization	Humility, respect, and a positive attitude	Teamwork, diversity and leadership skills	Virtual work environment and global assignments
Patience	Flexibility	Interaction time	Impatience and urgency

A mentor can be a person who offers knowledge, insight, perspective or wisdom that is helpful to another person in a relationship that goes beyond duty or obligation. A mentor creates opportunities for exposure, provides challenging and educational assignments, and serves as a role model and adviser to the mentee. Such relationships often evolve informally, but managers can encourage and formalize them. Effective mentoring requires listening, caring and other forms of involvement between mentors and mentees. According to experts, mentoring is often used to achieve the interests of special groups and populations, conserve and transfer special know-how, encourage mentee contributions, bring employees together in a new social environment, help people reach their full potential, enhance the competitive position of a person or department and develop better relationships around the globe.

Mentoring is a collaborative effort on the part of the mentor and the mentee. Effective mentoring is a relationship built on trust where the mentee confides personal information and characteristics to the mentor and the mentor guides the mentee toward growth and learning opportunities. A good mentoring program is usually focused on specific learning objectives where both the mentor and mentee receive training.

There are many deliverables originating from a mentoring program, including easier recruitment of the best talent; more rapid induction of new recruits; improved staff retention; improved opportunities, performance and diversity management; increased effectiveness of formal training; reinforcement of cultural change; improved networking and communication; and reinforcement of other learning initiatives. Successful organizations recognize the value of mentoring programs as an effective way to address diversity, manage organizational knowledge, retain stellar performers, and prepare for succession. There are many organizations that have found benefits in mentoring individuals from underrepresented groups, specifically women, Asians, Hispanics, Native Americans, and African Americans in the fields of business and education. According to experts, there are many roles that professional mentors play, including teacher or tutor, coach, friend, counselor, information source, nurturer, adviser, networker, advocate, and role model. Regardless of the mentoring location, highly effective mentors and leaders share some of the same characteristics. They:

- Are experienced and respected in the field.
- Have current knowledge.
- Are trustworthy, confident and show high self-efficacy.
- Use transformational leadership skills.
- Willingly share their knowledge and guide others.
- Remain approachable.
- Have great passion for their work.
- Know what to communicate, how to communicate, when to communicate, and how to help improve the mentee.
- Connect well and challenge mentees to reach their full potential.
- Get extraordinary results using a variety of skills to get their points across and to bring about the needed behavioral changes in their mentees.

Figure 14- Essential Change Management Skills

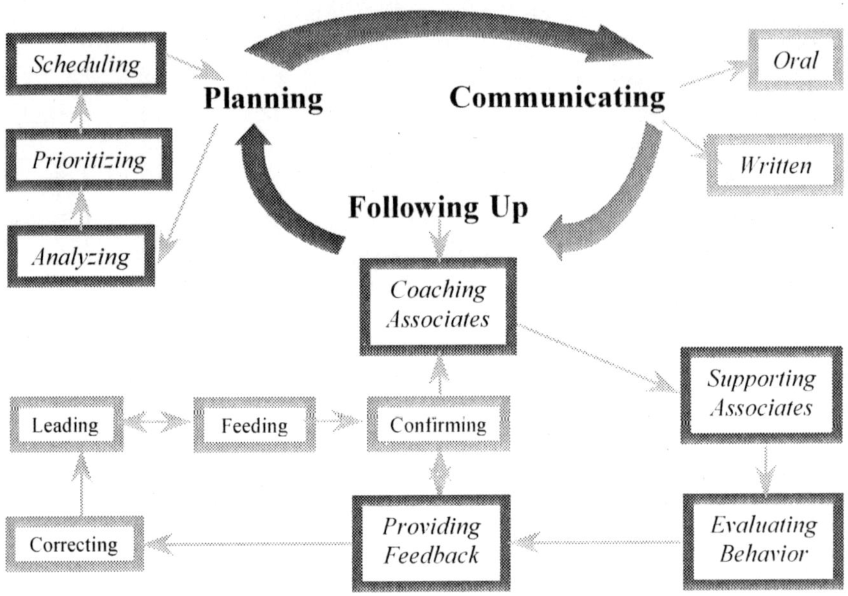

The goal of a mentoring program should be to help leaders, managers, coaches, and senior employees in a firm become highly skilled, self-aware, inclusive, energetic and creative, and to carry a zest for mentoring into the organization every day. Mentoring is not an easy task, but such is the obligation bestowed on the lucky ones. Highly effective mentors and leaders understand that developing others requires self-reflection, sensitivity, risk-taking, interdependency and teamwork among all parties (mentors, mentees, managers, peers, and senior officers). They also understand that such a synergy requires forging a partnership, inspiring commitment, growing both the mentor and mentee's skills, promoting persistency and shaping the environment so all parties can achieve their goals. At the minimum, both mentors and mentees should master the essential skills of change management, which are planning, communicating and following up, if they are to be effective change agents (see Figure 14).

Coaching Toward Performance and Productivity

While mentoring is a very useful tool, the value of managers coaching employees for maximum productivity amid major change must be emphasized. Due to the changing demographics of the business world such as more competition and the introduction of new technologies, organizations are discovering that traditional tactics of management are no longer enough to remain competitive. As such, coaching is becoming to be recognized and practiced as an effective tool to increase morale, performance and the bottom line through the success of each individual associate. For example, studies have shown that about 90% of employees who received coaching in their jobs say that it improved their job performance and professional success. In organizations where coaching is effectively practiced as a management style, the bottom-line performance is two to three times better than the traditional "command-and-control" type of organizations. Furthermore, it has been proven that employee commitment increases when there is a strong, positive relationship between the manager and his/her employees. These types of relationships are developed best as a result of effective coaching.

Effective relationship-oriented coaching creates more knowledgeable and competent employees, reduces errors and rework, and it greatly assists in bringing new changes to the culture. Both effective and ineffective managers tend to know what makes a good coach. The difference lies in being able to transfer this knowledge into successful actions with employees to increase their performance and success. Effective coaching skills make a manager's job easier as it enables greater delegation leaving him/her time to take on bigger projects. It builds the manager's reputation as a developer of people while increasing productivity since everyone will know the expectations and the fact that what they do matters. It also can develop trust and a good relationship between managers and employees. Last but not least, good coaching skills can increase creativity, innovation, morale, and teamwork since everyone will feel safe working in an inclusive environment.

So what is coaching? Simply stated, coaching is about developing a trusting relationship with employees so one can jointly clarify expectations and departmental goals thereby leading to specific action plans for their achievement. As such, there are many situations where coaching skills will be very effective and the following are some of them.

1. Reinforcing good performance.
2. Motivating employees to new heights and peak performance levels.
3. Orienting a new employee into the department or organization.
4. Providing new knowledge to individuals about changes and tactics.
5. Training a new skill for a new task that needs performing.

6. Following up on competencies passed on during a training session.
7. Explaining the current or new standards and how they can be achieved.
8. Setting priorities for effective time management with those employees who need it.
9. Inculcating someone into the cliques and groups which may exist within the political circles.
10. Clarifying expectations and correcting poor performance.
11. Increasing the self confidence of an employee about the task or new responsibilities and challenges.
12. Conducting a performance review.

Coaching is not an innate skill, but rather it is learned. It occurs through one's life personally and professionally. Effective coaching is the process of letting people know that what they do matters to you and to the organization. Furthermore, it is about letting them know that you are there to help them be the best they can be as their success is important because it matters to you. It is also about being sincere, specific and to the point about both good and poor performance so they can take personal responsibility for their achievements. From this perspective, coaching is and it can be one of the most important functions managers perform because it communicates performance levels, expectations, importance of the tasks and responsibilities, and it communicates a caring attitude. The following list summarizes some of the main elements involved in coaching.

1. Before beginning the coaching session, be sure to plan exactly what you want to achieve, and the potential benefits for the other person.
2. Start on a positive note and establish a common ground by having a supportive environment.
3. Communicate clearly, listen effectively, show that you care, and do not "beat around the bush." Clearly and caringly state the challenge, opportunity, and/or expectations.
4. Be respectful of the other person's feelings, honor and dignity. Create a non-threatening environment for the interaction, dialogue and discussion.
5. Be culturally sensitive by getting to know the other person's background, values, and anticipate his/her reactions.
6. Avoid value judgments, stereotyping and labeling the behavior of others.

7. Use empathic listening skills to clarify your understanding and the other person's perspective.
8. Stay with the point and do not get side tracked with other issues. Restate the purpose of the session and ask what specific things can be done to increase or improve performance. You can offer assistance, but avoid providing solutions –let the individual come up with the solutions. Your job is to lead them in the right direction.
9. Document and clarify the specific plan suggested by the employee, the expected level of performance and how the plan will improve performance. Seek agreement and summarize the conversation.
10. End on a positive note and thank the person for coming up with the specific plan.

Effective coaches encourage, inform, praise, raise awareness, collaborate, set clear expectations, serve as role models, empowers, helps, challenges, serve as vehicles for change, remove barriers, and enable others to reach their full potential. One should remember that coaching can be the single most important thing you do as a leader or manager. Also, managers and coaches never let good or poor performance go unnoticed. When effective coaches and managers see good performance, they say it and praise it. One should not let poor performance go unnoticed by saying privately and making it positive for future performance. For real personal issues and poor personal habits: first, prepare the teammate/associate, and second, be gentle and to the point in stating the problem that needs fixing. The video titled *"The Practical Coach,"* which has been used by corporations to train their managers, offers many insights and suggestions on coaching for all leaders. The video offers a concept called the *"Two Minute Challenge"* with the following steps:
◊ First, state what you observed.
◊ Second, wait for a response.
◊ Third, remind the person of the goal.
◊ Fourth, ask for a specific solution.
◊ Fifth, jointly agree on the solution and its implementation.

Managers have gotten where they are because somebody guided and helped them toward the right direction and eventually trusted their judgment. So, as a global change agent, be there for your people and effectively coach them toward maximum productivity amid personal, professional, societal, and cultural changes. Coaches can also make sure that that a Cross Cultural Change Management Process (as demonstrated in Figure 15) is used to deal with change initiatives in the global environment.

Figure 15- Cross Cultural Change Management Process

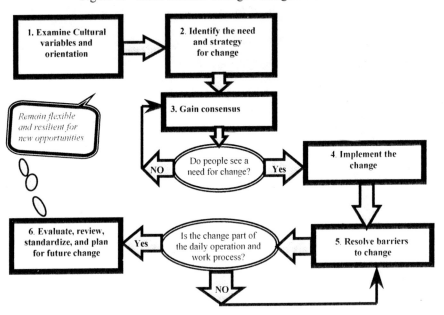

Embrace Continuous Change

Change is inevitable and it is continuous for human beings from birth to death. In today's flux work environment, an individual either changes positively in order to grow or one will most assuredly change...perhaps automatically for the worst. Twenty-first century change agents must realize that change is constant, therefore it requires managing; change can be threatening and cumbersome; change can create chaos and inefficiency; and change can cause people to respond quickly and reactively. Reactive responses are unplanned, situational, and may involve more time and cost; and proactive responses are based on values, planned, goal-oriented, more effective, and requires a change management plan. The best option during an inevitable change that has been introduced is to proactively begin the adaptation process and thus reap the benefits, as demonstrated in Figure 16.

Figure 16- Organizational Stages of Change

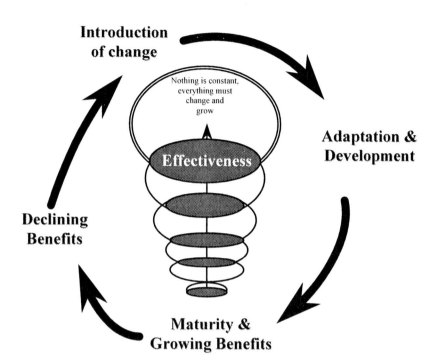

In the Organizational Stages of Change, the spiral represents the relationship or results (profits, productivity, sales, etc) and the amount of change that needs to take place for that result to become reality. The shadow represents "results" while the remaining part of the circle represents change, risk, and uncertainty. Proactive organizations and firms start planning and assess the need for improvement in the maturity stage of an implemented change. By doing this, one can avoid responding reactively to change and minimize losses during the decline stage. Proactive organizations and individuals prolong the maturity stage and decrease or totally eliminate the losses from the decline stage. Industry leaders who would like to stay leaders usually are prepared to go from maturity into the introduction of the new change in a short period of time with minimum or no losses. Leaders, managers, and all other change agents throughout the organization can proactively manage change by following the five steps included in the Change Management Process, as demonstrated in Figure 17.

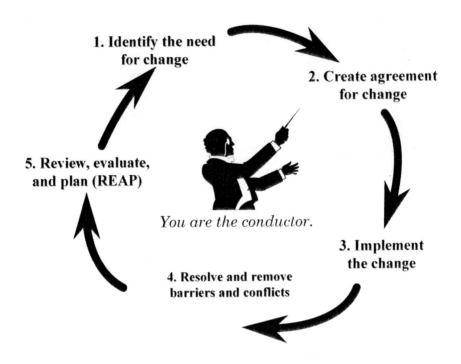388 | Bahaudin Mujtaba

Figure 17- The Change Management Process

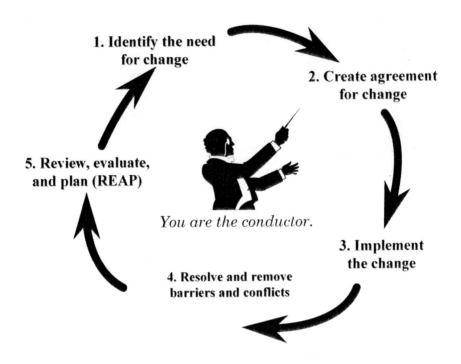

People grow like fruits, plants, and trees. Just as fruits are either green and growing or ripe and rotting, people can also be either growing or experiencing atrophy. Plants best flourish when they receive sufficient amounts of rain and sun. Too much of anything can kill them, but the right balance will help them grow. If you want to become successful, you must align yourself with changes and situations that offer opportunities for the achievement of your goals.

According to John P. Kotter and Leonard A. Schlesinger's 1979 March/April article in Harvard Business Review, which was titled "*Choosing strategies for change,*" among people there are four common psychological reasons for resisting change and they are:

1. Potential loss of something valuable such as authority, control, loss of job or status, freedom in procedures, etc.
2. Misunderstanding of prospective change and lack of trust in those initiating or implementing change. The common phrase is that top echelons are trying to get more (usually in terms of

profits) out of people without giving anything in return to their associates.
3. A belief that new change is not necessary and not needed which may be based on incomplete or wrong paradigms.
4. A belief that one may not be able to adapt to new change and may lose face among peers.

While there might be many other reasons that people resist change, there are also many strategies for effectively handling resistance to change. It is the responsibility of change agents to find out what the reasons for resistance are and work on reducing it. Change agents can use the Change Agent Responsibilities Flowchart, as demonstrated in Figure 18, as a guide.

Figure 18- Change Agent Responsibilities (CARs) Flowchart

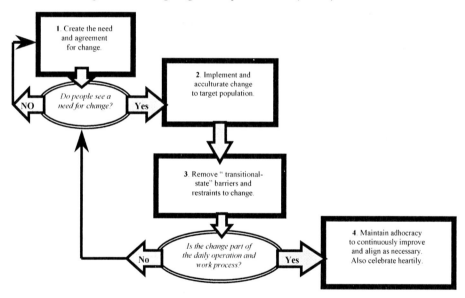

The following are some of the suggestions that can be applied by change agents to understand and effectively handle resistance to change.

Listen. Become an active or an empathic listener by seeing people's emotions, hearing them from the heart, and acknowledging their resistance. Try to sincerely understand their point of view and once you fully understand them, they feel understood, and they have overcome their anger, then try to explain the reasons for change and their role in making this change successful. It is important that you listen to them at their pace and not rush them because most people become strongly attached to how they have been doing things and change is usually seen as the enemy. So, be patient, listen with empathy and then help them understand the need for change and provide emotional support.

Involve people in the process. The greatest human need is probably involvement and recognition of one's contribution to worthwhile causes and services. Everybody wants to be involved and contribute to a greater cause or service; therefore involving people in the change process and asking for their cooperation from the outset would be the best way to expect successful implementation of change. Involvement and contribution creates "buy-in" which helps people become much more accepting of the change. Involving people from the outset helps them understand the need for change and consequently agree with the change. Involvement also increases trust and commitment on everyone's part thereby making them formal or informal change catalysts or agents. Some people fear that involving people in the process will create chaos and they might lose control; however, they do not realize that not involving them will create more hassles and chaos because people may remain resistant for a long time and may resort to shirking.

Educate and train people beforehand. Education is important because it provides knowledge about the change, and of course a little knowledge is appreciated by everyone. Training is the key in transforming knowledge into production. People say that "knowledge is power," which is not really the case because it is the application of knowledge that creates result which may or may not create power, depending on other variables such as the need for the result, the availability of the results from other sources, and so on. So, when people are trained and educated about the change then they may be fully prepared to deal with change, and thus, change will not be a threat to them as much as before.

Reward and recognize. People are motivated internally by different needs and those needs may become fulfilled by different rewards, incentives or recognition programs. It is important that appropriate monetary and non-monetary rewards are linked with implementing the change successfully. In order for people to change their way of doing things, the change should be supported or aligned with appropriate recognition and reward programs. Keep in mind that according to the principles of behavior modification, behavior that is rewarded will get repeated and behavior that is ignored may disappear.

Celebrate the change publicly. When the change is made public and celebrated with happiness and joy then people may become more accepting of it because they realize that it is not another fad or a thing that will go away when another fad becomes popular. People are better able to see that the change has been committed into the culture and that they are not alone because it is affecting others who will be going through the same difficulty of adjusting to the new change.

> What we see, and like to see, is cure and change, but what we do see and do not want to see is care, the participation in the pain, solidarity in suffering, the sharing in the experience of brokenness. And still, cure without care is as dehumanizing as a gift given with a cold heart (Henri Nouwen, as cited by in *The Magic of Conflict* by Crum, 1987).

Change Management Synopsis:[10] Impact on Stress and Conflict

Mankind has never before experienced so many changes in such short period of time, and this change characteristic of our modern century is a very pervasive one. Life itself is a process of change and adaptability. Our modern century of technological marvels and social revolutions has thrust upon us much unbearable conditions and consequences, some of which rage above our deepest sentiments and comprehension. Society today is bombarded on all sides with a series of drastic changes within all social institutions, and the degree at which these change factors and agents assault our minds and lives is overwhelmingly inexhaustible.

Managing change is a tactical and strategic affair which becomes increasingly dangerous and difficult as the number of change variables and agents increases. This is further complicated by conflict which is inherent in all human social affairs. Conflict is unavoidable in human affairs, and as such, serves as the bottleneck of progress! One of the major aims in change management and conflict resolution seems to be that of eliminating conflict. This is an almost impossible task we set ourselves whilst our differences remain as individuals. It is fully within our nature to agree and disagree with each other, and our added knowledge and information of today have both increased and decreased the threshold for disagreement under various circumstances.

Change is a frightening social and psychological experience when it requires entering new spheres and situations. Moreover, change today has a significantly wider scope than it did decades ago, as the factors of globalization and cultural diversity have become fundamental principles and paradigms upon which change is prefabricated. One must now have a variety of skills and a wider knowledge base to manage or even comprehend change as it takes place within the context of cultural and

---

[10] - This material is co-authored with Dr. Donovan A. McFarlane, City College of Fort Lauderdale.

social conflicts. The cross-cultural aspects of change and conflict further complicate their management and resolution.

Change is a social process because it is the human element that gives life and significance to change in any setting. Therefore, when managers and leaders consider change within their institutions or organizations they need to take a decisively behavioral or human approach to the management of change. Change is one of the most dominant characteristics of today's hard-pressing business environment in which fast-paced technology and high level competition are pushing individuals and organizations into new situations and environments. Entering into new competitive and social arenas can be highly stressful for employees and this amidst resulting conflicts internal and external to the organization. As a result of this awareness, managers and leaders must make change and conflict management a major part of their training and responsibilities. Teaching employees about the nature of change and its significance can be a first step in the process of effectively managing change.

Change is natural and expected within our lives. It is the nature and dynamics of change that can become stressful or cause conflicts, resistance and fear in us. The problem therefore is not change itself, but unplanned change. As human beings we like to plan and be able to manage our every aspect of life and living. Planned change is the catalyst around which we approach life; our education, training, socialization, communications, etc. However, life seems to offer more of the other for which we can be wholly unprepared to manage or accept; unplanned change. The field of strategic management has offered managers and leaders considerable knowledge in the area of planning; both short-term and long-term. However, planning for change is not an easy task, and this further complicates managing change. Change in today's society can offer many advantages as well as disadvantages, and this will depend on the degree of change, the context in which change unfolds, the scope of change, the mindset, knowledge base and skills of the individual undergoing change, the type of information and education the individual possesses, the source or sources of change, and the cultural and social experiences of the individual. Culturally, change can be a very destructive force, especially when assimilation of one's values, beliefs, customs, etc., becomes the major consequence. It is this aspect of change that becomes very stressful for both individuals and groups. All forms of change have cultural and social overtones that affect organizational progress and performance. Managers and leaders must become attuned to the fact that change within organizations means change within the social contexts of employees' work and lives. The field of industrial psychology still holds great knowledge benefits for those who would examine the effects of change in work environments and change management across all organizational boundaries. Furthermore, the lack of management initiatives and programs to deal with change and conflicts in immediate organizational settings are grossly lacking in twenty-first century institutions. Usually, we choose to react to change only when it arrives, and this is where conflict and resistance become major issues. We must prepare for change and then we will be better able to manage it within all contexts.

Conflict is inherent in all human affairs and this seems evident even from the onset of human history when we consider life from a Creationist perspective. Conflict seems to be part of the imperfect mind and nature of man as he strives to make decisions as to wrong or right, and those having to do with the allocation and distribution of limited resources. Conflict strives from individual differences; personal, social, psychological, cultural, physical and even the gender-related biological differences within our specie. Human conflict has both micro and macro origins; generated between individuals, groups, institutions or larger society, races or cultures. The nature of conflict as it exists within our lives rests heavily on our knowledge of selves and others and in our ability to foster tolerance and adapt to change within all contexts effectively.

Cultural exchange is the most fervent perpetrator of change and conflict as we each encounter different ways of behaving, different social values, norms, mores, attitudes, reactions and ideas to human thoughts and actions. With the proliferation in cultural exchange resulting from globalization and increased travel and communications, change and conflict have become increasing dominant in human personal and business affairs. There seems to be a silent cultural war wherein values and beliefs, social roles and behaviors clash to produce conflict in our daily interaction as leaders, managers, and followers. Change should be expected, as well as conflict given the differences between individuals and their social values and cultural training. The major issue therefore is the degree to which each individual embraces or refuses change and the reactionary stance such person chooses. This is what produces conflicts among us. Within business organizations, individual values are not secondary to organizational culture, and this must be taken into consideration when dealing with change. Though organizations have their own unique culture the individual's social values and cultural training through more fundamental societal institutions; namely, the family and religion will still have even more powerful bearing on their ability to adapt to change of any nature. We are social creatures and most of the change we experience takes place at the affective level where most of our experiences are translated into life-long meanings. Therefore, conflict should naturally be expected when changes arrive, whether they are planned or unplanned. Organizational leaders and managers must then act as effective supporters in the education and adaptation process when it comes to employees and followers accepting change and dealing with the conflicts which arise.

Leaders of the twenty-first century must practice being effective supporters in counseling their subordinates to deal with change and in managing conflicts. It is important that managers and leaders of the twenty-first century do not strive to be or exemplify themselves as propagators of radical or mass social and organizational changes, but rather as facilitators in the change process. This will better enable them to address resistance as well as to deal with conflict. Conflict and change management should be practiced alongside each other for the best result, since they are closely interrelated and change and conflict strive from and feed on each other. Managers and leaders of today's institutions and organizations must possess a wide knowledge base and familiarity with cultures and individuals' social values in order to effectively arrive at the heart of conflict and uniquely address issues and problems. Cultural diversity as an initiative of twenty-first century organizations has added much complexity to change and conflict as individuals from varied backgrounds and societies encounter each other in active working relationships.

Conflict like change cannot be avoided, it can only be dealt with, and managers and leaders must become aware of this fact. Our differences as individuals serve to perpetuate change and conflict; our language, ethnic and social differences, etc. Knowing this fact, life then is best seen as a process of adapting to change and dealing with conflict, and the best way we can approach this is by effective change management and conflict management. The field of conflict resolution has not done much for us as a society, and this is immediately evident in the widespread social problems we experience today. One of the grave issues is the speed at which social change takes place; so rapid that it is best termed social revolution. Social revolution has perpetuated conflict throughout all corners of our society and this conflict is multiple in character. There are conflicts which are gender-based, generational-related, economic-based, racially-based, culturally-based, and the list goes on. The rate at which change is taking place at all levels of our society is alarming and as such evades our ability and comprehension to deal with it effectively. The rapid nature of change has affected our ability to address conflicts across the board as we struggle to deal with several issues at once. This puts a strain on individual knowledge and scope, as well as on the limited resources we have available including time to resolve many conflicts. Resulting from this is the need for effective stress management. Stress is a major factor of social and other related problems in individuals and organizations. In fact, it seems to be a major health issue in highly developed and industrialized nations than in any other.

The relationship existing between stress, change, and conflict is one which becomes quite obvious when we consider the fact that they usually arise simultaneously within social contexts or situations or proceed immediately out of each other's existence (see Figure 19).

Figure 19 shows that the relationship between change, conflict, and stress is a highly interrelated one in so much that one does not exist without the other. This has great implications for leaders and managers. Stress management, conflict management and change management must become an integrated task if success is to be achieved in any of these. Leaders and managers of twenty-first century institutions and organizations must effectively integrate stress, conflict, and change management into a comprehensive program in order to effectively address the issues and problems stemming from globalization, cultural change, technological and social revolutions.

Figure 19 - The Relationship between Change, Conflict and Stress

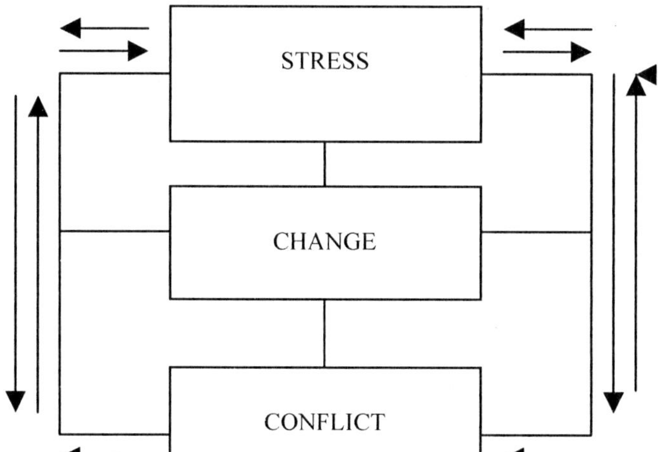

Change in today's society is alarmingly fast-paced and this is the major issue which most individuals seem to find difficult to confront. As human beings we like to feel comfortable in a safe zone where stability guarantees us certain psychological and social needs. Change can disrupt our lives and wreck our world into disaster, especially when change has the characteristic unpredictability it does in our technologically advanced society. Our twenty-first century society has the highest degree of uncertainty that our civilization has witnessed throughout generations thus far, and with individual knowledge of this fact, our resistance to change should come as no surprise. Change can be drastic and dramatic, devastating, devouring, disastrous, and destructive. Such is the type of change experienced by some people in Afghanistan and Iraq with the United States military intervention and invasion. Such change where culture, religion, way of life, survival, and life itself are crushed and trammeled is the most fearful and problematic, causing severe cultural, social and psychological stress and damages.

When change is natural it is a different issue than when it is change resulting from willful enforcement such as the change experienced by the people of Iraq and Afghanistan with the interference of outside forces. Forceful change does not allow for adaptation or negotiation; it imposes and penalizes and ridicules, and brings with it the most severe forms of stress and conflicts. This is the type of change we fear; change that rocks our worlds and turn them upside down. Example of such recent change has been that experienced by victims of the Tsunami of Asia and the hurricanes that have recently swept across the United States and the Caribbean. Change in human eyes is best when it is planned change, since it has a greater degree of manipulability and its lasting results are at best predictable.

Managers and leaders of twenty-first century institutions and organizations must not impose change without consensus, and when such change is introduced, implementation in an incremental manner is the best method or approach. Too much change too fast and in too little time can upset progress by affecting individual satisfaction, performance, concentration, skills, and ability to cope with tasks and responsibilities. Therefore, it is important to educate individuals about change and make them aware of the type of change and how it will affect them. This will reduce stress as well as conflict and the resistance to change.

As a civilization, we have perhaps individually and collectively experienced more of the devastating and negative side of change than the positive one. Dramatic change has shaped our entire progress, destiny and century. For example, World War I, World War II, The Gulf War, The Iraq Invasion, the Vietnam War, etc. All these have been examples of change in its most devastating aspect witnessed by our civilization, and which have affected our lives in numerous ways. Change can be beautiful or ugly, and it is the ugly type of change that people fear. Furthermore, within social contexts change is not always welcome as it affects human interaction and relationships; our most fundamental needs. For example, change in a relationship often affects one partner's comfort or may be initiated or experienced at some cost. Therefore; it is the cost-benefit factor that makes change something that causes stress and conflict. Change can be very costly as we have witnessed from the hurricanes which have hit the United States. When change is costly it displaces people mentally, physically, psychologically, socially, and emotionally.

Positive change is what we seek and require as individuals and when this fails to show itself we are confounded and stressed. When we plan change it often involves less stress and conflict. Managers and leaders of the twenty-first century must invest heavily in fostering and promoting positive change to motivate employees and deal with conflicts. Change can be the source of new growth or the precursor of failure and losses.

Summary

Change has been a part of everyone's life since birth, and change will continue to be with everyone until death. One becomes what he or she is because of changes experienced thus far. These changes are not always likable or enjoyable as they can also be tragic; yet they shape one's life and actions thereby making them who they are at this moment of their life (Deems, 1995). Change is all around, and it impacts people in many ways. Self-chosen change, be it personal or organizational is naturally the easiest and the best form for implementation. Change that is "imposed" on people tends to face more resistance, compared to 'self-chosen" change. When it comes to "imposed" change, people tend to see the "minuses" and often ignore seeing the "pluses" or positive sides of the change. With imposed change, there is a tendency to see how the change is uncomfortable, unfair, inconvenient, and untimely. What is important is to get involved in the organization's "imposed" changes on a proactive basis, thereby making it a "self-chosen" change in order to be successful in managing change in a cross-cultural business environment. Richard Deems (1995) states that change is a universal human experience, and people can make it work for themselves through proactive planning, communication, and staying focused on one's goals. Twenty-first century's global employees and change agents need to accept change, communicate their feelings regarding change to others, become "tempered radicals," and tackle their goals as per their current and new priorities and responsibilities.

As discussed in the preface and throughout the book, change is a reality of life and all human beings go through it personally, professionally, physically, mentally, socially, and spiritually in the progression of their life. Realistically speaking, change happens regardless of whether it is desired, needed, wanted, or invited. Another reality is that responses to change are often predictable and, thus, resistance toward a new initiative can be reduced or managed through proactive planning efforts. *Cross Cultural Change Management* (CCCM) has been about making sure that workers and professionals are able to see the positive side of the issue and, as change agents, they can make sure that every person impacted by the transition goes through the change process effectively and as quickly as possible. The book on *Cross Cultural Change Management* provided practical definitions and perspectives for change and discussed why change initiatives need to be managed through proactive planning. The book discussed how change can impact people and how individuals often react to change. *Cross Cultural Change Management* offered change management models and strategies for overcoming resistance to change. It also described the roles and responsibilities of leaders, managers, and change agents in change initiatives. People resist change mostly due to the loss of control over what they do or the perception this loss of control; therefore, it is the change agent's role and responsibility to reduce and eliminate this fear by instilling a sense of confidence in workers who are impacted by change as per the employee's level of readiness to accept the change or successfully complete the new task. It is recommended that managers and change agents use situational leadership concept and styles to effectively transition workers in the change process. Overall, the book offered various approaches and strategies for organizations and individuals to successfully initiate, execute, manage, and lead change in today's cross-cultural workplace. Change agents and managers can use a formal process or model for change management initiatives by identifying the problem, determining the solution, examining and evaluating both driving and restraining forces in a timely manner, assessing the value and ease of change for each force, selecting appropriate strategies for implementation, implementing the change, assessing the success of the change with each milestone, and remaining flexible to make appropriate adjustments as needed.

Figure 20- Restraining and Driving Forces for Change

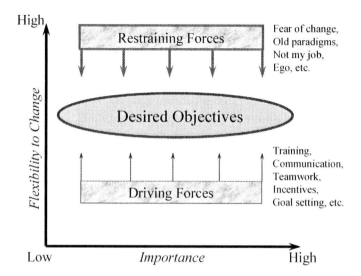

As demonstrated in Figure 20, change agents, managers, and "tempered radicals" must remain resilient, while reducing the restraining forces and increasing the driving forces to bring about successful change. It is important to reduce the fear of change among employees through sufficient training, effective communication, teamwork, appropriate incentives, and time-bounded goals. The increased focus on driving forces and expectations of everyone in the firm to adapt to the new process can also communicate the importance of change as it relates to the success of employees, managers, and the organization in today's competitive environment of business.

Tom Peters once said that "The business environment is no longer predictable; financial, technological, and market changes come fast and furious, and only flexible organizations that learn to live with the chaos will survive" (Tom Peters, 1987, author of *Thriving on Chaos)*. Peters (1897) continued to say that "The winners of the business environment, now and in the future, will be those organizations that can adapt quickly to meet the new market driven challenges." Furthermore, "The new leaders must love change and inspire the organization with a clear vision. Leaders must personify hustle and urgency and clear away bureaucracy and Mickey Mouse rules that slow the action" (Peters, 1987). It is clear that twenty-first century corporations need to increase their capacity for change and its acceptance. Today's global business environment is shifting at a rapid pace, and modern organizations must shift with it or face the consequences of atrophy and death. Of course, organizations don't change without individuals changing in a purposeful manner toward a brighter vision of the future. Average individuals know what change means to them financially, while leaders know what change means to their purpose and vision in life.

It is important that managers know how change is impacting their employees. Effective managers should openly, honestly, and consistently communicate with their employees in a timely manner about changes that impact them. Consistent, honest, and open communication builds trust and enhances the cycle of two-way communication between the manager and his/her employees. Some studies seem to indicate that professional employees who are in challenging jobs seem to be more ready for change, and more accepting of change when compared to those who are in passive jobs. There seems to be a positive relationship between high levels of education and people's willingness, readiness for change, and attitude toward accepting change. Employee loyalty and length of time with the organization or seniority also seem to be positively related to one's level of "readiness" for change. Overall, the more employees feel that they are a part of the organization and are involved in the success of the company the higher the probably that they will be more accepting of change and new initiatives to enhance the competitiveness of the firm. As such, effective managers should attempt to change passive jobs to dynamic positions in order to stretch the talents of their people while involving them in the problem solving process. Furthermore, effective managers should provide job enrichment, training and education opportunities, and personal development workshops for their workers in order to equip them with the right skills, attitudes, and the commitment needed to effectively manage change.

According to Tom Peters (1987), "There is no limit to what the average person can achieve if he/she is thoroughly involved. This power can most effectively be tapped when people are gathered in human-scale groupings we call self-managing teams." Professor Peter goes to say that "Change must become the norm, not cause for alarm. And today's incremental changes must support a larger bold goal to be achieved in record time. This means leaders at all levels must become obsessive about change and thrive on it." Socrates said: "Let him who would move the world first move himself." Similarly, change agents should be able to manage the change process with themselves first in order to succeed in helping others change successfully. This will enable change agents to be a good example for those who are impacted by the change. Intelligence, education, and drive are prime requisites for the successful achievement of major change initiatives with people. However, intelligence, education and drive are worthless without the discipline that enables one to transport his or her abilities to the work environment. A true cross cultural change agent is an individual who is working toward or has reached his or her full potential as it relates to the change in order to be a role model for others. In other words, in the Gandhian spirit, true change agents become the change that they would like to see in others.

The flow of communication between you (change agent) and everyone impacted by the change is greatly affected by the level of trust that exists between you and them. If the trust level is high, you have an environment that supports open and honest communication about the change. It is up to you, as a change agent, to help build an environment of trust with everyone around you. When people feel comfortable and safe from being judged prematurely and incorrectly, they are more willing to open up and speak their minds. If the trust level is low, then the opposite becomes true. So, you can make or "break" the level of trust between you and your colleagues through your character. Remember, who you are as a person communicates much more loudly, persuasively, and eloquently than anything you write, say, or do. To become a person of strong character, change agents need to be consistently compassionate, courageous, and honest in all of their dealings with everyone in the organization. Change agents must develop trust through consistency, compassion, courage, persistency and determination, and by continuously communicating a brighter vision of the "near" future while pointing to "the light at the end of the tunnel." Remember the poem that "There is one life that soon will pass – and only what is done with love will last." Help others transition through change with compassion, consideration, and unconditional love. Be a builder, never make "empty" promises, always deliver on your intentions, and "don't quit" striving for excellence.

As an effective cross-cultural change agent and tempered radicals, may you always have the hindsight to know where you have been, the foresight to know where you are going, and the insight to know when you are about to go too far. Remember, if you can perceive and believe it then you are very likely to achieve it as well. Good luck making great changes and giant strides toward greatness.

Don't Quit

When things go wrong as they sometimes will.
When the road you are trudging seems all up hill.
When funds are low and debts are high.
And you want to smile, but you have to sigh.

When care is pressing you down a bit.
Rest, if you must, but don't quit.
Life is queer with its twists and turns.
As everyone of us sometimes learns.

And many a failure turns about
When he might have won had he stuck it out:
Don't give up though the pace seems slow --
You may succeed with another blow.

Success is failure turned inside out --
The silver tint of the clouds of doubt.
And you never can tell how close you are.
It may be near when it seems so far:

So stick to the fight when you are hardest hit --
It's when things seem worst that you must not QUIT.

(Unknown)

Mr. "Meant To"

Mr. "Meant To" has a comrade
And his name is *"Didn't Do,"*
Have you ever chanced to meet them?
Did they ever call on you?

These two fellows live together
In the house of never win,
And I am told that it is haunted
By the ghost of *"might have been."*

Builder or Wrecker?

I watched them tear a building down
A gang of men from a busy town

With a Hi-he-hooh and a lusty yell
They swung a beam and a side-wall fell

I asked the foremen, are these men skilled?
The kind you would hire if you wanted to build

He laughed and said ohhh Noooh, indeed
Unskilled labor is all I need

If I could easily wreck in a day or two
What it takes a builder a year to do

I asked myself as I walked away
Which of these roles have I tried to convey

Am I a builder who works with care
Measuring life by the rule and square

And shaping my deeds to a well laid plan
Carefully doing the best I can

OR am I a wrecker that walks the town
Content in the labor of tearing down.
                                        (Unknown)

REFERENCES

Adams, S. M. (1999). Settling cross-cultural disagreements begins with "where" not "how". *Academy of management executive, vol.13* retrieved September 9, 2004 from EBSCO database.

Adler, N.J. (1984). "Women in international management: Where are they?" *California Management Review,* 26 (4): 78-89.

Adler, N.J., (1984a). "Women do not want international careers: And other myths about international management." *Organizational Dynamics,* 13 (2, Autumn): 66-79.

Afghanistan, (2005). *Afghanistan Independent Radio Moves towards Stability.* Retrieved 25 February 28, 2005 from: http://www.internews.org/regions/afghanistan.

Ahern, N.C., and Scott, E.L. (1981). "Career outcomes in a matched sample of men and women PhDs." Washington, DC: National Academy Press.

Ahmed, M. M., Chung, K. Y., & Eichenseher, J. W. (2003, March). Business students' perception of ethics and moral judgment: A cross-cultural study. *Journal of Business Ethics,* 43(1/2), 89.

Ampofo, A.; Mujtaba, B.; Cavico, F.; and Tindall, L. (September 2004). The Relationship between Organizational Ethical Culture and the Ethical Behavior of Employees: A Study of Accounting and Finance Professionals in the Insurance Industry of United States. *Journal of Business and Economics Research,* Vol.2, Number 9. Pages 13-24.

Anderson, W. T. (1992). *Reality isn't what it used to be.* San Francisco: Harper and Row.

Anderson, C., Glassman, M., & Pinelli, T. (1997). A comparison of communication practices among Indian and US scientists and engineers. Working paper, Old Dominion Univeristy.

Andreason, A.W. & Kinneer, K.D. (2004). Bringing Them Home Again. *Industrial Management, 46* (6). Retrieved May 12, 2005 from ABI/INFORM Global.

Appreciative Inquiry. *Public Personnel Management*, 30(1), 129. Retrieved September 30, 2004, from EBSCOhost database.

Armas, Genaro C. (2000). "More Women Take Executive Roles, but other Gaps Widen 'Glass Ceiling' is Cracking, but Gender Equality in the Workplace has a Long Way to Go, Analysts Say." *The Augusta Chronicle*. Augusta, Ga.: Apr 24.

Ash, Mitchell A (1992). Cultural Contexts and Scientific Changes in Psychology. *American Psychologist*, February pg. 198-207; and Lewin, Kurt (1931) "Environmental Forecast in Child Behavior and Development." Handbook of Child Psychology ed. C. Murchison, Clark University Press. Ph. 94-127. Worcester. MA.

Ashford, B.E. & Humphrey, R.H. (1995). *Emotion in the workplace*: A reappraisal. Human Relations, 48(2), 97-125.

Association of American Colleges and Universities. (2005). *Global Perspective*. Available from the AACU Web site, www.aacu.org

Association for Quality and Participation (AQP), 1995. "*The Spirit of Working Together*." The 17th Annual Spring Conference and Resource Proceedings. Pages 13- 100 are titled "Inspiring Change."

Avila, A. C.; Edward, A.; Fitzpatrick, T; Williams, C.; and Wohl, J. (2004). *Wal-Mart's Twenty First Century Management Practices*. Graduate team research project presented on March 13th at the Huizenga School of Nova Southeastern University.

Aylesworth, A. B., Goodstein, R. C., & Kalra, A. Effect of archetypal embeds on feelings: An indirect route to affecting attitudes? *Journal of Advertising, 28*(3), 73-81

Badaracco, J. L. (1997). *Defining moments: When managers must choose between right and right.* Boston: Harvard Business School Press.

Badaracco, J.L. (2001). *We Don't Need Another Hero*. Harvard Business Review, 78:8-92.

Babcock, P., (September 2005). A Calling for Change. *HR Magazine*. Pages 46-51.

Barinaga, M. (1992). "Profile of a field: Neuroscience (The pipeline is leaking)." *Science*, 13, March, 255: 1366-1367.

Berney, K. (1988). "Where women are welcome." *Nation's Business*, August: 26R-27R.

Barnett, John H; Weathersby, Rita; Aram, John. (Winter-Spring 1995). American Cultural Values: Shedding Cowboys Ways for Global

Thinking. *Business Forum. Vol. 20*, (n1-2), 9. Retrieved Feb. 8, 2005 from ProQuest database. Bartlett, C.A.,

Baruch, Y., Steele, D.J. & Quantrill, G.A. (2002). Management of expatriation and repatriation for novice global player. *International Journal of Manpower, 23* (7). Retrieved May 12, 2005 from ABI/INFORM Global.

Beck, C. E. (1999). *Managerial Communication/ Building Theory and Practice.* Upper Saddle River, NJ: Prentice Hall. ISBN 0-13-849886-5

Beck, C. E (1985). *The Open Door Policy: Communication Climate and the Military Supervisor.* Retrieved March 31, 2005 from http://www.airpower.maxwell.af.mil/airchronicles/aureview/1985/may-jun/beck.html

Becker, K, PhD. (2000). *Culture and International Business.* Binghamton: International Business Press.

Bennis, Warren. Why Leaders Can't Lead. Jossey-Bass Publishers. See 'ten keys to avoiding disaster during change.

Bennis, W., Parikh, J., & Lessem, R. (1994). *Beyond Leadership: Balancing Economics, Ethics and Ecology.* Cambridge, MA: Blackwell Publishers Inc.

Beyers, C. (1984). "Bridging the gender gap." *Family Computing*, August: 38-41.

Biesada, A. (2004). Wal-Mart Stores, Inc. Hoover's On-Line. Retrieved January 18, 2004 from http://www.hoovers.com/wal-mart/--ID-_11600--/free-co-factsheet.html

Black, S., Morrison, A. & Gregersen, H. (1999). *Global Explorers.* New York & London: Routledge . Pages 6-8

Blanchard, K., Zigarmi, P., and Zigarmi, D., (1985). *Leadership and the One Minute Manager.* Morrow and Company, Inc. New York.

Block, P. (1996). *Stewardship.* San Francisco: Berrett-Koehler.

Block, P. (1993). *Stewardship: Choosing Service over Self-Interest.* San Francisco: Berrett-Koehler Publishers.

Block, P. (1987). *The Empowered Manager: Positive Political Skills at Work.* San Francisco: Jossey-Bass.

Bloom, D. E., Mahal, A., King, D., Henry-Lee, A. & Castillo, P. Globalization, liberalization and sustainable human development: Progress and challenges in Jamaica. UNCTAD/ UNDP Kingston, February 21, 2001.

Blum, L., and Smith, V. (1988). "Women's mobility in the corporation: A critique of the politics of optimism." *Signs, Journal of Women in Culture and Society*, 13(3): 528-545.

Boddewyn, J. J., Toyne, B., & Martinez, Z. L. (2004). The Meaning of "International Management". *Management International Review, 44*(2), 195-212.

Bolino, M.C. & Feldman, D.C. (2000). Increasing the skill utilization of expatriates. *Human Resource Management 39*(4). Retrieved April 21, 2005 from Business Source Premier.

Bolman, L. G. and Deal, T. E. (1995). *Leading with Soul: An Uncommon Journey of the Spirit*. San Francisco: Jossey-Bass.

Bonner, B. (2004, Jan 4). Inner Grove Heights;Minn., Wal-Mart to open despite intense local opposition. *Knight Ridder Tribune Business News*. Retrieved April 8, 2004 from http://www.proquest.umi.com.novacat.nova.edu/

Booher, Dianna (1991). *Executive's Portfolio of Model Speeches for All Occasions*. Prentice Hall. ISBN: 0-13-296989-0.

Borgmann, A. (1993). *Crossing the postmodern divide*. Chicago: University of Chicago Press.

Bornstein, R. F., & Pittman, T. S. (1992). *Perception without awareness*. New York: The Guilford Press

Bowen, D.D. (1985). Were men meant to mentor women? *Training and Development Journal*, 39(2): 31-34.

Brewster, C. (2004). Repatriating valuable expatriates. *European Business Forum*, (19). Retrieved May 10, 2005 from Business Source Premier.

Broome, B. J., De Turk, S., Kristiansdottir, E. S., Kanata, T., & Ganesan, P. (2002). Giving voice to diversity: An interactive approach to conflict management & decision making in culturally diverse Work environments. *Journal of Business and Management*, 8(3), 239-265. Retrieved September 9, 2004 from ProQuest database.

Bryman, A. (1992). *Charisma & Leadership in Organizations*. London: Sage Publications

Buckley, P. J. (1993). The Role of Management in Internationalization Theory. *Management International Review, 33*(3), 197-207.

Buckley, P. J. (1996). The Role of management in International Business Theory: A Meta-Analysis and Integration of the Literature on International Business and International Management. *Management International Review, 36*(1), 7-54.

Bullock, A. (2004). *The secret sales pitch: An overview of subliminal advertising*. San Jose, CA: Norwich.

Buress, J. H. (2004). "The Gender Equity Gap in Top Corporate Executive Positions." *Mid-American Journal of Business*, 19(1): 55-63.

Burke, R.J. (1984). "Mentors in organizations." *Group and Organizational Studies*, 9: 353-372.

Burns, D. J. (1993). Coping with different ethical perceptions in America's increasingly diverse workforce. *Business forum*, 18, 41-44. Retrieved September 9, 2004 from InfoTrac OneFile database.

Business Week, 4/28/03, pp. 69-70.

Business Wire. New York. (Feb 3, 2005). ACLJ Encouraged by President Bush's Remarks on Values Issues in State of Union Address. 1. Retrieved Feb. 8, 2005 from ProQuest database.

Campbell, P.F., and McCabe, G.P. (1984). "Predicting the success of freshmen in a computer science major." *Communications of the ACM*, November, 27(11): 1108-1113.

Canavor, Natalie (2004). "Commentary: Women in Business: Moving ahead, slowly." *Long Island Business News*. Ronkonoma. Jul 9, 2004: 1

Cannon, Walter. B. (1932). *The Wisdom of the Body*. W.W. Norton, New York.

Cant, A.G. (Sep 2004). Internationalizing the Business Curriculum: Developing Intercultural Competence. *Journal of American Academy of Business. Vol.5*, (iss1/2), 177. Retrieved Feb. 6, 2005 from ProQuest databaseCavico, F., & Mujtaba, B., (2005). *Business ethics: Transcending requirements through moral leadership.* Boston: Pearson Custom Publications.

Capra, F. (1996/7). *The web of life*. New York: Doubleday.

Cavico, F. & Mujtaba, B., (January 2005). *Business Ethics: Transcending Requirements through Moral Leadership.* Pearson Custom Publications. U.S.A. ISBN: 0-536-85783-0. Web address: http://www.pearsoncustom.com/best/0536857830.html# .

Cavico, F. & Mujtaba, B. (2004). *Machiavellian Values "The Prince": Bullying, Begulling, Backstabbing, and Bargaining in the Twenty First Century Management.* The Association on Employment Practices and Principles (AEPP) Proceedings.

Cavusgul, S. & P. N. Ghauri. (1990). *Doing Business in Developing countries: Entry and negotiation strategies.* London; New York : Routledge.

Capozzoli, T. K. (1999, November). Conflict resolution–a key ingredient in successful teams. *Supervision, 60*(11), 14. Retrieved September 10, 2004 from EBSCO database.

Carr-Stewart, S., & Walker, K. (2003). *Learning leadership through Appreciative Inquiry.*

Challenger, John A. (1999). "Future Looking Brighter for Women in Workplace." *Daily News* [Valley Edition], Los Angeles, CA.: Jun 14, 1999, p. 15.

ChangingMinds.org, (2005). *Trompenaars' and Hampden-Turner cultural factors*. Retrieved on May 4, 2005 from the following URL: http://changingminds.org/explanations/culture/trompenaars_culture.htm

Checkland, P. & Scholes, J. (1999). *Soft systems methodology in action*. New York: Wiley.

Checkland, P. (1999). *Systems Thinking, Systems Practice: A 30-Year Retrospective*. New York, NY: John Wiley & Sons, Inc.

Chopra, D. (1993). The seven spiritual laws of success. San Rafael: Amber-Allen Publishing and New World Library.

Chopra, S., & Sodhi M., S. (2004). Managing risk to avoid supply-chain breakdown. *MIT Sloan Management Review, 46*(1), 53-61. Retrieved February 19, 2005, from EBSCOhost database.

Chuvala, B. (2001). Small business faces big challenges. *Fairfield County Business Journal, 40*(43), 19. Retrieved February 19, 2005, from EBSCOhost database.

Cohen, R. *Negotiating Across Cultures: Communication Obstacles in International Diplomacy*. Retrieved on May 5, 2005 from the following URL: http://www.colorado.edu/conflict/peace/example/cohe7517.htm

Collins. J.C. (2001). *Good to great: Why some companies make the leap...and others don't*. New York: Harper Collins.

Collis, B. (1985). "Psychosocial implications of sex differences in attitudes toward computers: Results of a survey." *International Journal of Women's Studies*, 8(3): 207-213.

Complaints, (2004). Number of complaints suggest Wal-Mart disrespects worker's, laws. (January 17). *St. Louis Post*. Retrieved April 1, 2004 from Nova Southeastern's ProQuest database.

Conflict Management skills. Retrieved Feb. 3, 2002 from: www.extension.unr.edu/CommDevBrd/CFLTMGMT.htm

Conflict Management Technique. Retrieved Jan. 31, 2002 from: www.col-ed.org/cur/misc/misc 33.txt.

Conflict Resolution Basics. Retrieved Feb.13, 2002 from: http://www.ivysea.com/pages/ct1297_2.html

Conner, Daryl R., 1992. *Managing at the speed of change: how resilient managers succeed and prosper where others fail*. Villard Books. New York.

Connor, P. E., Becker, B. W., Kakuyama, Y. (1993). A cross-national comparative study of managerial values: United States, Canada and Japan. Advances in International Comparative Studies, 8, 3-11.

Cooper, J., Hall, J., and Huff, C. (1990). "Situational stress as a consequence of sex-stereotyped software." *Personality and Social Psychology Bulletin*, 16(3): 419-429.

Cox Jr., T. (1994). *Cultural Diversity in Organizations: Theory, Research and Practice*. San Francisco: Berrett-Koehler.

Cox, T.H., Lobel, S.A., McLeod, P.L. (1991) *"Effects of Ethnic Group Cultural Differences on Cooperative and Competitive Behavior on a Group Task."* Academy of Management Journal. 34,4 827-847

Covey, S. R. (1995). *Principle-centered leadership*. New York: Simon & Schuster.

Crum, T. F., (1987). *The Magic of Conflict: Turning a Life of Work into a Work of Art*. Touchstone; Simon and Schuster.

Culpan, R. (2002). *Global Business Alliances*. London: Quorum Books.

Czinkota, M.R., Tonkainen, I.A., Moffett, M.H. (2005). *International Business* (7th Edition). Mason, Ohio: South-Western/Thomson Corporation.

Czinkota M., & Knight, G. (2005). Managing the terrorist threat. *European Business Forum. Issue 20*, 42-45. Retrieved February 19, 2005, from EBSCOhost database.

Dalton, M., Ernest, C., Deal, J., & Leslie, J. (2002). *Success for the New Global Manager: What You Need to Know to Work Across Distances, Countries, and Cultures*. San Francisco: Jossey-Bass, A Wiley Company.

Danon-Leva, E. (2005). Global Managers in the Age of Globalization. *Global Business and Economics Review, 7*(1), 16-24.

Dastoor, B.; Roofe, E.; and Mujtaba, B., (March 2005). Value Orientation of Jamaicans Compared to Students in the United States of America. *International Business and Economics Research Journal*, Volume 4, Number 3. Pages 43-52.

David, P. (2003). *National Jeweler*; Vol. 97 Issue 7, p30, 2/3p. Retrieved February 14, 2005 from the Business Source Premier database.

Davidson, Jeff (1997). *The Complete Idiot's Guide to Managing Stress*. Alpha Books. New York, NY.

D'Eugenio, D. P., (August 2005). *Transitional and Change Management: Assessment Application and Achievement*. Lecture Series Guest speaker at Nova Southeastern University on August 10, 2005.

Deems, Richard S., (1995). *Making Change Work for You: How to Handle Organizational Change.* American Media Publishing. American Media Incorporated.

Dessler, Gary (2001). *A Framework for Human Resource Management.* 2nd edition. Prentice Hall.

Devito, Joseph A. (1993). *Essentials of Human Communication.* Harper Collins college Publishers, New York.

DeGeorge, R. T. (1993). *Competing with Integrity.* Oxford: Oxford University Press.

Demby, E. R. (2004). *Two stores refuse to join the race to the bottom for benefits and wages. Workforce Management.* (February 2004). Pages 57-59.

Department of Advertising, the University of Texas at Austin. Advertising Laws and Ethics. Overview. Retrieved September 17, 2002, from the World Wide Web, MSN Search Engine.

De Pree, M. (1992). *Leadership Jazz.* New York: Currency Doubleday.

De Pree, M. (1989). *Leadership Is an Art.* New York: Doubleday.

DiDomenico, N. & Mujtaba, B. (October 2004). *Tempered Radicals: The Leadership Style for Making Changes Quietly.* The Association on Employment Practices and Principles. Published in the AEPP Proceedings, Pages 86-91.

D'Innocenzio, A. (2003, September 21). *Wal-Mart suppliers flocking to Arkansas. The State and wire service sources.* Retrieved February 20, 2004 from http://retailindustry.

Disaster Management: Calm in a crisis (2004). *The Lawyer.* Pg 19.

Discipline without Punishment. A CRM Learning Video. 2215 Faraday Avenue. Phone: (800) 421-0833. Also made available by the Performance Systems Corporation: The Walk the Talk Company. Retrieved on 10, 06, 2005 from: http://www.crmlearning.com/product.cwa?isbn=111472V

Doing business in dangerous places. (2004). *Economist. 372*(8388), 11. Retrieved February 19, 2005, from EBSCOhost database.

Donaldson, T., and Gini, A. R. (1994). *Case Studies in Business Ethics.* Englewood Cliffs, NJ: Prentice Hall.

Donaldson, T., and Werhane, P. H. (Eds.) (1996). *Ethical Issues in Business: A Philosophical Approach.* Upper Saddle River, NJ: Prentice Hall.

Dorfman, P. W., Howell, J. P. (1998). Dimensions of national culture and effective leadership patterns: Hofstede revisited. In R.N. Farmer & E.C. McGoun (Eds.), Advances in International Comparative Management, 3, 127-150.

Dougherty, L. (2004). Immigration to America. Retrieved November 23, 2004, from Northwest High School Library Media Center Web Site: http://www.kn.pacbell.com/wired/fil/pages/ listimmigratli.html.

Dowling, P.J., Welch, D.E. (2005). *International Human Resource Management: Managing People in a Multinational Context (4th Ed.)* Italy: Thomsom South-Western.

Downes, A (2003). *Productivity and competitiveness in the Jamaican economy.* Prepared for the Inter American Development Bank, Washington DC, USA.

Doz, Y. L., & Prahalad, C. K. (1991). Managing DMNCs: A Search for a New Paradigm. *Strategic Management Journal, 12,* 145-164.

Drucker, P. (2005). Sell the Mailroom. *Wall Street Journal,* Page B2; November 15, 2005. Originally published on July 25, 1989.

Duke's Fuqua School of Business. *Management Communication.* Retrieved on June 6, 2005 from the following URL: http:///www.fuqua.duke.edu/faculty/areas/manageme…/managem ent_communication_area.htm

Duxbury, L., & Mills, S. (1989). The electronic briefcase and work-family conflict: An analysis by gender. *ICIS Proceedings.*

Dworkin, G. Paternalism. *The Stanford Encyclopedia of Philosophy,* Winter 2002 ed., Edward N. Zalta (ed.). Retrieved on November 11, 2003 from http://plato.stanford.Edu/archives/win2002/entries/paternalism/ perspective. Journal of Economic Issues, 34, (2) 393-401.

Ecevit, Y, Gündüz-Hosgör, A, and Ceylan Tokluoglu (2003). "Professional women in computer programming occupations: The case of Turkey." *Career Development International,* 8(2): 88-98.

Edstrom, KRS, (1993). *Conquering Stress: The Skills You Need to Succeed in the Business World.* USA, Barron's: A Business Success Guide.

Elashmawi, F. & Harris, P. R. (1993). *Multicultural Management.* Houston: Gulf Publishing.

Ellis, Albert; Harper, Robert (1975). *A Guide to Rational Living.* N. Hollywood: Melvin Powers, Wilshire Book Company.

Ellis, Albert; Harper, Robert (1979). *A New guide to Rational Living.* Prentice Wall, Englewood Cliffs, N.J.

Ely, R. J., & Thomas, D. A. (2001). Cultural Diversity at Work: The Effects of Diversity Perspectives on Work Group Processes and Outcomes. *Administrative Science Quarterly* 46(2): 229-73.

Evans, Jennifer (2000). "Women Under-Represented in IT Industry." *Canadian HR Reporter.* Toronto: Mar 13, (13)5: 10.

Eysenck, Hans. J. (1988). Health's Character. *Psychology Today.* Pgs. 28-35.

Everard K.B and Morris, Geoffrey (1996*), Effective School Management.* London

False Advertising. Retrieved September 17, 2004 from the World Wide Web. MSN Search Engine. www.wpcu.com.

Fatehi, Kamal, 1996. International Management: A cross-cultural and functional perspective. A Prentice Hall publication.

Federal Trade Commission's Website. Corrective Advertising. Retrieved September 18, 2002 from the World Wide Web. MSN Search Engine. www.ftc.gov.

Fernandez, J.P. (1993). *The Diversity Advantage: How American Business Can Out-Perform Japanese and European Companies in the Global Marketplace.* New York: Lexinton Books.

Fishman, C. (1999). This is a Marketing Revolution. *Fast Company.* May/June pp. 204

Friedman, M. (1970). "The social responsibility of business is to increase its profits". In Hoffman W. and Moore J. (1990), *"Business ethics, readings and cases in corporate morality*: 153-157. NY: McGraw-Hill.

Fishman, C. (2003). The Wal-Mart you don't know. *Fast Company,* (77). Retrieved March 30, 2004 from http://fastcompany.com/magazine/77/walmart.html.

Foldy, E.G. (n.d.), (2004). Learning from Diversity: A Theoretical Exploration. Retrieved September 11, 2004, from from EBSCO database.

Frenkel, Karen A (1990). "Women & Computing." *Association for Computing Machinery: Communication of the ACM,* 33(11): p. 34.

Frazee, V. (1997). Welcome your repatriates home. *Workforce, 76*(4). Retrieved June 2, 2005 from General BusinessFile Internat'l.

Freud, S. (1950). *Collected Papers.* (Ed.), edited by Jones, E. New York.

Friedman Jack P., (2000). Dictionary of Business Terms. 3rd Edition. (New York: Barron's Educational Series).

Friedman, M; Rosenman, R. (1974). *Type A Behavior and your Heart.* Fancett, Greenwich, Conn.

FTC Charges "Miss Cleo" with Deceptive Advertising, Billing and Collection Practices: (FTC File No. 012 3084) Civil Action No.: 02-60226 CIV GOLD. Retrieved September 28, 2004 from the World Wide Web. www.ftc.gov/opa/2002/02

Gable, W., & Ellig, J. (1993). Introduction to Market Based Management. Fairfax, VA: Center for Market Process.

Gale Group (1999, Oct). Associates keystone to structure (Wal-Mart). Retrieved March 19, 2004 from http://www.findarticles.com/cf_dls/m3092/1999_Oct/57578936/print.html.

Gardiner, L. Rubbens, C. Bonfiglioli, E. (2003). Big Business, Big Responsibility. *Corporate Governance, 3, 3, 67-77.* Retrieved May 20, 2005 from ABI/INFROM Complete.

Gates, S. & Budman, M. (1996). Managing expatriates' expectations. *Across the Board, 33*(7). Retrieved May 10, 2005 from Business Source Premier.

Gazso, Amber (2004). "Women's Inequality in the Workplace as Framed in News Discourse: Refracting from Gender Ideology." *The Canadian Review of Sociology and Anthropology*, 41(4): 449-474.

Geller, Judith B. (1994). *A Manager's Guide to Human Behavior.* Fourth edition. American Management Association.

Gender Relations in Educational Applications of Technology (GREAT). (16 March 1998). "Special Issue: The Effect of Computers on the Gender Gap in Education—Gender Inequalities in Education: What's Been Done." Available from the Stanford University Web site, www.stanford.edu

Ghoshal, S., and Birkenshaw, J. (2004). *Transnational Management: Text, Cases and Readings in Cross-Border Management* (4th Edition). New York: McGraw/Irwin.

Gibson, J; Ivancevich, J.M. Donnelly J.H. Jr. Konopaske, R. (2005). *Organizations: Behavior, Structure, Processes.* McGRaw-Hill/Irwin-12th edition, New York, N.Y.

Gibson, Jane (1995). *The supervisory Challenge* (2nd. Ed.). Prentice-Hall.

Gibson, Jane (1991). *Organizational Communications*: A Managerial Perspective, 2nd edition. Harper Collins.

Gibson, Jane (1985). *Reading and Exercises in Organizational Behavior.* Academic PressGirlando, A., P. (1998) A study of the influence of national culture on Russian students in the US.

Greenberg J.S. (1993). *Comprehensive Stress Management.* Brown & Benchmark, Dubuque, IA.

Gregersen, H.B. & Stewart Black, J. (1996). Multiple commitments upon repatriation: the Japanese experience. *Journal of Management, 22*(2). Retrieved June 2, 2005 from General BusinessFile Internat'l.

Greiner, Lynn (2004). "Canadian Software Developers: Girls Just Wanna Write Code." *Computer Dealer News*. Willowdale: Jan 16, 20(1): p.18.

Griest, G. (2004, Jan). *Kmart Posts $250 Million Profit, 13.5 Percent Drop in Sales*. Retrieved March 29, 2004, from http://0-proquest.umi.com.novacat.nova.edu/ pqweb?index+13&sis= 1&srchmode=1&vins.

Gries, D., and Marsh, D. (1992). "The 1989-90 Taulbee survey." *Communications of the ACM*, January, 35(1): 133-143.

Griffith, R.W. & Pustay. (2003). *International Business (4th Ed.)*. New Jersey: Pearson Prentice Hall

Gorritz, C. M. & Medina, C. (2000). Engaging girls with computers through software games. *Commun. ACM* 43(1), p. 42. Available from the ACM Digital Library Web site, www.acm.org

Guillory, W. A., & Guillory, D. (2004). The Roadmap to Diversity, Inclusion, and High Performance; Healthcare Executive, Jul/Aug2004, Vol. 19 Issue 4, p24, 6p; Retrieved September 11, 2004 from EBSCO database.

Guy, V., & Mattock, J. (1995). *The International Business Book: All the Tools, Tactics, and Tips you need for doing Business across Cultures*. Lincolnwood: NTC Business Books.

Hacker, A (2003). *Mismatch: The Growing Gulf Between Men and Women*. New York, NY: Scribner.

Hafkin, N. & Taggart, N. *Gender, Information Technology, and Developing Countries: An Analytic Study*. Available from the Office of Women in Development, U. S. Agency for International Development Web site, pdf.dec.org

Hage, J., & Powers, C. H. (1992). *Post industrial lives: Roles and relationships in the 21st century*. Newbury Park, CA: Sage.

Higgins, C., Duxbury, L., and K.L. Johnson (2000). "Part-time work for women: Does it really help balance work and family?" *Human Resource Management*, 39(1): 17-32.

Higgins, C., Duxbury, L, and Catherine Lee (1994). "Impact of life-cycle stage and gender on the ability to balance work and family responsibilities." *Family Relations*, 43(2): 144-151.

Hambrick, D. C., Canney D. S., Snell, S. A. & Snow, C, C., (1998). When groups consist of multiple nationalities: towards a new understanding of the implications. Organizational studies, 19, 181-205

Hall, E. T. and Hall, M. R., (1987). *Understanding Cultural Differences*. Intercultural Press, Inc. USA.

Harris, P. R., Moran, R. T., & Moran, S. V. (2004). *Managing Cultural Differences: Global Leadership Strategies for the 21st Century* (6th ed). Burlington: Elsevier Butterworth-Heinemann

Hartman, L. (2001). *Perspectives in Business Ethics*. U.S. of America: The McGraw – Hill Companies, Inc.

Hatcher, T. (2003). Ethical compass. Executive Excellence. Provo: July 2003. 20 (7), 19. Retrieved September 22, 2004 from ProQuest database.

Henke, H. (1999). Jamaica's decision to pursue a Neoliberal development strategy: realignment in the state-business – class triangle. Latin American Perspectives 108, (26) 7-33.

Herald, 1/11/03, 4/24/03, pp. 1C, 3C, 4/28/03, p. 8B, 6/27/03, 9/13/03, pp. 1C, 2C.

Herbig, P. (2005). *Cross Cultural Negotiations Lecture 2. The Importance of Thinking Global*ly. Tri-State University. Retrieved on June 4, 2005 from the following URL:
http://www.tristate.edu/faculty/hergig/pahccn2.htm

_____, P. Cross *Cultural Negotiations Lecture 3. 'The Incredible Shrinking World'*. Tri-State University. Retrieved on May 4, 2005 from the following URL:
http://www.tristate.edu/faculty/hergig/pahccn3.htm

_____, P. Cross Cultural Negotiations Lecture 5: '*How to Succeed in negotiations without really trying*. Tri-State University. Retrieved on May 4, 2005 from the following URL:
http://www.tristate.edu/faculty/hergig/pahccn5.htm

_____, P. *Cross Cultural Negotiations Lecture 12: 'How do we agree? Let me count the ways.'* Tri-State University. Retrieved May 4, 2005from the following URL:
http://www.tristate.edu/faculty/hergig/pahccn12.htm.

Hersey, Paul and Campbell, Ron (2004). *Leadership: A Behavioral Science Approach.* ISBN: 0-931619-09-2.

_____, P. and Campbell, R., (2004). *Leadership: A Behavioral Science Approach* (Learning Journal). ISBN: 0-931619-10-6.

_____, P. (July 2004). *Personal Communication on Situational Leadership*. One-week workshop by Dr. Hersey and facilitators of 'The Center for Leadership Studies." Escondido, CA. July 11-18. Phone: (760) 741-6595.

_____, P.; Blanchard, K.; and Johnson, D., (2001). *Management of Organizational Behavior*. Eight edition. Prentice Hall. ISBN: 013-032518X.

_____, P. (1984 & 1997). *The Situational Leader*. Escondido, CA. The Center for Leadership Studies. ISBN: 0-931619-01-7. Phone: (760) 741-6595.

Hill, S.E.K., Bahniuk, M.H., and Dobbs, J. (1989). "The impact of mentoring and collegial support on faculty success: An analysis of support behavior, information adequacy, and communication apprehension." *Communication Education*, 38: 15-33.

Hodgetts, R. M., & Luthans, F. (2003). *International Management: Culture, Strategy, and Behavior* (5th ed.). New York: McGraw-Hill/Irwin.

Hoecklin, L (1995). Managing cultural differences: strategies for competitive advantages. New York: Addison – Wesley Publishing.

Hoffman, J., J. (1998). Evaluating international ethical climates: A goal-programming model. Journal of Business ethics, 17, 1861-1869.

Hofstede, G. (2003). *Geert Hofstede Cultural Dimensions*. Retrieved on October 9th 2004 from ITIM website http:// geert-hofstede.com/hofstede_united_states.shtml

_____, G. (2001). Culture's consequences: Comparing values, behaviors, institutions across nations. London: Sage

_____, G. (2001). *Culture's Consequences: comparing values, behaviors, institutions across nations*. London: Sage.

_____, G. (1997). Cultures and organization: Software of the mind. London: McGraw Hill.

_____, G. (1994). *Cultures and Organization: Software of the Mind*. London: McGraw Hill.

_____, G. (1993). Cultural constraints in management theories. *Academy of Management Executive, 7* (1) 81-90.

_____, G. (1983). The cultural relativity of organizational practices and theories. *Journal of International Business Studies, 14*, 75-89.

_____,G. (1980). *Culture's Consequences: international differences in work related values*. California: Sage Publications.

_____, G. (1994). Management scientists are human. *Management Science, 40*, 4-13.

_____, G., Van Deusen, C.A., Mueller, C.B., & Charles, T.A. (2002). What goals do business leaders pursue? A study in fifteen countries. *Journal of International Business Studies, 33(*4), 785-803.

_____, G., Neuijen, B., Ohayv, D.D, & Sander, G. (1990). Measuring organizational cultures: a qualitative and quantitative study across 20 cases. *Administrative Science Quarterly*, 35, 286-316.

Holder, W. (2002). "*Why Change Efforts Fail*." Refresher Publications, Inc.

Holmes, Thomas. H; Rahe, Richard, H. (1907). The Social Readjustment Rating Scale. *Journal of Psychosomatic Research.* 11:213-18.

Holt, D. H., Ralston, D. & Terpstra, R., H., (1994). Constraints on capitalism in Russia:
The managerial psyche. California Management Review, 124-141.

Holton, Bil and Cher, (1992). The Manager's Short Course. John Wiley & Sons. See the section on welcoming change.

Hosmer, L. R. (1996). *The ethics of management* (3rd ed.). Boston: Irwin/McGraw-Hill.

Hunt, D.M., and Michael, C. (1983). "Mentorship: A career development training tool." *Academy of Management Review*, 8: 475-485.

Hutinger, P. L. (1996). Computer applications in programs for young children with disabilities: recurring themes. *Focus on Autism and Other Developmental Disabilities*, 11(2), 105-124.

Impact Factory. *Communication Skills.* Retrieved on June 6, 2005 from the following URL:
http://www.impactfactory.com/p/effective.communication_skills.html

International Congress on Stress. Retrieved on October 12, 2005 from: http://www.sterss.org/cong.htm

Jamieson, D. & O'Mara, J. (1991*). Managing Workforce 2000: Gaining the Diversity Advantage*. San Francisco: Jossey-Bass.

Jassawalla, A., Connelly, T. & Slojkowski, L. (2004). Issue of Effective Repatriation: A Model and Mansgerial Implications. *S.A.M. Advanced Management Journal, 69*(2). Retrieved May 12, 2005 from ABI/INFORM Global.

Jelinek, M., and Adler, N. (1988). "Women: World class managers for global competition." *Academy of Management Executive*, 2(1).

Johanson, J., & Vahlne, J. (1977). The Internationalization Process of the Firm-A Model of Knowledge Development and Increasing Foreign Market Commitments. *Journal of International Business Studies, 8*(1), 23-32.

Johnson, G., & Leavitt, W. (2001). Building on Success: Transforming Organizations through an

Johnson, Bill & Weinstein, Art (2004). *Superior Customer Value in the New Economy: Concepts and Cases*. Boca Raton, FL; CRC Press LLC.

Johnson, M. (1990a). "Women under glass (women in information management)." *Computerworld*, December 3, 49(24): 3.

Johnson, M. (1990). "The feminine technique in IS; women in IS management carry distinctive personal skills." *Computerworld*, December 10, 50(24): 95-96.

Jones, G & George J. (2003). *Contemporary Management* (3rd ed.) New York: McGraw-Hill Irwin.

Jones, G. R., George, J. M. & Hill, C. W. L. (2000). *Contemporary Management*. Boston: Irwin McGraw-Hill.

Judson, Arnold (1991). *Changing Behavior in Organizations: Minimizing resistance to Change*.

Judy, R., & D'Amico, C. (1997). Workforce 2020: Work and workers in the 21" century. Indianapolis, IN: Hudson Institute.

Jue, A. L. (2004). *Towards a taxonomy of spirit-centered leadership as reflected in phenomenological experiences of entrepreneurial leaders*. Doctoral dissertation, University of Phoenix.

Jue, A. L., & Mujtaba, B. (2004a, October). *The new arena of spirit-centered leadership: An ethical bridge to the future.* Proceedings of the Association of Employment Principles and Practices 12th Annual International Conference, Ft. Lauderdale Beach, FL, October 7-9.

Jue, A. L., & Mujtaba, B. (2004b, October). *The practice of spirit-centered leadership: Empirical applications.* Proceedings of the Association of Employment Principles and Practices 12th Annual International Conference, Ft. Lauderdale Beach, FL, October 7-9.

Juran, Joseph M. (1989). Juran on Leadership for Quality. Macmillan Inc. See "Rules of the Road" for Handling Resistance In the Work Place.

Kaiser, E. (2004, Jan 27). U.S retailers give Wal-Mart a head start on RFID. *USA TODAY.* Retrieved April 1, 2004 from http://www.usatoday.com/tech/news/ techinnovations/2004-01-27-walmart-pioneers-rfid_x.htm.

Kalakota and Robinson (2003, Aug). From e-Business to Services: Why and Why Now? Retrieved April5, 2004 from http://www.informit.com/isapi/product.

Kanter, R.M. (1977). *Men and Women of the Corporation*. New York: Basis Books.

Karahalios, M. (2005). A Computer-based Nutritional Intervention to Teach Adolescents with Autism How to Make Healthier Food Choices. Unpublished dissertation proposal.

Kasamatsu, A; Hirai, T (1966). *Studies of EEG's of Expert Zen Mediators*. Folia Psychiatric Neurological Japonica 28:315.

Keirsey, David (2002). *The Four Temperaments*. Advisor Team: Harness the Power of Personality. Retrieved on February 13, 2002 from: www.col-ed.org/cur/misc/misc 33.txt.

Kennelly, J. J., & Lewis, E. E. (2002). Degree of Internationalization and Corporate Environmental Performance: Is there a Link? *International Journal of Management, 19*(3), 478-488.

Kent, S., (September 2005). Happy Workers Are the Best Workers. *Wall Street Journal,* September 6, 2005, p A20.

Kheng, L.G (1990). "WIT: The Singaporan Way." *The Computer Bulletin,* 2(1): 18-20.

Kieran-Greenbush, S. (1991). Respecting diversity: designing from a feminine perspective *Proceedings of the 19th ACM SIGUCCS Conference on User Services,* pp. 171 – 175. Available from the ACM Digital Library Web site, www.acm.org

Kiger, P. J. (2004) Workforce Management: 83 (12) pg 30.

Kim, Kwanghyun (November 2005). The Effects of Self-Monitoring on Expatriate Job Satisfaction. Presented at the *Southern Management Association Conference,* November 11, 05; Charleston, SC.

Kim, C. W. and Mauborgne, R. (August 1997). Fair Process: Managing in the Knowledge Economy. *Harvard Business Review.* Pages 65-66.

Kimura, G. H., Khandelwal, S., Zucker, H., & Greenfield, J. (2004). Using innovative technology for the health education of Afghan women and families. Presented at the Public Health and the Environment Conference, November 6-10, 2004. Available from the APHA Web site, apha.confex.com

Klaff, L.G. (2002) The Right Way to Bring Expats Home. *Workforce, 81* (7). Retrieved May 10, 2005 from Business Source Premier.

Kmart Corporation (2004). Hoover's Company Information. Retrieved March 19, 2004 from http://cobrands.hoovers.com/global/cobrands/proquest/factsheet. xhtml?COID= 10830.

Kmart Corporation (2004). About Kmart. Retrieved April 3, 2004 from http://www.kmartcorp.com/corp/.

Kobrin, S.J. (2005). Technological Determinism, Globalization and the Multinational Firm. In Buckley, P.J. (Ed.), *What is International Business?* (pp. 39-56). Great Britain: Palgrave McMillan.

Koch, Charles G. (1993). Introduction to Market-Based Management. Center for Market Processes

Koch, M. (1994). No girls allowed. *Technos* 3(3), pp. 14-19.

Kolata, G. (1984). "Equal time for women." *Discover,* January: 24-27.

Kooskora, M. (2001). Ethical Aspects of Decision Making. Master Thesis (EBS, Tallinn), 49-51

Kotler, P. (1997) *Marketing Management: Analysis, Planning, Implementation, and Control* (9th ed.). Englewood Cliffs, NJ: Prentice Hall.

Kotler, P., Armstrong, G. (1990). *Marketing: An Introduction* (2nd ed.) Englewood Cliffs, NJ: Prentice Hall.

Kotter, John P., 1990. A force for change: How leadership differs from management. Free Press publication.

Kotter, John P. and Schlesinger, Leonard H.(1979). Choosing Strategies for Change. *HBR*, Page 111. March/April issue.

Kram, K.E. (1985). *Mentoring at work.* Glenview, IL: Scott, Foresman and Co.

Krass, P. (1990). "Chief of the Year: Kathy Hudson." *Information Week*, December 24, 301(4): 40.

Kreitner, R. & Kinicki, A. (2003). Organizational Behavior (6th ed.). The McGraw-Hill Companies. Retrieved September 30, 2004, from Publisher Web site: http://www.mhhe.com/kreitner.

Kreuter, Eric A. (1993). Why Career Plateaus are Healthy (CPA in Industry). Retrieved September 10th 2004 from http://www.nysscpa.org/cpajournal/old/14522934.htm

Laukaran VH, Winikoff B, Myers D. (1986). The impact of health services on breastfeeding: common themes from developed and developing worlds. In: Jeliffe A, Jeliffe E, eds. *Advances in International Maternal and Child Health.* 121-128.

Lazarus, Richard. S. (1966). *Psychological Stress and the Coping Process.* McGraw-Hill Book Co, New York.

Lazarus, Richards (1984). Puzzles in the Study of Daily Hassles. *Journal of Behavioral Medicine* 7: 375-389.

Lazarova, M. & Caligiuri, P. (2001). Retaining Repatriates: The Role of Organizations Support Practices. *Journal of World Business 36*(4). Retrieved May 10, 2005 from EBSCOHost

LeBaron, M, (2005) *Culture-Based Negotiation Styles.* Beyond Intractability.org. Retrieved on May 4, 2005 from the following URL: http://www.beyondintractability.org/m/culture_negotiation.jsp?nid

Leininger M. (1985). Transcultural care diversity and universality: a theory of nursing. *Nurse and Health Care.* 6:209-212.

Lewis, M (2002). The Last Taboo. *Fortune*, October 28, pp. 137-44.

Lodge, G. C. and Vogel, E. F. (1987). *Ideology and National Competitiveness: An Analysis of Nine Countries.* Harvard Business School.

Lord, J. (1998). The Quote Center. Retrieved October 1, 2004, from Web site: http://www.appreciative-inquiry.org/AI-Quotes.htm.

Lundin, S. C., Paul, H., & Christensen, J. (2000). *Fish!* New York: Hyperion.

Macoby. (Jan/Feb 2005). Creating Moral Organizations. *Research Technology Management. Vol.48*, (iss.1), 59. Retrieved Feb. 6, 2005 from ProQuest database Madsen, T. G. (2001). *Five Classics*. Salt Lake City, UT: Eagle Gate.

Magnotta, L.; and Mujtaba, B., (2004). *Integrating Effective Training Techniques when Developing and Educating Diverse Adults in the Twenty First Century Workforce*. The Association on Employment Practices and Principles. AEPP Proceedings, Pages 162-168.

Maigman, I., Ralston, D. (2002). Corporate Social Responsibility in Europe and the U.S.: Insights from Businesses' Self-presentations. *Journal of International Business Studies*, 33, 3, 497-514. Retrieved May 20, 2005 from ABI/INFROM Complete.

Management in Education, 17(2), 9. Retrieved September 30, 2004, from EBSCOhost database.

Markham, Ursula (1993*) How to Deal With Difficult People*, Thorsons, London

Marquardt, M. & Berger, N. (2000). *Global Leaders for the 21st Century*. Albany, New York: State University of New York Press. Pages 1-32 & 175-189

Mattock, John. (Ed.). (2003). *Cross Cultural Communication; the essentials guide to international business.* (New rev. ed 2.). London ; Sterling, VA.

Maultsby, Maxie (1984). *Rational Behavior Therapy*. Prentice-Hall, Inc. Englewood Cliffs, N.J.

Mayer, J.D. & Salovey, P. (1993). *The intelligence of emotional intelligence. Intelligence.* 17, 433-442.

McCartney, T; Neville, M. (1998). The Therapeutic Learning Process as Effective Modality in Coping with Addictions. *OD intervention*, Bahamas Oil Refining Corporation, Freeport, Grand Bahamas.

McCartney, T. (2006). *The Professional Development Process in Managing Self, Others and Organizations.* Unpublished Manuscript, Ft. Lauderdale, Florida.

McShane, S. L., & Von Glinow, M. A. (2003). Organization Behavior: Emerging Realities for the Workplace Revolution (2nd ed.). The McGraw-Hill Companies. Retrieved September 30, 2004, from Publisher Web site: http://www.mhhe.com/mcshane2e.

Mead, R. (2005). *International Management: Cross-Cultural Dimensions (3rd Ed.).* Malden, Massachusetts: Blackwell Publishing.

Mead, R. (2005). *International Management: Cross-Cultural Dimensions (3rd Ed.)*. Malden, Massachusetts: Blackwell Publishing.

Melymuka, Kathleen (2003). "Glass Ceiling: Barrier or Challenge?" *Computerworld*, Mar 4, 2003, 36(10): 36.

Mendenhall, M., Kuhlmann, T. & Stahl, G. (2001). *Developing Global Business Leaders: Policies, Processes, and Innovations.* Pages 2-16, 54-55, & 75-80.

Mendenhall, M.E. & Stahl, G.K. (2000). Expatriate Training and Development: Where do we go from here? *Human Resource Management, 39(2, 3)*. Retrieved April 21, 2005 from Wiley Interscience Database.

Metzger, Michael B, Mallor, Jane P., Barnes, A, James, Bowers, Thomas, and Phillips, Michael, J., (1989). Business Law and The Regulatory Environment. 7th Edition. (Illinois: Irwin).

Meyerson, D. (2001). *Radical Change, the Quiet Way*. Harvard Business Review, 79:9-92.

Milkovich, George T. & Boudreau, John W. (1991). Human Resource Management (6th ed.). IRWIN. Homewood, IL 60430

Mincer, J. (2001). "Survey Finds Sex Discrimination in High-tech Jobs." *Kansas City Star.* June 6: C.1

Mitroff, Ian I., (2005). *Why Some Companies Emerge Stronger and Better from a Crisis: Seven Essential Lessons for Surviving Disaster*. AMACOM.

Mohebbi, Rayka; Derlatka, Karen; Watson, Lweis; and Suskind, Raphael, (2004). *Cultural and Ethical Conflicts in the Workplace: How to Control and Minimize Them*. Project submitted for "Managerial Communication and Ethics." October 6th 2004.

Molloy, M. (1991). "Women still face hurdles within networking arena: Execs offer advice on scaling corporate ladder." *Network World,* February 18, 7(8): 29.

Moncur, Michael. (1994-2004). The Quotations Page. Retrieved Feb 6, 2005, from www.thequotationspage.com.

Moore, S. (2004, Feb 18). Beaumont, California approves Wal-Mart; Critics say small businesses will suffer. *Knight Ridder Tribune Business news.* Retrieved April 11, 2004 from Nova Southeastern's ProQuest database http://0-proquest.umi.com.

Mujtaba, G. Bahaudin (2006). *Privatization and Market-Based Leadership in Developing Economies: Capacity Building in Afghanistan*. Llumina Press and Publications, Tamarac, Florida. ISBN: 1-59526-551-1. Website: www.Llumina.com

Mujtaba, G. B. (2006). *The Art of Mentoring Diverse Professionals: Employee development and retention practices for entrepreneurs and multinational corporations.* ISBN: 1-59427-052-X. Aglob Publishing Inc. Hollandale, Florida USA.

_____ (2005). *AFGHANISTAN: Realities of War and Rebuilding.* Aglob Publishing Inc. Hollandale, Florida USA.

_____ (2005). *The Ethics of Management and Situational Leadership in Afghanistan.* AGLOB Publishing Inc. ISBN: 1-59427-047-3. Fort Lauderdale, Florida USA. Website: www.aglobpublishing.com.

_____ and Jue, Arthur (February 2005). Deceptive and Subliminal Advertising in Corporate America: Value Adder or Value Destroyer. *Journal of Applied Management and Entrepreneurship* (JAME), Vol 10, Num 1.

_____ and Traylor, K. (2003). The "Bait and Switch" Strategy: Value Adder or Destroyer! Society for Advancement of Management (SAM) International Conference Proceedings on *"Trust, responsibility, and business."* April.

_____ (1999). Cross Cultural Marketing Ethics: Literature Review and Training Suggestions. *Journal of Global Competitiveness.* Volume 7(1). Pages 235 -251. ISSN: 1071-0736.

_____ (1998). International Marketing Ethics & Training. Published at the proceedings of *Australia New Zealand Marketing Academy Conference (ANZMAC98).* Conference was held in New Zealand.

_____ & Hinds, R. M.. (2004). Quality assurance through effective faculty training and development practices in distance education: The survey of Jamaican graduates. THE CARIBBEAN AREA NETWORK FOR QUALITY ASSURANCE IN TERTIARY EDUCATION (CANQATE). Inaugural Conference on November 3-4. Ocho Rios, Jamaica.

Murphy, Jim (1994). *Managing Conflict at Work.* American Media Publishing.

Nadler, David A.; Shaw, Robert B.; Walton, A. Elise, and Associates, (1995). Discontinuous Change: Leading Organizational Transformation. Jossey-Bass Publication.

Napier, N. & Peterson, R. (1991). Expatriate Re-Entry: What Do Repatriates Have to Say? *Human Resource Planning, 14*(1). Retrieved May 10, 2005 from Business Source Premier.

National Coalition for Women and Girls in Education (NCWGE). (2002). Title IX at 30: Report Card on Gender Equity.

Newman, H. L., & Fitzgerald, S. P. (2001). Appreciative inquiry with an executive team: Moving along the action research continuum.

Organization Development Journal, 19(3), 37. Retrieved September 30, 2004, from ProQuest database.

Nicholson, J.D., Stephina, L.P., & Hochwarter, W. (1990). Psychological aspects of expatriate training and effectiveness. In G. Ferris & K. Rowland (Eds.), Research in personnel and human resource management (Suppl. 2, 127-145). Greenwich, CT: JAI Press.

Nimmo, C. (1994). Autism and computers. *Communication*, 28(2), 8-9.

Noe, R. A., Hollenbeck, J. R., Gerhart, B., Wright, P. M. (1997). Human Resource Management: *Gaining a Competitive Advantage.* (2nd ed.). *IRWIN.* Chicago O'Toole, J. (1996). *Leading change: The argument for values-based leadership.* New York: Jossey-Bass.

Northrup, H. (1988). "Professional women in R & D laboratories." *Research-Technology Management,* July/August, 31(4): 44-52.

Oddou, G.R & Mendenhall, M.E. (1991). Succession Planning for the 21st Century: How Well Are We Grooming Our Future Business Leaders? *Business Horizons.* Retrieved May 10, 2005 from Business Source Premier.

Offermann, L. R. & Hellmann, P. S. (1997). Culture's consequences for leadership behavior: National values in action. Journal of Cross-Cultural Psychology, 342-351.

O'Keefe, Alice. (2004). "Focus: Equality at Work." *The Observer.* London (UK): Jan 11, 2004. pg. 20

Olesen, Erik, (1993). 12 Steps to Mastering the Winds of Change. Peak Perfomers Reveal How To Stay On Top In Times Of Turmoil. Rawson Associates, a □ofstede of Macmilllan Inc.

Ornstein, R; Sobel, D. (1987). *The Healing Brain: A new Perspective on the Brain and Health.* Semon & Schuster, New York.

O'Sullivan, S.L. (2002). The protean approach to managing repatriation transitions. *International Journal of Manpower, 23*(7). Retrieved May 10, 2005 from ABI/INFORM Global.

Page, Susan, (2005). *On Security, Public Draws Blurred Lines.* USA Today, August 4, 2005.

Panyan, M. V. (1984). Computer technology for autistic students. *Journal of Autism and Developmental Disorders*, 14(4), 375-382.

Parks, Elizabeth. (2000). "Gender Equality in Engineering Salaries." *Machine Design.* Cleveland: Jan 13, 72(1): 166.

Patten R. (2004, September/October). From implicit to explicit: Putting corporate values and personal accountability front and centre. *Ivey Business Journal Online, p. H1.*

Payne, N, (2005) *Cross Cultural Negotiations. Everoft.com.* Retrieved from the following

URL:http://developers.eversoft.com/article/business/negotiation/cross-cultural-negotiations.shtmlTucker, M., Benton, D & McCarthy (2002). *The Human Challenge* (7ᵗʰ ed). New Jersey: Prentice Hall

Peyrefitte, J., Fadil, P. A., & Thomas, A. S. (2002). The Influence of Managerial Experiences on Large Firm Internationalization. *International Journal of Management, 19*(3), 495-502.

Pohlman, R., (2004, September). *Adding Value to the Bottom Line.* SmartBusiness, Vol. 1, No.1, Page 8.

Pohlman R. A., & Gardiner, G. S. with Heffes, E. M. (2000). *Value Driven Management: How to Create and Maximise Value Over Time for Organizational Success.* AMACOM. N. Y.

Powell, Gary N. (2003). "Gender, Gender Identity, and Aspirations to Top Management." *Women in Management Review*. 18(1): 88-97.

Poznak Law Firm LTD, False Advertising. Overview. Retrieved September 10, 2004 from the World Wide Web. MSN Search Engine. www.jlp@poznaklaw.com.

Porter, Michael E., (1985). Competitive Advantage: Creating and Sustaining Superior Performance. (New York: The Free Press. Pages 3.

Princeton Study. (1989). *Student Stress Lowers Immunity*. Brain Mind Bulletin. 14:17

Pritchett, P. and Pound, R. (2005). *A Survival Guide to the Stress of Organizational Change.* Reviewed in 2005.

_____, P. and Pound, R (1993). *Business as Unusual: The Handbook for Managing and Supervising Organizational Change. 3ʳᵈ Ed.* Pritchett & Associates, Inc. Dallas, Tx.

_____, P. (1993) *Culture Shift. The Employee Handbook for Changing Corporate Culture.* Pritchett & Associates, Inc. Dallas, Tx.

_____, P. and Pound, R. (1993) *High-Velocity Culture Change: A handbook for managers.* Pritchett & Associates, Inc. Dallas, Tx.

_____, Price. New Work Habits For A Radically Changing World: 13 Ground Rules for Job Success In the Information Age.

_____, Price and Pound, Ron (1992). Team ReConstruction: Building a high performance work group during change. This is a hand book for managers.

_____, Price and Pound, Ron (1990). Change: The employee handbook for organizational change. Reprinted in 1993. 8ᵗʰ. Ed.

_____, Price and Pound, Ron (1988). Business As Unusual: The handbook for managing and supervising organizational change.

Ragins, B.R. (1989). "Barriers to mentoring: The female manager's dilemma." *Human Relations,* 42:1-22.

Ragins, B., and Cotton, J. (1991). "Easier said than done: Gender differences in perceived barriers to gaining a mentor." *Academy of Management Journal*, 34(4): 939-951.

Ralston, D. A., Gustafson, D. J., Cheung, F. M. & Terpstra, R. H. (1993). Differences in managerial values: A study of U. S., Hong Kong and PRC managers. Journal of International Business Studies, 24 (2) 249-275.

Ramaswamy, K., Kroeck, K. G., & Renforth, W. (1996). Measuring the Degree of Internationalization of a Firm: Comment. *Journal of International Business Studies, 27*(1), 167-177.

Ramsey, Jase (November 2005). The Role of Other Orientation on the Relationship between Institutional Distance and Expatriate Adjustment. Presented at the *Southern Management Association Conference*, November 11, 05; Charleston, SC.

Randolph, A. W. and Blackburn, R. (1989). *Managing organizational behavior*. Richard Dee Irwin, Inc.

Rasmussen, B., and Hapnes, T. (1991). "Excluding women from the technologies of the future: A case study of the culture of computer science." *Futures*, 23(10): 1107-1119.

Redding, S.G., Norman, A, & Schlander, A. (1994). The nature of individual attachment to theory: A review of East Asian variations. In H.C. Triandis, M.D. Dunnett, and L.M. Hough (Eds.), Handbook of industrial and organizational psychology, 4, 674-688. Palo Alto, CA: Consulting Psychology Press.

Reidenbach, R.E. and Robin D.P. (1989). *Ethics and profits.* NY: Prentice-Hall.

Reinicke, W. H. (1997). Global Public Policy. *Journal of Foreign Affairs, 76*(6), 127-131.

Reskin B.F., and Hartmann, H.I. (1986). *Women's Work, Men's Work: Sex Segregation on the Job.* Washington, D.C.: National Academy Press.

Rhode, D.L. (1990). "Gender equality and employment policy." In S. E. Rix (Ed.), *The American Woman, 1990-1991: A Status Report.* New York, NY: W.W. Norton and Company.

Ricks, D. A., Toyne, B. & Martinez, Z. (1990). Recent developments in international management research. Journal of Management, 16, 219-252.

Richards, L. (Feb. 3, 2004). Plan ahead to ensure repatriation success. *Personnel Today.* Retrieved May 12, 2005 from ABI/INFORM Global.

Rioux, M. (2003, Mar). Lessons Learned from Kmart. *IDEA Article*. Retrieved April 9, 2004 from http://www.naedtechnolgyinformer.com/feature_archive_4-04-03-2.html.

Robbins, S. (2001). *Organizational Behavior*. 9th edition. Prentice Hall.

Rogers, C. R., & Roethlisberger, F. J. (1952). Barriers and Gateways to Communication. *Harvard Business Review*.

Rubin, Ethics in Advertising. Retrieved September 10, 2004 from the World Wide Web MSN Search Engine. www.rubak.com.

Ryan, F., Soven, M., Smithier, J., Sullivan, W., & VanVuskirk, W. (1999). *Appreciative inquiry*.

Ryan, M. (1990). DAC, "Women and careers." *Electronic Engineering Times*, July 23, 600: 100.

Salovey, P. & Mayer, J.D. (1990). *Emotional intelligence. Imagination, Cognition, and Personality*. 9(1990), 185-211

Salter, Chuck (2001). Attention, Class! 16 Ways to Be a Smarter Teacher. Fast Company. Retrieved on 3/5/04 from: http://www.fastcompany.com/magazine/53/teaching.html

Sarkar, Pia. (2002). "Gender Gap/Computer Industry Skewed Toward Male Perspective Despite Users' Demographics." *San Francisco Chronicle*, Jan 30: B.1

Savage, J.A., (1989). "Ask CEO/Founder quits to publish her story." *Computerworld*, March 20, 32(12): 95-99.

Schwartz, F.N. (1989). "Management women and the new facts of life." *Harvard Business Review*, 89 (1, January-February): 65-76.

Schiemann, W. (1992). *"Why Change Fails" Across the Board*. April, 1992.

Schein, E. H. (1992). *Organizational culture and leadership* (2nd ed.). San Francisco: Jossey-Bass.

Schwartz, S.A. (1999). A theory of cultural values and some implications for work. *Applied Psychology: An International Review, 48(1), 23-47*.

Senge, Peter (1994). *The Fifth Discipline Field-book: Strategies and tools for building and learning*. New York, NY: Doubleday.

_____, P. (1992). *Learning Organizations and Human Resources*. American Society for Training and Development (ASTD) National Conference. New Orleans.

_____, P. (1990). *"The Fifth Discipline: The Art and Practice of the Learning Organization."* Doubleday, New York

Senge, P. (1998). Through the Eye of the Needle. In R. Gibson (Ed.), *Rethinking the Future* (pp. 123-146). London: Nicholas Brealey Publishing.

Science and Engineering Equal Opportunities Act (SEEA), Section 32(b), Part B of P.L. 96-516, 94 Stat. 3010, as amended by P.L. 99-159.

Seyle, Hans (1956). *The Stress of Life*. McGraw-Hill Books Co., New York.

Seyle, Hans (1974). *Stress without Distress*. J.B. Lippincott, New York.

Sfeir-Younis, A. (2002). The spiritual entrepreneur. *Reflections, 3*(3), 43-45. [Society for Organizational Learning and the Massachusetts Institute of Technology].

Sheinin, R. (1989). "Women as scientists: Their rights and obligations." *Journal of Business Ethics,* February/March, 8(2): 131-155.

Shelton, C. D., & Darling, J. R. (2004). From Chaos to Order: Exploring New Frontiers in Conflict Management, Organization Development Journal, Chesterfield: Fall 2004. Vol. 22, Issue. 3; pg 22, 20 pgs. Retrieved September 9, 2004 from ProQuest database.

Siegel, Barry (September 2005). The Business Case for Recruitment Process Outsourcing (RPO): How outsourcing can improve your company. *HR Florida Review*, Vol. 4, No. 2.

Sims, Randi (2005). Stress Management Concepts and Practices. Retrieved on October 30, 2005 from:
http://www.nova.edu/~sims/smmpover.html

Singh, B. R. (2002, June). Problems and possibilities of dialogue across cultures. Intercultural Education, 13(2), 215. Retrieved September 10, 2004 from EBSCO database.

Singhapakdi, Marta, Rawwas, & Ahmed (1999). A cross-cultural study of consumer perceptions about marketing ethics. *Journal of Consumer Marketing, 16(3), p. 257.*

Singhapakdi, M. & Vitell, S. J.(1993b). Personal and professional values underlying the ethical judgments of marketers. *Journal of Business Ethics, 12, p. 528.*

Smith, E. (1989). "The women who are scaling high tech's heights." *Business Week*, 3121 (August 28): 86-89.

Soeters, J. L. & Recht, R. (2001). Convergence or divergence in the multinational classroom? Experience from the military. International Journal of Intercultural Relations.

Spera, S. and Lanto, S., (1997). *Beat Stress with Strength: A Survival Guide for Word and Life*. Park Avenue: an Imprint of JIST Works, Inc.

Stanley, Alessandra (2002). "For Women, to Soar is Rare, to Fall is Human." *New York Times:* Jan 13: 3.

Stanton, William J, Etzel, Michael J., Walker, Bruce J., (1991). Fundamentals of Marketing 9th Edition (New York: McGraw-Hill Publishing).

Sternberg, E.N. (2000). *The Balance Within*. W.H. Freeman & Co. New York.

Steven Suranovic, 2004. *The Theory of Comparative Advantage: An Overview*. ©1997-2003. Retrieved on 2/17/04 from: http://internationalecon.com/v1.0/ch40/40c000.html.

Stoner, James A. F. and Freeman, Edward R. , 1989. Management. 4th edition. Prentice Hall Publication.

Strob, L.K., Gregersen, H.B. & Stewart Black, J. (1998). Closing the Gap: Expectations Versus Reality Among Repatriates. *Journal of World Business, 33*(2). Retrieved April 15, 2005 from Business Source Premier.

Stuart, P. (1992). New Direction in Training Individuals. *Personnel Journal*, 71, 86. Retrieved February 12, 2004 from ProQuest database.

Sugarman, K. (2000). *Leadership Characteristics*. [Online]. Retrieved on 4, 4, 2004 from URL: http://www.psywww.com/sports/leader.html

Sullivan, D. (1994). Measuring the Degree of Internationalization of a Firm. *Journal of International Business Studies, 25*(2), 325-342.

Sun Sentinel, 4/24/03, p. 3A

Swanson, J. (2000). What's the difference? Available from the Girl Tech Web site, www.girltech.com

Swettenham, J. (1996). Can children with autism be taught to understand false belief using computers? *Journal of Child Psychology and Psychiatry and Allied Disciplines*, 37(2), 157-165.

The Basics of Conflict Resolution: *Interpersonal Problem-solver Series*. Retrieved Feb. 13, 2002 from http://www.ivysea.com/pages/ct0200_1.html

The Stress Management Handbook, 1995. *A Guide to Reducing Stress in Every Aspect of Your Life*. Sixty-Minute Training Series. National Press Publications.

Thomas, Karen (2005). *Teen People Select Young and Powerful*. USA Today, August 4, 2005.

Thomas, G., Mujtaba, B., (2004). *Effective Global Leadership in the Twenty First Century and Preventing Disasters from Occurring in Developing Nations*. The Association on Employment Practices and Principles. Proceedings of Twelfth Annual AEPP International.

Ting-Toomey, S. (2005). *Cultural barriers to Effective Communication*. Conflict Research. Consortium. Retrieved on June 04, 2005 from the following URL: http://www.colorado.edu/conflict/peace/problem/cultrbar.htm

Tinkler, H. (2004, November 16). Ethics in business – the heart of the matter.

Tisch, J. (2004). *The Power of WE: Succeeding through Partnerships.* Introduction on Wall Street Journal's October 26th issue.

Triandis, H.C. (1982). Review of cultural consequences. International differences in work related values. Human Organization, 41, 86-90.

Training across cultures (1995). *Employee counselling [sic] Today*, 7, 17. Retrieved February 12, 2004 from ProQuest database.

Trauth, E. M. (2002). "Odd Girl Out: An Individual Differences Perspective on Women in the IT Profession." *Information Technology and People*, Special Issue on Gender and Information Systems, Volume 15, Number 2: 98-118.

Trauth, E. M., Quesenberry, J., Morgan, A. J. (2004). "Understanding the Under Representation of Women in IT: Toward a Theory of Individual Differences." Proceedings of the ACM SIGMIS Computer Personnel Research Conference (Tucson, AZ).

Trompenaar, Fons (1993). *Riding the Waves of Culture: Understanding Diversity in Global Business,* (New York: Irwin, NY).

Turkle, S. (1984). *The Second Self: Computers and the Human Spirit.* New York: Simon & Schuster.

Turkle, S. (1988). "Computational reticence: Why women fear the intimate machine." In C. Kramarae (Ed.), *Technology and Women's Voices.* New York: Routledge & Kegan Paul, Inc.

Twin, A. (2003, Dec). 2003's Biggest Losers. *CNN Money.* Retrieved March 30, 2004 from http://money.cnn.com/2003/12/12/markets/yir_biglosers03/.

University of Virginia. *Management Communication.* Retrieved on June 6, 2005 from the following URL: http://www.darden.virginia.edu/faculty/fac_mc.htm

Upbin, Bruce (2004). "*Wall to Wall Wal-Mart: The Retailer Conquered America and Made it Look Easy. The Rest of the World is a Tougher Battleground.*" Forbes: The World's 2000 Leading Companies. April 12, 2004 issue.

USA Today, (2005). *How U.S Divorce Rate Compares.* August 4, 2005.

U.S. Department of Labor (2001). Bureau of labor statistics data. Retrieved October 10, 2001, from www.bls.gov/data/.

Using personal narratives for initiating school reform. Clearing House, 72(3), 164. Retrieved September 30, 2004, from EBSCOhost database.

U.S. Department of Labor Statistics (1975,1990, 2003).

U.S. National Center for Educational Statistics (2000).

Verschoor, Curtis C. (Dec 2004). Strategic Finance. *Montvale. Vol. 86*, (iss.6), 15.

Verspejc, M.A. (1989). *The Ten Most Frequent Causes of Stress in the Work Place*. Industry Week (pg. 19, 20). New York.

Virovere, A., Kooskora, M., & Valler, M. (2002). Conflict as a tool for measuring ethics at workplace. Journal of Business Ethics. Dordrecht: August 2002. 39 (1/2), 75. Retrieved September 22, 2004 from ProQuest database.

Von Hellens, L. A., Nielson, S. H., Trauth, E. M. (2001). "Breaking and Entering the Male Domain: Women in the IT Industry." Proceedings of the ACM SIGCPR Conference, (San Diego, CA, April).

Vuong, Andy (2001). "Women Cite Divide in Digital Roles." *Denver Post*: June 5: C.01.

Wal-Mart Corporation (2004). Hoover's Company Information. Retrieved April 10, 2004 from http://cobrands.hoovers.com/global/cobrands/proquest/ops. xhtml?

Wal-Mart Corporation (2003, October 29). Wal-Mart Named America's Largest Corporate Cash Giver. *Wal-Mart News*. Retrieved March 30, 2004 from http://www.walmartstores.com/ wmstore/wmstores.

Wal-Mart Stores (2004), Home page. Retrieved April 9, 2004 from http://www.walmartstores.com/wmstore/wmstores/HomePage.jsp.

Walton, S. and Huey, J. (1992). Made in America. New York: Doubleday.

Watkins, J., & Mohr, B. (2001). Appreciative Inquiry: Change at the Speed of Imagination.

Wein, Harrison (2000). *A Report Firms the NIH World on health*. NIH Office of communications and Public Liaison. Retrieved on October 10, 2005 from: (http://www.nih.gov/news/wordonHealth/oct2000/story01.htm)

Welch, L. S., & Luostarinen, R. (1988). Internationalization: Evolution of a Concept. *Journal of General Management, 14*(2), 34-55.

Whyte, G. (1990). Companies put their faith in recycling the workforce. *Computer Weekly*, October 11, 1235: 86.

Wilkins, M. (2005). What is International Business? An Economic Historian's View. In Peter J. Buckley (Ed.), *What is International Business?* (pp. 133-152). Great Britain: Palgrave McMillan.

Williams, W.M. & Sternberg, R.J. (1988). *Group Intelligence: Why some groups are better than others*. Intelligence, 12, 351-377.

Wikler, Y. (2001). 7 days in September. *Kashrus Magazine. 22*(2), 20-21. Retrieved February 19, 2005, from EBSCOhost database.

Women's Educational Equity Act Resource Center (WEEA). (November 1999). "Connecting Gender and Disability." *Gender and Disability Digest*.

World Development Report 2005: *A Better Investment Climate for Everyone*. Retrieved February 15, 2005, from http://worldbankgroup.com/.

Wright, Barbara D., Myra Marx Ferree, Gail O. Mellow, Linda H. Lewis, Maria-Luz Daza Samper, Robert Asher, and Kathleen Claspell (Eds.). (1987). *Women, work, and technology transformations*. Ann Arbor: The University of Michigan Press.

Yerkes, L. A., & Decker, C. (2003). *Beans: Four principles for running a business in good times or bad*. San Francisco: Jossey-Bass.

Appendices

Author and Contributor Biographies

Bahaudin Mujtaba is an Associate Professor of International Management with NSU. Bahaudin has worked as an internal consultant, trainer, and teacher in the corporate arena. He also worked in retail management for 16 years. His doctorate degree is in Management, and he has two post-doctorate specialties: one in Human Resource Management and another in International Management. Bahaudin is author and co-author of several books and articles. During the past 20 years he has had the pleasure of working in the United States, Brazil, Bahamas, Afghanistan, and Jamaica. He was born in Khoshie of Logar province, and raised in Kabul, Afghanistan.

Timothy McCartney is a Clinical Psychologist and an Organizational Development Consultant. He is also a Professor at the H. Wayne Huizenga School of Business and Entrepreneurship, Nova Southeastern University, Ft. Lauderdale, Florida. He was educated in the Bahamas, USA, Switzerland, Jamaica, England, and France where he received his doctorate in clinical psychology from the University of Strasbourg, summa-cumlaude (tres honorable). Dr. McCartney returned to the Bahamas in 1967, and was appointed to serve in Ministry of Health of the Bahamas. He was the first Bahamian to obtain a doctorate in Psychology and directed to develop the profession of Psychology and Allied Health. He created many innovative programs in the field of mental health and was instrumental in starting organizations that focused on primary difficulties as well as wellness/preventive issues.

Donovan McFarlane completed a Masters of Business Administration degree at Nova Southeastern University. He received a Doctor of Metaphysical Science degree from the University of Metaphysics in California, a Doctor of Philosophy from the American Institute of Holistic Theology, Alabama. He is currently a University Research Associate, an instructor in business studies at the University of Fort Lauderdale, and a Distinguished Member of the International Society of Poets; Owing Mills, MD. He was born and raised in Jamaica and completed the latter part of his tertiary education in the United

States. As such, he has spent considerable amount of time studying and understanding cultural trends in the United Sates. His areas of research interests are gender, culture, leadership, philosophy, and management.

Kendrick D. Traylor received his Master of Arts in Organizational Management from the University of Phoenix and Bachelor in Business Administration in Marketing from Grand Valley State University. Kendrick has 14 years of experience in Marketing and Management while working in a variety of marketing positions to include Advertising Account Executive, Manager of Market Research, Market Development Associate and Market Analyst. Kendrick also has worked on a variety of consulting projects in new business development and Co –Authored a Paper entitled *Bait & Switch—Value Adder or Destroyer* with the Society for the Advancement of Management (SAM). Kendrick is a two time combat veteran of Operations Desert Shield/Storm and Operation Enduring Freedom. Kendrick has 16 years of military experience in the areas of Logistics and Personnel Management and currently serves as a Captain in the Army National Guard. In the near future, Kendrick plans to obtain his doctorate. and open a consulting practice.

Erica L. Franklin is a graduate student at Nova Southeastern University. She is currently in her second year of the Masters of International Business Administration program (M.I.B.A.), and her expected date of graduation is August 2006. Erica is from Memphis, Tennessee where she graduated from Whitehaven High School and attended Christian Brothers University. She obtained a B.S. in Business Administration with a concentration in Marketing from Christian Brothers and was a magna cum laude graduate. While attending Christian Brothers University she was a member of various student organizations, the most notable being a member of Sigma Beta Delta Business Honor Society. After completing her studies at Nova Southeastern University, Erica hopes to begin a career in the field of international marketing either as a consultant or marketing coordinator or in field of logistics and international supply chain management.

Nicholas DiDomenico received a Master of Arts in Organizational Management from the University of Phoenix in 2005. Nichalos has many years of experience in the corporate arena. Nicholas has worked on a variety of academic projects and recently co-authored a paper entitled *Tempered Radicals* with Dr. Bahaudin Mujtaba and it was presented in Fort Lauderdale, Florida, during November 2004 at the annual international conference held by the Association on Employment Principles and Practices (AEPP). Nicholas is an advocate of helping every person to effectively bring about the needed changes in his or her department and/or organization. Nicholas works, and lives with his family, in Milford, Pennsylvania.

Note: Other contributors can be contacted for background information using the contact information provided on the next page.

CONTRIBUTOR INFORMATION

Bahaudin G. Mujtaba, D.B.A.
Nova Southeastern University
3301 College Avenue
Fort Lauderdale, Florida 33314
Phone: (954) 262-5045
Email: mujtaba@nova.edu

Timothy McCartney, Ph.D.
Nova Southeastern University
3301 College Avenue
Fort Lauderdale, Florida 33314
Phone: (954) 262-5000
Email: mccartne@nova.edu

Erica Franklin, MIBA
Nova Southeastern University
4544 Paula Drive
Memphis, TN 38116
Email: efrankli@nsu.nova.edu

Rose Marie Edwards, MS/HRM
University of West Indies
27 Queensbury Drive, Meadowbrrok Estate
Kingston 19, Jamaica.
Email: rosemarie.hinds@scotiabank.com

Donovan A. McFarlane, Ph.D.
Nova Southeastern University
3301 College Avenue
Fort Lauderdale, Florida 33314
Email: donovan@nova.edu

Rick Pinelli, MBA
Nova Southeastern University
10103 Sherwood Lane, Apt. 141
Riverview, FL 33569
Email: Pinelli@timeinc.com or:
rpinelli0609@aol.com

Kendrick D. Traylor, MAOM
University of Phoenix-Online
Email: kendrick.traylor@us.army.mil or:
kdtraylor@email.uophx.edu

Nicholas DiDomenico, MAOM
University of Phoenix-Online
101 Field Place. Milford, PA 18337
Email: nicholas_f.didomenico@ROCHE.COM

Susan K. Key, Ph.D.
University of Alabama at Birmingham
1150 10th Avenue South
Birmingham AL 35294-4460
Phone: (205) 934-7338
Email: susankey@uab.edu

Philip F. Musa, Ph.D.
University of Alabama at Birmingham
1150 10th Avenue South
Birmingham AL 35294-4460
Phone: (205) 934-8844
Email: musa@uab.edu

LeJon Poole, Ph.D.
University of Alabama at Birmingham
1675 University Blvd.
Birmingham AL 35294-3361
Phone: (205) 934-1666
Email: lpoole@uab.edu

Elizabeth Danon-Leva, MSc., D.I.B.A.
Nova Southeastern University
5000 Valley Oak Drive
Austin, TX 78731
Work: (512) 750-2893
Email: danonlev@nova.edu

INDEX TABLE

Printed in the United Kingdom
by Lightning Source UK Ltd.
112769UKS00001B/190